Chomsky's Challenge to American Power

CHOMSKY'S CHALLENGE TO AMERICAN POWER

A Guide for the Critical Reader

Anthony F. Greco

Vanderbilt University Press ■ Nashville

© 2013 by Vanderbilt University Press
Nashville, Tennessee 37235
All rights reserved
First printing 2013

This book is printed on acid-free paper.

Library of Congress Cataloging-in-Publication Data on file
LC control number 2013007827
LC classification JZ1312.G74 2014
Dewey class number 327.73—dc23

ISBN 978-0-8265-1947-4 (cloth)
ISBN 978-0-8265-1948-1 (paperback)
ISBN 978-0-8265-1949-8 (ebook)

To Celia

Contents

Preface and Acknowledgments ix

Introduction 1

1. Vietnam 5
   America's War in Vietnam: A Synopsis 5
   The Vietnam War According to Chomsky 14
   Conclusions 39

   Indochina Afterword
      Chomsky and Cambodia 44

2. Cold War Empire 53
   American Foreign Policy during the Cold War:
   A Chomskian Overview 53
   America's Third World Empire:
   How Evil? How American? 57
   The American Empire: Some Observations 95

3. Domestic Power and Global Purpose 99
   The US Power Structure 99
   Explaining America's Cold War 109

4. Ideology, Illusion, and the Media — 121
    The Propaganda Model: The Framework — 123
    Case Studies — 127
    The Propaganda Model in Perspective — 142
    The Role of Intellectuals — 150

5. America in the Post–Cold War World — 160
    Empire Redux — 161
    Interventions: Assets Turned Rogue — 169
    Interventions: Humanitarianism and Kosovo — 180
    Varieties of Terrorism — 192
    Hegemony and Its Discontents — 201

Summary and Conclusions — 207
    How Chomsky Has Been Right — 207
    The Problems with Chomsky — 216
    The Chomsky Conundrum — 228

Notes — 231

Index — 251

Preface and Acknowledgments

PROFESSOR NOAM CHOMSKY IS A GIANT in the field of linguistics. This book is not about Chomsky the linguist. It is about Noam Chomsky the thinker-activist whose searing critiques of American foreign policy and politics have earned him a reputation as one of the world's leading public intellectuals. I am interested in exploring and evaluating Chomsky's writings on politics—"politics" understood broadly to mean the workings of government, and people's efforts to influence government, in both foreign and domestic affairs. Since the great bulk of Chomsky's writings on politics have been about American foreign policy, that subject takes up most of the book.

Whatever one thinks of Chomsky, no one can deny that during the course of his nearly fifty-year career as a public intellectual he has dealt provocatively with important issues worthy of the attention of informed citizens: the Vietnam War, America's broader international role (especially its interventions in the Third World), the structure of power in American politics, the role of the media and of intellectuals in forming public opinion, and American foreign policy in the post–Cold War world. My decision to write about Chomsky was motivated by the simple fact that he has written about things that I care intensely about—things that I think other citizens should care about as well. Ultimately, my interest is not so much in Chomsky personally as it is in his contribution to our understanding of these issues. Accordingly, this book is as much about the issues as it is about Chomsky's treatment of them.

I see the reader as a partner in this search for understanding: when I use the word "we" I mean not the editorial "we" (I prefer the first person singular) but the author and the reader joined in a common effort.

Chomsky is an unusually polarizing figure. His admirers tend to be fervent and his critics fierce. It is very hard to find perspectives on Chomsky between those poles. With this book I take up a spot on that lonely middle ground. I didn't set out to arrive there—I don't necessarily believe that the truth lies somewhere in the middle—but that is where I ended up. I believe that while much of Chomsky's work on politics is insightful and important, it is marred by glaring defects. Unfortunately, the value of his work can easily be obscured in the glare of those defects. I hope that a careful, balanced analysis of Chomsky's deficiencies as well as his merits will help to remove the glare and thus serve to reveal what is genuinely worthwhile. I expect that this book will displease Chomsky fans and foes alike, but my objective is to serve critical readers—readers seeking not confirmation of their biases, but genuine understanding. My aim is to help such readers to see patterns in Chomsky's work—to see where his strengths lie, and where his reliability may be subject to doubt.

Some aspects of Chomsky's political writings will not be examined here. They fall into two categories: things that I think do not require serious attention, and things that are deserving of attention but that I simply don't have room for in this book.

To take the second category first: The author of dozens of books and countless articles, Chomsky has been an amazingly prolific writer on a tremendous range of topics in politics and world affairs. A careful and truly comprehensive assessment of this corpus of work would take volumes. It would require an interdisciplinary team of social scientists and historians with expertise in several world regions. No such team is at my disposal. I have therefore had to be selective. Chomsky has written on many topics that are not treated in this book. My most important omission is Israel and Palestine, a subject about which Chomsky has written extensively and repeatedly. Many books have dealt with the respective merits of the opposing narratives in the historic conflict between Israelis and Palestinians. I don't see that I can add appreciable value to this literature in the context of this book.

The major subject in the category of things I do not believe require serious attention is Chomsky's political philosophy, the outlook that he sometimes calls anarchism, sometimes libertarian socialism. This omission may seem surprising: a book about a person's analyses of politics should, presumably, include a discussion of the philosophic underpinnings of those analyses. The omission is nevertheless justified on two grounds, both reflecting my primary interest in Chomsky's analyses of actually existing politics and society. First, while Chomsky's anarchism reflects a radical sensibility—a conviction that existing society needs to be radically transformed—it doesn't *specifically* inform his approach to political analysis. Unlike, say, Marxism, anarchism doesn't provide a set of theoretical constructs for or methodological approaches to political and social analysis. One can reject Chomsky's radical anticapitalist perspective and still agree with most of his assumptions and conclusions about how the real world works. Second, there is simply not that much to say about Chomsky's anarcho-socialism. Chomsky himself disavows any original contribution of his own to this field of thought, and he is right to do so. His vision of a libertarian socialist society, to the extent that he has described it, is both sketchy and utopian—utopian in that it is unconnected to any concrete analysis of real-world possibilities.

A second omission in the unmeritorious category is the notorious Faurisson Affair. In the mid-1970s Chomsky wrote a statement in defense of the right of Robert Faurisson, a holocaust denier, to express his views. That statement showed up as a preface to a book authored by Faurisson. Chomsky's culpability in this matter has been debated at length by his defenders and detractors. I see no intellectual payoff to attempting to sort out the tangle of claims and counterclaims advanced by the two sides. The issue ultimately is only relevant insofar as it bears on the charge, advanced more or less explicitly by some of his critics, that Chomsky is somehow anti-Semitic. That charge is directed at a Jew who grew up in a household immersed in Hebrew-language studies and later lived for a time on a kibbutz. It doesn't deserve serious consideration.

A final note on what this book is and is not about: It is a book about Chomsky's ideas and his approach to political analysis. It is not a biography, or even an intellectual biography—the latter meaning a work that seeks consistently to place its subject's ideas in the context of his life experiences and to explain their development over time. Nor am I interested here in analyzing Chomsky psychologically. I deal with the content of his writings and ask whether they make sense. I avoid speculating about psychological motivations that might explain what he says.

I WANT TO ACKNOWLEDGE the friends and scholars who have read and commented on portions of the manuscript or have otherwise given me help and encouragement in this project: Eric Alterman, Michael Bérubé, Fred Block, Daniel Greco, Jack Hammond, Wallace Katz, Peter Parisi, Edward Scher, Ida Susser, Jeffrey Tannenbaum, and Michael Teitelman. I owe thanks most of all to my wife, Celia Orgel, who has always been there for me all the way.

Introduction

It started with the Vietnam War. Long before the fateful escalation of the war in the mid-1960s, Noam Chomsky had won recognition as a seminal figure in the field of linguistics, but was little known outside that field. He was certainly not known as a commentator on politics. That is not to say that Chomsky was apolitical. As a child growing up in the Great Depression in Philadelphia he had had an early exposure to radical political views in his family and in the wider Jewish working-class culture his family inhabited. His lifelong interest in anarchism dates at least as far back as the tender age of ten, when he wrote an article on the Spanish Civil War for his school newspaper.[1] But it was not until the Vietnam War that Chomsky's radical views led him to public activism.

Chomsky was not alone. The war was the central, cataclysmic event of a decade of wrenching conflict in American society. Historians have used phrases like the "unraveling of America" and "the civil war of the 1960s" to characterize the years of upheaval that led to lasting changes in American life.[2] The dispatch of hundreds of thousands of American troops to Asia beginning in early 1965 brought hundreds of thousands of protesters onto the streets of major cities in the United States. Many if not most of the protesters undoubtedly had never before thought to question the wisdom and probity of their government's actions abroad.

Prominent intellectuals joined the dissenters—people like the novelists Norman Mailer and Mary McCarthy, the poet Robert Lowell, the literary critic Susan Sontag, and the political theorist Hans Morgenthau. The recently founded *New York Review of Books* became the prime organ of intellectuals who defined the war as a moral issue; it soon was the most influential journal read by the nation's intellectual elite. Noam Chomsky was one of its leading contributors; his "The Responsibility of Intellectuals" (February 1967) would become "the most important essay of the Vietnam generation."[3]

Chomsky was outraged by what the United States was doing in Vietnam. In articles in the *New York Review* and elsewhere, and in increasingly frequent speaking engagements, Chomsky employed his powerful analytic gifts and his talent for annihilating rhetoric to demolish the rationales the US government had set forth to justify its actions in Indochina. I present and assess Chomsky's antiwar critique in Chapter 1.

The end of the war did not lead Chomsky to step back from the political arena. The perspectives and themes that Chomsky developed in opposition to US intervention in Vietnam have continued to inform his views of political power in America and its role in the world: the brutality of American policy toward Third World peoples, the servitude of the mass media and much of the intellectual elite to established power, and the narrowness of the range of debate and "respectable" dissent in the United States. It was during the Vietnam War period that Chomsky first took aim at the deeply rooted, unexamined, and often implicit beliefs that underlie Americans' thinking about their country, centering on the notion that the United States serves as a unique beacon of freedom and democracy in the world. Chomsky's entire career as a public intellectual can be seen as a relentless assault on the myths of "American exceptionalism," a battle he launched long before that term entered into popular usage.

Chomsky had come to see the US involvement in Indochina as a natural outgrowth of long-established policy objectives pursued by America's ruling groups in business and government. US leaders invariably framed those objectives in terms of America's Cold War competition with the Soviet Union, but Chomsky saw the Cold War as a smokescreen for the real motivations of American policy, which were to construct a global empire open to the pursuit of profit by America's increasingly global giant corporations. America's defeat in Vietnam marked the loss of a piece of that empire, but the US government could be expected to continue to react ruthlessly to enforce its dominance around the world. In a series of books beginning with *The Political Economy of Human Rights* (1979, 2 volumes), Chomsky, sometimes working with coauthor Edward S. Herman, set himself the task of analyzing the American empire, exposing what he saw as its crimes and explaining the driving forces behind it. Chomsky's dissection of the American imperial power system and its impact on the rest of the world is the subject of Chapters 2 and 3.

One of Chomsky's early concerns as he formulated his opposition to the Vietnam War had been to try to understand how Americans could so readily accept the rationales their government offered for actions he regarded as patently barbaric. Thus began Chomsky's interest in what he came to call the doctrinal system—the complex of ideas, beliefs, and implicit assumptions about the world that serve to rationalize and legitimate the behavior of those in power. Crucial to the construction and maintenance of the doctrinal system have been the American mass media, which Chomsky has always seen as subservient to the nation's dominant power groups. Practically all of Chomsky's political writings are laced with acid commentaries on the media's uncritical acceptance and propagation of official orthodoxies. I examine Chomsky's media criticism in Chapter 4, along with his views on the role of intellectuals in creating and perpetuating the doctrinal system.

Since Chomsky never took the Cold War seriously as a driving force in American foreign policy, it is unsurprising that he sees the end of the Cold War as a marker of continuity more than of change in America's role in the world. In his view, the collapse of the Soviet foe has if anything given the United States more freedom to pursue its imperial objectives unimpeded, with often devastating consequences for the countries—usually in the less-developed word—that have been most vulnerable to American power. While acknowledging the horror of 9/11, Chomsky contends that Americans have been the perpetrators far more than the victims of terror. Chomsky's views on American power since the Cold War are scrutinized in Chapter 5.

WE BEGIN WITH THE SUBJECT that propelled Chomsky into his life-long commitment as a dissident intellectual activist—America's war in Vietnam.

CHAPTER 1

Vietnam

> There may have been a time when American policy in Vietnam was a debatable matter. This time is long past. . . . The war is simply an obscenity, a depraved act.
> —Noam Chomsky, 1969

A SURVEY OF 110 LEADING American intellectuals in the early 1970s ranked Noam Chomsky by far the most influential intellectual critic of America's war in Vietnam.[1] Chomsky's case against the war was essentially a moral indictment of US policy: it challenged the official justifications American leaders advanced for war and emphasized the devastating impact of US intervention on the people of Vietnam.

America's War in Vietnam: A Synopsis

Japan's wartime occupation of French Indochina laid bare the vulnerability of French colonial rule and spurred the growth of a Vietnamese national independence movement.[2] The nationalists were united in the Viet Minh, a coalition that was broadly representative of Vietnamese society but dominated by the Vietnamese Communists under their charismatic leader, Ho Chi Minh.

THE FIRST VIETNAM WAR

The collapse of the Japanese occupation in late August 1945 enabled the Viet Minh to take control of a significant portion of northern Vietnam. Ho Chi Minh followed up quickly with the proclamation of an independent Democratic Republic of Vietnam (DRV). By the end of 1946 the Viet Minh were in a full-scale war with France for national independence.

US policymakers viewed France's colonial war in Vietnam with ambivalence. On the one hand, the Americans saw European colonialism as an anachronism in the postwar world. On the other, they were focused on the emerging Cold War in Europe and were reluctant to alienate an important European ally over a distant conflict. Besides, a Communist-led regime in Vietnam was clearly not an acceptable outcome to the United States. Accordingly, Washington chose to support France's effort to maintain control of its colony. US concern for the future of Vietnam was heightened by the 1949 Communist victory in China and the outbreak of war in Korea in June 1950. Increasingly, US decision makers viewed Vietnam in a Cold War context: a Viet Minh takeover in Vietnam would represent a major victory for international Communism. American financial aid to the French colonial war began in 1950 and escalated exponentially over the next few years, but the Viet Minh resistance continued unabated.

France's will to continue the fight was clearly waning in early 1954 when the French prime minister accepted a Soviet proposal for an international conference on Far Eastern problems. The conference, held in Geneva, Switzerland, beginning in late April, was cochaired by Britain and the Soviet Union, with representatives of France, China and the Viet Minh's Democratic Government of Vietnam participating. The United States attended as an "interested nation," not as "a belligerent or principal in the negotiations."[3] The State of Vietnam, the nominally independent entity set up by France, attended in essentially the same capacity. The Geneva Conference took place against the backdrop of France's most catastrophic defeat in its long war against the Vietnamese resistance, the loss in March of the strategically pivotal military base at Dienbienphu. The decisive Viet Minh victory there put the DRV in an apparently strong bargaining position at Geneva.

The Geneva Conference produced two agreements in late July. The first, between the French and the Viet Minh, set a cease-fire and divided Vietnam roughly at the 17th parallel into two "regroupment zones."[4] The French were required to withdraw all troops from northern Vietnam but retained effective control of the South. The document made clear that the two zones were not separate nations, and that they would be eventually reunited as one nation through free elections held throughout Vietnam. The second agreement was a final declaration by most of the participants—a consensus document not formally signed or voted on—that recognized the Franco-Vietnamese agreement and stipulated that general elections were to be held throughout Vietnam in July 1956 under the supervision of an international commission, with arrangements to be made by consultations between "the competent representative authorities" of the two regroupment zones.[5]

The Viet Minh were somewhat disappointed at Geneva. They had naturally hoped that they would be rewarded for their military triumph with control of a united Vietnam. In agreeing to a compromise, they yielded to pressure from their Chinese and Soviet allies, who were interested in exploring accommodation with the West.[6] They also had excellent reason to expect that their broad popular support would bring them victory in the promised nationwide elections.

The United States, as a somewhat reluctant observer rather than a principal in the Geneva negotiations, did not sign any document. The US representative, Bedell Smith, did however pledge that the United States would not threaten or use force to "disturb" the agreements. He also asserted support for the unity of divided states through free elections, and said the United States would view any violation of the agreements as a threat to international peace and security. But US secretary of state John Foster Dulles had other ideas. A unified Vietnam would almost surely be a Communist Vietnam. The day after the end of the conference, Dulles told a National Security Council meeting that "the great problem from here on out [is] whether we [can] salvage" southern Vietnam.[7]

THE CREATION OF SOUTH VIETNAM

The Vietnamese point man in that salvage operation was to be Ngo Dinh Diem, an anti-Communist nationalist appointed prime minister during the Geneva Conference by Bao Dai, the figurehead emperor who "ruled" Vietnam on behalf of the French. Diem had an extensive network of politically influential contacts in the United States, where he had lived for a couple of years earlier in the decade. Diem became the focus of a strong and ultimately successful push by the United States to supplant French with American influence in the southern regroupment zone, enabling Washington to become effectively the Western sponsor of a new State of Vietnam.[8]

Diem was rather incongruous in the role of postcolonial leader of a new nation. He had not been a leader of the armed struggle against the French. He was attached to no political party or movement and had no mass base. A devout Catholic, he was a member of a religious minority whose special privileges had long aroused widespread resentment among the overwhelmingly non-Catholic majority.[9] His government was very much a family affair. Three of the six members of Diem's first cabinet were family members. In addition, his father was ambassador to the United States and his youngest brother ambassador to Great Britain. His brother Ngo Dinh Nhu, in the special office of presidential counselor, was believed by some to be as powerful as Diem himself.[10]

A critical issue dividing the French from the Americans and Diem was the Geneva provision for unifying elections. The accords set a deadline of June 1955 for the representatives of the northern and southern zones to begin consultations on election preparations. The French took seriously the pledges they made at Geneva and felt responsible for ensuring that the agreements, including the provisions for elections, were successfully implemented. Generally seconded by the British, they felt not only that the scheduling of elections was a treaty obligation, but that failure to hold elections could be a cause for renewed warfare.[11] Diem, however, had from the beginning made clear that he would not be bound by Geneva. Ignoring the urgings of both the British and the French, he repeatedly spurned requests by the DRV for the preparatory consultations, claiming that free elections would be impossible in the Communist-controlled North.[12]

For Washington, the issue of elections was troublesome. On the one hand, Washington did not relish the prospect of Diem facing an electoral test; the Americans in early 1955 brushed aside a French proposal for the British, the French, and the Americans to develop a common approach to the issue of elections. On the other, to explicitly advise Diem, even in private, to resist elections could be embarrassing if it became public knowledge. The United States, after all, had been waving the banner of democracy and free elections since the outset of the Cold War. Washington settled on a policy of going through the motions of gently nudging Diem to acquiesce in consultations, but never really pushing him.[13]

The Viet Minh had counted on French support to ensure that elections would take place; they had no way of foreseeing the speed with which the Americans would move to take control of events. Once the June 1955 deadline for consultations had passed, it was increasingly clear to all parties that the elections were unlikely to happen. Still, the Viet Minh persisted, staging demonstrations and parades calling for consultations throughout South Vietnam. But with their Chinese and Soviet allies disinclined to exert any pressure for implementation of Geneva, the Viet Minh had to swallow their disappointment as the July 1956 deadline for elections came and went.[14]

While the implementation of the Geneva provisions for reunifying elections foundered, the regroupment of forces envisioned by the agreements was effected in reasonable time. About 130,000 southern Vietnamese affiliated with the Viet Minh, two-thirds of them guerilla fighters, went to the North.[15] (An estimated five to ten thousand former guerillas remained in the South.)[16] The population movements in the opposite direction were much larger. Estimates vary, but probably upwards of one million people—Vietnamese Catholics, French or Vietnamese military personnel and their dependents, French civilians, and Vietnamese tribesmen who had served the French as auxiliary troops—fled the North for the South. The resettlement of Catholics in the South helped Diem by providing him with a badly needed if limited political base.[17]

With his American support now firm and the French moving out of the way, Diem solidified his rule by staging a referendum in October 1955 that deposed Bao Dai and made Diem president of a newly created Republic of Vietnam (RVN). Diem received 98 percent of the vote in the well-rigged election. After a January 1956 ordinance that effectively outlawed all organized political opposition, elections to a National Assembly in March 1956 followed the pattern of the October referendum. Ninety of the 123 legislators elected were essentially hand-picked by the Diem government.[18]

Around the same time Diem moved to forestall challenges to central government authority by abolishing the elected village councils that had been set up by Bao Dai. The councils were replaced by committees appointed by the province chiefs, who in turn were to be selected directly by the president. Vietnamese Army (ARVN) officers, often corrupt cronies of Ngo Dinh Nhu and his coterie, were heavily represented among the province chiefs. The committee posts were disproportionately occupied by Catholics who had come from the North and were basically unknown and unsympathetic to the villagers.[19]

The installation of a new political and administrative elite in the countryside roughly coincided with and facilitated the restoration of a traditional elite—the landlords. During the war against the French, the Viet Minh had confiscated French-held land and large Vietnamese-owned estates, distributing land to the landless. Where land was still rented, they placed limits on rental rates and instituted a variety of measures to protect tenants' rights. The Diem regime reversed many of these reforms, and compelled tenants to sign contracts reaffirming the landlords' rights to their land. Diem's subsequent "land reform" program, instituted tardily under pressure from the United States, was largely ineffective, being ridden with loopholes and poorly enforced. Only a tiny percentage of peasants gained any benefits.[20]

Diem thus employed the trappings of constitutionalism to establish an oligarchic dictatorship. He also used brute repression. With the Denunciation of Communism campaign, begun in late 1955, Diem's regime cast a dragnet that swept up anyone suspected of links with the North. The historian Eric Bergerud writes, "Predictably, the Cong An, Diem's police, were hardly discriminating. It proved easy to accuse any potential enemy of having Communist affiliations. Jails filled, and an uncommonly large number of prisoners were shot while attempting to escape."[21] Different estimates of the numbers jailed and executed are roughly consistent. One historian puts the average rate of killings at 150 per month through 1957, with the rate of arrests at 5,000 per month.[22] Another cites figures of 2,000 killed and 65,000 arrested in 1957 alone.[23] A later study by the US Defense Department acknowledged that "there can be no doubt . . . that innumerable crimes and absolutely senseless acts of suppression against both real and suspected Communists and sympathizing villagers were committed. Efficiency took the form of brutality and a total disregard for the difference between determined foes and potential friends."[24]

In the short run, the Denunciation of Communism campaign was a great success. A small, rudimentary Communist Party apparatus had remained underground in the South after the regroupment mandated by Geneva, but it was devastated by Diem's anti-Communist campaign.[25] By the end of 1957 Communist Party membership fell to about one-third of its prior strength of five thousand. Morale within the party dropped precipitously, with some members expressing a sense of betrayal in reaction to their abandonment by their northern comrades.[26]

REVOLT

Soon, however, the Communists started fighting back, aided in their recruitment efforts by resentment stirred by Diem's repression. Clashes between the ARVN and armed units led by former Viet Minh began as early as 1957, with one thousand casualties on both sides before the end of that year. The fighting escalated over the next few years, with casualties reaching eleven thousand during 1959. The Viet Minh also retaliated with a campaign of terror against Vietnamese government personnel and supporters. Beginning in mid-1957, village officials, police and security personnel, and civilians such as schoolteachers and social workers became targets.[27]

Hanoi observed the rising level of unrest in the South with some disquiet. The Vietnamese Workers (Communist) Party in the spring of 1956 gave its southern followers permission to engage in limited self-defense measures in reaction to the anti-Communist campaign, but the party leadership refused to countenance armed rebellion. This stance reflected Hanoi's conclusion that with the shelving of the elections mandated by Geneva the reunification of their country would have to be put on indefinite hold; accordingly, priority would go to consolidating the Communist regime in the North. The Hanoi regime's nonintervention policy also reflected the belief that the weak and corrupt Diem regime would eventually collapse on its own without any help from outside.[28]

It wasn't until January 1959, after often acrimonious internal debate, that Hanoi responded to its southern cadres' repeated pleas for permission to organize an armed resistance.[29] That May, a supply route to the South (the beginning of the famous Ho Chi Minh Trail) was created, and southern Communist regroupees began returning from the North to lend strength and guidance to the growing insurrection. By the end of 1959 the guerillas, including returnees, numbered about five thousand; by late 1960, twelve thousand.[30] The Communists gave the insurgency a political identity in December 1960 with the founding of the National Liberation Front (NLF). The NLF, like the Viet Minh before it, was ostensibly a broad coalition; its components included representatives of the Buddhists, the Catholics, and other non-Communist political and religious groups. The leadership of the NLF nevertheless was definitively in the hands of the Communist Party.

By the time the administration of US president John F. Kennedy took office in January 1961, it was clear that the insurgency posed a serious threat to the government of South Vietnam. It was clear, that is, to the Americans. A good part of the problem, in the view of American policymakers, was the Diem regime: its narrow basis, its corruption and incompetence, its refusal to implement meaningful reforms, and—as a consequence of all the foregoing—its failure to capture the allegiance of the people.[31]

The Kennedy administration nevertheless steadily and substantially increased US support for Diem's regime in dollars, personnel, and military hardware. During 1962 the number of US military advisers to the South Vietnamese armed forces increased to nine thousand, a tenfold increase over the Eisenhower level. Washington established the Military Assistance Command, Vietnam (MACV), and tripled total economic and military aid to Saigon.[32] Still, the Viet Cong (the name that the Americans and their South Vietnamese supporters attached to the NLF forces) continued to score military successes.[33]

Essential to the Viet Cong's achievements in combat was a broadly integrated political/military strategy that involved the construction of an alternative state structure that in many areas of the countryside effectively supplanted the Saigon regime. The historian Marilyn Young cites a US Army report based on captured documents that described how the NLF developed its infrastructure in one village beginning in 1959. NLF cadres launched their campaign with agitation over the abuses of the landlords and Diem-appointed local officials. As the landlords were intimidated into leaving, their holdings were distributed to peasants. (In other areas, the landlords were allowed to remain, but compelled to accept lower rents.) With the similar departure of local administrators, the NLF took over critical public health, sanitation, and education functions and even helped peasants in the marketing of their produce. Young recounts how in time, "the village, now totally removed from Diem's administrative control, was nevertheless still entirely part of the country Diem ruled." Eventually, the village became a full-fledged "combat village" where battalion-strength guerilla units moving at night would camp for short periods of time, gathering food and information from the villagers before moving on to elude the ARVN.³⁴

The authority of the Diem regime came under increasing pressure in the cities as well as in the countryside during 1963. Buddhist resentment of the regime's favoritism toward Catholics led to a series of demonstrations by Buddhist priests, capped in June by a cleric publicly burning himself to death in Saigon. Another priestly self-immolation followed in August. The regime, led by Diem's brother Ngo Dinh Nhu, responded with repression. Buddhist pagodas throughout the country were raided and monks arrested; several monks who resisted arrest were killed.

Washington's patience with Diem was finally exhausted. The US government quietly supported a coup planned by top ARVN generals, but the coup was aborted on August 31 after Diem learned of the conspiracy. A second plot, in late October, was successful after the generals acted despite mixed signals from the United States. In the course of the coup, Diem and his brother were murdered, an outcome not sought or anticipated by the American leadership.

The replacement of Diem led neither to political stability in South Vietnam nor to a more effective prosecution of the war. The next year and a half saw a succession of coups in Saigon, some successful, some not, but none productive of a really authoritative government. Meanwhile the NLF continued to expand its influence and control in the countryside.³⁵ During the course of the year, top policymakers in the administration of President Lyndon Johnson increasingly came to the view that it would soon become necessary to expand the military role of the United States in Vietnam, including possible attacks on the Communist regime in the North. Their thinking was that the key to ending the war in the South was to pressure Hanoi into calling off the insurgency.

ESCALATION

In mid-summer 1964 President Johnson seized an opportunity to lay the basis for a possible future expansion of the US war effort. On August 2, the US destroyer *Maddox* was attacked by North Vietnamese warships in the Gulf of Tonkin after it conducted operations within the twelve-mile coastal limits claimed by North Vietnam. A second, murkier incident, involving the US destroyer *Turner Joy*, occurred two days later and was also characterized by the administration as a deliberate attack by North Vietnam. The Gulf incidents provided the president with the ammunition to present Congress with a resolution that in substance had already been in preparation for some months. The so-called Gulf of Tonkin Resolution not only authorized an immediate armed response to attacks on US military forces; it also granted the administration broad discretion in responding to what it regarded as aggression in Southeast Asia.

The first major step in the escalation of the US war effort came in February 1965 with Operation Rolling Thunder, a sustained bombing campaign against targets in both North and South Vietnam. Launched in mid-February, Rolling Thunder flew twenty-five thousand sorties against North Vietnam during its first year, a number that would triple during 1966.³⁶ Parallel with the escalation of the air war was a massive increase in the presence of American ground forces. At the beginning of 1965, there were twenty-three thousand US troops in Vietnam. A year later there were 184,000; by year-end 1966, the number stood at 385,000, and by early 1968, at 535,000.³⁷ The ARVN, plagued by morale problems and internal squabbling, continued to play a role in the war, but an increasingly subordinate one. The war was becoming Americanized. At the same time, the war on the Communist side was being "northernized" as increasing numbers of North Vietnamese regular troops entered the fight. The US forces alone vastly outnumbered those of the Communists. Viet Cong regular troops, which numbered about thirty-five thousand in 1963, stood at sixty-four thousand by late 1967. North Vietnamese troops, which first appeared in small numbers in late 1964, numbered fifty-four thousand by late 1967.

THE WAR GOES ON . . . AND ON

The rapid escalation of the US military commitment in Vietnam produced something of a stalemate. The disaster that seemed imminently possible in 1964–1965 was averted, but a decisive blow against the insurgency proved elusive. Despite heavy casualties and the punishing bombardment of the North, the Communist leadership showed no indication of a readiness to sue for peace. President Johnson for his part chose to stay the course.

Developments in the South Vietnamese government offered Americans opportunities to view the glass as either half-full or half-empty. An apparently stable South Vietnamese government took power in the spring of 1965 with a coup that installed General Nguyen Van Thieu as president and Air Marshal Nguyen Cao Ky as prime minister. Together with another general, Cao Van Vien, they led the Directory, a committee of generals and colonels that constituted itself as the supreme governing authority in South Vietnam. But the Directory soon confronted a critical challenge. As before, the leading urban protest force was the Buddhists, now joined by an increasingly assertive student movement and even some sectors of the military. Once again, a South Vietnamese government sent troops to attack Buddhist dissidents lodged in pagodas, as well as dissident ARVN units. The government managed to crush all resistance by the end of June. The end result was a new political stability of sorts—the power of the Directory was reinforced, but at the expense of a further weakening of South Vietnamese civil society.³⁸

The Directory followed up this success with a presidential election in the summer of 1967. Washington was heavily involved in the election planning. The field of candidates excluded Communists and avowed neutralists. General Duong Van Minh, the leader of the coup that had overthrown Diem in 1963, was also barred from the ballot. Minh, a Buddhist long suspected of an inclination to negotiate an end to the war, was perhaps the Thieu-Ky ticket's most formidable potential challenger. Aided by a large field that split the vote among ten opponents and by some careful manipulation of the election laws, the Thieu-Ky ticket managed to win with 35 percent of the ballots. Most of the losing candidates filed election fraud charges, which were ignored. The Thieu-Ky showing was considered disappointing, but the Johnson administration nevertheless applauded the election as a milestone in Vietnam's democratic development.[39]

On January 30, 1968, the beginning of Tet, Vietnam's most important holiday, North Vietnamese and NLF forces totaling over eighty thousand men launched attacks in thirty-five of the South's forty-four provincial capitals, sixty-four district capitals, and five of the South's largest cities. In Saigon, NLF units blasted through a wall of the US embassy and attacked the city's airport, the headquarters of South Vietnam's general staff, and the presidential palace.

Militarily, the Tet offensive was a defeat for the Communists. After a couple of weeks of heavy fighting, they were forced to withdraw from most of their positions, incurring huge casualties.

Whatever its impact in South Vietnam, Tet struck at America with shock and awe. Notwithstanding their defeat, the Communists' ability to mount such a large-scale offensive and resist as long as they did clashed head-on with the Johnson administration's effort to project an optimistic picture of the war's progress. The last Gallup poll before Tet had found that 60 percent of Americans described themselves as "hawks" in their view of the war; 24 percent as "doves." After Tet, the numbers were 41 percent and 42 percent.[40] Media perceptions of the war also changed: emblematic was the reaction of CBS anchor Walter Cronkite, often dubbed "the most trusted man in America." After a trip to Vietnam to observe the impact of Tet firsthand, Cronkite expressed to his television audience his newly acquired doubt that the war could end with an American victory. It was time, he said, for this country to find a negotiated way out.[41]

Cronkite wasn't the president's only problem. In early March, Minnesota's Senator Eugene McCarthy, a war critic engaged in a seemingly quixotic campaign to deny Johnson renomination for the presidency, scored a near-win in the bellwether New Hampshire primary. Soon afterward, the president convened a meeting of his panel of foreign policy advisers, the so-called Wise Men. The Wise Men included both senior officeholders in the current administration and veteran stalwarts of the US foreign policy establishment like former secretary of state Dean Acheson. During their last convocation the preceding November, the Wise Men had urged the president to stay the course. This time, they urged him to seek a negotiated settlement of the war. Days later, the president in a nationally broadcast television address announced a halt to the bombing over most of North Vietnam as a peace offering toward getting negotiations started with the Communists. In the same speech, he shocked the nation with his pledge not to seek or to accept his party's nomination to a second term as president. The president soon dispatched veteran diplomat Averell Harriman to Paris where Harriman, assisted by his deputy, Cyrus Vance, entered into a six-month dialogue with the North Vietnamese. Negotiations in one form or another continued on and off for more than four years.

NIXON'S WAR

In November 1968 Richard Nixon was elected to the White House. During his campaign Nixon had assured the American people that he had a secret plan to end the war. He now had to somehow follow up on that promise. His solution was "Vietnamization": the United States would gradually draw down its forces in Vietnam while assisting the South Vietnamese to strengthen their capacity to deal with the enemy. The president announced the first reductions in US troop strength in Vietnam in mid-1969. By the end of 1970, total US forces there had been reduced to 335,000; by early 1972, to 68,000. The Nixon administration, however, remained determined to demonstrate that Vietnamization didn't signal a flagging of American resolve. To maintain the pressure on the enemy, the Nixon administration extended the war to enemy sanctuaries in Cambodia and made wider use than ever of US air power.

THE END

A breakthrough in negotiations followed some of the worst violence of the war in 1972. In January 1973 an agreement between the United States and North Vietnam provided for a cease-fire and a rapid withdrawal of all American troops while allowing the North Vietnamese to keep (but not augment) their forces in the South. The Thieu government could remain but it would accept the legitimacy of the NLF with a view toward forming a coalition government.

The agreement marked the end of direct US involvement in the war—as provided, the last US troops left Vietnam in a matter of months. For Vietnam, however, the cease-fire never really took effect, and fighting raged for two more years. The United States provided some financial assistance to Saigon during this period; the US Congress, understanding that the American people wanted out of Vietnam, refused the Nixon and Ford administrations' requests for more substantial aid. Renewed US military intervention was of course out of the question. Eventually Hanoi prevailed over the politically rickety South Vietnamese regime and its equally rickety army. Communist troops overran Saigon on April 29, 1975. Vietnam's reunification finally was at hand.

The Vietnam War According to Chomsky

Moral outrage pervades Chomsky's writings on Vietnam. The war was an abomination—a "savage battering" of a defenseless people that was "unique in the history of warfare."[42] According to Chomsky, the US government's stated justification for the war—that it was defending the South Vietnamese from aggression from the North—was bogus. The insurgency the United States sought to defeat represented a genuinely indigenous revolt against a succession of oppressive governments backed by the United States. This country's core objective in Vietnam, then, was to impose on the South Vietnamese people a regime congenial to us but unwanted by them. This was necessary, from the US standpoint, because any government truly representing the people of South Vietnam would have been unduly influenced if not controlled by Communists. The United States thus wasn't fighting an outside aggressor; it was fighting the Vietnamese people, who supported our enemy. As a result, the United States "was compelled to undertake a war of annihilation to destroy the society in which [the enemy] gained its support."[43] It follows that the war was reprehensible not only because its objective—the denial of a people's right to self-determination—deserved to be condemned. It was criminally wrong because the means by which it was fought necessarily involved massive violence against an innocent civilian population.

That the military intervention in Vietnam—the US "invasion," in Chomsky's lexicon—was a criminal act, and not simply the result of a series of well-meaning but misguided efforts by US policymakers, is a recurrent theme in Chomsky's writings on the war. Chomsky is explicit and vehement that his critique of the war is based on moral and not merely pragmatic grounds. As opposition to the war mounted in the United States beginning around 1967, Chomsky took pains to attack the positions of war critics whose disaffection reflected the conclusion that the war had become too costly to the United States to be worthwhile. He was notably scornful of the historian Arthur Schlesinger Jr., who, in arguing for a change of course, acknowledged that if the war effort were to turn out to be unexpectedly successful, "we may all be saluting the wisdom and statesmanship of the American government."[44]

SOME PRELIMINARY CONSIDERATIONS: MORAL JUDGMENT AND WAR

Because Chomsky's antiwar stance is so critically based on moral considerations, it would be well to anticipate a fundamental objection that could be leveled at his whole line of argument. Absolutist adherents of the so-called realist school of international relations theory hold that moral concerns should not come into consideration in the evaluation of foreign policy. In a pure realist view, anarchy rather than law governs international politics, which in its fundamentals differs little from a classically Hobbesian war of all against all.[45] Accordingly, the international environment confronting statesmen is one of extreme constraint: "The struggle for power is identical with the struggle for survival and the improvement of the relative power position becomes the primary objective of the internal and the external policy of states. All else is secondary."[46] Given their compulsory preoccupation with power, statesmen can't afford to indulge in moralizing when they make foreign policy decisions. It follows that citizens should not allow moral concerns to influence their evaluations of the foreign policies their leaders pursue.

This isn't the place for an extended discussion of international relations theory; a brief argument should suffice for our purposes. Realism offers many useful insights into international behavior, but in its most dogmatic formulations, it presents a caricature of the international political system, grossly overstating the constraint and understating the discretion available to foreign policy decision makers. It is utterly implausible to claim that the quest for power is so universal and unceasing that the foreign policies of great powers like the United States must be exempt from moral scrutiny. As one critic has observed, "Many moral objectives can be pursued at a cost far less than national survival, sometimes even at little or no cost to the national interest defined in terms of power."[47] Most realist theorists recognize as much, often qualifying their more categorical claims in ways that rob their theories of what initially seems to be a practically iron determinacy. Even the über-realist Hans Morgenthau, for example, acknowledged in 1960 (long before he became a leading critic of the Vietnam War) that "nations recognize a moral obligation to refrain from the infliction of death and suffering under certain conditions despite the possibility of justifying such conduct in the light of . . . the national interest."[48]

Chomsky holds that it is not only appropriate, but it may well be imperative, for responsible citizens to evaluate the moral implications of their countries' foreign policies. I agree. But before we go into the substance of Chomsky's critique, it will be helpful to make one more brief digression into the realm of theory—this time the theory of just and unjust wars.

Rooted in medieval religious discourse and developed over the centuries by secular as well as religious thinkers, just war theory has come to be used by contemporary philosophers as a guide in forming moral judgments about war. While Chomsky doesn't employ the vocabulary of just war theory, its concepts are highly relevant to his arguments. Most critically, just war theory distinguishes two areas of concern in the moral evaluation of war-making: *jus ad bellum*, the justice (or injustice) of war, which concerns whether it is right or wrong to fight a particular war; and *jus in bello*, justice in war, which is concerned with the *way* a war is fought The political philosopher Michael Walzer explains:

> *Jus ad bellum* requires us to make judgments about aggression and self-defense; *jus in bello* about the observance or violation of the customary and positive rules of engagement. The two sorts of judgment are logically independent. It is perfectly possible for a just war to be fought unjustly and for an unjust war to be fought in strict accordance with the rules. . . . It is right to resist aggression, but the resistance is subject to moral (and legal) restraint.[49]

In Chomsky's view, American's war in Vietnam was unjust to start with—the United States had no right to intervene militarily in Vietnam (*jus ad bellum*). To make matters worse, the means the United States employed in Vietnam—the massive destruction of civilian lives—were unconscionable (*jus in bello*).

CHOMSKY'S CRITIQUE IN BRIEF

Chomsky never produced a single synthesis of his critique of US policy in Vietnam. His views are to be found in a number of different articles and books he wrote beginning in the mid-1960s. We can summarize his main arguments as follows:

1. The rationale for the war most often cited by the US government—the need to defend South Vietnam from aggression—was bogus. There was no aggression

by the North Vietnamese regime; it was the United States whose intervention in South Vietnam—its determination to create and sustain a US client regime in the South—constituted "aggression."
2. A second rationale touted by the US government—the protection of the South Vietnamese right to self-determination—was equally bogus. US intervention worked directly counter to the South Vietnamese right to self-determination.
3. Still another justification for the war—the need to stand up against international Communist expansionism—was unsupportable. The Vietnamese fighting the United States weren't tools of Moscow or Peking—they were fighting their own battle for national independence.
4. The US war effort was conducted with callous disregard for human life. The effective prosecution of the war in fact necessitated an unconscionable level of violence directed deliberately against civilians—a "war of annihilation."

We will consider all four arguments in turn.

Was the United States fighting "aggression" in South Vietnam? The official, publicly stated rationale for US military intervention in Vietnam centered on the claim that the United States was responding to the request of a legitimate government for assistance in its defense against external aggression. The infiltration from North to South Vietnam of personnel who would engage in guerilla war constituted a clear-cut case of aggression by the Hanoi regime against the South.

While Washington's case for the war centered on Hanoi's role in attempting to subvert the Saigon regime, Chomsky's critique emphasizes the indigenous nature of the southern insurgency. He notes correctly that the insurrection began fairly spontaneously in the South even as Hanoi stood aloof, that "even according to American propaganda," there was no significant infiltration into the South until 1959–1960, and that most of the infiltrators were in fact native southerners. Even as late as 1965, surveys of Viet Cong prisoners and defectors found most guerillas unaware of any direct Hanoi role in the war.[50]

In stressing the indigenous nature of the southern insurrection, Chomsky and others in the antiwar movement cited the findings of several contemporary historians, including the Frenchmen Philippe Devillers and Jean Lacouture and the American George McT. Kahin. But even before the war ended, information in captured documents and other sources started becoming available, indicating that these historians had understated the operational unity of the Vietnamese Communist Party. Whatever their discontents, the southern Communists were loyal and disciplined members of a single Vietnamese Communist Party; they never significantly overstepped the bounds set for them by Hanoi, to whom they looked for leadership, guidance, and support. It seems unlikely, according to one historian, "that the unrest would have achieved enough coherence and dynamic force to challenge the power of the Saigon regime without the organizational genius provided by the Party leadership in Hanoi."[51]

But Chomsky's case against the war doesn't stand or fall on the assumption that the guerillas were independent of Hanoi. After all, he argues, Vietnam was one country, not two; hence, there can be no possibility of external aggression by the Vietnamese. Chomsky's argument rests solidly on Vietnam's history, most recently as recognized in the Geneva agreements. Chomsky quotes the Final Declaration at Geneva, which states explicitly that "the military demarcation line is provisional and should not in any way be interpreted as constituting a political or territorial boundary" and that Vietnam should be united through elections under international control.[52] Indeed, even the 1967 constitution of *South* Vietnam states that "Vietnam [not South Vietnam] is a territorially indivisible, unified, and independent republic."[53] So, according to Chomsky, "even if Ho Chi Minh were to have sent his entire army to South Vietnam, he would not have been guilty of 'aggression,' but only of insurrection and subversion."[54]

Moreover, the North's aid to the insurrection in the South was fully justified given the southern regime's refusal to abide by the Geneva Accords. Chomsky correctly observes that the Viet Minh had "accepted the Geneva Accords in good faith and made a serious effort to initiate discussions that would lead to the elections promised in 1956. The American-instituted regime in the South took advantage of this naiveté to institute an extensive repression."[55] In response to this repression, an insurrection broke out. The insurrection was purely indigenous, and viewed in fact with some wariness by Hanoi. Eventually the rebels were joined by Vietnamese coming from the North, but who were overwhelmingly of southern origin; they were former Viet Minh who had gone north after 1954 in observance of the Geneva Accords, expecting that the promised reunifying elections would enable them to return to their homes. Hanoi encouraged and facilitated this infiltration, but "it is difficult to see why this should be impermissible, after the subversion of the Geneva Agreements and the American and Saigon violations of the Geneva Accords, the Diemist repression, and the renewal of guerilla war in the South in 1957."[56] Hanoi, having in effect been cheated out of half the victory it reasonably felt it had won by 1954, was fully justified in coming to the aid of that insurrection.

The war in Vietnam, then, was a civil war, but a civil war with a major external participant—the United States. In fact, if there was an external aggressor in Vietnam, it was the United States, which deliberately subverted the 1954 Geneva agreements for the peaceful reunification of Vietnam. US aggression first took the form of a variety of political, economic, and military efforts to establish an independent state of South Vietnam, in violation of the Geneva Accords. Chomsky quotes a Defense Department analyst writing in the Pentagon Papers:

> South Vietnam . . . was essentially the creation of the United States. Without U.S. support Diem almost certainly could not have consolidated his hold on the South during 1955 and 1956. Without the threat of U.S. intervention, South Vietnam could not have refused to even discuss the elections called for in 1956 under the Geneva settlement without being immediately overrun by the Viet Minh armies. Without

U.S. aid in the years following, the Diem regime certainly, and an independent South Vietnamese regime almost as certainly, could not have survived.[57]

Increasingly, the US participation took the form of military intervention, in further blatant violation of the Geneva Accords. Chomsky likes to point out that the US military presence in Vietnam at every stage outpaced that of Hanoi. US military assistance to the South began long before the 1959 North Vietnamese decision to aid the southern rebellion. And, by mid-1965, American troops in South Vietnam had increased to forty-five thousand, while regular North Vietnamese regular troops still numbered far below ten thousand.[58] (Native southern infiltrators from the North numbered in the tens of thousands at the time.) US troops in South Vietnam in fact continued to vastly outnumber North Vietnamese and NLF troops combined until after Vietnamization was well underway in 1970.

OF COURSE, DEFENDERS OF THE US intervention had responses to most of these arguments.

One response that Chomsky correctly dismisses is that the intent of the Geneva Accords was somehow ambiguous—that it wasn't clear that the division of Vietnam was truly intended to be only temporary.[59] Most of the participants at Geneva in fact genuinely expected the provision for reunification of Vietnam through elections to be implemented. It was only later, as Diem seemed to be prevailing in his resistance to elections, that this expectation faded.[60]

Another counterargument, advanced by Diem himself in 1955–1956, is that free and fair elections could not have been held given the totalitarian control of North Vietnam by the Communists.[61] This claim might have had more credibility if Diem had at least consented to consult with the North Vietnamese on setting up elections, but it is also disingenuous: all informed observers, including US intelligence and Defense Department analysts on up to the president of the United States, expected that the Viet Minh would win free elections had they been held in the period specified by Geneva.[62] Diem wasn't afraid of rigged elections; he was afraid of elections, period. (Diem, of course, showed that he himself was no slacker when it came to rigging elections.) In any case, any obstacles to free elections were known or easily foreseeable at the time of the Geneva Conference; the later claim that such obstacles made it impossible to implement the conference provisions thus can have no validity.[63]

A more compelling defense of US intervention, which I think Chomsky dismisses too cavalierly, is that regardless of the Geneva agreements, two de facto states of Vietnam existed by 1959; the use of force by one against the other therefore constituted aggression.[64] South Vietnam by the late 1950s had won diplomatic recognition from several dozen nations and was a member of numerous international organizations, including specialized agencies of the United Nations. Its membership in the United Nations, proposed by the United States in 1957, had been vetoed by the Soviet Union. But before their veto, the Soviets, to the consternation of the North Vietnamese, had proposed admission of both North and South Vietnam (a compromise rejected by the United States). So, the argument goes, South Vietnam, like its Northern counterpart, was a de facto international entity, if not a de jure state: "Since disputes about the legality of the origin of territorial entities or exercises of authority over territory are common, it would greatly undermine the basic prohibition on unilateral use of force in international relations to allow unilateral resort to force to change a continuing *de facto* exercise of authority."[65]

One problem with this argument is that it legitimates the US fait accompli of establishing the state of South Vietnam in contravention of the Geneva agreements. It says in effect that the United States succeeded in creating a new reality, and the North Vietnamese just had to live with it. Advocates of this point of view will argue that world order rests on implicit ground rules that necessarily reflect the realities of power in the international system. Great powers like the United States get to set those rules; small countries like North Vietnam are perforce bystanders. Might does indeed make right.

This line of argument will certainly appeal to faithful believers in the role of American power in the world: if American foreign policy is fundamentally beneficent, then more power to it. Chomsky, of course, is not such a believer. Instead, he repeatedly criticizes the assumption that great powers like the United States have a right to impose their will on smaller countries. Chomsky is convincing in arguing that this assumption, though usually implicit and cloaked in rationalizations, was widespread in US elite opinion.[66]

Moreover, Chomsky argues that even if we accept that the division of Vietnam created two de facto national entities, North Vietnam's aid to the southern insurrection was justifiable—certainly no less justifiable than US aid to Saigon, given the South Vietnamese government's fragile hold on power. It would clearly be unjust, in Chomsky's view,

> to hold . . . that governments recognized by the major powers are legally permitted to call in outside force to put down a domestic insurgency, while insurgents are not entitled to seek outside help. Suppose further that this rule applies even where the insurgents constitute the only effective government in large areas and the only mass-based political organization, and where these insurgents are asking support from a state from which they have been arbitrarily separated by great-power intervention and subversion.[67]

Chomsky here is evidently utilizing an argument about external involvement in civil conflicts developed by the legal scholar Richard Falk. Falk poses the question, "To what extent does the constituted elite—the incumbent regime—enjoy a privileged position to request outside help in suppressing internal challenges directed at its control?" According to Falk, "Traditional international law permits military assistance to the incumbent regime during early stages of an internal challenge. However, once the challenging faction demonstrates its capacity to gain control and administer a substantial portion of the society, most authorities hold that a duty of neutrality or nondiscrimination governs the relations of both factions to outside states."[68]

Accordingly, Falk argues that even if it is conceded that the North Vietnamese contribution to the rebellion in the South was significant, the US involvement in the South would have had to be proportionate to that of North Vietnam. But, US aid to the South was consistently disproportionate to the North's aid to the rebels, and necessarily so, given the indigenous strength of the Viet Cong and the weakness of the Saigon government. He further argues that US support of Cuban exiles in the Bay of Pigs was a far more flagrant use of exiles to overthrow a constituted government: the United States had less claim to control Cuba than North Vietnam had over the South, and Castro's regime was domestically viable in a way that no Saigon regime ever was. "It seems more destructive of world order to help overthrow a firmly established government than to assist an ongoing revolution against a regime incapable of governing."[69] Indeed, it is surprising that Chomsky neglects to make the obvious polemical point that if Hanoi was guilty of aggression, so too was the United States repeatedly during the course of the twentieth century, most recently in its interventions to overthrow established regimes in Iran (1953) and Guatemala (1954) as well as in Cuba.

Falk does not, however, claim that his legal argument is conclusive; he acknowledges that the "doctrinal ambiguity [of international law] is greatest with respect to internal war with significant external participation. International law offers very little authoritative guidance on the central issue of permissible assistance to the contending factions."[70] Other prominent legal scholars came to essentially similar conclusions as to the inadequacy of existing international law to provide a firm answer to the question of the legitimacy of US intervention in Vietnam.[71]

In sum, defining "aggression" in the case of the Vietnam War is an exceedingly difficult task; the argument that the US intervention in Vietnam was an appropriate reaction to aggression is therefore dubious at best. It must rest, ultimately, on an argument for force majeure: the North Vietnamese were properly obliged to respect the fait accompli by which the United States effectively scuttled the Geneva agreements. A rationale in terms of force majeure is a far cry from the noble-sounding "defense of an ally against aggression" that was the principal justification for war advanced by successive US administrations. Even then, it is hard to justify intervention on behalf of a regime with a tenuous claim to legitimacy.

The issue of the Saigon government's legitimacy is closely linked to our next question.

Was the United States protecting the South Vietnamese right to self-determination? Certainly not, in Chomsky's view. On the contrary, the US objective in Vietnam was "to ensure the domination of those elements that will enter into partnership with us."[72] Unfortunately, the Vietnamese people were not inclined to be governed by "those elements." Their preferences went instead to the Viet Minh and their successors. As one Pentagon analyst recognized, "For many [Vietnamese peasants], the struggle which began in 1945 against colonialism continued uninterrupted throughout Diem's regime: in 1954, the foes of nationalists were transferred from France and Bao Dai, to Diem and the U.S. . . . but the issues at stake never changed."[73] Hence the need, in Dean Acheson's words, for the French to "overcome opposition of [the] indigenous population" in order to defeat the Viet Minh; the need to avoid the elections mandated by the Geneva Accords; and the need thereafter to support dictatorial regimes that could not permit free and fair elections.[74] A US National Intelligence estimate completed in August 1954 opined, "If the scheduled national elections are held . . . the Viet Minh will almost certainly win," an outcome that was clearly unacceptable to the US government.[75] Throughout the history of US involvement in Vietnam, US policymakers were determined to impose a non-Communist regime regardless of the preferences of the Vietnamese people.

It is undoubtedly true that none of the Saigon regimes that enjoyed the support of the United States enjoyed widespread popular backing. As Chomsky notes, the Thieu-Ky regime that eventually succeeded Diem was probably even more narrowly based, and even more corrupt, than its notorious predecessor. Even under the manipulated conditions of the 1967 election, Thieu and Ky only managed to win 35 percent of the vote. (Thieu didn't take any chances for his reelection in 1971—he made sure he got over 90 percent of the vote in an essentially one-man show.)

It is equally undoubtedly true that the National Liberation Front did enjoy widespread popularity. Just how popular the NLF was is impossible to say; public opinion polls were not a part of the Vietnamese political landscape in the 1960s, and the NLF of course never had the opportunity to compete in an election. But American leaders and policy analysts consistently recognized the broad-based popularity of the former Viet Minh and later their successors. Chomsky quotes Pentagon analysts acknowledging in the twilight of the Diem regime that "only the Viet Cong had any real support and influence on a broad base in the countryside" while the Saigon government, even after Diem's fall, continued to decline in legitimacy.[76] Chomsky also cites Douglas Pike, a strongly pro-war USIA officer who served for several years in Vietnam, who estimated that perhaps half of the overall Vietnamese population at least tacitly supported the Viet Cong in 1963.[77] As Chomsky pointedly observes, 50 percent support is an impressively high level in a largely peasant country where it would be reasonable to expect a large portion of the population to be apolitical.

Regional and village-level studies of Vietnam at war similarly point to the formidable popular support achieved by the Viet Cong, and the corresponding unpopularity of the Saigon governments. James Trullinger, who studied a village near Hue, estimated that the guerillas had achieved a 75 percent level of popular support by the early 1960s.[78] The historian David Elliott described the "overwhelming popular support" achieved by the NLF in a province at the other end of Vietnam by the early 1960s, reflecting "the benefits of land distribution and rent reduction, the elimination of oppressive GVN [Government of Vietnam] local officials . . . and a deep-rooted feeling that the revolution was the authentic face of Vietnamese nationalism and that the [Diem regime] was merely an extension of foreign domination." People greeted Viet Cong cadres as a welcome relief to the oppression of the Saigon government and its officials, and participation in the revolution was broad-based and often spontaneous.[79] As the historian Eric Bergerud explains,

> The peasantry perceived the GVN to be aloof, corrupt and inefficient. . . . The GVN lacked legitimacy because, in most important respects, it represented a continuation of the political and social structure established over the years by the French colonial administration. South Vietnam's urban elite possessed the outward manifestations of a foreign culture and often professed an alien faith. . . . In sharp contrast to GVN officials, Front cadres were perceived by most peasants as honest, efficient, and coming as they did from the ranks of the peasantry more responsive to the rural population.[80]

As late as 1966, a member of the South Vietnamese junta admitted, "We are very weak politically and without the strong political support of the population which the NLF have. . . . We are without a political instrument that can compete with the Communists in the south. Such a political instrument we must now begin to create, a process that will take a generation."[81]

We can only guess at the likely results of elections that were never held. But the preponderance of evidence is clear: had genuinely free elections been held at any point between the early 1950s and the mid- to late 1960s, the Communists and their allies would almost surely have captured a plurality, if not an outright majority, of the vote nationwide.[82] Which is why none of the governments in Saigon ever allowed such elections to take place. And, of course, why there was never any pressure from Washington for Saigon to hold such elections.

Chomsky, then, is correct: the US intervention in Vietnam from the beginning served to frustrate, not protect, Vietnamese self-determination. And it could not be otherwise, given the US determination to maintain a non-Communist regime in a country whose people inconveniently tended to prefer the Communists.

But there is a counterargument, which Chomsky does not entertain. Communist regimes, once installed, notoriously do not hold free elections and do not yield power. Even if a Communist regime in South Vietnam had come to power with the initial support or acquiescence of its people, it would have denied that people any future opportunity to change their mind. The American insistence on maintaining a non-Communist regime in Saigon thus served to maintain the South Vietnamese people's long-term possibilities for self-determination. Skeptics will point to the obviously Orwellian ring to this argument: "We must deny the Vietnamese their right to self-determination in order to preserve that right." It's also an argument just too conveniently and universally serviceable in America's Cold-War contest with Communism: practically by definition, it becomes impossible for any people ever to choose to be ruled by Communists, even if they do so choose. Skeptics will further note that the prospects of the Vietnamese achieving democratic self-determination under American tutelage reasonably had to be regarded as problematic: the Thieu regime might have yielded to a democratic order had the war been won, but it might not have. Other US-sponsored Asian dictatorships, notably Taiwan and South Korea, eventually did develop into democracies, but those developments took several decades to unfold. And, on the other hand, it is at least conceivable that a Communist regime in South Vietnam would have retained the support of its people indefinitely, even in the absence of Western-style free elections.

In sum, America's war in Vietnam was fought to maintain a US-friendly government in a country whose people, we had good reason to fear, would vote Communist if allowed to. The claim that America was protecting the South Vietnamese right to self-determination is empty: it is barely plausible only if based on speculative future possibilities. Even then it fails, because as far as self-determination is concerned, there was no clear-cut choice between a certainly good future for a South Vietnam under American tutelage and a certainly bad future under the Communists. American intervention actually served to block any immediate possibilities for the South Vietnamese to choose their own rulers. The promise of democracy in some uncertain future cannot serve as a justification for denying a people's right to democratic self-determination in the present.

Was the war necessary to contain Soviet or Chinese expansionism? Nonsense, says Chomsky, but the specter of international Communism served the need of successive administrations to bolster their weak public rationale for intervention in Vietnam: "It would have been difficult to convince Americans that Ho Chi Minh posed a threat to their welfare or survival. The Soviet Union or Dean Rusk's billion Chinese are another matter." (Actually, by the 1960s, it was China, rather than the Soviet Union, that US leaders usually cited as the instigator of the Vietnam War.) Chomsky cites the Sino-Soviet split and rumblings in Eastern Europe as evidence that international Communism wasn't monolithic, and points to "the admitted refusal of North Vietnam, even in its present desperate straits, to kowtow to its powerful allies." Indeed, the historical antagonism between China and Vietnam, reflected in the known attitudes of some members of the North Vietnamese leadership, suggests that "if we were really interested in containing Chinese expansionism, we should presumably be supporting Ho Chi Minh, along with all popular, indigenous forces on the border with China, whatever their domestic character."[83] Privately, US decision makers understood that a unified Vietnam under Communism would most likely reassert its traditional hostility to China.[84]

We don't need to devote much space to this question. There is no reason to doubt that the North Vietnamese Communist Party was a committed and loyal member of the international Communist movement, and was tied by bonds of ideological solidarity with both China and the Soviet Union. Hanoi's leaders certainly consulted regularly with their Soviet and Chinese counterparts. But there is no credible evidence that Hanoi acted at the behest of either of the major Communist powers in making its commitment to the conflict in the South.[85] There is, instead, considerable evidence that both Chinese and Soviet Communists counseled patience to their Vietnamese comrades; the Vietnamese were urged to seek unification through a long-term diplomatic and political effort, awaiting more favorable conditions rather than relying on military means. Many Vietnamese Communists resented the Soviet Union for its line of peaceful coexistence. And, decades later, Vietnamese Communists speculated that China preferred a divided Vietnam, because the division prevented Vietnam's emergence as a regional power rival to China.[86]

North Vietnam did receive a great deal of critical aid from both Russia and China during its war with the United States, but, as a contemporary observer noted, "Because of the Sino-Soviet dispute, [the North Vietnamese] can take the aid from both and the advice from neither. Thus neither side has much leverage."[87] A later historian recounted that "the wary Vietnamese did not permit their powerful northern neighbors to share in decision making" and "developed into an art form the exploitation of divisions among their allies."[88]

In sum, Chomsky was undoubtedly correct that in fighting a war of liberation in the South, Hanoi was acting for itself, not as an agent of either Communist major power. This is not to say that America's war in Vietnam had no implications for its conflicts elsewhere in the world with its Communist adversaries. It was certainly plausible that a Communist victory in Vietnam would strengthen Communist-led insurgencies elsewhere. (As we shall see in the next chapter, Chomsky himself held that view.) The point is that American intervention in Vietnam was not a response to aggressive designs by the Soviet Union or China, and the attempt to sell it as such was bogus.

Did the United States wage a "war of annihilation" against the Vietnamese peasantry? In late 1969 news reports surfaced of a horrific massacre in the village of My Lai a year and a half earlier. A company of American troops entered a village expecting to engage enemy fighters. Instead they found only unarmed villagers. They proceeded to kill some five hundred people—overwhelmingly women, children, and old men—in cold blood. The My Lai revelation rocked US public opinion. To Chomsky, however, it was unremarkable: "In fact, it is difficult to understand the surprise or concern over My Lai, considering the relative triviality of this incident in the context of the over-all American policies in Indochina."[89]

In Chomsky's view, massive violence knowingly directed against civilians was integral to the US war effort. This violence aimed to cripple the guerillas, who depended critically on their ability to recruit and draw support from Vietnam's peasant population. The guerillas had gained that support through years of activism at the grass roots of rural life. To defeat the enemy—to cut them off from the life support provided them by their popular base—it was necessary effectively to destroy rural society: "Massacre and forced evacuation of the peasantry, combined with rigorous control over those forced under American rule, is the essence of American strategy in Vietnam . . . [because] there is no other technique that can be effective against a 'people's war.'"[90] Thus, the strategy was as rational as it was ruthless: "The savagery of the war does not reflect some peculiar streak of barbarism in the United States command. Rather, there was no other way to solve the problem . . . of destroying the nationalist movement that the Communists had 'captured.'"[91]

According to Chomsky, then, the "context" of My Lai was a wide-ranging assault on Vietnamese rural society, an assault that was carried out primarily by air power and supplemented by artillery bombardment. The US air war in South Vietnam began in earnest in mid-1965, roughly coincident with the initiation of regular bombing of the North. Chomsky points out that while public attention generally focused on the US bombing of North Vietnam, the South was in fact bombed far more heavily than the North. He approvingly cites the French Vietnam expert, Bernard Fall, who in October 1965 asserted that "what changed the character of the Vietnam War was *not* the decision to bomb North Vietnam; *not* the decision to use American ground troops in South Vietnam; but the decision to wage unlimited aerial warfare inside the country at the price of literally pounding the place to bits."[92] Chomsky's claim that the battering South Vietnam received was "unique in the history of warfare" is inarguably correct: South Vietnam was hit by four million tons of bombs between 1963 and 1973—a larger tonnage than the US dropped in all theaters combined during World War II—making it the most bombed country in history.[93]

Chomsky's view of the Vietnam War as an annihilating assault on Vietnamese rural society can be assessed under two closely related topics: the creation of refugees, and physical attacks—via air power, artillery bombardment or land operations—on the civilian population.

The war turned Vietnam into a nation of refugees. Estimates of the number of refugees generated during the course of the war range between 3.5 and 5 million people, not counting people who were only temporarily displaced.[94] Most refugees were displaced for two or more years. These are staggering numbers, considering that the population of South Vietnam stood at just about eighteen million in 1970. For the Vietnamese peasant, refugee status generally meant impoverishment. Most refugees had to leave everything they owned—livestock, furniture, and farm implements. Craftsmen had to leave their tools; shopkeepers left their stock.[95] The loss of homeland was psychologically traumatic as well as economically disastrous: "In the eyes of their inhabitants, villages were much more than places to live or cultivate; they were revered as shrines, the natural world around them was the home of the spirits they prayed to and the graves of their ancestors were symbols of death and reincarnation. Leaving these places was unthinkable except in dire emergency."[96]

Peasants who were forced to leave their villages either found their way to the cities, or were resettled in refugee camps. The task of accommodating the needs of the huge refugee population was naturally tremendous, one which the US and

South Vietnamese authorities evidently were not up to performing effectively. Refugee camps were little better than open-air prisons, and in many ways worse, since living conditions often were far below acceptable standards for prisons in the United States. A Government Accounting Office (GAO) report described a 1970 visit to a refugee camp on Vietnam's central coast:

> We observed there were no latrines, no usable wells, no classrooms, and no medical facilities. The shelters were crudely constructed from a variety of waste material, such as empty ammunition boxes and cardboard. We observed that the number of shelters would not adequately house these people. . . . The [American] refugee adviser stated that there were no plans to improve the living conditions at this site.[97]

Another camp—considered one of the worst of sixty-eight camps in its province—was described as surrounded by concrete walls, barbed wire, and armed soldiers. No one was allowed out during the day and the gates were locked at night. There was little food or shelter, and most occupants were forced to sleep outdoors even in monsoon season because there were few wooden barracks. Hunger was common, as were malaria, dysentery, and infectious hepatitis.[98]

Peasants who took refuge in the cities were hardly better off. By 1968 practically every major city and provincial and district capital had on its outskirts a squalid slum peopled with refugees living in abysmal conditions, typically lacking basic sanitation facilities and adequate water supplies.[99]

What caused this huge refugee flow? Wars inevitably disrupt normal everyday life, and people often flee their homes to avoid the crossfire of contending armies. The Vietnam War was distinctive, however, in that the generation of refugees was central to one side's military strategy. The strategy was based on the belief that the forcible relocation of civilian population from areas subject to Viet Cong influence was the most effective way of depriving the guerillas of supplies and manpower—of draining the water in which they swam.[100]

The population relocation strategy had antecedents in earlier efforts by the South Vietnamese government to fight the insurgency by separating the peasants from the guerillas. The "strategic hamlet" program, launched in 1962, sought to concentrate the rural population in fortified villages, where they would be "protected" from the Viet Cong. The program met with resistance: "In practice, the strategic hamlets became instruments of control rather than pacification. The peasants resented having to leave their homes and gardens and being herded into fortified stockades which the government forced them to build without compensation for their labor."[101] Despite the support of the US government and vastly inflated claims of success by Saigon, implementation of the program fell far behind target, and it was abandoned soon after Diem's death.

The strategic hamlet concept was long outlasted, however, by an associated strategic innovation: the creation of "free-fire zones." These were designated by the commander of the ARVN as areas subject to bombardment by artillery and air strikes in order to drive the population into strategic hamlets. There were 105 such zones by November 1962, from which several tens of thousands of refugees already had fled.[102]

The population relocation strategy was reinvigorated soon after the major escalation of the US war effort in 1965. Chomsky cites a December 1965 encounter between the MAVC supreme commander General William Westmoreland and journalists, in which the general explains the rationale for the strategy:

> In the past year we have seen an escalation to a higher level of intensity in the war. This will bring about a moment of decision for the peasant farmer. He will have to choose if he stays alive. Until now the peasant farmer has had three alternatives: he could stay put and follow his natural instinct to stay close to the land, living beside the graves of his ancestors. He could move to an area under government control. Or he could join the VC. . . . Now if he stays put there are additional dangers. The VC can't patch up wounds. If the peasant becomes a refugee, he does get shelter, food and security, job opportunities and is given a hope to possibly return to his land. The third alternative is life with the VC. The VC have not made good on their promises; they no longer have secure areas. There are B-52 bombings, the VC tax demands are increasing; they want more recruits at the point of a gun, forced labor to move supplies. The battle is being carried more and more to the enemy.[103]

When Westmoreland was asked, "Doesn't that give the villager only the choice of becoming a refugee?" He replied, "I expect a tremendous increase in the number of refugees." Thus, peasants were made to understand that they could not rely on the NLF for protection ("They no longer have secure areas"); those who refused to come under GVN control were subject to extermination.

The use of violence or the threat of violence against civilians to achieve political objectives is conventionally described as terrorism. Westmoreland doesn't use the word, of course, but it is clear that he is talking about using terror to induce the peasants to relocate. Two years later, Westmoreland again described the relocation strategy: "The success of the communist insurgency program is dependent upon control of the people. . . . In order to thwart the communist's [sic] designs, it is necessary to eliminate the 'fish' from the 'water,' or to dry up the 'water' so that the 'fish' cannot survive." There were two ways to do that, he explained: either drive the Communists out of the populated areas or relocate people. The first is expensive and time consuming, making the second the method of choice.[104]

The American military's use of terror against the civilian population is summarized in careful euphemisms (in my added italics) by the historian Guenter Lewy, a supporter of the war's legitimacy:

> In view of the great difficulties experienced in bringing *security* to the people it was considered easier to bring the people to security, and until late 1968 the prevalent but uncodified policy was that of compulsory relocations and *displacement by*

military pressure through combat operations, crop destruction and the creation of *specified strike zones* [i.e., free-fire zones].[105]

Here "security" for the people is a code word for separation from the Viet Cong. Lewy evidently sees no irony in a policy of making people more secure by bombing them, thus inducing them to seek security.

Often, population relocation was carried out systematically by US and ARVN troops in conjunction with the planning of military operations. For example, Operation Cedar Falls was launched in January 1967 in the so-called Iron Triangle, an NLF bastion northwest of Saigon. The operation's mission was to scour the area for enemy installations and clear it of all civilians so that it could be declared a specified strike zone (the new euphemism for "free-fire zone," a term that had come under criticism for its connotation of indiscriminate violence). Over the course of nineteen days, over six thousand civilians—all presumed Viet Cong sympathizers—were removed with their belongings and livestock in a carefully organized mass evacuation. Bunkers and tunnels were then blown up and houses and other structures were leveled. In April 1967, eight thousand Montagnard tribesmen were relocated for the multiple purposes of denying food and manpower to the Viet Cong, bringing more people under GVN control, and creating a free-fire zone along the Cambodian border where the Ho Chi Minh Trail entered Vietnam. An even larger relocation was carried out the following month in the demilitarized zone for the purpose of clearing areas of North Vietnamese troops and artillery without fear of civilian casualties. Thirteen thousand people were taken from their homes to the Cam Lo resettlement area twenty miles away.[106]

This last operation was described in vivid detail by William Corson, a US Army lieutenant colonel who had taken part in it. According to Corson, military urgency had made it necessary to launch the operation without advance notice to the villagers, who were overwhelmingly women, children, and old men:

> Loudspeaker bullhorns were used to call the people from their homes and fields, where the rice harvest was due in three weeks. . . . Those who failed to move with sufficient alacrity were prodded w. clubs and bayonets. When "the word" was passed about what was to happen, a groan escaped from the people because they knew their crops would either be destroyed or rot in the fields. . . . When the destination of Cam Lo was announced another groan rose from the crowd.[107]

The first groan, he explained, reflected their dismay at being turned into paupers and stripped of their dignity as productive human beings. The second groan reflected the fact that 90 percent of the villagers had never traveled further than ten kilometers from their homes. They feared that Cam Lo would be a point of no return—a frightening prospect for Buddhists who dreaded dying in a strange place, which might impede their possibility for passing on to the Buddhist version of heaven. "Without a shot being fired, we had conspired with the GVN to literally

destroy the hopes, aspirations and emotional stability of 13,000 human beings....
Within three weeks the crops had rotted in the fields, [and] the hamlets around
Trung Luong were ghost towns."[108]

Peasants venturing back into free-fire zones—a common occurrence, given
the peasants' resistance to leave in the first place—were subject to the general rule
that anything that moved was a fair target. Westmoreland explained this rule during a June 1967 visit to troops in the field: "If the people are in relocation camps,
they're green, so they're safe. We leave them alone. The Vietcong and NVA are red,
so we know they're fair game. But if there are people who are out there—and not
in the camps—they're pink as far as we're concerned. They're Communist sympathizers. They were not supposed to be there."[109]

Population movements weren't always a consequence of planned relocations.
Often, refugee flight was a spontaneous response to the dangers posed by allied
military operations. Sometimes the creation of free-fire zones was preceded only
briefly by warning infantry sweeps or leaflet drops or loudspeaker announcements. Peasants not reached by these communications became the victims of allied bombardments and artillery fire. Villages could become targets of air and
artillery bombardment even in the absence of free-fire zone designation. The
American military's rules of engagement required that the population be warned
before attacks on settled areas, but this principle was a matter of discretion: the requirement to inform residents in advance ceased to apply as soon as a commanding officer believed that the element of surprise was necessary for the success for
his operation. And commanding officers decided whether and in what circumstances such warnings were repeated. "Once warned always warned" became a GI
stockphrase.[110]

There were also numerous cases of air strikes against villages and other targets "suspected" of harboring the Viet Cong in cases where there was no ground
engagement. One journalist recounted a story of a paratroop unit that drew half
a dozen rounds of small-arms sniper fire when it approached a small village. The
unit halted and called in an air and artillery strike that leveled the village. "It
seemed an extraordinary response to a few rounds of sniper fire."[111] The historian
Jeffrey Race recounted an almost identical incident in 1967 in the village he studied, and added that the commander's decision to call in the air and artillery strike
was not only consistent with but positively mandated by the military's rules of
engagement.[112] According to Lewy, refugee studies in different regions in 1966 and
1967 showed that between 31 percent and 65 percent of refugees cited artillery fire
and bombardment as the principal reason for their leaving their homes.[113] Most
of the new arrivals to the cities were also in similar flight, according to a US Army
staff study.[114] Of course, not everybody made it.

Chomsky cites numerous examples, mostly from press reports, of the mayhem
inflicted on civilians by MACV and ARVN operations. A particularly egregious
case was recounted in a letter to the editor of the *New York Times* by the journalists Jonathan and Orville Schell, who had spent six months in Quangngai Province during 1967:

The "pacification" camps became so full that Army units were ordered not to "generate" any more refugees. The Army complied. But search-and-destroy operations continued.

Only now peasants were not warned before an air-strike was called in on their village. They were killed in their villages because there was no room for them in the swamped pacification camps. The usual warnings by helicopter loudspeaker or air dropped leaflets were stopped. Every civilian on the ground was assumed to be enemy by the pilots by nature of living in Quangngai, which was largely a free-fire zone. . . .

Village after village was destroyed from the air as a matter of de facto policy. Air strikes on civilians became a matter of routine.[115]

Many more such stories were compiled by antiwar activists during the 1960s.[116] *New York Times* reporter Neil Sheehan in November 1965 reported on the fate of Duchai, a complex of five fishing villages on the coast, also in Quangngai Province:

> In mid-August United States and Vietnamese military officials decided the Communists were using Duchai as a base for their operations in the area and that it should be destroyed. For the next two months . . . it was periodically and ferociously shelled by Seventh Fleet destroyers and bombed by Vietnamese and American planes. . . . At least 198 civilians died during Duchai's two months of agony. Some reasonable estimates run as high as 600. . . . When an American visits Duchai these days, villagers . . . [tell] him horror stories of how many of the 15,000 former inhabitants were killed by bombs and shells.
>
> "There," said a fisherman pointing to a bomb crater beside a ruined house, "a woman and her 6 children were killed in a bomb shelter when it got a direct hit."[117]

Sheehan reported that at least 10 other villages in the province had been destroyed as thoroughly as the 5 in Duchai, while 450 other villages had been under intermittent attack by US and Vietnamese planes. The provincial hospital in Quangngai Town was admitting six hundred to one thousand civilians per month wounded by bombs, shells and bullets; about 30 percent required major surgery.[118]

Similar stories emerge from interview-based local and regional studies of Vietnam at war. The historian David Elliott, whose monumental study of a Mekong Delta province is the most exhaustive of the works of this genre, recounts the "massive and indiscriminate firepower" employed by the US Ninth Infantry Division in an "incessant bombing and shelling of the countryside" that produced a "catastrophically high level of civilian casualties."[119] Like Chomsky, Elliott questions the significance of My Lai, which he says can be attributed to the behavior of a few officers, while the extensive carnage resulting from air and artillery operations was a consequence of official policy.[120] The exceptional attention given to My Lai does indeed reflect a curious fact of human perception: homicide from a distance—by air or artillery—tends to be seen as less horrifying, and more likely to be justifiable in terms of military necessity, than homicide in which the killers and victims meet face-to-face.

But it is wrong to suggest that My Lai was insignificant. There is by now a mountain of evidence that while My Lai was almost surely exceptional in the number of people killed, many hundreds if not thousands of comparable smaller incidents occurred during the course of the war. Much of the evidence comes from official US government sources. One of these sources was a commission set up under General William Peers to examine the My Lai incident but went on to investigate other similar cases. The Peers Commission's research generated over one hundred archive boxes of material. Peers submitted a four-volume report in March and April 1970, which became public in 1975. A second US Army source is the research output of the Vietnam War Crimes Working Group (VWCWG), also set up by the army shortly after the Peers Commission, to review all accusations of US war crimes and atrocities. The VWCWG eventually created a 10,000-page archive covering 246 cases. Following a Freedom of Information Act inquiry, the archive was released to the National Archives in 1994. These data sources have been largely untouched by academic historians, though they have been the subject of books and Pulitzer Prize-winning articles by journalists.[121]

Along with statistical analyses, memoranda, and other internal reports, these archives contain hundreds of sworn statements and letters from soldiers and veterans who committed or witnessed rapes, tortures, murders, massacres, and other atrocities. Every major division that served in Vietnam was represented. Journalists working through the Peers archive alone counted over three hundred allegations in cases that were substantiated by the army's own investigations. Five hundred additional allegations couldn't be proved or hadn't been fully investigated. According to officers who helped compile the records, those numbers represented only a small fraction of the atrocities committed in Vietnam.[122] Among the documents was a letter from a "concerned sergeant" writing in May 1970 about his company's activities during Operation Speedy Express the previous year:

> In these ambushes we killed anything or anybody and a lot of these weren't VC. We used Claymores on any people or any boat that passed and sometimes it would be a sampan with a load of bannanas [sic] and a couple of women or sometimes a papasan [male Vietnamese] with a hoe. No big thing, they were VC as soon as we killed them. . . . I asked my platoon leader about this and he said it was ok to zap them if they move during curfew. But he couldn't answer when I asked if they knew it was curfew. He just said hardcore . . . to zap them. . . . This thing happened 15 or 20 times in my platoon. . . . Sure, there was some real big fights with a hard core unit, but *very* few. . . . If I am only 10% right, then I am trying to tell you about 120–150 murders, or a My Lay [sic] each month for over a year.[123]

Not all American troops engaged in atrocities, of course—some refused orders; a few, like the "concerned sergeant," sought to alert the higher echelons in the chain of command to what they had witnessed. It is impossible to quantify the number of such incidents, or the casualty toll they exacted. Still, atrocities were so widespread and frequent—for some units practically a matter of routine—that they cry out for explanation.

Obviously, gratuitous murders, not to mention rapes, were not sanctioned by the MACV. How, then, could so many American soldiers have performed acts that to all appearances must be described as heinous or even depraved? One level of explanation focuses on the psychological and situational factors confronting American soldiers: the tremendous strains inherent in fighting a guerilla war in which the enemy easily blended into the general population or the surrounding jungle. Guenter Lewy explains: "Troops would tramp for days in tropical heat through swamps and irrigated rice paddies, wade through streams and canals, climb hills and fight dense jungle growth without making contact with the evasive foe. Meanwhile they suffered the deadly depredations of enemy activity—ambushes, snipers, mines and booby traps. Buddies were killed and maimed, yet no enemy was in sight on whom one could revenge these losses."[124] Tales were told of women and children tossing concealed grenades. And many combat deaths resulting from mines or booby traps occurred during or after passing hamlets, so "it became the prudent thing to doubt the loyalty of every villager. Feelings of hatred and vengeance were difficult to control, and the hostility toward the unseen enemy was often transferred to the civilian population which in looks, language and dress was indistinguishable from the elusive guerilla. The value of civilian life grew cheaper."[125] It is quite possible, too, that an increasingly debased perception of the value of Vietnamese lives reflected infantrymen's awareness of the death and destruction that the US war effort was raining from the skies.

But an explanation of atrocities that focuses exclusively on the strains on and the perceptions of the troops on the ground misses a larger point. American troops came to see the civilian population as hostile because in fact much of it *was* hostile in varying degrees to the American war effort. That was inherent in the war America was fighting. It was a war against an enemy that had won the active support of a significant segment of the rural population and the sympathy of a much larger segment—very likely an outright majority—of rural Vietnamese. A fairly common attitude was expressed by one GI: "They're all VC or at least helping them—same difference. You can't convert them, only kill them. Don't lose any sleep over those dead children—they grow up to be commies too. . . . This is a war and we have to stop the commies any way we can, using whatever we've got."[126] Shocking, but reflecting a genuine reality. The strength the guerillas achieved in the countryside—their substantial success in recruiting the peasantry to their side and enlisting their active and passive support—led US soldiers to an expansive definition of "the enemy." My Lai-type atrocities were a natural consequence.

So, do we have evidence of a "war of annihilation" against the Vietnamese peasantry? It is clear that there was a strategy of population removal that caused massive suffering among the peasants. If we understand "violence" broadly to include not only the infliction of bodily harm and death but also the deprivation of freedom and decent living conditions, then there is no question that American war strategy deliberately subjected the rural Vietnamese population to massive violence. But awful as it is, large-scale forced population removal by itself falls short of "annihilation" as most people would understand the term. More to the point is the ample evidence that the American military killed Vietnamese noncombatants in large numbers both to implement the population removal strategy and in frequent disproportionate reactions to enemy fire in presumably hostile territory. To further scrutinize the charge of annihilation, we need to consider questions of scale and of intentions. "Annihilation" of a population after all implies very large numbers of dead people: how many noncombatants did American forces actually kill and maim? And did the American leadership—military and civilian—consciously and deliberately eradicate noncombatants in large numbers, or was the death toll a tragic but more or less unintended consequence of the war strategy?

The question of scale leads to a discussion of the thorny issue of war casualties—"thorny" because most Vietnam War historians agree that we will probably never know with any degree of confidence just how many casualties there were in that conflict. Estimates of the total number of deaths—civilian and military together—for all of Vietnam range from 1.35 million to over 3 million. Any discussion of civilian casualties is a speculative exercise based on uncertain data. But we have to wade in nevertheless.

A good starting point is an analysis by Guenter Lewy. Extrapolating from hospital admission statistics, which he acknowledges are of highly doubtful reliability, Lewy arrives at an estimated civilian death toll for South Vietnam of 301,000 for the period 1965–1974.[127] He makes a final adjustment to reflect the likelihood that a large proportion (he estimates one-third) of ostensible enemy combatant deaths were actually noncombatants. This leads to an adjusted total (which Lewy doesn't break out separately) of 523,000. This is undoubtedly an underestimate: many of the villages subject to heavy bombardment or drawn into battle zones were beyond the range of medical help, and villages wiped off the map without a trace would not register in hospital data.[128] On the other hand, Edward S. Herman, in an analysis cited approvingly by Chomsky, came up with a very high estimate of 1.1 million civilian deaths between 1965 and 1969 alone. Herman's calculations start with an estimate of seventy-two thousand deaths for the year 1965 made by a prominent French journalist and assume for subsequent years a one-for-one relationship between civilian deaths and the quantity of US ordnance expended.[129] But in addition to its reliance on a loosely supported base-year estimate, Herman's analysis founders on its unsound assumption of a simple relationship between civilian deaths and US ordnance explosions. Artillery and aerial bombardment wasn't the only cause of noncombatant deaths: people died in mine and mortar attacks (most of them laid by Viet Cong) and in the cross-fire between opposing forces. The Viet Cong, too, were guilty of attacks on civilian populations. It is probably reasonably safe to say that the actual number of civilian casualties was somewhere between Lewy's 523,000 and Herman's 1.1 million, and almost certainly closer to the former.

How many of these deaths were attributable to US firepower? Again, the only available data is at best suggestive. Chomsky cites estimates that 90 percent of war casualties at the Hue hospital, and 70 percent at Quangngai, were caused by US air and artillery fire. On the other hand, CIA director William Colby presented an analysis to Congress in 1971 that suggested that only about one-third of total civilian casualties between 1967 and 1970 were caused by air and artillery bombardment.[130] Colby's analysis, again, was based on hospital data, which would tend to underestimate casualties inflicted in areas not under US control; presumably, a disproportionate number of those casualties would have been caused by air and artillery fire. On the other hand, the data end in 1970, when air and artillery attacks were declining. Applying Colby's possibly low ratio to Lewy's probably low total for civilian deaths, we get about 175,000 civilian deaths due to air and artillery fire. It would be reasonable to round this figure up to two hundred thousand, which very roughly jibes with a Senate committee staff's estimate that three hundred thousand people died in free-fire zones between 1965 and 1968.[131] But again, we are at best groping for an approximation. And of course we are not counting deaths due to miscellaneous mini–My Lai–type actions or deaths of unlucky people caught in the midst of shootouts between opposing military forces.

What about intentions? Did the US leadership—civilian and military—understand the magnitude of the suffering and death our forces were inflicting on the Vietnamese?

Officially, the policy of the US military was to minimize civilian casualties. General Westmoreland, in his four years as MACV supreme commander, repeatedly sent letters to all commanders warning against the excessive deployment of firepower in populated areas; on one occasion, he expressed the concern that "an attitude of disaffection toward the Vietnamese may be developing among our personnel. . . . Comments such as 'the only good village is a burned village' are indicative of the trend."[132] MACV order 535-3 in October 1966 called on commanders to recognize the need for striking a balance between the force necessary to accomplish a mission and the high importance of minimizing noncombatant casualties. The rules of engagement (ROE), designed to limit civilian casualties, were revised regularly and delivered to all units with the instruction that the men should be made fully aware of them. But the ROE were riddled with ambiguities and exceptions. Open as they frequently were to opposite interpretations, it was possible to read them more as recommendations than obligations. As we have already seen, they allowed for the destruction of whole villages in response to limited sniper fire. In any case, there is abundant evidence that the officer corps regarded the ROE with attitudes ranging from indifference to hostility. Instruction in the ROE for all newly arriving soldiers, formally mandatory, was in practice at best perfunctory.[133]

Clearly, there was a divergence between official policy and actual practice with regard to respecting noncombatant life. It is hard to dismiss as overly cynical the opinion of the *New York Times*' Sheehan that "all of those directives issued by the American military headquarters in Saigon about taking care to avoid civilian casualties, about protecting the livestock and the homes of the peasantry, were the sort of pharisaic prattle you hear from many American institutions. Whenever you say the institution is not behaving as it says it should, the institution can always point to a directive and say you must be mistaken."[134]

Did the administration in Washington understand what it was doing to the people of Vietnam? Of course they did, says Chomsky. He cites the fact that Henry Cabot Lodge, between his two stints as ambassador to Vietnam, wrote the introduction to a book by the journalist Malcolm Brown that described the gruesome impact of the war on the peasantry.[135] The *Times*' Sheehan agrees, pointing to the many information sources available to Washington decision makers.[136] Chomsky also cites Sheehan's reporting of a secret study done for the US embassy and military headquarters in Saigon in the summer of 1966; the study recommended that the policy of unrestricted bombing and shelling be carefully reexamined, given the attendant suffering and possibly counterproductive consequences.[137] The proposal for a reexamination was vetoed at the highest levels of American authority in Saigon. Sheehan reasonably infers that "by deciding not to reconsider, the American leadership in Saigon was deciding to ordain the practice, to establish a de facto policy." Asking why, Sheehan answers his own question: "Because devastation had become a fundamental element in their strategy to win the war."[138] During a trip to Vietnam in 1965, Secretary of Defense Robert McNamara told reporters he had been disturbed by stories that American pilots were killing civilians in their raids over the South. He said he had asked many pilots about it during his five-day tour of Vietnam, and none of them said they were killing civilians.[139] It is reasonable to assume that the pilots McNamara spoke to knew the answer he wanted and expected to hear. It is no less reasonable to assume that McNamara knew that they knew.

The destructiveness of the war on Vietnam's civilian population probably peaked in 1968 or 1969. General Creighton Abrams, who took over from Westmoreland in June 1969, upgraded the priority assigned to a "hearts and minds" pacification strategy that emphasized winning the support of the peasantry. MACV now saw population relocation as more of a double-edged sword that, whatever its short-term military value might be, impeded the longer-term goal of wresting the allegiance of the rural population from the Viet Cong. This new perspective, along with a change in the character of military engagements, probably contributed to the marked reduction in allied bombing and shelling in South Vietnam between 1969 and 1972.[140] In any case, by 1969 the US war in Vietnam had destroyed hundreds of villages, degraded the lives of millions of people forced to live as refugees, and killed somewhere around two hundred thousand noncombatants through shelling and bombardments alone. It had also ravaged the natural environment: American forces dropped nineteen million gallons of herbicides on South Vietnam during the 1960s. The objectives were to destroy crops that might feed guerillas (but that also, of course, fed the villagers who grew them) and to clear the dense jungle foliage in which the guerillas found hiding places.[141]

Whatever we think of the ultimate motivations for entering into the war, can

America's conduct of the war possibly be justified? Or, to use our just war terminology: setting aside considerations of *jus ad bellum*, isn't it clear that the US war effort shredded *jus in bello*? Guenter Lewy offered a systematic, if qualified, defense of the US conduct of the war in his *America in Vietnam*. In a review, Chomsky showered Lewy's book with withering scorn.¹⁴² Lewy, however, is not a completely uncritical apologist for the US military's behavior: he acknowledges that avoidable civilian casualties, including even some definable as war crimes, did occur too often. In part, these unfortunate occurrences reflected the nature of the war; they also reflected insufficiently vigorous promulgation of the rules of engagement. Supreme MACV commander Westmoreland bears a heavy responsibility for the latter: Westmoreland should have known

> that in the Vietnam environment inadequate understanding of the ROE could and would lead to violations of the law of war.... MACV was undoubtedly aware of the high civilian casualties resulting from fighting in and around hamlets and villages, of the existence of command pressure for a high body count and of the belief of many soldiers in the "mere gook rule"—that the lives of Vietnamese were cheap and not protected by the law of war. Indeed, the constantly repeated expressions of intense concern of MACV with the question of civilian casualties can be read as an acknowledgment that [the ROE were] not applied and enforced as they should have been.¹⁴³

Overall, however, Lewy concludes that the US record in Vietnam did not violate prevailing standards of human decency in time of war. His argument, in short, is that international law recognizes war as a dirty business in which the suffering and death of civilians may well be inevitable. If said suffering and death is in reasonable proportion to the military objectives sought, it is justifiable. Thus, forced population relocation, whether or not it was ultimately effective, was justifiable in terms of military necessity because it deprived the guerillas of supplies and manpower. Furthermore, while it was "incontrovertible" that the US war effort made "lavish use of firepower," resulting in "a large number of civilian casualties," this was a reflection of the nature of the war. The Viet Cong's use of fortified hamlets made it necessary for allied forces to bring the fighting to populated areas. And, while it may seem disproportionate to answer sniper fire by obliterating an entire village, the commander in such cases faced a difficult judgment call, given the murky circumstances of a war without clearly defined fronts: "What if there are five snipers blocking an important bridge situated in a hamlet? How can a commander make a precise estimate of the size of the enemy unit which is firing upon his men? One sniper using an automatic weapon can sound like a platoon." Moreover, it is erroneous to assume that all noncombatants in the war were "innocent civilians," given the various ways in which villagers collaborated with the guerillas: "It is well-established that once civilians act as support personnel they cease to be noncombatants and are subject to attack."¹⁴⁴

But Lewy misses the point. He seems unaware that his defense of US war conduct in terms of military necessity actually supports the arguments of Chomsky and others. He thinks that if the deliberate targeting of presumptively Viet Cong villages for bombardment was militarily opportune, it was justified, provided that it achieved or reasonably promised to achieve military objectives that were proportionate to the death and destruction inflicted. We can leave aside the obvious consideration that the killing of an unknown number of civilians to combat an unknown number of enemy soldiers means that any idea of proportionality goes out the window: no proportion can be estimated if neither side of a ratio is known. More fundamentally, the thrust of Chomsky's argument is that it is precisely *because* such violence against civilians was militarily opportune, given the special circumstances of this war, that the war itself must be condemned. The US war effort was morally reprehensible because massive violence against civilians was intrinsic to the war effort.

In viewing civilian casualties as acceptable, Lewy elides the fundamental distinction between civilian casualties as collateral damage and civilian casualties as a direct objective of military strategy. Just war doctrine does indeed recognize that civilian casualties may be an unavoidable result of military operations, and allows that they may be acceptable if proportionate to the military objectives sought. It does not condone the deliberate targeting of civilians, except in exceptional cases, like the case of civilians working in armaments factories that supply the enemy forces. Lewy implicitly invokes this kind of exception in asserting that civilians acting as support personnel can be regarded effectively as combatants. But killing civilians in their homes is not equivalent to killing them in armaments factories. In the latter case, they are being targeted for a specific militarily relevant activity. In the former case, they are being targeted not for any specific activity, but essentially for *who they are*—supporters of the guerilla enemy. A very large portion of the Vietnamese population fell into that category. To claim that the targeting of such a large portion of the civilian population of a country can be justified in terms of military necessity is to stretch just war doctrine beyond reason.

A "people's war" in which the guerillas have become deeply embedded among the civilian population is a war in which something resembling a "strategy of annihilation" may indeed be a rational if ruthless response to the insurgency. In such a war, the distinction between *jus ad bellum* and *jus in bello* collapses: the war must be judged unjust because it can only be fought unjustly. Michael Walzer explains that

> whenever ordinary soldiers (who are not moral monsters and would fight by the rules if they could) become convinced that old men and women and children are their enemies . . . it is unlikely that the war can be fought except by setting out systematically to kill civilians or to destroy their society and culture. . . . In the theory of war . . . considerations of *jus ad bellum* and *jus in bello* are logically independent, and the judgments we make in terms of one and the other are not necessarily the same. But here they come together. . . . The struggle against [the guerillas] is an unjust struggle as well as one that can only be carried on unjustly.[145]

Did the United States, then, wage a "war of annihilation"? Arguably, that characterization goes a bit over the top. Chomsky does indulge in flights of rhetoric that invite derision; for example, claiming that "the Nazi-like barbarity of U.S. war policy was the most salient and unforgettable feature of the war. . . . The American leadership was sadistic."[146] Even genuine horrors can be exaggerated: words like "annihilation" and "Nazi-like" can be understood to imply a deliberate US policy of genocide.[147] Clearly, the American leadership did not set out with the goal of eradicating a people, nor did it come anywhere close to effecting such an outcome. And characterizing American leaders as "sadistic" is plainly silly as well as gratuitous, given Chomsky's attribution of rationality to US policy. But it is certainly correct to say that the United States waged a war whose logic compelled the use of massive, systematic violence against the noncombatant population. Shorn of its rhetorical excesses, Chomsky's moral indictment of the war is powerful.

Conclusions

As readers have undoubtedly gathered by now, I think Chomsky was mostly right about Vietnam. The United States wasn't fighting aggression, it wasn't fighting a proxy for Communist China, and it certainly wasn't fighting to enable the people of South Vietnam to determine their own fate. It *was* wreaking large-scale death and devastation on that country in order to ensure the survival of a regime friendly to the United States.

Chomsky did get some things wrong. Along with many others in the antiwar movement, he overstated the autonomy of the South Vietnamese insurgency from Hanoi. That misconception also led him to misunderstand the Johnson administration's motivations for the bombing of North Vietnam. As Chomsky saw it, Operation Rolling Thunder was little more than a propaganda sideshow to buttress the administration's rationale for intensifying the war in the South.[148] That was a reasonable supposition, given his assumption of NLF autonomy: if Hanoi had little influence over the southern guerillas, why else would Washington attack the North? But it is clear from all the accounts we have of decision making in the Johnson administration that Washington did, indeed, believe that Hanoi controlled the southern insurgency and could call it off if it chose to.

Also, Chomsky's view of the Vietnamese Communists was exceedingly benign. Though he acknowledges the use of terror by the guerillas, he generally avoids the subject of atrocities by their side. Chomsky instead is explicitly critical of those who believe that a "balanced" account of the war requires a full consideration of atrocities by the Communists as well as by the US side. He argues that American war crimes far exceeded those of the Communists; moreover, there is no moral equivalence between terror employed by insurgents resisting a dictatorial regime and terror employed by that regime and its American sponsor. He asserts that GVN/US terror "long preceded and also always outweighed by a considerable margin the terrorism of its Vietnamese antagonists."[149] But while these arguments may well be defensible, that can only be demonstrated through a willingness to openly and consistently confront the considerable evidence of NLF terrorism. Atrocities by the guerillas are a relevant part of the story of the Vietnam War. They go to the issue of what kind of people the insurgents were, with what kinds of values, and therefore what kind of society they would construct.

Chomsky's refusal to deal with these issues mars his credibility as an analyst of the war; it brands him as a partisan. And Chomsky clearly is an unblinking partisan. He is no less certain than the decision makers in Washington that the war is an uncomplicated conflict between good guys and bad guys; he just disagrees as to who is good and who is bad. His partisanship is evident in his account of his 1969 trip to North Vietnam.[150] His praise of the achievements of the Communist regime and the courage of its people is free of the slightest hint of skepticism or doubt. The powerfully acute critical sensibility that Chomsky brings to bear on American policy is nowhere in evidence.

This is not to say that partisanship is always necessarily bad. A partisan may be willing to advance unpopular arguments on behalf of his cause that more "objective" analysts will shy away from. In the process, he may even uncover evidence neglected by others. Such was the case with the question of the potential consequences of a Communist victory in South Vietnam. Defenders of American policy argued that the United States was preventing a likely "bloodbath" against non-Communists that would likely occur in the event of a Communist takeover. As evidence, they pointed to the brutal campaign accompanying North Vietnam's collectivization of agriculture in the 1950s, in which, it was widely believed, fifty thousand resisting peasants were killed by the Communist regime. Citing original research by the young Asia scholar Gareth Porter, Chomsky pointed out that the original source of the fifty thousand figure was a highly dubious analysis conducted by an individual closely connected with the CIA and the South Vietnamese government. The actual number of deaths, in the Porter estimate publicized by Chomsky, was under 2,500.[151] Later research showed that the death toll in fact was probably close to the Porter estimate, in the low single-digit thousands, and surely under fifteen thousand.[152]

Chomsky again raised reasonable questions about a generally accepted "fact" of the Vietnam War by challenging prevailing accounts of the Hue massacre of 1968. In their retreat from Hue during their Tet offensive, the Communists brutally murdered a large number of civilians they regarded as South Vietnamese collaborators. Historians have estimated the number killed at 2,500 and up.[153] Chomsky, again drawing on work by Gareth Porter and others, points credibly to a number of grounds for questioning what actually happened in Hue, giving a much lower estimate—under one thousand—of the number of deaths caused by the Communists.[154] Porter and Chomsky may or may not be correct, but their concerns are plausible enough to merit investigation. To my knowledge, no historian has pursued this. Most don't even acknowledge the Porter/Chomsky thesis. It is reasonable to suppose that this failure might reflect a lack of interest by "objective" historians in taking up what could seem like a "partisan" cause.

IN HIS WRITINGS ON THE VIETNAM WAR, Chomsky devotes almost as much attention to criticizing how Americans thought and talked about the war as he did to the war itself. In Chomsky's view, the proper reaction to the war in Vietnam was outrage, but outrage was strikingly missing from most commentary on the war in the U.S. media. He marvels at how news reports of the death and destruction wrought by allied forces in the village of Ben Suc in early 1967 failed to ignite widespread indignant protest. He is equally dismayed by reviewers of Jonathan Schell's book on the topic for their refusal to draw the obvious moral judgments that Schell's account pointed to. "One can hardly decide which is the more scandalous, the events themselves or the muted response."[155]

In part, Chomsky attributes the muted response to bedrock American beliefs in this country's goodness and probity. That our leaders might be engaged in a morally reprehensible war against a defenseless people defies credulity because it flies in the face of Americans' fundamental conceptions of their national character and role in the world. A recurrent theme in Chomsky's writings on Vietnam—and one that we shall see recur again and again in his writings—is Americans' misguided belief in the essential rectitude of this country's actions in the international arena: a "sentimental faith in American benevolence."[156] "Responsible" critics of American foreign policy may cite our leaders' mistakes or misconceptions in the conduct of foreign affairs, but it is practically unthinkable to suggest that their motives might be morally questionable.[157] This "unshakable belief in American goodwill and generosity . . . stultifies political thinking and debases political discourse."[158]

Chomsky is particularly disturbed by the refusal of liberals to make tough moral judgments about American behavior. Thus, he criticizes a *Washington Post* editorial at the war's end that saw the war as a case where, in the words of the editorial, "good impulses came to be transmuted into bad policy. . . . For the fundamental 'lesson' of Vietnam surely is . . . that we are capable of error—and on a gigantic scale."[159] Anthony Lewis, the liberal columnist for the *New York Times,* similarly sums up the early American decisions on Indochina as "blundering efforts to do good."[160] And Richard Strout of the *New Republic* sees the war as "not wickedness; it was stupidity."[161]

Not wickedness? Chomsky would have us ask why it is so hard to characterize a war that involved massive violence against civilians—killing and terrorizing hundreds of thousands and displacing millions—as wicked. "The beauty of nationalism is that whatever the means your state employs, since the leadership always proclaims noble objectives, and a nationalist can swallow these, wickedness is ruled out and stupidity explains all despicable behavior."[162]

To adhere to a cherished belief in the face of contravening evidence generally requires a degree of self-deception, and indeed "it is remarkable to see how easily perceptive and informed commentators succeed in deluding themselves as to the character of American actions and policies."[163] Self-deception was often the basis for the unshakable belief in American good intentions. Thus, the *Washington Post* editorial I cited in the previous paragraph actually ascribes American's war motives in part to "the hope that the people of Vietnam would be able to decide on their own form of government and social order."[164] But in fact US policy consistently sought to deny the South Vietnamese the opportunity to freely "decide on their own form of government and social order." How can a *Washington Post* editorialist so blithely ignore that historical record? That the United States was seeking to advance democratic self-determination in South Vietnam is simply a premise, an assumption for which no evidence is necessary.

Policymakers in government were also prone to utilizing various forms of self-deception to rationalize their decisions. Chomsky quotes former assistant secretary of state Roger Hilsman, who describes the strategic hamlet program as an effort to provide peasants a "free choice" between the Viet Cong and the government. That "free choice" was to result from isolating the peasants from the Viet Cong and ensuring through careful police work that no VC agents penetrated the hamlets. Hilsman laments that VC agents usually did manage to get inside; he seems unaware that his Orwellian idea of "free choice" is one in which the peasants have no opportunity to choose the Viet Cong.[165]

Chomsky finds in the Pentagon Papers a similar "inability to perceive facts that are inconsistent with the requirements of official propaganda." For example, the Pentagon analysts tended to see the Viet Minh and their NLF successors one-dimensionally as agents of foreign aggression. They consistently refused to acknowledge the genuine popularity achieved by the guerillas among the peasantry. "To concede this would discredit the American enterprise.... Accordingly, government spokesmen and the press, generally, speak only of the 'control' of the peasants by the Viet Cong ... That the peasants might have some positive reason for supporting the NLF was a possibility too remote for consideration." Chomsky notes that the dubious public rationales for American intervention are consistently echoed in documents not intended for public consumption: "There is a striking similarity of internal to external rhetoric and expressed beliefs. What had to be believed for the justification of American policy was, apparently, efficiently internalized. Lying is not quite the right term for this kind of behavior."[166]

Much of Chomsky's writing on Vietnam, then, can be seen as an anguished plea to Americans to face the harsh realities of this country's war policy and to draw the appropriate moral conclusions. His basic procedure is to set forth the facts as he sees them and to puncture what he considers the ideological blinders or filters that impede perception and judgment.

It is useful to view Chomsky's antiwar stance in the perspective of the many volumes on the war written by professional historians in the decades since the war's end. Most historians have judged the war to have been a disastrous mistake for the United States—a mistake variously attributable to hubris; to a failure to understand Vietnam's history and particularly the strength of nationalism; to misguided reliance on a client regime that never achieved necessary legitimacy; to underestimation of the indigenous strength of the guerilas and the determination and resilience of Hanoi; and to excessive attachment to outdated Cold War assumptions, particularly regarding the workings of international Communism.

(A minority of historians—often dubbed "revisionists"—has viewed the war as a worthwhile cause that was ultimately lost because of avoidable errors or an absence of sufficient determination by the United States.) Typically, historians have sought to answer questions like, how did we get into such an awful mess, and why did it take us so long to get out?[167]

But historians have been less interested in scrutinizing the morality, as opposed to the wisdom, of our Vietnam debacle.[168] Most histories of the war fail to convey the extent to which American firepower was aimed at civilian targets. There is very little historiography that asks, how could we have done such terrible things to the people we were supposedly defending? Even after forty years, historians have generally not addressed the question posed by former under secretary of the Air Force Townsend Hoopes about the US political leadership: "Why did so many intelligent, experienced and humane men in government fail to grasp the immorality of our intervention in Vietnam?"[169] Perhaps the historians' reticence reflects a professional inclination to stick to facts and avoid value judgments. But there are plenty of facts to work with, facts that most of our historians have shied away from confronting. It is telling that the two gold mines of information on atrocities by US forces in Vietnam discussed earlier—the archives of the Peers Commission (available since 1975) and of the Vietnam War Crimes Working Group (available since 1994) have been largely untouched by American academic historians.[170]

I suspect our historians' reluctance to grapple with the moral issues posed by the war reflects a continued unwillingness or inability to contest that "unshakable belief in American goodwill and generosity" and "sentimental faith in American benevolence" that Chomsky attributed to respectable opinion in the 1960s. The historian Marilyn Young, introducing a collection of articles on the war, comments acidly on her professional colleagues' failure to follow the mounting evidence of atrocities by US forces to its logical moral conclusions: "By definition, the United States cannot wage aggressive war, commit war crimes or crimes against humanity.... When the evidence that these things have occurred is overwhelming, understanding has nowhere to go but the particular: this low-level guard, that misunderstood order, the soldiers grieving for comrades under great stress."[171] She cites the cri de coeur of another historian, participating in a symposium in a leading journal, in the face of his colleagues' inattention to the moral issues raised by the war: "Am I the last crank fighting the forgotten political battles of an earlier age against ghostly antagonists who have now sensibly moved on? If so, why? How did that happen?"[172] As long as such questions are worth asking, Chomsky's challenge to the myths of American benevolence and rectitude remains on target.

Indochina Afterword

Chomsky and Cambodia

IN JUNE 1977 CHOMSKY AND A COAUTHOR, Edward S. Herman, wrote a review article on three books about the recent revolutionary upheaval in Cambodia.[1] Chomsky and Herman challenged the findings of two of the books, which reported widespread murderous brutality by Cambodia's new Communist rulers. They praised the third book, which presented a highly positive picture of the Cambodian revolution, one entirely lacking in the murderous imagery of the other books. In 1979, Chomsky and Herman published their own book, *After the Cataclysm*, whose extensive discussion of Cambodia expanded on the views they expressed in the earlier review article.

Chomsky and Herman's writings on Cambodia sparked a controversy that continued to rage—first in print, later over the Internet—for decades. The controversy is no longer over the nature of the Cambodian revolutionary regime. No one questions that that regime was, in fact, guilty of mind-numbing crimes against humanity on a staggering scale. The controversy continues, however, over Chomsky and Herman: were they, as some critics charge, apologists for a genocidal regime? Or were they merely raising well-justified questions about the reliability of the horribly sensational reports coming out of Cambodia?

Background

It was ultimately impossible for Prince Norodom Sihanouk, Cambodia's head of state, to keep his country from becoming embroiled in the Vietnam War, which was raging on Cambodia's eastern borders. After the US escalation of the war in 1965, the Vietnamese Communists used Cambodian territory as bases for their troops and for the resupply of forces fighting in Vietnam. But the Vietnamese presence made Cambodia a target for the United States. In an effort to wipe out the Vietnamese sanctuaries, President Nixon in March 1969 approved a covert bombing campaign that over the next four years devastated large swaths of the Cambodian countryside and took tens of thousands, perhaps hundreds of thousands, of civilian lives.

The expansion of the war into Cambodia accelerated after a pro-US coup overthrew Sihanouk in March 1970. Within six weeks, the Nixon administration took advantage of the opportunity to invade Cambodia, hoping to score decisively against the Communist enemy. The US campaign met with only limited success, and troops were soon withdrawn in the face of a furious domestic reaction to the

Nixon administration's expansion of the war. The US move into Cambodia did, however, have the effect of driving the Vietnamese deeper into the Cambodian heartland, where they made common cause with the Cambodian Communists, known as the Khmer Rouge. The coup had catalyzed the Khmer Rouge's own armed insurrection, already under way in the late 1960s. Benefiting initially from the extensive engagement of North Vietnamese troops and from popular resentment at the authoritarianism and corruption of the Khmer Republican regime that the coup had installed, the Cambodian Communists by late 1970 controlled about half the country. After four and a half more years of bloody civil war, the Communists overran the regime's last bastion, the capital city of Phnom Penh.

On April 17, 1975, the Khmer Rouge launched the new regime of Democratic Kampuchea (DK), which became more generally known as the Pol Pot regime, after its leader. Intent on a rapid revolutionary transformation of the country into an agrarian Communist society, the new rulers immediately ordered a mass evacuation of all major cities, including the capital, whose pre-civil-war population of six hundred thousand had swollen to nearly two million as refugees fled the fighting in the countryside. The forced evacuation applied to all city dwellers, including the old and infirm and hospital patients. One historian has estimated that about twenty thousand people died during the evacuation of the capital, half of them executed either for their associations with the old regime or for resisting orders to move; the other half—mostly the elderly, the very young, and the sick—weren't able to withstand the weeks-long trek to their newly assigned locations.[2] The erstwhile city dwellers—whom the Khmer Rouge tended to regard suspiciously as bourgeoisie hostile to the revolution—were subject to harsh and often brutal discipline as they were assigned forced labor roles in a hugely expanded agricultural workforce. Over the course of the next four years, somewhere around 1.5 to 2 million people—one quarter of the population—died as a result of regime policies and actions.[3] Many of these were executed outright; others expired after overwork, starvation, or mistreatment.

DK lasted less than four years. A series of border disputes with its Communist neighbor, Vietnam, sparked intermittent armed clashes as early as 1975, culminating in a major Vietnamese incursion into Cambodia in late 1977. The Vietnamese soon withdrew, but a renewed, full-scale invasion at the end of 1978 led to the rapid collapse of the Khmer regime. The victorious Vietnamese installed a new regime, called the People's Republic of Kampuchea, early in 1979.

The Controversy

Chomsky and Herman's review article, "Distortions at Fourth Hand," appeared in the *Nation*'s June 25, 1977, issue. The authors begin by surveying media coverage—especially US media—of postwar Vietnam, decrying what they see as the media's relentlessly negative images of the Communist regime in the now reunified country. In their view, the media's negative portrayal of postwar Vietnam served to retrospectively rationalize the US war effort, demonstrating the grimness of the Communist fate from which American intervention had sought to preserve the people of Vietnam. The new Communist regime in Cambodia, they argued, was getting a similar media treatment. In support of that view, they reviewed three books. One of them, presenting a generally favorable view of the new Cambodia, was being generally ignored by the media. The other two, replete with horror stories, had received widespread attention and acclaim.

Chomsky and Herman have only praise for *Cambodia: Starvation and Revolution,* the book by George Hildebrand and Gareth Porter that shows the revolutionary Cambodian regime to be dealing efficiently and humanely with daunting problems of postwar recovery and reconstruction.[4] Hildebrand and Porter see the evacuation of Phnom Penh as a rational response to the humanitarian crisis of a city facing mass starvation. They discount reports of executions and brutality in the forced mass exodus from the capital, citing instead stories of kindness and patience shown by Khmer cadres in assisting the departing city dwellers. Chomsky and Herman praise Hildebrand and Porter, too, for putting Cambodia's problems in the proper historical context of the destructive American impact on that country.

Chomsky and Herman are far from enthusiastic about a second book, François Ponchaud's *Cambodia Year Zero.*[5] Ponchaud, a Khmer-speaking French missionary with ten years of experience in Cambodia, drew on hundreds of interviews with refugees, most of them in Thailand but others in Vietnam, Laos, and Malaysia. The refugees told numerous stories of the Cambodian revolutionaries' terrible cruelty, including casual mass murders during the evacuation of Phnom Penh and afterward. Chomsky and Herman have some kind words for Ponchaud but find his book badly flawed. Ponchaud's heavy reliance on refugee accounts is a critical shortcoming, in their view: refugees tend to have a biased view of the regime they have fled, and they will often tailor their accounts to their perceptions of what their new hosts (e.g., the pro-US government of Thailand) would like to hear. Chomsky and Herman also point to a number of Ponchaud misstatements and numbers that don't quite add up, suggesting that he is a less than completely reliable reporter.

Chomsky and Herman's sharply skeptical attitude toward Ponchaud's book is mild compared to their treatment of the third book, *Murder of a Gentle Land,* by the journalists John Barron and Anthony Paul.[6] Barron and Paul's findings—also based largely on interviews with refugees—are consistent with Ponchaud's, but they get no respect whatsoever from Chomsky and Herman. Chomsky and Herman cite apparent inaccuracies in some of the stories recounted by Barron and Paul as evidence of the general unreliability of their reporting. They also criticize Barron and Paul, as they criticize Ponchaud, for failing to take into account various reports of people traveling in Cambodia during and since the Khmer Rouge takeover who saw no atrocities. Pointing also to the authors' utilization of US and allied government resources and their failure to acknowledge any role by the United States in creating Cambodia's misery, Chomsky and Herman dismiss

Murder of a Gentle Land as a third-rate propaganda tract that collapses under serious scrutiny.

Actually, Chomsky and Herman's article fares worse under scrutiny than Barron and Paul's book. Let's start with Chomsky and Herman's unqualified praise for Hildebrand and Porter. Whatever its authors' intentions, Hildebrand and Porter's book is closer to a propaganda tract than Barron and Paul's. As one Chomsky critic points out, the book contains not a single sentence critical of the Khmer Rouge.[7] And, while Chomsky and Herman criticize Barron and Paul for use of official sources, they say nothing about Hildebrand and Porter's much heavier reliance on official sources. In their final crucial chapter on Cambodia's agricultural revolution, thirty-three of the last forty-three citations pertaining to the new regime are of sources affiliated with the regime; another six are of Hsinhua, the official news agency of Communist China, DK's superpower patron.[8] Hildebrand and Porter's book provides useful background on conditions in Cambodia before 1975, but for the period beginning with the Khmer takeover the book is basically a credulous account of the new Communist leaders' version of events; it provides little independent information about what is actually happening in Cambodia. That Chomsky and Herman can praise it as a "carefully documented study" while castigating B&P as carriers of official propaganda is remarkable.

Chomsky and Herman's case against both Ponchaud and Barron and Paul rides on the credibility of the refugees whose testimony provides the core of both books. Chomsky and Herman are certainly correct that refugee testimony should be treated with a certain amount of caution. Ponchaud, in the introduction to the English-language version of his book, credibly asserts his awareness of this issue.[9] Barron and Paul are rather more vulnerable to charges that they were too quick to pass on hearsay testimony, including some stories that turned out to be false.[10] Still, the evidence they compile, taken as it is from hundreds of refugees in multiple locations over the course of a year, is for the most part credible and compelling—all the more so for being consistent with Ponchaud's reporting. Chomsky and Herman do cite a number of contrary reports, by different individuals present in Cambodia during and after the Khmer takeover, who saw no atrocities, or very limited atrocities. But the existence of such "saw no evil" reports hardly qualifies as evidence that atrocities didn't take place; it proves only that atrocities didn't take place everywhere at all times. Supporters of US intervention in Vietnam could similarly cite "saw no evil" accounts of the behavior of American forces.[11]

That Chomsky and Herman have no interest in dealing fairly with Barron and Paul is evident from their misleading capsule summary of the book:

> [Barron and Paul's] point of view can be predicted from the "diverse sources" on which they relied: namely, "informal briefings from specialists at the State and Defense Departments, the National Security Council and three foreign embassies in Washington." Their "Acknowledgments" mention only the expertise of Thai and

Malaysian officials, U.S.A. Government Cambodian experts, and Father Ponchaud. They also claim to have analyzed radio and refugee reports.

The implication is that Barron and Paul mostly relied on information handed out by US and pro-US government official sources. Almost as an afterthought, they acknowledge that Barron and Paul "also claim to have analyzed" refugee reports, whose origin Chomsky and Herman don't identify. This is a gross misrepresentation of the book, which is based overwhelmingly on refugee testimony that Barron and Paul, aided by interpreters, took first hand.

Chomsky and Herman's treatment of Ponchaud is also curious. Calling the book "serious and worth reading," they tell us that Ponchaud has given a "grisly account of what refugees told him about the barbarity of their treatment at the hands of the Khmer Rouge." But there is no discussion whatsoever of the wealth of credible grisly detail that Ponchaud provides. Instead, most of their discussion of the book is of the alleged shortcomings of Ponchaud's method and of the media's sensational treatment of the book. The reader is left wondering why they think the book is worth reading, since they have almost nothing good to say about it that is at all specific.

Where Chomsky and Herman do engage Ponchaud on specifics, their treatment is one-sidedly critical. For example, they challenge Ponchaud's view that the evacuation of Phnom Penh wasn't motivated by a desire to avoid famine, citing sources that indicated a dangerously short supply of food remaining in the city. But they make no mention of Ponchaud's point that the Khmer Rouge had been pursuing a policy of radical de-urbanization since 1972, sending the inhabitants of villages and towns they occupied into the forests, and often burning the residents' homes to forestall their return. Nor do they mention his observation that the new regime's order to evacuate wasn't limited to Phnom Penh, but applied uniformly to all the towns and villages in the country.[12] Both of these points, of course, would cast doubt on the benign explanation of the evacuation favored by Chomsky and Herman. So, too, does the fact that the Khmer regime turned down offers of food aid from several nongovernmental organizations (NGOs) and foreign countries. And so does the complete and indiscriminate scope of the urgent evacuation order, which hardly comports with the image of a rational response to a practical problem. Here, too, Chomsky and Herman's failure to convey any of Ponchaud's grisly details suggests an unwillingness to really confront his narrative. For example, Ponchaud's *own* eyewitness account (not that of a refugee) of the forced evacuation includes the following: "I shall never forget one cripple who had neither hands nor feet, writhing along the ground like a severed worm, or a weeping father carrying his ten-year-old daughter wrapped in a sheet tied around his neck like a sling, or the man with his foot dangling at the end of a leg to which it was attached by nothing but the skin."[13]

Given their evident lack of enthusiasm for Ponchaud, why are Chomsky and Herman so much harsher on Barron and Paul? Undoubtedly, the two reporters' affiliation is part of the explanation: they were working for *Reader's Digest*, which

Chomsky and Herman regard not unreasonably as a purveyor of Cold War propaganda. Also, Barron and Paul's brief discussion of pre-1975 developments in Cambodia gives no hint that the United States had anything to do with Cambodia's problems. Nothing in their book would raise hackles with the crassest apologist for US intervention in Indochina. Ponchaud, on the other hand, recounts the devastation and terror wrought by US intervention and the brutality and corruption of the pro-US regime that preceded the Khmer Rouge takeover, which he says he had welcomed. In short, it is hard to see Ponchaud as an anti-Communist propagandist; it's not so hard to see Barron and Paul that way. But whatever the shortcomings of the latter's work, it merits serious consideration. Chomsky and Herman's wholesale dismissal of the book is simply not reasonable; it can only be the product of a deep and determined bias against its authors and/or their conclusions.

Chomsky and Herman end their article with a disclaimer. Noting the sharp divergences between Ponchaud's account and that of Hildebrand and Porter, they tell us that "we do not pretend to know where the truth lies amidst these sharply conflicting assessments," and claim that their main concern is with the allegedly one-sided treatment of the Cambodian regime in the media. But this disclaimer seems a bit disingenuous. The plain fact is that they have reviewed three books that purport to provide factual accounts of current developments in Cambodia. One of those books has nothing but good things to report about the Khmer regime, and Chomsky and Herman have nothing but praise for that book. The other two books report widespread horror stories about the regime; Chomsky and Herman treat one of those books with skepticism and the other with disdain. Even if they don't claim to *know* where the truth lies, it is obvious that they strongly *believe* it is probably much closer to the favorable Hildebrand and Porter account of the Cambodian revolution than to the dark pictures painted by Ponchaud and Barron and Paul. That belief could not have come from an unbiased reading of the three books in the context of the evidence available to them even in the spring of 1977.

Chomsky and Herman's *After the Cataclysm: Postwar Indochina and the Reconstruction of Imperial Ideology* was published two years after the *Nation* "Distortions" article and several months after the collapse of the Khmer regime. It was undoubtedly written mostly before the Vietnamese takeover in Phnom Penh initiated a flood of new information that allowed the outside world to begin more reliably to assess the extent of the horrors wrought by the Khmer Rouge. The authors state that their main concern is not to establish the facts with regard to postwar Indochina, but rather to examine how "these facts have been interpreted, filtered, distorted or modified by the ideological institutions of the West."[14] The book represents a shift in emphasis from the *Nation* article: media criticism, which was essentially an overlay in the article, now becomes their major theme.

The 160-page chapter on Cambodia in *After the Cataclysm* largely repeats Chomsky and Herman's earlier arguments, now buttressed with many more "saw no evil" references and expanded documentation. They are now considerably harsher in their treatment of Ponchaud, whom they say "cannot be taken very seriously because he is simply too careless and untrustworthy."[15] On the other hand, they now explicitly admit that the Khmer regime was associated with terrible atrocities: "There can be little doubt that the [civil] war was followed by an outbreak of violence, massacre and repression, and it seems that bloody purges continued throughout the period under review," and "the record of atrocities in Cambodia is substantial and often gruesome."[16] But they argue that this record needs to be viewed alongside what they see as significant positive achievements by the regime. For example, they expand on their earlier favorable review of Hildebrand and Porter's claim that the evacuation of Phnom Penh averted many deaths from starvation. And they speculate that the new order may reflect a very mixed and messy picture: "There may be a good deal of local variation rather than [a] coordinated campaign of state-directed genocide.... The worst atrocities [may] have taken place at the hands of a peasant army, recruited and driven out of their devastated villages by U.S. bombs and then taking revenge against the urban civilization that they regarded, not without reason, as a collaborator in their destruction and their long history of oppression."[17]

But the main thrust of *After the Cataclysm*, in contrast to the 1977 *Nation* article, is to question the media coverage of events in Cambodia, rather than to support one or another version of those events. They cite various instances of sensationalism and apparent exaggeration of atrocity reports, as well as neglect of contrary evidence and of dissenting views of various Indochina experts, to argue that the media's treatment of Cambodia was grossly unbalanced. Anticipating their "propaganda model" of the mass media (see Chapter 4), their concern is with what they see as the excessive eagerness of the media to present a picture of foreign enemies—in this case the revolutionary regime in Cambodia—that comports with prevailing assumptions of US foreign policy.

The shift in tone and emphasis from "Distortions" to *After the Cataclysm* is subtle, but real. Chomsky has not acknowledged the change, and it has gone largely unremarked by both his critics and his defenders. In *After the Cataclysm*, Chomsky and Herman explicitly recognize that at least some of the Khmer revolutionaries were guilty of atrocities, and that abuses may have been widespread. They even concede that "when the facts are in, it may turn out that the more extreme condemnations [of the Khmer Rouge] were in fact correct." Still, they go on to insist, "But even if that turns out to be the case, it will in no way alter the conclusions we have reached on the central question addressed here: how the available facts were selected, modified or sometimes invented to create a certain image offered to the general population."[18] In short, Chomsky and Herman's claim to be primarily concerned with the workings of the media, rather than with promoting a particular account of what was actually happening in Cambodia, is more credible in *After the Cataclysm* than in "Distortions." In effect, they are saying, "OK, the regime may be guilty of terrible things, but it's not clear that it's as awful as the media say it is, and anyway the media is only interested in portraying the regime in the worst possible way."

I don't think this can fairly be characterized as apologetics for the Khmer Rouge. Chomsky and Herman do make a strong case that the media were little interested in a balanced presentation of the facts about the regime. Western and especially US media are overwhelmingly anti-Communist; some, too, are inclined toward sensationalism. The emerging stories from Cambodia provided grist for sensational anti-Communist propaganda, including some reports that were grossly distorted or demonstrably false.[19] The temptation to exaggerate horrors, particularly when they can be associated with a widely hated ideology, is powerful.

But the fact that horrors have been exaggerated doesn't mean that they aren't gargantuan in any case, and therein lay the rub for Chomsky and Herman. Clearly, they wanted to believe in the Cambodian revolution, and they were suspicious of a narrative that they thought could be used retrospectively to justify the US war in Vietnam and future wars against revolutionary nationalist movements. For a time, the conflicting reports coming out of Khmer Cambodia left just enough room for hopeful leftists to cling to a benign view of the Cambodian regime. Objectively, it wasn't enough. Chomsky and Herman chose to highlight those reports that suggested a positive or mixed picture, and berated the media for neglecting those reports. While they scored some points, their analysis—even as revised in *After the Cataclysm*—lacked balance. The significant story coming out of Cambodia in the late 1970s was one of a revolutionary regime perpetrating unspeakable horrors. In the face of that reality, Chomsky's critique of the media seemed—and was—a quibble, a large misplacement of emphasis at best. There may have been some slender basis for doubt, but the preponderance of evidence, certainly by mid-1978, pointed toward a horrendous picture of the new regime.[20] Chomsky and Herman stubbornly did their best to point the other way.

Eventually, Chomsky did come to acknowledge that the Pol Pot regime was guilty of large-scale atrocities, but this acknowledgment was unaccompanied by any hint of a mea culpa. Quite the contrary: Chomsky in the late 1980s asserted flatly that "I am aware of no error or misleading statement that has been found in anything that we wrote" about Cambodia. The basis for that avowal is the claim that he and Herman had not been trying to establish the facts of what had happened in Cambodia, but only to critique the media's handling of the available evidence.[21] But at the same time, Chomsky, without acknowledging the inconsistency, asserted that he and Herman had written about the regime's atrocities in the *Nation* article, which is to say, that they *had* written about the facts.[22] The truth, of course, is that Chomsky and Herman in that article wrote not about the atrocities but about books that documented the atrocities, books they sought to discredit. Soon afterward, Chomsky again stated that he and Herman had written about the facts: that they had showed that the bloodbath in Cambodia was comparable to the slaughter inflicted by Indonesia in suppressing East Timor's quest for independence.[23]

Chomsky and Herman also claimed retrospectively that in the *Nation* article they "were clear and explicit . . . that refugee reports left no doubt that the record of Khmer Rouge atrocities was 'substantial and often gruesome' and that . . . 'there is no difficulty in documenting major atrocities and oppression primarily from the reports of refugees.'" Both parts of this claim are false.[24] As Bruce Sharp points out, there was no acknowledgment whatsoever in the *Nation* article of "atrocities and oppression" under the Khmer regime; that acknowledgment came only two years later, in *After the Cataclysm*.[25] The *Nation* article, moreover, emphasized the "extreme unreliability" of refugee reports, and even in *ATC* the authors' major thrust was to urge great caution in their use.

Chomsky retrospectively tries to have it both ways: he says that he wrote not mainly about the facts of the Cambodian holocaust, but about how the media distorted the facts; not long afterwards he claims to have written about the facts. He also says he knows of having made no incorrect or misleading statements about what happened in Cambodia, but makes false and misleading statements about what he said. Chomsky's credibility would have suffered far less with a frank mea culpa.

CHAPTER 2

Cold War Empire

CRITICS AND SUPPORTERS OF America's role in Indochina have widely agreed that the Vietnam War was not an aberration. The US commitment to war in Indochina was a natural and logical consequence—though perhaps not an inevitable one—of basic assumptions and strategies that had underpinned American foreign policy since at least the end of World War II. This is certainly Chomsky's view, but his understanding of American foreign policy and its objectives departs radically from mainstream views.

American Foreign Policy during the Cold War: A Chomskian Overview

Most students of history see American foreign policy after World War II as dominated by the Cold War—the nearly half-century confrontation between the United States and the Soviet Union. To most Americans, the Cold War reflected an essentially defensive effort by the United States and its Western allies to contain the expansionist ambitions of a Soviet Union bent on imposing its Communist system throughout the world. This view of the Cold War was eventually challenged by some historians who saw the Cold War as a more interactive process in which the American side was hardly less aggressive than the Soviet. But even in this "revisionist" view the Cold War usually remained the central reality of international politics.[1]

Chomsky, instead, believes that the Cold War was something of a smokescreen. It served the needs of both superpowers for an excuse to consolidate their control over their respective empires. The American empire wasn't characterized for the most part by direct ownership of foreign lands; it was, instead, an empire of influence and control, utilizing economic, political, and military power. Its core objective was to serve American business in the pursuit of profits.

Chomsky recounts that the United States after World War II enjoyed a position of unprecedented international primacy; no other country remotely approached this country in economic or military power. Anticipating this fortunate position, US policy planners even before the war's end had set to work planning the reconstruction of the international economic system, a system that would surely be dominated by American capitalism. A liberal internationalist system of open markets and unrestricted investment opportunities would naturally accrue to the advantage of firms of the dominant economic superpower. In this system, the countries of what came to be called the Third World were to play their traditional roles as suppliers of raw materials and outlets for exports and investment by international corporations based in the West.[2]

American leadership did largely succeed in reconstructing the world capitalist system, but the vision of a "balanced" international economy, with poorer countries playing their allotted subaltern roles, was to be threatened repeatedly by outbursts of revolutionary nationalism in the Third World. The most dramatic case, of course, was Vietnam. American policy planners in the early 1950s saw Indochina as a critical source of raw materials and market opportunities for the advanced capitalist economies—in particular, that of Japan, which was to serve as the pivot of the American-dominated world capitalist system in Asia. Should Vietnam withdraw from that system (to be followed, via the domino effect, by the rest of Southeast Asia), Japan could find itself compelled to turn to the Communist world for its economic lifelines. Thus, in Chomsky's words, "the Vietnam War is simply a catastrophic episode, a grim and costly failure in this long-term effort to reduce Eastern Asia and much of the rest of the world to part of the American-dominated economic system."[3]

Third World revolutionary movements were especially worrying to Washington because they could spread: the domino theory, derided by some critics of the Vietnam War, contained "an important kernel of plausibility, perhaps truth. National independence and revolutionary social change, if successful, may very well be contagious."[4] A successful revolutionary regime in a unified Vietnam, for example, might present an attractive model of development for other countries in Asia and even beyond.

The first challenge to the reconstructed world capitalist system had come from the Soviet Union, whose expansion and consolidation of its own empire impeded the reintegration of the Eastern European countries into the economies of Western Europe. Chomsky explains that the Soviet Union's "autarkic command economy interfered with US plans to construct a global system based on (relatively) free trade and investment, which, under the conditions of mid century, was expected to be dominated by US corporations. . . . The Iron Curtain deprived the capitalist industrial powers of a region that was expected to provide raw materials, investment opportunities, markets and cheap labor."[5]

Thus, it was the closure of Eastern Europe to the reach of the capitalist world economy, and not a fear of Soviet aggression, that brought the United States into conflict with the Soviet Union. According to Chomsky, US leaders understood that the Soviets didn't pose a real military threat to Western Europe, but the emerging Cold War facilitated US assertion of its leadership of the Western alliance. Because they understood the functionality of the Cold War to the US-led international system, US leaders repeatedly spurned feelers by the Soviet Union in the 1950s and early 1960s to reduce Cold War tensions in Europe.

In the Third World, the Cold War exigency of battling international Communism anywhere and everywhere it threatened to gain ground came to serve Washington as an ever-ready pretext to fight indigenous revolutionary movements whose aspirations clashed with the needs of American business and the world system it dominated. US policy called for Third World regimes that were amenable to penetration by Western business. But revolutionary nationalist regimes posed obstacles to US-based and other transnational corporations. The threat of nationalization was only the most severe. The maintenance of a favorable climate for business called for free trade, minimal restrictions on capital movements, lax regulation, low taxes, cheap labor, and a relatively docile labor force. All of these are less likely to be obtainable in countries seeking independent, noncapitalist paths to development. The American crusade against Communism, then, was really directed against "the efforts of indigenous movements to extricate their societies from the integrated world system dominated largely by American capitalism and to use their resources for their own social and economic development."[6]

Regimes or revolutionary movements that resisted their assigned model of economic integration incurred the opposition of the United States. Often, US opposition took the form of CIA-sponsored covert subversion of the recalcitrant regime through encouragement and assistance to local counterrevolutionaries, usually including the military. Chomsky notes that there were eighteen military coups in Latin America between 1960 and 1979. Many of these were aided or encouraged by the United States, and most of the resulting juntas enjoyed strong US support after taking power. Occasionally, US opposition to Third World nationalism took the form of outright American military intervention, as in the Dominican Republic in 1965 and, less successfully, in Vietnam. Invariably, an alleged danger of Communism served as the pretext for US intervention. In many if not most of the US interventions, the role of Communists in the offending regime was far less prominent than claimed by US officials. Even where the Communists did have a leading role in revolutionary nationalist movements, as in Vietnam, they typically represented genuinely indigenous popular forces yearning for change. Instead, Washington portrayed its Third World adversaries as agents, or at best unwitting dupes, of Moscow or Peking or both.

But the repression of nationalist aspirations in the Third World was often an unavoidably nasty business. The "cleanup" after a resisting regime was overthrown, as in Iran in 1953 and Guatemala in 1954, often involved harshly repressive measures aimed at the former regime's leaders and supporters. Since the reintroduction of democracy might bring the offenders back into power, continued reliance on authoritarian repression was necessary. Democratic rhetoric notwithstanding, Washington had no trouble recognizing the virtues of Third World dictatorships, which often proved more accommodating to US foreign policy objectives than democracies. According to Chomsky and Herman, "The operative principle [of US foreign policy] has been and remains *economic* freedom—meaning freedom for U.S. business to invest, sell, and repatriate profits—and its two basic requisites, a favorable investment climate and a specific form of stability. Since these primary values are disturbed by unruly students, democratic processes, peasant organizations, a free press, and free labor unions, 'economic freedom' has often required political servitude."[7]

Chomsky convincingly demonstrates a recurrent, positive relationship between US foreign aid and increasing human rights violations in ten countries following successful coups in the 1960s and 1970s. In what looks like practically a predictive model, the two variables apparently correlate because of their relationship to a third: the restoration of a favorable business climate. Pro-US coups were almost invariably followed by a variety of concessions to US business in areas like taxes, profit repatriation, and minerals claims.[8] Washington gladly showed its appreciation for such cooperative behavior.

In its efforts to make the Third World safe for American business, the United States over time constructed a neocolonial "evil empire." (Chomsky applied the term only after it was coined by Ronald Reagan.) It was composed of Third World "fascist" states that mocked democracy, brutally repressed dissent and terrorized their own populations but reliably served American interests.[9] Fascism in the Third World also suited the interests of local economic elites who had their own reasons to fear popular aspirations. It also enabled political and military officeholders to enrich themselves. A practically universal feature of Third World fascist regimes was widespread systemic corruption. These were "shakedown states," where an arbitrary distribution of power and privilege fed a pervasive cynicism, fostering the perception that the command of public power is a natural means to private enrichment.

Chomsky strongly suggests that the US empire was no less "evil"—and perhaps even more so—than its Soviet counterpart. The worst crimes of Stalinism were in the 1930s. On the other hand, the much more recent if not current crimes of some US client regimes—notably, the Indonesian military regime of the 1960s and 1970s and the Central American regimes of the 1980s—reached genocidal magnitudes. He cites an Amnesty International study of the mid-1970s showing that the practice of torture had largely disappeared in the Soviet empire, but was flourishing in Latin America, within the US sphere of influence. And he quotes a Guatemalan journalist who in 1990 noted that the Czechs had been "lucky" to have the Soviet Union as their oppressor: the student uprising in Prague had been possible because the Czech police didn't shoot to kill, unlike the security forces in Guatemala and El Salvador, who killed freely.[10]

Lest anyone argue that abuses of human rights in the American empire reflected excesses in the fight against international Communism, Chomsky points to continuities in US policy with the pre-Cold War era. There was nothing new about US policymakers' aggressive determination to keep poorer countries open to penetration by American business. Both Democratic and Republican presidents had routinely and repeatedly employed gunboat diplomacy to assure US dominance of the countries of the Caribbean basin. The pretexts, of course, were different then—there was no Communist bogey to combat but there was always the need to restore order in chaotic lands that couldn't govern themselves. During World War I, the specter of German penetration of the hemisphere could be invoked. Democracy and freedom, always proclaimed as core American values, were readily subordinated to stability and the promise of a favorable business climate when it came to judging a regime's acceptability to the United States. Thus, Chomsky points out that US officials cheered Benito Mussolini's accession to power in Italy: not only did Il Duce lay low the threat of Communism, he made clear that Italy actively sought investment and trade relations with the United States. The Nazi conquest of power in Germany also initially got favorable (if somewhat more reserved) reviews from US officials. It was only with the heightening aggressiveness of the two fascist countries in the second half of the 1930s that the United States showed its clear disapproval of those regimes' policies.

The Cold War thus provided a new and highly useful rationale for US foreign policy objectives that were long-standing, while US primacy in the postwar era offered new opportunities for pursuing those objectives on a global scale:

> The United States itself has a long history of imposing oppressive and terrorist regimes in regions of the world within the reach of its power, such as the Caribbean and Central American sugar and banana republics. . . . Since World War II, with the great extension of U.S. power, it has borne heavy responsibility for the spread of a plague of neofascism, state terrorism, torture and repression throughout large parts of the underdeveloped world. The United States has globalized the "banana republic."[11]

To summarize: Chomsky provides a broad explanatory framework for understanding American foreign policy during the Cold War as well as a considerable body of detailed descriptive accounts of the impact of American policy on various countries in the Third World. What emerges from those accounts is a picture of the US role in the world that differs dramatically from the image held by most Americans. The remainder of this chapter is devoted to assessing the accuracy of the picture that Chomsky has drawn. Was "Third World fascism" as bad, or nearly as bad, as he claims? To what extent was it a product of US policy? How responsible was the United States for human rights violations by its Third World allies?

America's Third World Empire: How Evil? How American?

The broad Chomsky argument is that America's involvement in the Third World has repeatedly been indifferent to and destructive of basic democratic values and human welfare. So, we are interested in the nature of "Third World fascism" as described by Chomsky and the role of the United States in fostering it. While the broader explanatory question—how do we account for American foreign policy during the Cold War?—will be the subject of the next chapter, we will also be interested here in whatever evidence we can glean about why America's involvement with "Third World fascism" took the forms that it did.

Chomsky's writings on American foreign policy have covered over two dozen countries on five continents. As I indicated in the Preface, selectivity is unavoidable in any serious attempt to assess Chomsky's work. In this chapter, I will be focusing on just five countries that Chomsky describes as suffering the impact of American imperialism: two in Asia and three in Central America. I've chosen these five because they usefully illustrate the variety of historic circumstances under which the United States established and maintained its Cold War empire. The two Asian countries include a carryover from America's early twentieth century foray into formal imperialism, the Philippines; and an important Cold War addition to the empire, Indonesia. The three Central American countries were all long-standing client states of their northern neighbor, but their different historic experiences present useful variations for comparative analysis.

A few words on terminology: Back in the 1960s, when Chomsky first came to prominence as a public intellectual, talk of "American imperialism" was mostly the province of radical leftist critics of American foreign policy. People generally agreed that "imperialism" was bad but disagreed over whether America was, in fact, imperialist. In more recent decades, references to American imperialism have gained wider currency, and the term has taken on more neutral—sometimes even positive—connotations. I am going to use the terms "empire" and "imperialism" in a neutral sense. Other terminology could certainly be chosen—it is common to speak of US global hegemony, for example, or of its worldwide sphere of influence. "Imperialism" and "empire" are convenient shorthand for characterizing the global system of power that the United States constructed largely after World War II.

I will also follow Chomsky in his characterization of these five countries—like many other Third World countries—as "clients" of the United States. In international politics, "clientelism" is often understood to signify a bilateral relationship between two countries of grossly unequal power, in which the stronger country exerts a high degree of influence over the affairs of the other. All five countries examined here fit this broad definition of US client, although the degree of influence exerted by the United States varied widely among the five.

For each country, I will initially lay out Chomsky's narrative, at times adding background information and details or corrections based on evidence that became available after Chomsky wrote his interpretation of events. My own commentary will follow.

ASIAN OUTPOSTS OF EMPIRE: THE PHILIPPINES, INDONESIA, AND EAST TIMOR

The Philippines: Chomsky's narrative. The Philippines until 1946 was one of the few outright colonial possessions of the United States, acquired as a result of the Spanish American War of 1898. Chomsky recounts how the US defeat of Spain opened up Filipino hopes for national independence, but the victorious Americans, in their country's first great flush of imperialist fervor, had other ideas. The United States crushed the Filipino independence movement in a nearly decade-long war marked by "massacres of civilians, burnings of villages, torture, and the other appurtenances of pacification." Hundreds of thousands of Filipinos were killed. Subsequently under US colonial rule, the Philippines "was characterized by economic and political domination by US administrators and a local and US-based economic elite. The local elite was made up largely of major landholders whose interests were cemented to those of the United States."[12]

With formal independence in 1946, the Philippines became an oligarchic democracy in which political and economic power was concentrated in a small elite known as "the four hundred families." The country's heavy dependence on the United States continued as a result of extensive US direct business investment and a network of business, financial, and military linkages. Corruption was widespread, in the private sector but especially in government, which was widely perceived to be an instrument of the wealthy. A peasant revolt was successfully suppressed during the 1950s, but renewed unrest led to the declaration of martial law in 1972 by President Ferdinand Marcos. Numerous opposition figures were arrested and strict limits were placed on the press. At the same time, Marcos abrogated a recent Filipino Supreme Court ruling that the United States could no longer enjoy a privileged position in land ownership; US citizens and corporations would now have been subject to the existing general ban on foreign ownership of Filipino land. Chomsky cites a *Business Week* article stressing the newly authoritarian regime's friendliness to US business. According to one oilman quoted in the magazine, "Marcos says 'We'll pass the laws you need—just tell us what you want.'"[13]

Marcos used the declaration of martial law to effectively establish himself as dictator. By 1977, sixty thousand people had been arrested under the martial law decree. The regime freely employed torture, described in fairly grisly detail by Amnesty International. On occasion, dissidents "disappeared" under suspicious circumstances.[14] But the suppression of democracy and human rights hardly disturbed US-Philippines relations. On the contrary, the familiar pattern of *increased* US military and economic aid and investment following the overthrow of democracy held for the Philippines. International Monetary Fund (IMF) and World Bank lending to the Philippines also increased exponentially after 1972. Chomsky acknowledges that Marcos did eventually have to endure mild pressure from the United States to improve the human rights situation in his country. Marcos accordingly became adept at making token gestures like the release of prisoners or the holding of rigged elections when Philippine aid was coming up for review in the US Congress or when a dignitary like Vice President Walter Mondale was visiting. In any case, the US government was like an indulgent parent, easily reassured.

The Philippines: My commentary. How accurate is Chomsky's chronicle of Philippine history? How well does it support his broad explanation of American Cold War foreign policy's servitude to business?

Chomsky is entirely accurate in his description of the brutal suppression of the Philippine independence struggle in the early years of the twentieth century, which must surely rank as one of the most shameful episodes in US history. Estimates of Philippine noncombatant deaths range from two hundred thousand to six hundred thousand.[15] And, while US colonial rule in the Philippines deserves credit for introducing and encouraging the growth of formally democratic institutions, it was also complicit in the highly unequal development of Philippine society, enabling a small, wealthy elite to continue to dominate politics even after the achievement of independence and democracy in 1946.[16]

Chomsky's account of US government relations with the Marcos regime, and of the brutality and corruption of that regime, is also correct in most important respects. In imposing martial rule, Marcos acted without any prompting from the United States; indeed, the US ambassador to the Philippines tried to dissuade him. But Marcos reasonably interpreted the absence of any direct objection from Washington as at least tacit acquiescence. (Accounts differ, but it seems that Marcos spoke at least once with President Nixon by telephone in the days before his proclamation, and encountered no objection to his plans.)[17] A Rand Corporation study found that there was "considerable evidence" that martial law was carried out through US collusion in order to advance American economic and strategic interests. Alejandro Melchor, a trusted Marcos confidante sent to Washington to gauge US reaction, received enthusiastic support for martial law from Thomas Moorer, chairman of the Joint Chiefs of Staff. A National Security Council representative told Melchor that the United States had no problem with martial law as long as it posed no threat to US business in the Philippines. (The US Chamber of Commerce in the Philippines had in fact promptly announced its support for martial law.) Meeting with World Bank president Robert McNamara, Melchor obtained a promise of a doubling of the bank's loans to the Philippines. The promise was more than kept. US military aid increased even more dramatically, nearly tripling during the first year of martial law.[18]

The advent of President Carter's human rights policy changed little. Patricia Derian, Carter's assistant secretary of state for human rights, visited Manila and warned Marcos of a possible withdrawal of US support for international lending to the Philippines, but she was angrily rebuffed by the dictator. Derian was no more successful in her struggle within the administration for a tougher US stance toward Marcos. The administration even fought off a congressional proposal for a modest reduction in military aid to the Philippine regime.[19]

Chomsky's Philippines narrative essentially ends in the late 1970s with his and Edward S. Herman's book *The Washington Connection and Third World Fascism*; in his later writings, Chomsky makes only brief references to the Philippines. He does allude in passing to the events leading to the fall of Marcos in 1986: he observes correctly that US support for a favored dictator was withdrawn only after it became clear that his retention in power had become a hopeless cause. Chomsky asserts, quite reasonably, that even after the restoration of democracy, Philippine society remained scarred by extreme inequalities in economic and hence political power—an "elite democracy" in which the urban and rural poor found little voice.[20]

Why was the US government so tolerant of a brutal and notoriously corrupt dictator?[21] Chomsky's clear answer is that the US government valued Marcos as a willing servant of US business interests. Chomsky also notes that the US desire to retain its two huge military bases in the Philippines was an additional factor in US government decision making. The Subic naval base was reputed to be the largest US naval installation in the world outside the United States; it was located at the center of the Seventh Fleet's area of responsibility, well poised for the projection of naval power in the Indian Ocean, the Persian Gulf, and the South China Sea. Clark Air Force Base was the largest US overseas air base and also the largest US military installation in Asia.[22] The United States wanted to keep those bases, which could have been threatened by a hostile or unstable regime in the Philippines.

Chomsky cites an argument that the bases had lost most of their strategic value, but he doesn't acknowledge that this view, which first acquired currency during the Carter administration, was highly controversial in US policy circles, and remained so well into the 1980s.[23] Utilized extensively during the Vietnam War, the two Philippine bases took on added importance after the war's end: the United States lost its important base in Cam Ranh Bay, which the Vietnamese turned over to the Soviets in 1979. Chomsky asserts that Marcos used his apparently tough negotiations over rent for the bases as a bogus demonstration of his independence from his indulgent parent. But Chomsky is too ready to dismiss Marcos as a mere puppet: Marcos enjoyed a strong bargaining position, and he played it for what he could get.

Undoubtedly, then, both business interests and military strategic concerns were at play in shaping US policymakers' friendliness toward the Philippine ruler. Which was the more important? From what we know of internal discussions in the Carter and Reagan administrations, the bases appeared to be the more salient concern. That was also the perception of the American business community in the Philippines.[24] The weight of the available evidence indicates that the military-strategic interest was very probably more important than the business interest in conditioning US policy.[25]

In summary, America's coziness with Ferdinand Marcos lends partial support to Chomsky's view of US Cold War foreign policy. The Philippines under Marcos provides an excellent fit with Chomsky's observed pattern of US aid and investment increasing in tandem with concessions to US business interests following a "fascist" seizure of power. The United States had little trouble living with a brutal and corrupt dictator. If this country had any interest at all in democracy promotion, that interest took a cramped back seat to other concerns, whether of an economic or military-strategic nature. US leaders could have tried to push Marcos toward more humane governance, but chose not to; the *best* that can be said of the three US administrations that dealt with the Marcos dictatorship is that none was willing to take significant risks to advance human rights or democracy. On the other hand, the clear primacy that Chomsky assigns to business interests in determining US policy is not supported by the evidence.

Indonesia: Chomsky's narrative. For much of the post war period until the early 1960s, most US officials considered Indonesia more important to American interests than

Indochina.²⁶ Its large population, and its location and geographic expanse (Indonesia is an archipelago stretching three thousand miles east to west) made it of obvious strategic importance. American policymakers saw it as an important trading partner for Japan, whose industrial expansion would draw on Indonesia's abundant natural resources of oil, tin, and rubber. But Indonesia's charismatic president for life, Sukarno, was never a favorite of the United States. Sukarno maintained an aggressively neutralist stance and over time became increasingly close to Indonesia's large Communist Party, the PKI. In 1958 the CIA lent covert aid to an unsuccessful regional rebellion that would have undermined Sukarno's rule.

On October 1, 1965, a military coup effectively toppled Sukarno, installing General Suharto as the new ruler of Indonesia. Over the course of the next fifteen years Suharto's regime twice was responsible for acts of mass murder on a genocidal scale. Throughout this period Indonesia enjoyed friendly and cooperative relations with the United States.

Coup, countercoup, and bloodbath. The October 1 coup—sometimes referred to as the "countercoup"—followed by one day an apparent attempt at a seizure of power by a group of left-wing army officers. Six leading figures in the Indonesian military were assassinated in this abortive coup, which provided the Indonesian military establishment a pretext for a massive, bloody campaign against the PKI, which, at three million members, was the third largest Communist party in the world. The PKI and the army had coexisted in an uneasy balance in Indonesia's semi-authoritarian "guided democracy" under Sukarno. On the pretext of PKI involvement in the initial coup attempt, the countercoup leadership took the opportunity to eliminate its institutional rival for power while Sukarno looked on in intermittent, futile protest. Increasingly a figurehead, Sukarno was finally forced to abdicate in 1967 in favor of Suharto.

The mass killings began with isolated incidents during the first half of October; they spread rapidly later in the month and raged through November and part of December, with occasional incidents into 1966. The victims were ostensibly PKI leaders and party supporters at all levels, although undoubtedly many non-Communists—sometimes entire villages—were also enveloped in the slaughter. The PKI, which was organized as a conventional political party (i.e., for contesting elections and holding seats in parliament), had no military capability; it was able to put up almost no resistance. Estimates of the number of dead range from two hundred thousand to one million or more, with more recent estimates generally closer to the higher figure.²⁷ Up to a million people or more were arrested. The killings were sometimes carried out directly by the armed forces, and in other cases by local anti-Communist religious or nationalist groups encouraged and assisted by the military and inflamed by the government's lurid anti-Communist propaganda campaign. Taking full control of the radio and print media, the government fanned popular anger and fear with false claims that the murdered generals had been grotesquely tortured before being killed, and that the PKI had drawn up plans for killing sprees of its own.²⁸

Although he makes no claim of direct US involvement in the October 1 coup or its bloody aftermath, Chomsky notes that the Pentagon and the CIA had built an extensive network of connections with the Indonesian military. One-third of the Indonesian general staff and half of the officer corps had received training in the United States, and there were many personal bonds between the militaries of the two countries. At least one of the leaders of the countercoup had long-standing CIA connections. American policymakers had viewed these relationships, along with the considerable military aid the US extended to Indonesia, as useful for developing the Indonesian military in recognition of its role as a competitor for power with the PKI.[29]

In his first account of the coup, written in the late 1970s, Chomsky observes that American policymakers generally expressed satisfaction at the changed political situation in Indonesia, usually preferring to ignore the massacres. In a book written fifteen years later, he asserts, "There is no doubt Washington was aware of the slaughter, and approved."[30] No US congressman denounced the horrors on the floor of Congress. The new Indonesian government soon obliged US business interests with a foreign investment law passed in early 1967 that lifted import restrictions and offered tax and other incentives. A major inflow of US and Japanese investment followed. In one important respect, however, the new regime was less than ideal from the standpoint of international business: it was riddled with corruption. "Licenses to do business, to import, to export, to exploit timber or mineral resources, government contracts, and state bank credit are all up for sale by the military elite," who were able to use the funds thereby gained together with political leverage to build personal business empires.[31]

Indonesia: My commentary. Chomsky's account of the Indonesian coup and bloodbath is noteworthy for the relatively limited claims that he makes. He observes correctly that the United States had long cultivated the Indonesian military as a possible contender for power with the PKI, but he doesn't claim that the United States had any direct role in the coup. With characteristic irony, he classifies the bloodbath as a case of "constructive terror" from the US viewpoint, because the elimination of the PKI served long-standing US objectives. In *The Washington Connection* Chomsky is curiously inconsistent in describing the actual reaction of US leaders to the bloodbath. Early on he asserts without citing any evidence that US political leaders were "enthusiastic" about the massacres. Later, he asserts merely that the US response was "restrained."[32] But he makes no claim that the US government deliberately encouraged, much less assisted, the Indonesian army in the slaughter. Chomsky seems to leave it to the reader to speculate about the possible culpability of the US government.

Chomsky's initial reticence on the question of possible US government involvement in the coup and its bloody aftermath is appropriate; the evidence available at the time he first wrote about Indonesia was very limited. Even in his later *Year 501,* Chomsky acknowledges that the limited documentary evidence available leaves open questions regarding the US role. He does assert that "through

1965, the main question in Washington was how to encourage army action against the PKI."[33] Chomsky doesn't cite any source for this claim, which seems to be unsupported by any available evidence. By mid-1965, American policymakers, while favorably disposed toward the rumored possibility of a coup, had become pessimistic about their ability to decisively influence the Indonesian political situation; as Chomsky acknowledges, they were caught unawares by the dramatic events of September 30 and October 1.[34]

But, as Chomsky correctly observes, the Americans quickly realized that the coup represented a long-awaited opportunity for the realization of US objectives in Indonesia. Within days of the coup, the US embassy in Jakarta was in almost daily contact with Indonesian army leaders. On October 4, Undersecretary of State George Ball told columnist James Reston, "This is a critical time for the army. If the army does move they have [the] strength to wipe up [the] earth with [the] PKI and if they don't they may not have another chance."[35] Mass executions began during the first week after the coup, with 150 PKI leaders shot in Jakarta and preparations for similar executions elsewhere. This bloody beginning clearly didn't raise any problem for US ambassador Marshall Green, who reported on October 20 that the army "has been working hard at destroying PKI and I, for one, have increasing respect for its determination and organization in carrying out this crucial assignment."[36] By the end of October, the embassy had reports of killings throughout Java. One US military adviser, for example, returned from Bandung in late October reporting that villagers were "clearing out PKI members and affiliates and turning them over to Army" for arrest or execution.[37]

What was Washington's understanding of the violence? Documentary evidence that wasn't available to Chomsky makes it possible for us now to fill in some of the blanks he had to leave. A piece titled "Editorial Note," included in the State Department's documents published three decades later, clearly seeks to promote a benign interpretation of American official behavior. It suggests that the embassy's understanding of events in October and November 1965 was hampered by the "general chaos and confusion" in areas outside the Indonesian capital. At first, the embassy allegedly viewed the violence as a possible military-guerilla conflict, and was unable to determine whether some of the killings were reactions to acts of terror or sabotage by the PKI, or eruptions of Muslim anti-Communist fervor. The note characterizes the continuing reports of massacres as anecdotal.[38] As late as November 9, a CIA memo forecast a likely insurgency, even while acknowledging the armed forces' overwhelming military superiority.[39] Retrospectively, speculation about an active armed resistance by the PKI can be dismissed as groundless—we know now that the party lacked arms or preparedness for any such role—but it may have seemed plausible at the time.[40]

Still, the State Department's retrospective effort at self-exculpation is less than convincing. Certainly, US officials couldn't have been clear about the full scale of the bloodletting—questions about the death toll persist to this day. And up to a point there may have been some room for honest confusion about what was happening. But the embassy already knew of mass executions in Jakarta in early October. In early November, Ambassador Green reported that the Indonesian army was "moving relentlessly to exterminate PKI." In Jakarta, he said, the army was avoiding a further frontal attack on the PKI leadership, but "smaller fry" were "being systematically arrested and jailed or executed." Such statements don't suggest uncertainty or confusion about what was going on. The State Department documents show that the embassy continued to receive reports of cold-blooded massacres throughout the month of November.[41] At some point, accumulating "anecdotal" reports amount to an avalanche of evidence. Surely by early December, and probably well before, American policymakers had to have understood that the regime they were supporting was engaged in a deliberate, ongoing campaign of mass murder.

In the first few weeks after the coup, Washington had been wary of taking on too active a role in support of the army. It wasn't immediately clear that Sukarno might not be able somehow to stage a comeback, and any covert US aid to the military posed risks of being discovered.[42] US officials also debated whether to attach strings to US aid, particularly regarding Indonesia's treatment of American oil companies. Sukarno had initiated plans for a takeover of the companies. American policymakers were now hoping that the new regime would look more favorably on American oil interests. Francis Galbraith, the second ranking official at the US embassy, suggested to his Indonesian army contact in early November that doubts about this issue could be an obstacle to American aid; still, Galbraith assured the Indonesian that the United States was "sympathetic to and admiring of" what the army was doing.[43] The United States soon afterward decided to approve an Indonesian army request for medical supplies. Around the same time, the White House authorized the CIA station in Bangkok to provide small arms in order to "arm Muslim and nationalist youth in Central Java for use against PKI." Other material aid followed.[44] In early December the US embassy turned over to the Indonesian army lists it had been compiling from PKI sources of PKI leaders and cadres around the country. The chief of the embassy's political section later claimed that the Americans didn't expect the Indonesian regime to kill the Communists so identified rather than just arrested them.[45]

In sum, Chomsky is clearly correct in asserting that "there is no doubt that Washington was aware of the slaughter, and approved."[46] The leading historian of the postcoup period, Bradley Simpson, is unequivocal: US officials were strongly supportive of the bloodletting: "Washington continued its assistance long after it was clear that mass killings were taking place and in the expectation that US aid would contribute to this end. Not a single US official, however, ever expressed concern in public or private about the slaughter."[47] As one State Department official put it, "No one cared, as long as they were Communists, that they were being butchered."[48] President Johnson himself authorized a covert payment to an anti-Communist death squad organization in early December, at close to the height of the massacres.[49]

Would the Indonesian army have carried out a genocidal-scale campaign even without US support? Undoubtedly. Could American influence have restrained or moderated the Indonesian holocaust? Perhaps, but there is nothing in the documentary record to suggest that American decision makers ever pondered that question, or were in any way disturbed by the bloodletting.[50] Chomsky correctly observes, too, that mass murder was essentially a nonissue for the Washington foreign policy community and the US mass media, which greeted the changes in Indonesia with general satisfaction, if not approbation.[51] (It is worth noting, however, that one elected official did raise his voice. Robert Kennedy in a January 1966 speech asked why Americans had not spoken out against the "inhuman slaughter" in Indonesia.)[52]

It is more than a bit chilling to read the unapologetic account written over twenty years later by Marshall Green, US ambassador during the period. Green barely acknowledges the role of the Indonesian army in the bloodbath. He basically blames the victims for their deaths: the Communists, with their atheism and class-based appeals, had stirred up animosity in the countryside. Describing the situation as of December 1965, he notes the "recent improvements in the political climate," in Indonesia, but lists a number of continuing problems, including inflation, travel restrictions, threatened expropriation of foreign oil companies, and the need to purge the armed forces of residual Communist influence. Absent from his list is any concern to minimize further loss of life, or to protect the rights of the hundreds of thousands of arrestees.[53]

East Timor: Chomsky's narrative. On December 7, 1977, Indonesian armed forces invaded the former Portuguese colony of East Timor, less than a day after President Gerald Ford and Secretary of State Henry Kissinger met with Suharto in Jakarta. Over the next four years, the Indonesian army battled the proindependence movement on the island (East Timor shared the island with Indonesian West Timor), seeking to "incorporate" East Timor into Indonesia. The Indonesian forces inflicted massive, frequently gratuitous brutality on the civilian population. Decades later a UN truth commission concluded that between 100,000 and 180,000 East Timorese (out of a total population of 628,000) died as a result of Jakarta's campaign of "extermination."[54] The US government did nothing to stop the Indonesian onslaught; on the contrary, according to Chomsky, it provided Jakarta with critical material and diplomatic support. For Washington, the maintenance of smooth relations with a reliable client state was clearly a higher priority than the protection of human rights and life in East Timor.

The Portuguese announcement in April 1974 that it would give independence to its colonies spurred the formation of political parties in East Timor. The largest of these was Fretilin, which Chomsky describes as "a moderate reformist national front . . . calling for gradual steps toward complete independence, agrarian reform . . . and a foreign policy of non-alignment."[55] Fretilin won between 50 percent and 55 percent of the votes in local elections held in March through July 1975. Fretilin's closest competitor, the Timorese Democratic Union (UDT), was led by Catholics, many of whom were administrative officials or small landholders and were close to the colonial regime. A third party, Apodeti, was pro-Indonesian, and enjoyed the support of only about 5 percent of the population.

After a failed UDT coup attempt left Fretilin in firm control, Indonesia turned to direct military intervention. A series of border raids by Indonesian ground forces began in mid-September, supplemented by a campaign of air and naval bombardment beginning in November. After Indonesian rejections of Portuguese and Fretilin calls for a negotiated settlement, and with an Indonesian invasion apparently imminent, Fretilin declared East Timor independent on November 28. The Indonesian invasion followed by nine days. The Indonesians quickly captured the capital city of Dili, but encountered stubborn Fretilin-led resistance in the countryside.

Chomsky cites compelling circumstantial evidence that the US government anticipated the Indonesian invasion of December 7 and "not only took no significant action but gave its tacit or explicit approval."[56] Among other things, he quotes an August 1975 cable by Richard Woolcott, Australian ambassador to Indonesia, leaked in May 1976. Noting Jakarta's determination to take over East Timor, Woolcott reports that his American counterpart in Jakarta had been instructed by Henry Kissinger not to get involved in discussions on Timor and accordingly intended to "allow events to take their course."[57] During his December 6 visit to Jakarta, Kissinger told newsmen that the United States would not recognize the newly declared independent East Timor and that the United States "understands Indonesia's position on the question."[58] Challenging a journalist's assertion that there was no evidence that Ford and Kissinger had given their approval to the impending invasion, Chomsky remarks, "It takes quite an act of faith to believe that the invasion was not discussed" at the Ford-Kissinger-Suharto meeting of the 6th.[59]

The American "understanding" of the Indonesian position was reflected in the US votes in the United Nations. The United States abstained on a December 12 General Assembly resolution strongly deploring Indonesia's military intervention and calling on it to withdraw from East Timor (the resolution passed 72 votes to 10, with 43 abstentions, mostly close US allies). The United States did support a December 22 compromise resolution in the Security Council that called for Indonesian withdrawal, but the weak language of the resolution was regarded as a major concession to Indonesia's position. In April 1976 the United States abstained on a similar Security Council resolution, while in December the United States voted against a General Assembly resolution that rejected Indonesia's claim to East Timor (the resolution passed 68 to 20 with 49 abstentions). By March 1977, the US State Department was taking the position that "Timor has effectively become part of Indonesia." Under questioning in Congress at that time, the department's legal representative declined to "second guess" Indonesia on whether it had violated "international standards or norms of conduct" in the seizure and annexation of East Timor. To raise such questions "would not serve our best interests in light of the importance of our relations with Indonesia."[60] Consistent with this position, the United States continued to support Indonesia on Timor UN resolutions in the years that followed.

A remarkably resilient East Timorese resistance to the Indonesian takeover continued into 1979, and Indonesian atrocities also continued until the end. The United States, however, never acknowledged any extraordinary human rights problems in East Timor. Chomsky notes that the State Department's March 1977 Human Rights Report makes no mention whatsoever of East Timor. He remarks sarcastically that the 1978 report "rectifies" this omission with the following, which constitutes the report's total commentary on East Timor:

> Questions have been raised concerning atrocities by Indonesian troops in East Timor in 1975 and 1976 prior to the incorporation of East Timor into Indonesia. The Indonesian Government withdrew and disciplined offending units guilty of individual excesses, but most of the human losses in East Timor appear to have occurred prior to Indonesia's intervention.[61]

Chomsky points out that the last statement is a blatant lie.[62] The 1979 report is less egregiously mendacious, and even acknowledges that Timor "may" have been an exception to an allegedly improving human rights situation in Indonesia, "but the conflicting claims and lack of access into Timor by non-Indonesians make it difficult if not impossible to ascertain the loss of life."[63] As Chomsky documents extensively, the US government had long since possessed more than enough information to attempt an estimate of the loss of life.

The US government's complicity in the Indonesian onslaught on East Timor extended beyond diplomatic support and the whitewashing of atrocities. It included material support in the form of arms aid. A brief, pro forma suspension of arms aid in December 1975, in observance of US law prohibiting the supply of arms to countries engaged in aggression, had no effect, since arms shipments in the pipeline were allowed to go through. Eventually, the Carter administration actually increased military aid to the Jakarta regime. A State Department representative told Congress in 1980 that the United States had not asked Jakarta how it was using the aid.[64] The aid included counterinsurgency aircraft: ten OV-10s delivered between September 1976 and March 1978, and sixteen A4 Skyhawk IIs promised by Vice President Mondale in a visit to Jakarta in May 1978.[65]

East Timor: My commentary. Chomsky's account of Indonesia's assault on East Timor, and of Washington's cooperation with Jakarta, is accurate in all important respects. His hunch that Jakarta had gotten "tacit or explicit approval" from Washington before launching its December 7 invasion was not only reasonable; we now know that it was, in fact, correct. The administration of President Gerald Ford had been aware of Indonesia's interest in annexing East Timor for nearly a year. In a meeting in Washington in July, Suharto told Ford that East Timor was too small to be economically viable as an independent nation, so "the only way" would be its integration into Indonesia. A majority of East Timorese supported this route, he told Ford, but the majority were subject to the pressure of an "almost Communist" minority that wanted independence. Ford didn't respond.[66]

At the December 6 meeting in Jakarta, Suharto again raised the East Timor issue with Ford and Kissinger. Citing Fretilin's unilateral declaration of independence, and implying once again that the East Timorese favored integration with Indonesia, Suharto asked the US leaders for their "understanding if we deem it necessary to take rapid or drastic action." Evidently prepared for the conversation, Ford unambiguously replied, "We understand and will not press you on the issue. We understand the problem and the intentions you have." Kissinger noted that the use of US arms could be a problem, but suggested that Indonesia's action could be "construed" as self-defense. He added, "It is important that whatever you do succeeds quickly." While expressing understanding of the need to act quickly, Kissinger asked Suharto to wait until Ford and Kissinger returned to the United States; they would thus be in a better position to influence the reaction in America. He added, "Whatever you do, however, we will try to handle in the best way possible." Kissinger also asked Suharto if he anticipated a long guerilla war. Suharto replied that there probably would be "a small guerilla war."[67] Suharto waited for the Americans' plane to take off before launching his invasion.

There is no way of knowing whether Ford and Kissinger believed Suharto's claim that a majority of East Timorese wanted to be absorbed by Indonesia; certainly, they should have been aware that it was false, given Fretilin's solid majority victory in the July elections. They should also have known that Suharto's labeling of Fretilin as "almost Communist" was a long stretch at best. A November 1975 State Department briefing paper described Fretilin as "vaguely leftist," a reasonable characterization of a movement with an eclectic but mainly nationalistic ideology.[68] That didn't stop Kissinger—characteristically eager to find an anti-Communist rationale for policy—from referring to Fretilin in December as "a Communist government in the middle of Indonesia."[69]

Would Suharto have gone ahead with the invasion even if the American leaders had withheld their approval on December 6? Probably not. Concerned about reaction from the West, Suharto had moved cautiously on Timor even after Fretilin had crushed the UDT coup attempt in August. There is evidence that he only reluctantly acceded to pressure from his hawkish advisers to take radical action on East Timor. He was clearly eager to maintain friendly ties with the United States. There is very good reason to believe that a red light from Washington would have halted the planned invasion. But there is no evidence that the Ford administration ever considered discouraging Suharto's designs on East Timor. Washington's stance reflected a belief that East Timor was too small and primitive to merit self-government, as well as a desire to maintain good relations with the Suharto regime.[70]

In summary, US relations with Indonesia in the 1960s and 1970s lend strong support to Chomsky's contention that US government concern for the interests of American business trumped any concern for democracy or human rights in the Third World. Indonesia was host to heavy investment by US companies, particularly in oil and other natural resources. An appreciation of the country's importance to US business surfaces repeatedly in internal US government communications as well as in discussions between representatives of the two governments. US policymakers wanted to maintain a friendly and cooperative relationship with the Indonesian government; the Suharto regime's authoritarianism, and its proclivity for genocide, clearly posed no obstacle to that objective.

TRADITIONAL CLIENTS: GUATEMALA, EL SALVADOR, AND NICARAGUA

During the 1980s, Chomsky focused on US policy in Central America with an intensity and persistence that recalled the passion with which he had earlier opposed America's war in Vietnam. Chomsky's activism was a response to a heightened US involvement in the region, where a historical American sphere of influence was jeopardized by a recently triumphant revolution in Nicaragua and by threats of similar outcomes in Guatemala and El Salvador.

Central America is one of only two world regions (the other being the Middle East) to which Chomsky has dedicated a whole book, *Turning the Tide* (first published in 1985). Still, Chomsky's writings on Central America have a frustratingly sketchy and disjointed quality. This may well reflect Chomsky's work style. He has said, "I almost never work from an outline or follow a plan. The books simply grow by accretion."[71] The resulting work products are somewhat uneven. Whereas *Washington Connection* (coauthored with Edward S. Herman) provided a reasonably linear core narrative for each of the two Asian countries discussed earlier in this chapter, none of Chomsky's books offers a similarly straightforward exposition of the course of events for two of the three Central American countries I discuss here. (Chomsky's collaborative works with Herman seem to be more systematically organized than most of Chomsky's solo works.) In the sections that follow, I have pieced together Chomsky's narrative from *Turning the Tide* and other writings, but observant readers may still note apparent gaps in the exposition—relevant context and details omitted and obvious questions not raised, much less answered—that reflect the somewhat discontinuous nature of the source material.

El Salvador: Chomsky's narrative. Chomsky begins with a brief account of the *Matanza*, a 1932 massacre in which several thousand protesting peasants and workers were killed by the security forces of the authoritarian regime. For the next three decades memories of the *matanza* served effectively to inhibit dissent and preserve the power of the oligarchy, "about 100 major families, who enriched themselves and foreign investors while much of the population starved or emigrated."[72] This relative stability was disturbed briefly in late 1960 by a junior officers' coup that established a moderately leftist government. The new government fell after a few weeks to a countercoup prompted by pressure from elements of the traditional oligarchy and the United States.

The new military regime quickly gained recognition and strong support from the US government, which through the CIA established close links with the Salvadoran military and security forces. These links enabled the Salvadoran government to establish a military and paramilitary apparatus that was to become an instrument of regime-sponsored mass murder and terror in the coming years. Chomsky cites in particular the CIA's role in the organization and training of the rural paramilitary force ORDEN.[73] ORDEN was to become increasingly linked to death squad activity as resistance to the regime by newly active peasant associations, labor unions, and church-based self-help organizations acquired increasing force in the 1970s.

A move toward democracy in 1972 failed when presidential elections apparently won by the Christian Democrat Jose Napoleon Duarte were overturned by fraud and intervention by "two loyal U.S. clients, Guatemala and Nicaragua."[74] A second election result in 1977 was also negated by fraud.

In a context of increasing unrest, including a nascent guerilla movement, a reformist junta took power in a coup on October 15, 1979. Once again, however, the reformist complexion of the junta was modified, this time through US intervention to ensure that power was in the hands of elements on whom the United States could rely for support. The reorganized junta included Duarte, who had returned to El Salvador from a long exile. In early 1980, the Carter administration announced its intention to resume military aid to the Salvadoran government, which had been suspended in 1977 because of human rights violations. The announcement elicited an impassioned plea to President Carter by El Salvador's Archbishop Oscar Romero, who argued that power was in the hands of the armed forces who "knew only how to repress the people and defend the interests of the Salvadoran oligarchy."[75] A renewal of military aid, he predicted, would increase injustice and sharpen repression.

Carter declined the archbishop's request and sent the aid. According to Chomsky, Carter's decision reflected "the very essence of U.S. policy," which was to increase the repression and destroy the possibility of independent popular organizations challenging military rule.[76] The archbishop was assassinated in March, presumably by a right-wing death squad. "The war against the peasantry began in May with major massacres; . . . the university was destroyed in June; the leadership of the political opposition was murdered in November; the independent media were terrorized and eliminated; and in general the popular organizations were crushed with large-scale killings and torture."[77] Church sources eventually counted over eight thousand "verified" murders by the security forces of the state in 1980.[78]

Chomsky places responsibility for the violence squarely on the United States, treating the Salvadoran government essentially as a tool of Washington. He repeatedly uses phrases like "Carter's war against the peasantry" to describe the actions of El Salvador's security and armed forces in 1980.[79] The widely respected Duarte, who became president of the junta in December 1980, provided a democratic fig leaf for the slaughter; US spokesmen repeatedly acclaimed Duarte as a moderating force, doing his best to reduce the level of violence. In fact, he was a figurehead who functioned to lend legitimacy to the regime. The situation as summarized by Chomsky was that "the government was wholly illegitimate, a foreign implant supported by military forces that are hardly more than mercenaries of the foreign power that is responsible for the violent attack against the population off El Salvador under the facade it had created."[80]

As bad as this was, "the US-organized massacres escalated as Reagan took over."[81] During the first year of Ronald Reagan's presidency, some thirty thousand civilians were killed and six hundred thousand made refugees. "When the country was sufficiently terrorized and any hope of independent politics was eliminated, the US ran staged elections . . . ; the farce was repeated in 1984."[82] By that time, an expanded air war, assisted by US reconnaissance planes, was supplementing ground attacks on civilians in guerilla-controlled areas. Refugees reported the widespread use of incendiary bombs, with some entire villages burned to the ground, as well as the use of napalm and antipersonnel fragmentation bombs directed against noncombatants. Chomsky comments acidly on the credulity of US press reports that American reconnaissance assistance had "not enabled" the Salvadoran military to reduce civilian casualties in its war against the guerillas, as if it were the military's objective to reduce civilian casualties.[83] By 1984 about one-quarter of all Salvadorans had become refugees, either forcibly expelled from their homes or in flight from air or ground action by government forces. Salvadorans seeking asylum in the United States were almost invariably denied.

Chomsky ridicules the notion, repeatedly propagated by the Reagan administration, that a significant portion of the violence against civilians was attributable to the guerillas, or to right-wing death squads opposed to the government. He cites a variety of sources offering evidence that the Salvadoran military and security forces were heavily involved in protecting and supporting death squad activity.[84] And the number of civilians killed by guerillas was dwarfed by the numbers killed by government forces.

El Salvador: My commentary. Chomsky's account of recent Salvadoran history resembles a morality tale in which the US government is not only consistently aligned with the forces of evil; it is almost invariably the spearhead of those forces. Like many caricatures, Chomsky's contains important elements of truth. The United States bears a heavy responsibility for the suffering inflicted on the people of El Salvador by a succession of repressive governments. But as real as US responsibility is for El Salvadorans' misery, Chomsky often overstates the US role; he also ignores the few, albeit often ambivalent and ineffective, efforts by US governments to improve the lives of ordinary Salvadorans and advance human rights. In his lack of balance, Chomsky occasionally crosses the line separating overstatement from absurdity.

After a coup in 1931 overthrew a democratically elected government, El Salvador for all practical purposes was governed by the same regime for over half a century. Coups came and went and the composition of governments changed, but the regime remained essentially stable: El Salvador was ruled by a small oligarchy—reputedly "Fourteen Families" but really somewhat more than that—closely linked to the military, who maintained order and often occupied top government positions. El Salvador's regime was always a reliable supporter of American business interests in El Salvador and enjoyed warm relations with the United States.

Chomsky is correct that the United States pre-approved the countercoup that reversed the left-oriented coup of late 1960; the United States subsequently played a major role in fostering a repressive state security apparatus. On the other hand, he fails to acknowledge that the US government—under the banner of President John F. Kennedy's Alliance for Progress—did make some real effort to foster progressive social change in El Salvador and elsewhere in Latin America. The Salvadoran government that emerged from the countercoup soon after Kennedy's inauguration was highly responsive to Washington's new interest in enacting social reforms to mitigate ancient social inequities. Working with the US ambassador, the Salvadoran government announced a number of proposals for modest reform, including new taxes on income and wealth and expansion of government services in education, housing, and public health. But the reform program foundered on opposition from the oligarchy, some of whose members actually lobbied (unsuccessfully) for the State Department to replace its "pro-communist" emissary.[85]

El Salvador's experience was fairly typical of the Alliance for Progress. The alliance, motivated in good part by the desire to prevent another Castro/Cuban-style revolution in the Western Hemisphere, had two tracks: a social reform/economic development track and a military/security track. Social reform was seen as preventive of social revolution, but the possibility that armed insurgencies would break out in any case had to be anticipated. The second track (which is Chomsky's practically exclusive focus) therefore aimed to improve Latin American governments' ability to deal with armed insurgencies. In El Salvador as elsewhere, the United States was instrumental in promoting the development and expansion of the state's security and intelligence capabilities.[86]

Unfortunately, the security ties developed between the United States and its Latin American allies usually proved to be more consequential and durable than the efforts at social reform. The latter, to be effective, would have required a more consistent and forceful confrontation with the interests of local elites than US policymakers were willing to undertake. The Alliance for Progress thus was crippled by a major internal contradiction. In the words of the historian William LeoGrande, "By arming existing regimes to contain insurgency, Washington would end up arming the very conservative elites it sought to replace with reformers. Once armed, incumbents would have little incentive to accept even modest change."[87] Sympathetic critics have called the Alliance for Progress a "noble failure" because it generally failed to promote democracy or socioeconomic progress.[88] But the "failure" reflected a clear ordering of priorities—democratic reform and increased social justice were indeed objectives, but ultimately secondary to the overriding goal of averting more radical change, a goal that often involved strengthening repressive regimes.

A continuing lack of progress in ameliorating poverty and social inequality in El Salvador spawned an increasingly active and organized opposition during the course of the 1970s. Composed of peasant organizations, labor unions, student groups, and others, the opposition had the support of much of the Catholic Church hierarchy, influenced by liberationist theology. The protests following the stolen presidential election of 1972 were repressed brutally by the military, which followed up with continuing waves of repression that effectively demolished the organized political parties that the military regime had allowed to exist. Many opposition leaders, including Jose Napoleon Duarte, went into exile. Some joined one of several emerging guerilla forces.

Increasingly the Salvadoran repression got the attention of the outside world. The US Congress in 1974 passed legislation requiring that the administration evaluate human rights in countries receiving security assistance. In 1976, a series of congressional hearings brought to Americans' attention a shocking pattern of human rights abuses—including torture, extrajudicial executions, and disappearances. Only with the advent of the Carter administration in early 1977 did the US executive branch take seriously its legal obligation to link security assistance to human rights conditions. The new approach was forceful enough to induce several Latin American countries, including El Salvador, to refuse further US military aid rather than submit to intrusive human rights scrutiny.[89]

Resistance to Carter's human rights policy wasn't limited to the foreign governments affected; it was widespread within Carter's own government. Carter appointees seeking to implement the new approach to human rights found themselves engaged in a constant battle with veterans within the foreign policy bureaucracy who were uncomfortable with policies that created friction with long-valued allies in Latin America. Thus, reflecting entrenched State Department attitudes, Carter's first assistant secretary of state for inter-American affairs accused aggressive human rights advocates of being zealots with an inherent bias against established authority.[90] The US ambassador to El Salvador, Frank Devine, was another internal critic, so much so that he elicited a reproving message from a later Carter assistant secretary of state, Viron Vaky, who informed the ambassador that "there are those who take the position that if our admitted objectives of advancing human rights and containing Castroism were to conflict with each other, the contradictions should be resolved in favor of the latter. I do not think the President would agree with that. In any case, there is an element of obsession with the Cuban/Soviet 'menace.'"[91]

These conflicts within the Carter administration have no place in Chomsky's simple morality tale, but they are an important key to understanding US policy during the remainder of Carter's term of office. We commonly speak of "the US government" or "the administration" as if the government were in effect a single person with a clear will of his or her own—what social scientists call a "unitary actor." Chomsky's writings typically suggest a coherence and single-minded purposiveness characteristic of a unitary actor. In fact, government policy is often a less than consistent resultant of competing interests and policy preferences, and this was particularly true of the Carter administration on El Salvador. There was a genuine desire within the administration to curb the abuses of the Salvadoran regime and even prepare the way for a transition to democracy. Alongside those objectives, and increasingly in tension with them, was a concern to avoid a political destabilization that could result in a radical regime hostile to the United States.

The first opportunity for a significant shift toward democracy in El Salvador came with the October 15, 1979, coup. The two months following the coup were marked by a byzantine power struggle among factions of the new junta, including reform-minded civilians and reform and conservative groups within the military. By year's end, the older, more established and conservative elements in the military had gained the upper hand. Chomsky's account implies that US intervention was unequivocal and decisive in producing this outcome. The reality is somewhat more complex: the conservatives in the military may well have gotten the upper hand without US assistance, but it seems clear that the Carter administration's actions strengthened the forces of conservatism. Evidently, the administration's reformist impulses were trumped by its fear of radical change, now heightened by the recent triumph of the leftist Sandinistas in Nicaragua.[92]

By early January 1980, El Salvador had a new government, formed through a deal brokered by the United States. The new government, like the one that preceded it, was a military-civilian hybrid, but the preponderance of power now lay clearly with the military. During the course of the year, the political balance in the new government shifted ineluctably to the right. By March, following several resignations, the civilian membership of the junta was limited to a relatively conservative Christian Democratic faction headed by Duarte. By May, the most conservative elements in the military had achieved clear dominance over their more reformist colleagues.

1980 was also the bloodiest year yet in recent Salvadoran history. The hopes and freedoms unleashed by the October coup had given rise to a wave of organized political activity and protest. The regime's military and security forces responded with practically unrestrained brutality. Nearly twelve thousand civilians were killed by agents of the state in 1980, an increase from under two thousand in 1979 and less than one thousand in 1978. The victims included labor organizers, priests and Catholic lay activists, teachers and members of nascent guerilla cells, and opposition political party leaders. The agents of death prominently included the internal security forces—the National Guard, the Treasury Police, and the National Police—as well as private "death squads" who enjoyed tacit official protection.[93] Apologists for the Salvadoran regime—including, notably, spokesmen for both the Carter and Reagan administrations—often argued that much of the violence was the responsibility of the guerillas, while official violence was due to rogue elements in the security forces. The death squads were strictly private operations of the oligarchy. None of these excuses withstands scrutiny.[94]

So, by 1980, if not before, El Salvador had indeed become a "terror state," as Chomsky puts it.[95] What was the Carter administration doing during this terror?

Chomsky asserts that the US government was actually organizing the massacres; he even claims that Carter was waging a "war against the peasantry."[96] These assertions aren't hyperbole; they're ridiculous. The Carter administration (and again we need to keep in mind that the "Carter administration" was not a unitary actor) did not order any massacres, much less organize them. It did seek to curb official violence in El Salvador. Arguably, it didn't try hard enough. After losing confidence in Devine, Carter appointed a new ambassador to El Salvador, Robert White, who had a reputation as a strong human rights advocate. Shortly after taking office in March, White pointed out that the US embassy had been sending mixed messages to the military. White soon earned the widespread bitter enmity of the Salvadoran right and its allies in the security forces. (They also had allies in the US Congress. Republican senator Jesse Helms called White "an extreme leftist" whose appointment was "like a torch tossed in a pool of oil.")[97] But to have a chance of success, White's human rights efforts needed to be backed by a forceful US stance in support of the civilians in the government and the struggling reformists in the military. There were several opportunities during the first half of 1980 to pursue such a course, but the administration was unwilling to risk a fracture in the military that might open the floodgates of radicalism. That concern was especially salient to the Carterites in an election year in which the administration was already vulnerable to the charge of having "lost" another Central American country, Nicaragua, to the revolutionary left.[98] Chomsky's writings on El Salvador show no recognition whatsoever of these political pressures and dilemmas confronting the Carter administration.

The Carter administration clung to the figure of Jose Napoleon Duarte as its great "moderate" hope, gambling that progress in economic reforms would strengthen the political center at the expense of the right and the left. Duarte was in fact able to push through a limited agrarian reform program, even as the slaughter of dissidents (including some of Duarte's fellow Christian Democrats) intensified. But Duarte had already moved from left to right of center, and real power in any case lay with the security forces.[99] Instead of building a centrist counterweight to the security forces, Duarte became an apologist and a democratic facade for official violence, as Chomsky argues and as White pointed out as early as July.[100] Chomsky's relentlessly harsh portrayal of Duarte is largely justified, but it needs to be tempered by the recognition that Duarte was in a sense a prisoner in his own house, seeking to win greater freedom for himself by currying favor with his military captors and proclaiming their virtues. The Carter administration, rather than directly challenge the military, sometimes joined Duarte in his apologetics.

In short, the Carter administration can reasonably be accused of naiveté in its efforts to build on a political center that had already collapsed. It can reasonably be accused of a failure to act vigorously to counter atrocities, and of an unwillingness to confront obvious evil in its prioritization of political stability over human rights. But as a plain matter of fact, it did not order or organize mass murder, as Chomsky claims it did. The Salvadoran right—along with their Guatemalan counterparts—despised Jimmy Carter and celebrated with lavish parties on the night of the US presidential election in November 1980.[101] Now, they believed, they would have a true ally in the White House in the person of Ronald Reagan.

The new administration did, indeed, mark a significant shift in emphasis from its predecessor. If Carter's human rights effort in El Salvador had been inconsistent and largely ineffectual, Reagan's was practically nonexistent. Only under pressure from Congress did the administration eventually make some gestures in defense of human rights.

In 1981 Congress passed legislation that made continued military aid to El Salvador conditional on the US administration's certification that the Salvadoran regime was making a serious effort to curb human rights abuses, including indiscriminate murder and torture, and that it was making progress in moving toward democracy and land reform. The certification was required every six months. The administration's first certification, in January 1982, was thoroughly mendacious. The administration claimed that civilian deaths had declined during 1981, when it was well known that they had risen, and it denied that death squads were linked to the regime, even though it had recently received information to the contrary. It repeated the familiar false claim that a significant share of noncombatant deaths was due to guerilla activity, and it questioned the motives of human rights groups in El Salvador that were trying to monitor the slaughter. As Massachusetts Democratic congressman Gerry Studds put it, "The president has just certified that up is down, and in is out, and black is white. I anticipate his telling us that war is peace at any moment."[102] Over the course of three subsequent certification reports, the administration only gradually qualified its exculpation of the Salvadoran military and security forces for atrocities.[103]

Over time, the administration did feel compelled to take some action in defense of human rights in El Salvador. In part, the compulsion reflected the need to respond to the publicity attendant to some particularly sensational killings. In part, it reflected military successes by the guerillas, who during 1983 came to control one-third of the national territory. More aid would be needed to prevent the collapse of the Salvadoran armed forces, but Congress, sensitive to human rights abuses, held the purse strings. (Reagan utilized a variety of ways to get around congressional restrictions on aid, but Congress remained an important actor.) In early 1983, President Reagan called the recently elected provisional president of El Salvador to urge action to prosecute the guilty parties in the murder of two American aid workers in a widely publicized incident two years earlier. Not only was Reagan's plea ignored, but one of the accused was actually promoted.

A State Department policy review in July 1983 lamented that the Salvadoran government had "not been motivated to take the minimal actions required to help us sustain our support." If the Salvadorans wanted the military aid they needed to win the war against the guerilas, they would have to meet US demands, including ending "military participation in death squads."[104] The policy review led to no immediate action. The following fall, however, as private diplomacy failed to elicit any response by the military, the administration went public: US officials candidly discussed the death squads with journalists, even naming some of the officers suspected of involvement. But at around the same time, President Reagan undercut that message with a pocket-veto of the bill to link aid to El Salvador to certification of progress in human rights. *New York Times* correspondent Raymond Bonner cites the lack of responsiveness to Reagan administration pleas for human rights improvement as evidence of Washington's lack of control over Salvadoran events. But his own account suggests a somewhat different interpretation: "The Reagan administration lacked either the power or the will to convince the Salvadoran military to reform. The administration's actions spoke louder than its stern lectures. The financial spigot was never turned off; indeed, it was opened wider."[105] In short, the Reagan administration may not have been happy about its client's human rights abuses, but it was not inclined to take forceful action to curb them.

The Reagan administration, then, was deeply complicit in the atrocities of the Salvadoran regime that it supported, aided, and defended. Still, Chomsky's contentions that the Salvadoran regime was no more than a tool of the United States—that the US government was the motor force behind regime atrocities—fail even in the case of the Reagan administration. The Salvadoran regime had its own class and institutional interests in pursuing mass murder. The United States did not generate those interests, but they happened to coincide with Washington's interest in forestalling a revolutionary leftist victory in El Salvador. Accordingly, the Reagan administration was disinclined to take really meaningful action to stem the mayhem inflicted by its Salvadoran allies. Complicity in atrocities is morally reprehensible, but the distinction between complicity and agency is a valid and important one. It is a distinction that Chomsky tends to ignore. Even the Reagan administration was less constant and single-minded in its Salvadoran policies than Chomsky's account indicates.

Chomsky was right, however, to draw attention to the extensive human rights abuses of the army in its counterinsurgency campaign; these tended to get much less publicity than the more urban-centered death squad activities. It is hard to fault Chomsky for deriding the expectation that US military assistance might have enabled the Salvadoran military to reduce civilian casualties. Deliberate large-scale violence and terror against civilians was in fact a major feature of the Salvadoran armed forces' campaign against the guerillas, who had achieved widespread popular support in the countryside. The strategy was based on a familiar counterinsurgency theme: the ocean needed to be drained to get at the fish.[106] The development of this counterinsurgency strategy in the early 1980s coincided with a fivefold increase in the size of the Salvadoran army, an increase whose effectiveness depended significantly on extensive US training missions.[107] It is unclear what influence the American trainers (the word "advisers" was generally avoided because of its association with the escalating US involvement in Vietnam) had over the Salvadoran army's human rights practices. The use of American advisers was frequently justified in part as a means of educating their charges in the norms of war, including notably respect for human rights. There are reasonable grounds for skepticism that more than lip service was paid to this aspect of the trainers' mission. One US manual used for training Salvadoran military personnel included less than six hours of lectures on human rights subjects in a four-month course of study.[108]

Chomsky also has good reason to mock US government claims that El Salvador in the early 1980s was a "fledgling democracy" (a phrase that Chomsky always puts in quotation marks).[109] The Reagan administration cited as evidence of democratization El Salvador's 1982 elections for a constituent assembly and provisional president, but it is disingenuous at best to claim that democratic elections can be meaningful in a context of widespread terror. The 1984 elections, now under a new constitution, were also held, in Chomsky's words, in an "'atmosphere of terror and despair': the country had been sufficiently terrorized to eliminate any hope for a genuinely independent opposition."[110] (Chapter 4 will provide a closer examination of the El Salvador elections of 1982 and 1984.) The 1984 voting is sometimes viewed as a genuine, if flawed, beginning to the Salvadoran democracy that eventually emerged in the 1990s.[111] While that view may have some merit, the fact remains that the election result served to rationalize further US support for a military/security apparatus that continued to engage in egregious (though gradually declining) human rights abuses while ceding only limited power to the elected civilian leadership. Just days after the 1984 elections, the US House of Representatives, handing the Reagan administration a major victory, narrowly passed an aid package for El Salvador.

In summary, Chomsky's account of the US role in recent Salvadoran history is schematic; occasionally, it lapses into downright nonsense. But Chomsky's outrage is well founded. The people of El Salvador suffered for decades under oppressive governments. US policymakers found it convenient to live with those governments and helped ensure their survival. Even when oppression turned to terror and mass murder in the 1980s, American support for its Salvadoran ally was never in serious doubt.

Guatemala: Chomsky's narrative. In 1944, a reformist government came to power in Guatemala's first democratic elections. An archetypical "banana republic," Guatemala historically had been run by a tiny oligarchy closely aligned with foreign economic interests—notably, the United Fruit Company, by far the country's largest landowner. Now, for the first time, a government was genuinely committed to improving the condition of the poor Indians who constituted the great majority of the country's population. Democratic reforms in Guatemala, however, not only threatened the dominance of the traditional local oligarchy; they impinged on the privileged position of United Fruit and other US-based companies. Acting in defense of those interests, the US government sponsored a coup in 1954 that put an end to Guatemalan democracy. The new military regime, closely aligned with the oligarchy, found it increasingly necessary over the next three decades to engage in murderous mass repression to maintain its power. The United States actively supported and participated in the repression, even as it reached genocidal magnitudes in the 1980s.

Chomsky describes the democratic government that took power in 1944 as "mildly reformist"; its aim was to develop Guatemala as a modern "capitalist democracy."[112] Still, the government soon aroused concerns in the State Department because of its institution of a labor code whose worker protections imposed unprecedented obligations on United Fruit to treat its employees fairly. A 1952 agrarian reform law that threatened to expropriate unused land belonging to United Fruit heightened the concern in Washington. The United States was faced with an "excess of democracy" in a Third World country where American business was heavily invested.[113]

Washington initiated a diplomatic and propaganda war against the Guatemalan regime that accelerated after Dwight D. Eisenhower became president in 1953. The new US administration soon began planning a regime change; the coup, orchestrated in Washington, took place in June 1954.[114] The junta was ruthless in wiping out the old regime and its organized support. According to Chomsky, eight thousand peasants were murdered in the two months following the coup in a terror campaign that particularly targeted United Fruit Company union organizers and Indian village leaders.[115] The US government actively assisted, providing lists of alleged Communists for the government's dragnet (and subsequent incarceration). A large injection of US economic aid soon followed. The new regime showed its appreciation for its northern patron with a series of measures to make Guatemala a friendlier place for US business: the agrarian reform law was rescinded (as was the 1947 labor code, surprisingly not mentioned by Chomsky) and United Fruit got its land back. US investment in Guatemala doubled during the 1960s.

Elections scheduled for 1963 were blocked by a new coup that enjoyed the support of the United States. The military tightened its grip on the country through successive waves of terror, murdering large numbers of suspected supporters of the resistance. The terror continued through the 1970s and reached new heights in the 1980s, with the regime always enjoying the active support of the US government. During the 1980s "over 440 villages were totally destroyed and well over 100,000 civilians killed or 'disappeared,' up to 150,000 according to the Church and others, all with the enthusiastic support of the Reagan administration."[116]

By the mid-1980s, the government had succeeded in eliminating all effective resistance, finally crushing a guerilla movement that had lost popular support because of its inability to protect its supporters from the depredations of the government forces. Elections held in 1985 enabled the US government to justify its support of the Guatemalan regime as a "fledgling democracy" but real power remained in the hands of the military; death squad activity, though abated at times, continued to be a major factor in Guatemalan politics and society through the end of the decade.

Guatemala: My commentary. Chomsky's picture of Guatemalan history is broadly accurate. A ten-year experiment in democratic reform was ended by a US-organized coup in 1954. In the following decades, Guatemala was ruled by a succession of narrowly based military dictatorships. Chomsky characterizes Guatemalan governance during this period in terms of waves of terror inflicted by the state on its own people, resulting in widespread suffering and death. This is an entirely reasonable characterization given the generally recognized estimate of two hundred thousand violent deaths (over 90 percent caused by government security forces) over the course of thirty years.[117] The United States bears major responsibility for this staggering toll, both because of its initial role in destroying Guatemalan democracy in 1954 and because of the support and assistance it lent Guatemala's brutal rulers in the succeeding decades. Still, Chomsky's account deserves scrutiny, particularly with regard to two issues: the US reaction to Guatemalan democracy in 1944–1954 and the US government's culpability in the increasing repressiveness of Guatemala's rulers in the 1970s and 1980s.

Explaining the 1954 coup. Chomsky's characterization of the democratic Guatemalan governments of 1944–1954 as "mildly reformist" is reasonable but perhaps a bit too simple. Arguably, the programs of the Juan Jose Arevalo (1944–1950) and Jacobo Arbenz (1950–1954) governments were no more radical than those of Franklin Roosevelt's New Deal or the British Labor government of 1945–1950.[118] Still, in the context of Guatemalan history and particularly the history of Guatemala's relations with the United States, these governments were quite radical. That is not to say that the reforms they implemented weren't desirable or necessary, but they did radically threaten long-standing power relations both within and across borders.

The threat, from Washington's perspective, increased during the Arbenz government as the Communist Party was legalized. (Washington during the 1940s had pressed all Latin American governments to outlaw their countries' Communist parties. Arevalo had made no move to legalize the already banned Guatemalan party.) The Communists grew in strength and influence in Guatemalan society in the 1950s, particularly in the labor movement, and they enthusiastically supported Guatemala's democratic reformist governments. Arbenz openly recognized and appreciated the Guatemalan Communists' enthusiasm and dedication to his cause. Privately, Arbenz by 1952 had come to adopt a pro-Communist worldview, but he did not see Communism as a practical objective for Guatemala, which was at the heart of the American empire, and which, he believed, still needed in any case to undergo a capitalist revolution.[119] He appointed no Communists to his cabinet, and Communist participation in his administration was limited mainly to its agrarian reform agency.

As Chomsky sees it, Washington's hostility to Guatemalan democracy was a straightforward reflection of the American government's stalwart dedication to the defense of US business interests. This is certainly a plausible explanation. The major corporation aggrieved by Guatemala's democratic governments, United Fruit, was remarkably embedded with the foreign policy bureaucracy in Washington. Practically every Truman and Eisenhower administration official with a role in Latin American policy making had some tie with United Fruit. John Foster Dulles, Eisenhower's secretary of state, was a member of Sullivan and Cromwell, the law firm that had represented United Fruit in Guatemala and elsewhere. Other officials down the line had been directors or major shareholders of United Fruit or associated with financial institutions serving the agricultural giant.[120]

Nevertheless, a leading historian of the Guatemalan coup, Richard Immerman, has offered a different interpretation of American motivations.[121] As early as 1948 American policymakers suspected the Guatemalan government and the movement supporting it of Communist leanings; over time, that suspicion hardened into a firm conviction. The internal documentary record shows that American policymakers genuinely believed that the Guatemalan government was Communist, or at least subject to Communist control. How can one explain that belief, based as it was on scarce evidence?

Immerman argues that the heightening Cold War confrontation between the United States and Soviet Union had spawned in American policy circles what he calls the "cold war ethos": a generally exaggerated view of Communist threats and opportunities. This ethos, in combination with a traditional presumption that the United States' Central American neighbors would serve US interests, determined the increasingly alarmist view of Guatemala that took hold in Washington. That a Guatemalan government would take steps that threatened US business interests was seen as prima facie evidence of Communist influence. "In the cold war ethos, it was a simple step to interpret the enactment of a long-overdue agrarian reform, official opposition to Yankee-supported Latin American dictators, labor legislation, or other nationalistic policies that failed to coincide with those of the United States as proof of Communist intrigue."[122] This perception was fanned by a masterful public relations and lobbying campaign by United Fruit and by overwrought reports on Guatemalan Communism supplied to the State Department by hostile neighboring right wing dictatorships and by J. Edgar Hoover's FBI.[123]

Chomsky's response to Immerman's analysis is interesting, and bears on important broader issues of historic explanation. Chomsky acknowledges that Immerman "may well be right" in arguing that US leaders really believed the Guatemalan government's moderate reforms were evidence of Communism, "but the point is of little significance except for the (rather boring) study of the psychology of leaders and ideologues. It is a rare individual who consciously believes that what he or she does is genuinely evil; . . . [instead,] it is easy enough to come to believe whatever is convenient. . . . True interests are disguised in propaganda, perhaps even disguised to those who propound it."[124] Since it is considered unacceptable to base policy on crass servitude to greedy business interests, policymakers will naturally find other, more commendable rationalizations for action; and they will tend to believe their own rationalizations. That shouldn't prevent us from seeing the real motivations for policy. When concrete material interests point toward a particular course of action, we can safely assume that the explanation for the course chosen lies with those interests, rather than the rationalizations policymakers use to legitimate their actions.

Chomsky's counterargument is compelling. If normally intelligent and well-informed people believe something that is not supported by evidence, it seems unsatisfactory to explain their actions as a simple reflection of that belief. We feel compelled to ask *why* they believe what they do; if ulterior interests can be demonstrated, it is reasonable to point to those interests as the likely "real" basis for action.

Further complicating the issue, it is possible to point to still other ulterior interests that might serve as the "real" explanation for American policy. As Immerman notes, the United States has historically been the dominant power in the Caribbean, and has generally expected to have its way with the region's "banana republics." It is quite possible, as one former member of the overthrown Arbenz government suggested, that the United States would have staged the coup even if Guatemala grew no bananas.[125] Defending United Fruit coincided with other US policy objectives—namely, maintaining US dominance of the Caribbean. Even if Communism was not an imminent danger, independence from US control was clearly threatened. That threat in and of itself may have been enough to exercise American leaders concerned with maintaining this country's traditional sphere of influence, particularly while engaged in a competition for power in other areas of the globe.[126]

In sum, Chomsky credits only the first of three possible approaches to explaining US hostility to Guatemala's leftist nationalist governments: economic interests, ideology, and geopolitical power considerations. Untangling these three strands of explanation is no easy task; it is one to which we will return in Chapter 3 in assessing Chomsky's broad approach to explaining US foreign policy.

The American role in Guatemalan government repression. Chomsky justifiably speaks of successive "waves of terror" conducted by Guatemalan regimes in the decades after 1954, but his narrative is surprisingly spare in details.[127] He gives the reader no clue as to what might have prompted those waves of terror, or who they were directed against—did the Guatemalan military engage in random, capricious slaughter? Large numbers of noncombatants were indeed slaughtered, in increasing numbers over time, but the reader would naturally be interested in knowing that the slaughter was in fact the regime's brutal response to guerilla rebellion. Armed insurgency first developed in the early 1960s, but was crushed, with major US assistance, by the end of the decade. A significant guerilla rebellion again emerged in the early 1970s and by 1980 the rebels seemed close to victory. It is not until he gets to the late 1970s that Chomsky's narrative includes any allusion to guerillas, and then only in passing.

As Chomsky points out, a 1963 coup that preempted a political comeback by Guatemala's first democratic president, Arevalo, was apparently preapproved by the Kennedy administration.[128] In 1966, the US government convinced the military to allow a free and fair presidential election that was won by a Christian Democrat, Julio Mendez Montenegro. Mendez was allowed to take office only after signing a pact, brokered by the United States, that guaranteed the military substantial power and autonomy. Mendez got no help from the United States as his modest reform proposals were blocked by the business elite.[129]

The Guatemalan military, on the other hand, did get tremendous assistance from the United States during the same period that Mendez was struggling with his reformist program. US assistance to the Guatemalan military and police forces had begun in the early 1960s, in line with Alliance for Progress planning and in response to the first stirrings of armed insurgency. US involvement became really extensive and intimate in 1966, with the guerilla movement now a significant threat. The Guatemalan military utilized US training, especially by the US Special Forces (i.e., the "Green Berets"), as well as bomber planes, radar detection devices, and other sophisticated technology in putting down the revolt, a task that was fairly complete by 1970. It is not clear just how decisive the US aid was in the military's success, but it is certain that it at least enabled the military to achieve a swifter result. In the absence of US aid, pressures to negotiate with the rebels could have become hard to resist; in that case, the military might not have achieved the dominance of Guatemalan politics that it enjoyed in the succeeding decades.[130]

The counterinsurgency campaign took deadly aim at civilians suspected of guerilla sympathies. Villages in areas of guerilla strength were bombed freely, and peasants were subject to assassination by local bands of "civilian collaborators" of the armed forces.[131] An estimated three thousand to eight thousand Guatemalans were assassinated by rural or urban death squads between October 1966 and March 1968 alone. There is considerable evidence that US military personnel were active collaborators in the Guatemalan government's terror campaign. In some cases, US aircraft apparently piloted by Americans flew from bases in Panama to bomb villages targeted as guerilla haunts. US Special Forces "trainers" frequently accompanied Guatemalan army patrols on combat missions and advised on the formation of paramilitary units that became death squads.[132] In an anguished memo, Viron Vaky, the second-in-command at the US embassy in Guatemala City, deplored the US role in "rationalizing murder":

> After all hasn't man been a savage from the beginning of time so let us not be too queasy about terror. I have literally heard this from our people.... We have not been honest with ourselves. We *have* condoned counter-terror; we may even in effect have encouraged or blessed it. We have been so obsessed with the fear of insurgency that we have rationalized away our qualms and uneasiness. This is not only because we have concluded we cannot do anything about it, for we never really tried. Rather we suspected that maybe it is a good tactic, and that as long as Communists are being killed it is alright. Murder, torture and mutilation are alright as long as our side is doing it and the victims are Communists.[133]

Chomsky accordingly is on solid ground in citing US involvement in Guatemala's "wave of terror" in the 1960s. He does, however, fail to mention a cooling of relations between the two countries that began in the 1970s when the United States sided with its British ally against Guatemala in a territorial dispute over neighboring British Honduras (Belize). Nor does he acknowledge that US-Guatemalan relations deteriorated further during the Carter administration, when Guatemala joined El Salvador and other Latin American nations in refusing US aid linked to human rights progress. US training of the Guatemalan military largely ended in 1977. Carter administration pleas for restraint went unheeded as a renewal of guerilla warfare again elicited harsh countermeasures by the Guatemalan regime. Guatemalan officers and right-wing civilians took to routinely referring to the US president as "Jimmy Castro." Sometime in mid-1980, top Guatemalan officials simply stopped dealing with American diplomats, preferring to work with the presidential campaign of Ronald Reagan, whose victory they eagerly anticipated.[134]

By the time of Reagan's inauguration the regime was facing defeat in its war with the guerillas. It responded with a campaign whose brutality dwarfed even that of the 1960s. The strategy centered on the familiar "drain the sea" counterinsurgency theme of depriving the guerillas of their civilian support base by depopulating areas of guerilla strength through scorched earth burnings, massacres of whole village populations, and massive forced relocations.[135] Early estimates of the death toll just for the period from 1980 to 1984 were in the range of ten thousand to twenty thousand, but later figures put it at fifty thousand to seventy-five. The count of villages destroyed has been raised from the 440 cited by Chomsky to 626. As many as one million people were displaced, becoming internal or external refugees. Even refugee camps in Mexico were not immune to machine-gun attack by Guatemalan helicopters. The ultimate target of this devastation and carnage was a guerilla force estimated to number under ten thousand.[136]

By 1985, the counterinsurgency campaign was largely successful. The Guatemalan military achieved this success without significant help from the United States. The Reagan administration did try to obtain military aid for Guatemala's counterinsurgency campaign, but was unable to overcome congressional objections to Guatemala's human rights record.[137] What, then, can we make of Chomsky's claim that the atrocities of the Guatemalan regime enjoyed the "enthusiastic support of the Reagan administration?" He refers at other points to the "huge slaughter carried out by the US with the aid of its clients" and claims that "the Reagan Administration was not merely supportive but enthusiastic about the achievements [i.e., the successful slaughter and terror] of their friends."[138]

As with El Salvador, Chomsky again elides the distinction between complicity in atrocities and agency: the United States clearly did not "carry out" the undeniable slaughter in Guatemala. The Guatemalan regime, its survival threatened, was pursuing its own interests in crushing the insurgency. Those interests coincided with Washington's antirevolutionary agenda, and so the Reagan administration was disinclined to disturb the Guatemalans' brutal course. Instead, in its efforts to enlist aid for the regime's counterinsurgency, the administration repeatedly whitewashed the Guatemalan horror show.

The State Department Human Rights Report for 1981 fully exonerated the Guatemalan government of atrocities, while the administration denounced as Communist dupes or worse Amnesty International and other human rights organizations that reported differently. The United States stood practically alone, accompanied only by a small group of its closest allies (mostly dictatorships), in opposing a December 1982 UN resolution condemning the Guatemalan regime for massive human rights violations. That same month, President Reagan, having recently ordered a resumption of economic aid to Guatemala, visited Guatemala City and praised the current junta leader, Efrain Rios Montt. Reagan followed up by lifting the US arms embargo to permit a shipment of helicopter parts and other equipment for the Guatemalan military. Administration spokesmen did pay lip service to human rights concerns and publicly urged the Guatemalan regime to democratize, but privately, the Americans signaled to their Guatemalan counterparts their conviction that the guerillas needed to be defeated, even if the war was understandably dirty.[139]

Do these actions constitute evidence of "enthusiastic" support for mass murder? Chomsky is ever ready to attribute the most evil imaginable motives to American policy. On the basis of currently available evidence there is no way of knowing whether the Reaganites were enthusiastic about or merely tolerant of the depredations of their "friends." Perhaps they viewed the Guatemalan slaughter with distaste, but saw no alternative path to ensuring a guerilla defeat. In any case the Reagan administration undeniably did knowingly tolerate and at least indirectly facilitate large-scale atrocities. The Guatemalan regime undoubtedly would have engaged in mass murder even without the complaisance of the United States. But Washington was not helpless in the face of atrocity. The United States had numerous means of exercising pressure on its Central American clients. It could have joined, rather than resisted, the international community's condemnation of the Guatemalan regime. It could have threatened economic sanctions. It could thus have imposed some inhibitions on the Guatemalan megakillers, saving an unknowable but possibly considerable number of innocent lives. Instead, through inaction, as well as intangible and some tangible support, the United States condoned and facilitated mass murder. Once again, Chomsky's outrage is well placed even though his account of the US role in the crimes of other governments is overstated and over-simple.

Nicaragua: Chomsky's narrative. Nicaragua was ruled continuously for over four decades by a single family dynasty—the Somozas, who came to power after the US Marines in 1933 ended a lengthy occupation of that country. Chomsky tells us that while the notoriously corrupt Somozas ran Nicaragua like a private fiefdom, they were "careful to acknowledge U.S. hegemony and their own dependent status and 'special relationship'" with the United States, and to maintain a highly favorable climate for foreign investment, with a favorable tax regime and abundant low-cost labor.[140]

By the late 1970s, however, the Somoza regime had managed to alienate practically every sector of the population—including, critically, business groups, who could no longer abide the routine corruption and institutionalized cronyism that enabled Somoza family interests to gain unfair competitive advantage over legitimate private enterprise while looting the national economy. An unusual confluence of business opposition and guerilla insurgency brought the regime to a crisis in the summer and fall of 1978. After guerillas succeeded in capturing the national palace in the capital city of Managua, businessmen called a national strike, and other major cities throughout the country fell to the guerillas. The response of the Nicaraguan armed forces, led by the National Guard, was brutal. Widespread atrocities by the Guardsmen were reported in the crushing of the revolt, in which whole cities were largely destroyed and several thousand Nicaraguans were killed. Chomsky cites a *Wall Street Journal* correspondent who described "a bloody war between lightly armed teenagers and National guardsmen."[141]

The revolt posed a dilemma for the Carter administration. It was becoming increasingly clear in Washington that Somoza was no longer a guarantor of stability in his country, but the administration could not bring itself to take any really forceful steps against the longtime US ally. Indeed, a letter of praise that Carter sent to Somoza in the summer of 1978 may have had a role in provoking the disorders that followed. Accordingly, Washington must be assigned a heavy responsibility for the official violence. "The Carter Administration would have liked Somoza to resign and be replaced by 'moderates,' but it did not openly call for his resignation or entirely withdraw support from him. This vacillation set the stage for Somoza's forceful suppression of a virtually unified Nicaraguan population."[142] Chomsky reminds us that the National Guard was US-trained and equipped with US-supplied helicopters, gunships, and other sophisticated weaponry.[143]

Initially, the Carter administration sought to mediate between the Nicaraguan regime and its opposition. Only as that effort failed, and it became clear that Somoza was losing his grip on power, did the Carter administration begin a search for an alternative. Washington hoped that the radical guerilla movement, the Sandinistas, could be excluded from a major role in a new regime. When that goal became clearly untenable, US policymakers worried about how best to "moderate" the Sandinistas once in power.[144] An important concern was to keep intact the National Guard, since that institution, with its long-standing links to the United States, could provide a salutary counterweight to the new government. The Sandinistas took power in July 1979.

That didn't stop the Carter administration from preparing a counterrevolution: National Guard commanders were evacuated in a clandestine operation on US planes disguised with Red Cross markings. Chomsky asserts that within six months of the overthrow of Somoza, the administration initiated a destabilization campaign; the Argentine dictatorship acted as "a proxy for the United States," training and directing the Nicaraguan National Guard forces. At the same time, the administration sought to achieve some influence with the Sandinista regime with a $75 million economic aid package. Washington denied Nicaragua's request for military aid and training.[145]

The counterrevolution began in earnest under President Ronald Reagan, who was determined to destroy the Sandinista regime. Almost immediately, the administration initiated economic warfare, by cutting off bilateral economic assistance. Soon afterward, Washington used its influence to dry up credit to Nicaragua by the major multilateral lending institutions, notably the World Bank and the Inter-American Development Bank. Finally, in 1985 the White House announced a full trade embargo on Nicaragua.

Even more damaging, however, was Washington's employment of a proxy army, called the "contras," to wage a campaign of sabotage and terror inside Nicaragua. The contras, largely composed of former National Guardsmen, were organized and funded by the US government, which itself played a direct and active role in the contra war and also enlisted Latin American client governments to help. The contras freely employed terror against Nicaraguan civilians. Chomsky recounts several grisly stories of contra atrocities: rapes, kidnappings, torture, and murder. He quotes the former contra commander Edgar Chamorro, who described how the contras "would arrive at an undefended village, assemble all the residents into the town square, and then proceed to kill—in full view of the others—all persons working for the Nicaraguan government, including police, local militia members, party members, health workers, teachers and farmers" working on government cooperatives.[146]

The administration's initial justification for supporting the contra "freedom fighters" was to block alleged arms transfers from Nicaragua to the rebels in El Salvador. Before long, however, it became clear that the real objective of US policy—proclaimed from the outset by the contras and eventually acknowledged implicitly by the president himself—was the overthrow of the Nicaraguan government. According to Chomsky, the proxy war sought to weaken and eventually topple the Sandinista regime by forcing it to divert resources that might otherwise be devoted to constructive social programs, and driving it to adopt repressive measures, thus depriving itself of popular support. At the least, the Americans aimed "to sow enough terror and destruction to avert the danger that the 'virus' of successful development might 'infect'" neighboring countries.[147]

What exercised the Reagan administration was the threat of Nicaragua's "bad example"—the potential demonstration effect of a regime that pursued a strategy of development that prioritized the needs of the poor and asserted its independence of United States. The threat was real because the Nicaraguan regime did achieve significant progress in its economic and social goals. Chomsky tells us that in a relatively short period of time under the Sandinistas,

> infant mortality fell so dramatically that Nicaragua won an award from the World Health Organization for the best health achievement in a Third World nation, health standards and literacy sharply improved, a successful agrarian reform was carried out, . . . and Nicaragua came closer to self-sufficiency than any other Central American nation and made the most impressive gains of any Latin American

nation in the Quality of Life Index of the Overseas Development Council, based on literacy, infant mortality and life expectancy.[148]

Of course, the administration advanced other justifications for its war against Nicaragua: the Sandinista regime threatened to become a base of Communist subversion in the Western Hemisphere—that is, "another Cuba"; it refused to restore democracy and it repressed civil liberties; and it persecuted Nicaragua's Meskito Indian minority. Chomsky refutes each of these allegations. Almost invariably, he contrasts Nicaragua's behavior favorably to that of its neighboring Central American countries, which enjoyed the warm support of the United States.

One of the early charges hurled against the Sandinistas by the Reagan administration was that the Nicaraguans were aiding the Salvadoran rebels. Chomsky implicitly acknowledges that the administration was able to present some valid evidence for that charge in 1981, but points out that it was never able to prove further Sandinista involvement in insurgencies outside Nicaragua. Instead, in "torturing" Nicaragua the administration sought to implement a self-fulfilling prophecy: by driving the Sandinista regime into dependence on the Soviet bloc, the war would legitimate the administration's claims that the Sandinista regime was an agent of international Communism.

The Sandinistas' failure quickly to restore democracy through free elections figured prominently in Washington's indictment of Managua. Chomsky is dismissive of this complaint—the Sandinistas had made no promises about the timing of elections, and in any case, Nicaragua's record on this score compared favorably with neighboring US client states. (See Chapter 4.) Chomsky points out that the elections eventually held in 1984 were won handily by the Sandinistas and judged by a variety of credible foreign observers to have been conducted freely and fairly. Chomsky acknowledges that the powerful Sandinista propaganda apparatus, which dominated the television airwaves, helped shape the conditions under which the elections were held. But he points to the tremendous resources commanded by the opposition, "including inherited wealth, control over much of the economy, support from the influential Church hierarchy strongly backed by the Vatican in a predominantly Catholic country and . . . the nation's largest newspaper, subsidized by the country organizing the ongoing military attack against Nicaragua."[149]

Another major Reagan administration charge against the Sandinistas was that they engaged in the suppression of civil liberties, notably in their harassment and censorship of the major opposition newspaper, *La Prensa*. But, pointing to *La Prensa*'s open support of the contras, Chomsky asks what the United States would do to a newspaper lending its support to "an unimaginable power" that was attacking this country: "the editors and anyone remotely connected to them would be in concentration camps; recall the fate of Japanese during World War II."[150] More broadly, Chomsky claims that through the 1980s, Nicaragua has been quite unusual in the openness of its society in a time of crisis. Hostile journalists ... travel and report freely throughout the country. Bitterly anti-Sandinista U.S. officials and other advocates of the U.S. terrorist attack are permitted to enter and deliver public speeches and news conferences, calling for the overthrow of the government, and to meet with the U.S.-funded political opposition.... Domestic media that identify with the attack against Nicaragua ... have been subjected to harassment, censorship, and periodic suspension; but neither they, their editors and staff, nor opposition figures with the same commitments have faced anything remotely like the repression of media and dissidents in the U.S.-backed [Central American countries].[151]

Chomsky cites the example of Fernando Chamorro, a former contra leader who returned to Nicaragua in 1988 and was named a regional president of the pro-contra Conservative Party. Chamorro was able to live and work without fear, in sharp contrast to the experience of Adolfo Majano, a former Salvadoran member of the reformist military coup of October 1979. Having lived in exile for seven years, Majano returned to El Salvador in the late 1980s, and was the target of three assassination attempts, one of which succeeded in killing two bodyguards.

In sum, Chomsky argues that the Reagan administration's war against the Sandinistas reflected a determination to crush a revolutionary nationalist regime that refused to conform to the model of a typical US client state. The Sandinista regime jeopardized the US government's long-standing interest in keeping Latin America, and particularly Central America, subservient to US power and friendly to US business. Such a regime must not be allowed to exist, because it threatened to provide an attractive model for emulation by neighboring countries.

Beginning in 1984, a succession of attempts to bring peace to Central America were put in motion, initially at the initiative of the so-called Contadora countries (Panama, Colombia, Venezuela, and Mexico). The Contadora Process was succeeded by the Esquipulas (Guatemala) Process, which culminated in an agreement in August 1987 among five Central American countries, including Nicaragua. The Esquipulas II Accord provided for a number of measures to promote peace, including cease-fires, democratization, and the termination of external assistance to irregular forces. The Reagan administration's view of the peace initiatives ranged from wariness to contempt; the administration did its best to influence the process, and when it could not successfully determine outcomes, it simply ignored them. Thus, the United States continued to fund the contras in blatant violation of Esquipulas II.[152] The administration wasn't interested in a negotiated end of hostilities that left the Sandinistas in power.

Ultimately, the Reagan administration won its war against the Sandinistas, even though the victory came after Reagan left office. In the 1990 Nicaraguan presidential elections, Sandinista Daniel Ortega lost to the opposition candidate, Violeta Chamorro, in a surprising upset. Chomsky's explanation for this outcome is uncomplicated—the Nicaraguan people had been bludgeoned into submission. The economic embargo and the toll taken by contra subversion had severely damaged the Nicaraguan economy. Nicaraguans knew that their country would continue to be assaulted economically and militarily if the Sandinistas were returned to power. President George Bush, hosting Violeta Chamorro in Washington, had promised to lift the trade embargo and assist Nicaragua's reconstruction if the Sandinistas were turned out. "The embargo and other economic warfare were a clear message to Nicaraguan voters: if you want your children to eat, vote the way we order you to. . . . It took no great genius to perceive that the US would continue to torture Nicaragua . . . until it restored US clients to power."[153]

Nicaragua: My commentary. Chomsky's writings on Nicaragua amount to a partisan brief—an indictment of US policy combined with a defense of the Sandinista regime that the United States targeted. Like any partisan statement, his is generally one-sided and selective in its presentation of the relevant facts. Chomsky, does, however, have a strong case—one that generally stands up to critical scrutiny.

Chomsky is certainly correct that the long-standing Somoza regime, corrupt and brutal as it was, was a loyal client of the United States. The linchpin of the bilateral relationship was in the two countries' military ties. The Nicaraguan military had been essentially created by the United States during the Marines' occupation, when the Americans founded the Nicaraguan military academy. Cadets spent their fourth year in an American school. Nicaragua's central military institution, the National Guard, from 1956 until its demise in 1979, was commanded by West Point graduates.[154] President Anastazio Somoza, the last of his dynasty, was himself a West Pointer; according to counterinsurgency expert Todd Greentree, Somoza "spoke and acted like, and essentially considered himself an American army officer. For him, the U.S. military was the real power. . . . Virtually all officers were thoroughly oriented to the United States through training, contacts and careful cultivation, with anticommunism the ineluctable coin of the realm."[155]

The first significant disturbance to US-Nicaraguan relations came with the advent of the Carter administration. Chomsky, inclined to emphasize the continuity of US policy, gives Carter too little credit for the genuine efforts expended by his administration to pressure Somoza to respect civil liberties and move toward democratic reform. The Carter administration aimed to nudge Somoza into yielding power, thus paving the way for a moderate, pro-US democratic regime to succeed him. Unfortunately, the Carterites' pressure on Somoza tended to lag behind the rising tide of domestic opposition to the dictator.

Chomsky is correct that the Carter administration, faced with an increasingly revolutionary situation in Nicaragua in 1978–1979, proved unwilling to push forcefully for Somoza's ouster until it became practically inevitable. Chomsky suggests that a more aggressive US stance could have effected Somoza's departure sooner, saving the thousands of lives extinguished by the National Guard's brutal suppression of the growing popular revolt against Somoza. That is a reasonable speculation. In any case, the Carter administration clearly was more preoccupied with ensuring a pro-American regime than it was with securing an early Somoza departure.

Chomsky generally downplays or ignores the importance of US partisan politics on foreign policy decision making, but domestic political pressures did play a role in the administration's caution with respect to influencing change in Nicaragua. Indicative was a letter sent to the president by over one hundred members of Congress in June 1979. The letter urged Carter to support Somoza as a traditional ally, warning that his departure would lead to a Communist government. The letter was reprinted in a full-page *New York Times* ad under the heading, "Congress Asks: Please, Mr. President, Not Another Cuba."[156] Carter did, indeed, incur recurrent criticism and resentment from conservatives both in the United States and in Central America for having failed to stand by Somoza and other US-friendly dictators.

Once the Sandinistas achieved power, the administration sought to make the best of the situation. The Carterites were conscious of the contribution US hostility had made to the radicalization of the Cuban Revolution in 1959–1960, and aimed to avoid making the same mistakes. The administration provided $15 million in emergency assistance immediately following the Sandinista triumph, and followed that up with $8.5 million in economic assistance. In the fall of 1979, the administration submitted to Congress an $80 million foreign aid request for Central America, of which $75 million was allotted for Nicaragua. The Nicaraguan portion encountered considerable resistance in Congress, but finally passed in May 1980.[157]

Here again, Chomsky gives the Carter administration too little credit. The administration's evident willingness to coexist with a Central American regime whose leaders were clearly sympathetic to Marxism and to Fidel Castro was a clear break from past US policy. Even Castro himself, speaking at the Sandinistas' celebration of the first anniversary of their revolutionary triumph, complimented Carter for adopting a "more intelligent and constructive policy" toward Nicaragua than previous administrations had adopted toward Cuba.[158] Chomsky, instead, sees Carter's stance as little more than a prelude to the active hostility of the Reagan administration that followed. Partly in response to the Sandinistas' tightening of their hold on power, Carter did, in fact, initiate covert payments to opposition groups within Nicaragua late in 1980. But Chomsky's suggestion that the Carter administration employed Argentina as a proxy to prepare for covert warfare against Nicaragua is unsupportable.[159] The Argentine dictatorship in the late 1970s had taken upon itself a responsibility for combating Communism throughout Latin America. This posture in part reflected the Argentines' desire to fill what they viewed as a vacuum created by the Carter administration's excessive moralism and insufficient zeal in the anti-Communist struggle. Argentine military intelligence did work with Nicaraguan exiles during 1980 to establish operations in Florida for a counterrevolutionary campaign, and there is evidence that they utilized long-standing CIA contacts in that effort.[160] These activities were not sanctioned by the Carter administration; both Carter and his CIA director Stansfield Turner later denied that the administration had supported or funded any of the contra groups eventually sponsored by the Reagan administration.[161]

Chomsky is certainly correct, however, that Carter's successor was implacably dedicated to the overthrow of the Sandinista regime. That is not to say that even the Reagan administration was monolithically single-minded in its Nicaragua policy. At least through Reagan's first term, there were recurrent divisions between hard-liners determined to destroy the Sandinistas and pragmatists who could envision negotiating some kind of coexistence with the Nicaraguan regime. Ultimately, however, the hard-liners prevailed, if only because Reagan himself was firmly in their camp.[162] Chomsky is accurate in his account of the United States' hostility to the Contadora and Esquipulas peace processes, and of the usually contrasting flexibility of the Sandinistas.

Did Nicaragua under the Sandinistas really threaten to become "another Cuba"? Chomsky very plausibly argues that Washington's policies actually tended to strengthen the hard-liners among the Sandinistas and push the regime closer to the Soviet bloc. He notes dryly that Washington had some "true allies" among the Sandinistas—namely, "the elements committed to a Leninist model of totalitarian mass mobilization and control."[163] He suggests that if Washington had been really interested in moving Nicaragua toward democratic pluralism, it would have called off the contra war and negotiated with the Sandinistas. That raises the question, which Chomsky doesn't examine in any detail, of what kind of regime the Sandinistas really wanted to build.

As Chomsky hints, there were significant ideological differences among the Sandinistas, reflected in loose factional groupings. Most if not all of the Sandinista leaders, however, were in varying degrees sympathetic to Marxism. Like many Third World revolutionaries, they had a relatively benign view of the Soviet Union, which they looked to as a potential ally against Nicaragua's historic oppressor to the north.[164] In March 1980, a high-level Sandinista delegation visited Moscow and signed a party-to-party pact between the Sandinista National Liberation Front (FLN) and the Soviet Communist Party. Similar agreements were signed with the Bulgarian, Czech, and East German Communist parties.[165]

Still, it is unlikely that the Sandinistas were bent on constructing a Marxist-Leninist state. The Sandinistas abstained from major nationalizations of private property and never publicly renounced their commitment to a mixed economy. In contrast to its counterpart in Cuba, the Nicaraguan business class didn't flee the country, and remained an influential force. In particular, the private sector controlled nearly all of the country's export-producing capacity, which the Sandinistas not only refrained from nationalizing but actually subsidized heavily in order to earn foreign exchange.[166]

Even if the Sandinistas were inclined to follow a more orthodox Marxist path, they understood that they faced strong geopolitical constraints. These were recognized by their Soviet and Cuban friends, who advised them against following a Cuban path to socialism. That advice accorded comfortably with the views of the moderates among the Sandinistas, whose goal was a welfare state with a substantial private sector. The moderates were skeptical of the value of a too-close embrace of the Soviets and wanted a modus vivendi with the United States. The new Nicaraguan regime did, indeed, abjure the reflexively pro-US foreign policy that Washington had come to expect of its Caribbean clients. Like many other Third World countries, they sided more often with the Soviet Union than with the United States in UN votes, but their voting record also more closely matched Mexico's than it did that of the United States. The Sandinistas' independence from Moscow was also facilitated by the substantial economic aid they initially received from other Latin American and European governments. That support waned over the years in response to US pressure, but the Sandinistas were never as diplomatically isolated as Castro had been in the early years of his revolution. In any case, the Sandinistas came to learn that they couldn't rely on the Soviets for the amount of help they wanted. Moscow wasn't interested in taking on a second expensive ward in Latin America.[167] In short, the prospects for Nicaragua to become "another Cuba" were quite remote.

Chomsky is arguably too forgiving of the Sandinistas' initial postponement of free elections. But the Nicaraguan elections that were finally held in 1984 were at least as valid as the ones held around the same time in Guatemala and El Salvador. The fact that the Sandinistas actually were defeated, and yielded power, after free elections in 1990 is certainly hard to reconcile with the claim that they had established a totalitarian state.

On the broader issue of human rights and democratic freedoms, Chomsky is also right to compare Nicaragua favorably to its neighbors, not to mention the many other Latin American dictatorships that enjoyed warm relations with the Reagan administration. Granted, Chomsky is less than candid about the extent of human rights violations in Nicaragua. Opposition groups were subject to a variety of petty and not so petty harassments, including arrests (usually for short periods). The largest non-Sandinista labor union confederation, for example, reported that between 1983 and 1986 five hundred of its members, including all seven directors, had been temporarily imprisoned.[168] Many instances of cruel treatment of prisoners were reported, including some that would qualify as torture. (At least one case of waterboarding was documented.) The Sandinistas were credibly accused of tolerating if not encouraging mobs (*turbas*) that disrupted meetings of independent groups, assaulted opposition figures, and destroyed and vandalized the property of those figures. Other forms of coercion included property confiscations, dismissals, and the denial of credit and food rations to independent agricultural and union groups. But there were no death squads in Nicaragua, no disappearances, and no scorched-earth bombing attacks or other large-scale atrocities by security forces—nothing remotely comparable to what was occurring in El Salvador and Guatemala. Even at the height of the contra war, business, professional, and religious organizations were outspokenly critical of the government. No fair-minded person can seriously challenge Chomsky's claim that Nicaragua's human rights violations were mild compared to its neighbors.' According to Americas Watch, the most egregious violators of human rights in Nicaragua as of the mid-1980s were the contras.[169]

Notwithstanding its shortcomings, Chomsky's critique of the US assault on

Sandinista Nicaragua is powerful. The Reaganites' claim that the United States was somehow defending freedom, democracy, or human rights in Nicaragua was ludicrous, given the administration's record elsewhere in Latin America. More plausible, but still unconvincing, was the claim that the Sandinistas threatened to become an agent of Soviet power in the United States' backyard, though the hostility of the Reagan administration pushed the Sandinistas in that direction. A more moderate and tolerant stance by the United States might have enabled the two countries to come to an agreement that ensured Nicaragua's neutrality. But the Reaganites were uninterested in testing that possibility: nothing less than an overthrow of the revolutionary Nicaraguan regime was acceptable to them. The result was a decade of war in which over thirty thousand Nicaraguans died (a comparable death toll in the United States would be over two million) and Nicaragua's already badly impoverished economy plunged to new depths, heightening the suffering of its people.

The disastrous economy was decisive in the Sandinistas' electoral defeat in 1990. Part of the blame for the economic disaster can be assigned to poor economic management by the Sandinistas, but the challenges they faced were overwhelming. US economic and military warfare inflicted huge damage on the Nicaraguan economy; neighboring El Salvador, fighting a home-grown guerilla war, averted economic collapse only with massive US aid.[170] Violeta Chamorro, Nicaragua's opposition candidate in 1990, received covert aid as well as open praise from the administration in Washington. The election offered the Nicaraguans an opportunity to escape the implacable hostility of their powerful northern neighbor. Partisans will disagree, but Chomsky is almost surely right: the 1990 election result largely reflected the successful intimidation of a small, poor country's people by a great power. In 1985 Ronald Reagan had allowed that he might be willing to let up on the contra war if the Sandinistas said "uncle." In 1990, the Nicaraguan people said "uncle."

The American Empire: Some Observations

In *The Washington Connection*, Chomsky writes, "The basic *fact* is that the United States has organized under its sponsorship and protection a neo-colonial system of client states ruled mainly by terror and serving the interests of a small local and foreign business and military elite. The fundamental *belief*, or ideological pretense, is that the United States is dedicated to furthering the cause of democracy and human rights throughout the world" (emphases in the original).[171] Much of Chomsky's critique of US foreign policy has been devoted to establishing the "fact" and demolishing the "belief" described here. The five country histories examined in the preceding section provide powerful support to Chomsky's effort. Certainly, Chomsky's narratives—especially for Central America—do not constitute full, balanced accounts of events: Chomsky tends to be selective in his use of evidence, and more than occasionally he makes assertions that he cannot support. Still, putting aside reasonable questions over semantics (what constitutes "neocolonial"?) and allowing for some predictable hyperbole (ruled *mainly* by terror?), Chomsky has a strong case for his broad assertion of "fact."

The five countries examined in this chapter were all ruled for part or all of the Cold War period by dictatorships. All these dictatorial regimes were closely allied with the United States, some through formal treaties and others through a variety of informal economic, political, and military ties. The military linkages were especially important—the United States trained, armed, and equipped the military of all five countries; in the case of the Central American countries, the military and security apparatus was practically an extension of the US armed forces. And the military in all five countries was critical to the maintenance of dictatorial rule.

All five dictatorships were brutal, but not equally so: their crimes ranged from Marcos's routine, repressive thuggery to the quasi-genocidal horrors of Sukarno's Indonesia. US responsibility for its clients' crimes is of course a principal Chomsky theme. And there is no question that the United States, as the incomparably stronger country in its bilateral relations with each of these regimes, bears some responsibility for its partners' crimes. But Chomsky paints with a broad brush. Eager to depict America's role in the darkest possible hues, he ignores important distinctions.

At least two questions have to be explored relating to US culpability in its clients' crimes. First, to what extent did the client regime owe its existence to US patronage? Would the regime have existed and survived even without American aid and support? Second, to what extent did American policymakers participate in those crimes? Various levels of participation in abuses are possible, ranging from proactive (actual instigation), to passive (mere tolerance).

The five countries we have examined represent a range of answers to the first question. The Guatemalan dictatorship owed its very existence to the United States: it was US intervention that put an end to Guatemalan democracy. Somoza's regime in Nicaragua was also practically a US implant. At the other end of the spectrum, we can be quite sure that Suharto would have taken on dictatorial power in Indonesia with or without US aid; the United States did not in fact play a role in Suharto's coup, and his regime could almost surely have survived for many years even without the support it received from the United States. As for the Philippines, a clear veto from President Nixon would probably have deterred Ferdinand Marcos from formally declaring martial law, but Marcos could have found other ways to realize his authoritarian ambitions, perhaps with somewhat greater restraint. In El Salvador, the US joined forces with existing or evolving structures of repressive rule. That dictatorship would probably have come to an earlier end without US support, but it would have come about and persisted for a long time in any case.

A relevant contrast is with the Soviet empire in Eastern Europe. The American empire, unlike its Soviet counterpart, was for the most part not built by military conquest. It was to a large degree an "empire by invitation": it grew as national leadership groups sought and obtained US aid and protection.[172] Chomsky has asserted that "the U.S. sphere of client states is as homogeneous—and as agreeable to the interest of the dominant power—as the states of Eastern Europe in relation to the USSR."[173] This is nonsense. The Soviet Union's Eastern European satellite regimes all came into being under force of Soviet arms. All of them were single-party states on the Soviet model, which was imposed on them. They collapsed rapidly with the withdrawal of Soviet support in the late 1980s, and would probably have done so at almost any earlier point in their existence. Except in rare, climactic crisis situations (e.g., El Salvador in the early 1980s) none of the US client regimes was so utterly dependent on its patron's support for its survival.

Answers to the second question, regarding US participation in its clients' crimes, also vary. The US participation in the Indonesian genocides was mostly indirect; this country lent verbal, diplomatic, and some material support, but otherwise stood on the sidelines. Also, contrary to Chomsky's claim, the United States played no direct role in the Guatemalan mass murders of the 1980s, though it lent diplomatic and propaganda support. On the other hand, the United States did apparently play a critically important supportive role in the more limited but still gruesome Guatemalan government-directed terror of the 1960s, and in the Salvadoran rural terror of the 1980s. As for Marcos and Somoza, the United States didn't actually instigate those dictators' crimes, but it did generally maintain a friendly and supportive attitude toward their regimes in apparent indifference to their abuses.

In short, the picture of US culpability for the evil in its empire is a good deal more variegated than the one painted by Chomsky, but it is a pretty ugly picture nonetheless. Chomsky is certainly right that repression in much of the American empire was often far more brutal than in the average Soviet satellite, but this observation should be offset by the acknowledgment that the American role in that repression was generally less direct than the corresponding Soviet role. Chomsky's comparison of the two empires also fails to note that the Soviet Union patronized a number of brutal regimes outside of its Eastern European direct sphere of influence. A fair, comparative assessment of horrors would require a broader definition of the Soviet empire to include client states, making it more analogous to its American counterpart.[174]

How representative of the American empire are the five countries we have examined? The inclusion of Indonesia and Guatemala does tip this "sample" toward the high end of the range of horrors committed by US client regimes. Otherwise, the five are reasonably illustrative of the variety of relationships and circumstances characterizing the American empire in the Third World. Other examples of US-nurtured police states of varying degrees of awfulness could be found across the globe; at different times the empire included much of Latin America and the Middle East and parts of Central and Eastern Asia. We have looked at just one example of an actual overthrow of a democratic regime assisted by US covert action (Guatemala), but other significant examples (Iran, Brazil, Chile, etc.) could just as well have been explored.

The historical record certainly justifies Chomsky's cynicism regarding the "pretense . . . that the United States is dedicated to furthering the cause of democracy and human rights throughout the world." American patronage has often empowered repressive oligarchies in their resistance to popular aspirations for social justice and democracy. US leaders have shown themselves to be perfectly comfortable in warm, supportive relationships with a wide variety of despots—including, in some cases, quasi-genocidal mass murderers. Both Democratic and Republican presidents have been more than willing to dispense with democracy overseas, overthrowing democratically elected governments that stood in the way of US policy objectives. Conversely, there is not a single example during the Cold War of a dictatorial regime overthrown by US overt or covert action with the objective of establishing democracy.

How, then, do we explain this record? Chomsky's explanation, as we have seen, is fairly straightforward: the United States promotes "Third World fascism" in order to protect and advance the interests of American business around the world—in his felicitous terms, to promote the "freedom to rob and exploit." The relevant evidence we have seen so far is inconclusive. A concern with protecting American business interests certainly motivated US policy in Indonesia, but US government motivations in the other cases were either less clear or mixed. In the next chapter we take a broader look at US politics and foreign policy during the Cold War in search of explanations.

CHAPTER 3

Domestic Power and Global Purpose

WHY DID AMERICA BUILD its Cold War empire? Statesmen, political scientists, and pundits often speak in terms of "national interests" that a nation's leaders seek to defend as they chart their country's course in international affairs. Chomsky, instead, firmly rejects the very idea that there can be "national interests" presumably shared by all of the people of a country. It is a "mystification," he writes, to speak of "the nation, with its national purpose, as an agent in world affairs." For Chomsky, the key to understanding America's role in the world lies instead in understanding the structure of political power at home. Statesmen pursue the interests of those who wield political power, who invariably constitute a small segment of the population, even in formally democratic countries. "In the United States, as elsewhere, foreign policy is designed and implemented by narrow groups."[1]

The US Power Structure

Who are those "narrow groups"? In a capitalist country such as the United States, Chomsky identifies them with the leaders of the private corporate economy. Chomsky isn't fussy about terminology. Sometimes he talks of a "ruling class," sometimes of "dominant social groups," sometimes of "the private business sector" or simply "the powerful."[2] His basic idea is that economic power in the United States is tremendously concentrated in a relatively small number of large corporations whose owners and managers share broad interests in determining the course of government policy. The concentration of economic power translates into dominant political power. For the sake of consistency, I am going to use a single term—"the corporate class"—to refer to the dominant power group in American society as Chomsky understands it.[3] Chomsky makes no effort to define the boundaries of the corporate class—would they be the top shareholders and managers of the five hundred largest US corporations? The two thousand largest? Ten thousand? But that open-endedness poses no problem to his basic concept of political power.

How does the corporate class manage to control government in a democracy, where elected leaders must presumably respond to the interests and demands of a broad voting public? As Chomsky sees it, the most fundamental basis for corporate control lies in the simple and familiar fact that in a capitalist economy, the business of the nation *is* business: because the national welfare rides on the smooth functioning of the economy, the interests of the corporate class naturally define and limit what government leaders can and cannot do. "Actions that 'erode business confidence' would lead to capital flight, investment cutbacks, and in general an intolerable deterioration of the social and economic climate."[4] Speaking to a friendly audience, Chomsky crisply explained how control of the corporate economy sets powerful constraints on policy reform:

> So suppose all of us here convinced everybody in the country to vote for us for President, we got 98 percent of the vote and both Houses of Congress, and then we started to institute very badly needed social reforms that most of the population wants. Simply ask yourself, what would happen? . . . There would be disinvestment, capital strike, a grinding down of the economy. . . . So long as power remains privately concentrated, everybody, *everybody,* has to be committed to one overriding goal: and that's to make sure that the rich folk are happy . . . because if they're happy, then they'll invest, and the economy will work, and things will function, and then maybe something will trickle down. . . . But if they're *not* happy, everything's going to grind to a halt, and you're not even going to get anything trickling down.[5]

A related point is that in most capitalist societies, and particularly in the United States, the scope of politics is relatively limited—the really important decisions that affect people's lives are, for the most part, made in the private sector:

> In our society, real power does not happen to lie in the political system, it lies in the private economy: that's where the decisions are made about what's produced, how much is produced, what's consumed, where investment takes place, who has jobs, who controls the resources, and so on and so forth. And as long as that remains the case, changes inside the political system can make *some* difference—I don't want to say it's zero—but the differences are going to be very slight.[6]

Attempts to change this state of affairs—to enlarge the scope of government in such a way as to threaten the prerogatives of private capital—would risk the erosion of business confidence that political leaders instead must seek to maintain.

Chomsky makes no claim to being a social or political theorist—he is, in fact, rather disdainful of what he regards as social scientists' pretensions. He seems to believe that a few relatively simple propositions suffice for a basic understanding of the drivers of politics and power in American society. Consistent with that stance, Chomsky does not explicitly identify himself as a Marxist, nor does he cite Karl Marx's writings or the writings of contemporary Marxists in explicating his own views. Still, his intellectual debt to Marx is clear. He has said that certain of Marx's concepts, notably the "general idea" of social class analysis, are "indispensable" to the understanding of contemporary society, though he questions whether Marx's formulations were historically accurate or applicable to current realities.[7] On one occasion, he asserted justification for a "Marxist anarchist" perspective, but gave no explanation of what that would entail.[8]

Chomsky's concept of government (or, in the common European parlance, "the state") as ultimately subject to the functional requirements of the capitalist system is consistent with a school of thought known as "structural Marxism": structural Marxists believe that the corporate class need not consciously exert direct control over government in order to "rule"; the very structure of capitalist society ensures corporate dominance as a matter of course. The structural perspective is distinguished from "instrumental" Marxism, which views the state as a fairly direct instrument of a conscious, purposive ruling class. In the structural perspective, government leaders enjoy substantial autonomy—they need not and usually do not take orders from capitalists. Ultimately, they must serve the interests of the capitalist class, but that servitude is effected indirectly and spontaneously, as it were, through an intervening mechanism. That mechanism is the need to maintain satisfactory national economic performance, which government leaders critically depend upon for their survival. A smoothly functioning economy, in turn, requires that the state accommodate capitalists' needs—"to make sure that the rich folk are happy," as Chomsky puts it.[9]

Chomsky's structural view of class dominance doesn't require that members of the corporate class actively collaborate among themselves to enforce their rule. Chomsky nevertheless does sometimes hint at a more instrumental view of corporate class rule. Asked at a public forum about his opinion of the traditional Marxist view of the state as merely the executive committee of the capitalist class, Chomsky initially responded, "Well, there is something to that, I think," but soon clarified by observing that the corporate class does have internal conflicts, which seem to refute any notion of a monolithic ruling class. He pointed to the "regulatory capture" of the Interstate Commerce Commission by the railroad industry as an example of a segment of the corporate class using state power in ways that may not have served the interests of other segments.[10]

Chomsky thus has no trouble acknowledging that in a complex, diversified economy, conflicts of interest among and within industries and sectors are inevitable. A major function of the state, in fact, is to govern on behalf of the *general* interests of the corporate class. Sometimes, the special interests of even very large corporations—oil companies, for example—will conflict with those general interests. In such cases, "the state, representing the long-term global interests of US capitalism, generally prevails." Such instances help to foster the impression that the state is independent of business interests, an impression which, Chomsky says, is "largely an illusion, though not entirely so."[11]

Probably the most important example Chomsky gives of an apparently independent power center operating within the broader context of corporate class dominance is what President Eisenhower called the military-industrial complex—the Pentagon-centered nexus of government agencies and military contractors that promotes high levels of military spending. The military-industrial complex, in Chomsky's view, has played an important role in the government's management of the national economy. Military spending has provided critical stimulus to domestic demand while subsidizing high technology industry. Following the theories of the economist John Maynard Keynes, government spending became a major tool of economic management in the postwar economy, but the corporate class generally prefers what Chomsky calls "military Keynesianism" as a means of boosting demand over "welfare Keynesianism"; the latter, by enhancing the security and raising the expectations of ordinary people, tends to shift power away from the corporate class.[12] The alarmist rhetoric needed to justify gargantuan military budgets also has conveniently served to rationalize the drive to extend American power into every corner of the world.[13] But despite its apparent power, the military-industrial complex must be viewed ultimately as subject to corporate class rule: "It could be liquidated by the real ruling class at any moment by simply withdrawing its resources."[14] Here, Chomsky's perspective shows some affinity to instrumental Marxism, implying the possibility of conscious, unified action by a ruling class capable of so momentous a change as the "liquidation" of a major political power center.

It is noteworthy that Chomsky's discussions of the military-industrial complex include no mention of the important role of Congress, and particularly congressional committees, in supporting the Pentagon system. Chomsky is largely uninterested in the stuff of American politics that tends to preoccupy the attention of pundits and political scientists—political parties and elections, interest group activities, executive branch decision making, and the congressional process. This relative lack of interest undoubtedly reflects Chomsky's belief that most of these activities really don't matter very much—they all take place within a context that is critically conditioned by corporate dominance. "The basic contours of domestic and foreign policy are determined by institutional structures of power and domination. Since these are stable over long periods, policies vary little."[15] Although he does not quote C. Wright Mills, the elite theorist of the mid-twentieth century, Chomsky clearly shares Mills's view that much of what passes for political conflict in the United States takes places at the "middle levels of power" where serious challenges to elite groups seldom surface. As Chomsky sees it, "There is essentially one political party, the business party, with two factions. . . . The ideological system is bounded by the consensus of the privileged. Elections are largely a ritual form."[16]

The "ideological system" mentioned at the end of the last paragraph is another key element in Chomsky's analysis of American politics. While the structural argument is most fundamental in his explanation of political power in the United States and other capitalist democracies, he sees corporate class rule as reinforced by a number of other mechanisms of control. One is what Chomsky also sometimes calls the "doctrinal system": influence over public opinion and perceptions. Indeed, a distinguishing feature of American democracy is the degree to which the dominance of business ideology successfully restricts policy debate to a relatively narrow range of alternatives that are unthreatening to corporate class interests. The structural constraints on government policy—political executives' need to maintain the confidence of the corporate class, thus avoiding disinvestment and economic decline—seldom come into active play in the United States because policy proposals that are genuinely threatening to corporate class interests don't get serious consideration.[17] Chomsky's analysis of the doctrinal system is the subject of Chapter 4.

Still another mechanism of corporate dominance is the staffing of key decision-making positions with representatives of the corporate class. This is particularly important in the making of foreign policy. According to Chomsky, "Study after study reveals the obvious: Top advisory and decision-making positions relating to international affairs are heavily concentrated in the hands of representatives of major corporations, banks, investment firms, the few law firms that cater to corporate interests, and the technocratic and policy-oriented intellectuals who do the bidding of those who own and manage the basic institutions of the domestic society."[18] It is in his view of American foreign policy that Chomsky's instrumental view of government shows most clearly. The constant guiding purpose of American foreign policy, according to Chomsky, is to serve the international interests of the US corporate class. Those interests, determined by the search for profit, center on the goal of "maximizing the free access by American capital to the markets and human and material resources of the world, the goal of maintaining to the fullest possible extent its freedom of operation in a global economy."[19]

The question of whether American politics is dominated by a relatively small ruling group or class is at least as old as C. Wright Mills's *The Power Elite,* published in 1956. Mills's book challenged the "pluralist" view prevailing among American political scientists, who generally saw political power as fairly widely dispersed among a variety of "interest groups," no one of which was capable of consistently controlling government policy. With a particular interest in foreign policy, Mills identified the "power elite" as a triumvirate of high officeholders in business, in the civilian executive branch of government, and in the military.[20] Critics lost no time in attacking Mills's arguments for their lack of methodological rigor. Robert Dahl, a leading pluralist theorist, pointed out that Mills had made no attempt to cast his elite theory in the form of empirically testable propositions about policy decision making that could be proved or disproved.[21]

Still, the pluralist paradigm of American politics came under increasing assault in the 1960s and 1970s by a number of social scientists—mostly on the political left—who pointed to evidence that the unequal distribution of political power in the United States was associated primarily with economic inequality. Yes, there was a plurality of interest groups operating more or less effectively in American politics, but some interest groups—notably, those representing business—were more equal than others, while large segments of the population were essentially unrepresented in the system.[22] Anticipating Chomsky, some of these critics pointed to the relatively narrow range of policy debate in the United States: the pluralists' insistence on the analysis of decision making failed to account for "non-decisions": issues (or "non-issues") that were effectively excluded from the policy agenda.[23]

The debate about the nature of American democracy has continued into the twenty-first century, with a new skepticism emerging within the political science establishment regarding the egalitarian promise of American politics. The new skepticism has undoubtedly reflected objective changes in the US political arena—notably, the increased political organization and assertiveness of business interests and the decline of organized labor as a political and economic force. The skepticism was reflected in the establishment by the American Political Science Association of its Task Force on Inequality and American Democracy, whose findings demonstrated striking inequalities in political influence that mirrored disparities in people's wealth.[24]

One study that built on this work found a strong correspondence between the votes of US senators in the 1980s and 1990s and the views of their more affluent constituents; the association was remarkable especially because there was *no* correspondence between senators' votes and the views of low-income constituents.[25] Another study that examined actually enacted policies similarly found that US government performance strongly reflected the views of wealthy Americans over lower-and middle-income citizens.[26]

These and other studies have led two political scientists to pose the question of whether the US political system can be considered an oligarchy, which they define as a system in which "the wealthiest citizens deploy unique and concentrated power resources to defend their unique minority interests."[27] It might seem, then, that Chomsky's broad views on the political power structure in the United States are not very far from the mainstream of current American political science: gross disparities in political influence based on wealth, as demonstrated in the aforementioned studies, don't quite equate to corporate class dominance or rule, but they surely suggest something similar.

Still, in attempting to explain political inequality, the new skeptics have generally focused on considerations that Chomsky tends not to emphasize: the inherent advantages enjoyed by business in the American political game, including party competition, lobbying, and congressional procedures and politics.[28] Chomsky's dismissal of party politics, in particular, is not supported by research findings. On the contrary: an abundance of studies of both national and state politics in the United States support the proposition that partisan differences matter: Democratic Party control of government is associated with policies more favorable to the interests of lower-income groups, while Republican governance favors the affluent. These findings are consistent with comparative political research showing similar differences in government policy between conservative and social democratic governments in Europe.[29]

Of course, whether you regard even demonstrable differences in government policy as significant depends on your perspective. If you believe that capitalism is an intolerably oppressive system, then even apparently substantial improvements in the welfare of the oppressed can be regarded as insignificant. If you regard capitalism as somewhat less than intolerable and in any case likely to be around for a long time, you will accord greater value and significance to reforms within the system. Chomsky's view of the two US parties as mere factions of the same business party might suggest the former perspective, but Chomsky in fact has frequently expressed a positive view of the achievements of social democratic reformism in Europe and even of its more limited achievements in the United States.

But if significant, worthwhile policy reforms *are* possible under capitalism, how far can reform go before provoking the kind of capital disinvestment and economic downturn Chomsky envisions if the rich folk aren't kept happy? Chomsky doesn't ask, much less try to answer, this question. The fact that most capitalist countries have gone much further along a social democratic path than has the United States suggests that the structural constraints on reform under capitalism are not as clearly identifiable and rigid as implied by Chomsky's remarks quoted earlier in this chapter. Chomsky himself has noted the relative backwardness of social policy in the United States compared to other advanced countries—its failure to provide adequate health care for its citizens, for example.[30] That failure has a great deal to do with the nitty-gritty peculiarities of American politics in which Chomsky shows little interest.

While Chomsky has paid scant attention to the "middle levels of power" in capitalist democracy, political scientists have generally not focused on the economic structural explanation for corporate power stressed by Chomsky. An important exception was Charles Lindblom. In 1977 Lindblom published his magisterial *Politics and Markets,* an analytic survey of the varieties of political-economic systems.[31] In a chapter entitled "The Privileged Position of Business," Lindblom argues that in a market (i.e., capitalist) economy, business is not just another interest group. In any market system, a wide variety of decisions that critically affect the national well-being—decisions about technology, work organization, the location of industry, market structure, and resource allocation—are in the hands of business men and women, who thus exercise what are effectively public functions. A major function of government accordingly must be to facilitate businesspeople's effective performance of their jobs:

> In the eyes of government officials, therefore, businessmen do not appear simply as the representatives of a special interest, as representatives of interest groups do. They appear as functionaries performing functions that government officials regard as indispensable....
>
> Any government official who understands the requirements of his position and the responsibilities that market-oriented systems throw on businessmen will therefore grant them a privileged position. He does not have to be bribed, duped, or pressured to do so. Nor does he have to be an uncritical admirer of businessmen to do so. He simply understands ... that to make the system work government leadership must often defer to business leadership.[32]

Government officials thus will be reluctant to undertake policies that threaten to seriously displease the business community. Businesspeople "need only point to the costs of doing business, the state of the economy, the dependence of the economy's stability and growth on their profits or sales prospects—and simply predict, not threaten, that adverse consequences will follow on a refusal of their demands."[33]

Lindblom, a sometime collaborator of Robert Dahl's, is no Marxist. He doesn't use expressions like "class dominance" or "class rule," and in fact prefers to speak of a "duality of leadership" by business and government in which the two partners stand in a symbiotic relationship. But while he doesn't say so explicitly, the thrust of his argument points to business as the senior partner. The differences separating him from Chomskian structural Marxism seem more semantic than substantive.

Part of the reason for political scientists' neglect of economic structural determinants of business power undoubtedly lies in the fact that they are very hard to measure in a clear-cut way.[34] The needs to maintain business confidence and to facilitate or induce business performance are constant but relatively diffuse concerns for political leaders. How do we know when they are operative, and to what effect? Often, it is a matter of policymakers seeking to encourage, anticipate, or prevent possible reactions by business leaders: "We need to implement Policy A in order to enable business to do B and certainly not do C." But it is much more difficult to observe anticipation than to observe reaction after the fact. We can make inferences, but often they will inevitably seem speculative.

Certainly, there are instances where a structural explanation of business power seems highly relevant. Early in his presidency, Bill Clinton, in consultation with his business-friendly advisers, and to the frustration of his liberal secretary of labor, decided that his administration must pursue a policy of fiscal restraint in order to maintain the confidence of the financial markets.[35] That perceived structural constraint was surely consequential for a whole series of budgetary decisions by the administration, but there is no way of demonstrating that any single decision represented a specific response to pressure by business interests. This clearly poses a difficult challenge to the quantitatively oriented political scientist seeking to analyze government decisions as an indicator of relative interest group strength.

But for all the methodological difficulties it poses, a recognition of economic structural constraints must surely be a major part of any explanation of how political power works in the United States. That is, at least with regard to domestic policy. Foreign policy making, however, is a different matter. We can agree that political leaders must consider how domestic policy decisions will affect business activity and thus the general economic well-being, but it is much harder to see how they might make similar connections between foreign policy decisions and the nation's prosperity. Would a failure by the US government to intervene in Guatemala in 1954, or in Nicaragua in the 1980s, have so upset business behavior as to threaten negative economic consequences at home? It seems safe to dismiss any such hypothesis as wildly implausible.

It is hard, indeed, to imagine specific US foreign policy decisions that would be so consequential for the functioning of the US economy as to compel political leaders' deference to the interests of the corporate class. The most likely such scenarios would be in foreign economic policy. Statesmen under certain circumstances might, for example, feel obliged to maintain the value of the national currency, or, alternatively, to deflate it. Another possibility could involve a proximate threat to the availability of a natural resource—oil would be the obvious case—deemed critical to national economic prosperity.[36] Such cases would tend to be exceptional, however. Clearly, the structural approach has only limited usefulness in explaining foreign policy decision making.

Chomsky shows no awareness of this problem; he seems to imply that the structural explanation of corporate class dominance applies equally to foreign and domestic policy, but he doesn't try to show how structural constraints might mandate specific foreign policy decisions by political leaders. He asserts that "foreign policy is guided by the primary commitment to improving the climate for business operations in a global system open to exploitation" by US business, but this is quite different from a structural explanation. It suggests that statesmen are motivated by an understanding of the long-term needs of the economy as defined by the interests of the corporate class, rather than by a sensitivity to the relatively short-term requirements of economic management that politicians must attend to. It suggests, in other words, an instrumental view of corporate class dominance; indeed, Chomsky is effectively an instrumental Marxist in matters of foreign policy.

Chomsky clearly believes that the extensive presence of members of the corporate class in positions of authority in the foreign policy-making apparatus is the principal mechanism for assuring the subservience of US foreign policy to corporate class objectives. When, for example, Arthur Schlesinger Jr. pointed out that the Pentagon Papers showed no evidence of business attempts to influence American policy in Indochina, Chomsky replied that business didn't need to intervene actively—it already had its representatives in the key staff positions.[37] Chomsky would presumably respond similarly to the historian Melvyn Leffler, who reported that in his investigation of the origins of America's Cold War strategy, he found little evidence of business leaders actively seeking to influence US foreign policy in the 1940s and 1950s.[38]

It is certainly hard to argue with the observation that representatives of big business—particularly bankers, financiers, and corporate lawyers—have held a disproportionate number of influential positions in the government agencies responsible for making US foreign policy. One analysis tallied the individuals named to the very top national security positions—the secretaries of state and defense and of the three armed services, the chairmen of the Atomic Energy Commission, and the directors of the CIA. Seventy of the ninety-one people who held these positions in the early postwar decades were businessmen, lawyers for businessmen, or investment bankers.[39] Another study looked at a larger number of positions in a broader range of agencies, including the Departments of Treasury and Commerce as well as the national security-related agencies. Of 678 positions surveyed for the period 1944–1960, 60 percent were filled by individuals from the worlds of business, finance, and law (usually corporate law). Thirty-two percent were filled by career officials (some of whom also spent time in the private sector) and 8 percent from nonprofit organizations.[40] The extensive presence of business leaders in the national security apparatus is, moreover, a bipartisan phenomenon.

The elite that shaped US foreign policy under Democratic as well as Republican administrations during and after World War II was top-heavy with representatives from the world of international banking, finance, and corporate law, including Dean Acheson, Averell Harriman, James Forrestal, John Foster Dulles, and John J. McCloy.[41]

The heavy representation of big business in the counsels of state is surely consequential. People tend to understand and respond to other people like themselves. We would expect business people to find ready access and sympathetic ears among the makers of American foreign policy. That would certainly seem to place limits on the types of foreign policies we would expect government to pursue. We would be very surprised, to put it mildly, to find investment bankers and corporate lawyers actively promoting socialism and the expropriation of American firms in Third World countries. But it is easier to predict, on the basis of their social and economic class background, what decision makers will *not* do than to predict what they *will* do. If a business-dominated government pursues policies A, B, and C, we can reasonably assume that A, B, and C are probably not broadly detrimental to the business community, but we cannot reasonably assume that those policies were actually generated by the needs or demands of the business community. They may reflect concerns that are unrelated to typical business interests. A businessman entering a public office will surely bring to his duties a perspective reflecting his social class background, experience, and interests, but these may not completely determine his posture toward his new responsibilities.

Evidence that government decision makers do seem to respond to the wishes of business leaders comes from a study, which Chomsky cites, by political scientists Lawrence Jacobs and Benjamin Page. Jacobs and Page analyzed surveys of the foreign policy views of various elite groups in and out of government as well as of the general public across a period of over twenty-five years. They found a high degree of responsiveness among government decision makers, particularly in the executive branch, toward executives of companies involved in international business. Another elite group that demonstrated a high level of apparent influence on governmental decision makers was foreign policy experts—academic specialists and occupants of think tanks—but even the experts seemed to be strongly influenced by business. Weaker relationships were found between the views of labor leaders and those of the government decision makers, while public opinion had even less influence on decision makers. The authors conclude that "internationally oriented business leaders exercise strong, consistent, and perhaps lopsided influence on the makers of U.S. foreign policy."[42]

The Jacobs and Page study lends strong support to the Chomskian view that the interests of the corporate class are a major influence on American foreign policy. Still, it is not conclusive proof of Chomsky's thesis that US foreign policy objectives during the Cold War were a fairly simple and direct function of corporate class interests. Most importantly, while Jacobs and Page show that business leaders were very influential, and more influential than anyone else, their findings come nowhere near to demonstrating that business interests were the exclusive or even quasi-exclusive determinant of foreign policy. Also, the Jacobs and Page data start in the year 1974, over a quarter century after the onset of the Cold War. The underlying assumptions and objectives of American Cold War foreign policy had been formed early in that preceding quarter century.

In sum, the evidence we have on the structure of political power in the United States is in itself not quite sufficient to evaluate Chomsky's claim that US political leaders built and maintained a Cold War empire largely to serve the international interests of the American corporate class. The search for an answer will require a broader look at Cold War history.

Explaining America's Cold War

Is American foreign policy mainly about advancing the interests of American business? The popular, alternative explanation of American foreign policy objectives during the Cold War stresses the United States' worldwide competition with a dangerous rival, the Soviet Union. The two superpowers were locked in a worldwide struggle for power and influence. In that struggle, the United States sought what allies it could find; in the Third World, those allies were frequently unsavory despots. Whether wise or unwise, necessary or reprehensible, the United States' association with "Third World fascism," in this perspective, was largely a result of its Cold War competition with the Soviet Union, rather than an outgrowth of the promotion of US business interests.

THE COLD WAR AND ITS ORIGINS: A CONTINUING DEBATE

Practically since its onset, historians have been trying to explain how and why the Cold War got started and what kept it going for so long. At least two schools of thought are distinguishable in Cold War historiography. The orthodox school, dominant in the 1950s, presented a narrative that differed only in richness of detail from that of the popular culture: the Cold War was the inevitable and necessary defensive response by the United States and its allies to threats posed by an aggressive Soviet Union. This view could accommodate a range of interpretations of Soviet behavior, but whether Soviet policy was seen as ideologically or geopolitically motivated, whether the regime's goals were limitless (world domination) or more modestly opportunistic, the cause of East-West conflict was identified clearly as Soviet expansionism.[43]

As the US foreign policy consensus started cracking under the strains of the Vietnam War, Cold War orthodoxy came under serious challenge from a revisionist school of historians. Revisionists assigned a heavy share of responsibility to the United States for the onset of the Cold War and for its perpetuation. Rather than strictly defensive, American behavior at the end of World War II was highly ambitious and even aggressive; it reflected US policymakers' efforts to shape a world congenial to US interests. Most revisionists traced those interests to economic concerns: American leaders sought to construct a global economic order open to trade and investment by US business—that is, a global "open door" for the world's first truly global power. That objective clashed with the Communists' closure of a substantial portion of the globe to the Americans' new world order. In some revisionist accounts, it was the Soviet Union that reacted defensively to the ambitions of its far more powerful capitalist rival. US demands for self-determination in Eastern Europe threatened the Soviet Union's desire for friendly regimes in countries that had served as historic invasion routes into Russia. American determination to revive the economies of Russia's historic enemies, Germany and Japan, exacerbated Soviet suspicions.[44]

Chomsky's views are decidedly revisionist. In particular, Chomsky has drawn heavily on the work of the New Left historian Gabriel Kolko. In treating the Cold War as an excuse and a smokescreen for its imperialist objectives, Chomsky reflects Kolko's view that the very term "Cold War" is a misrepresentation of the nature of global conflict. Kolko sees US ambitions for constructing an integrated world economy under the aegis of American business as a critical factor in the onset of US-Soviet conflict. But, according to Kolko, the "defining fact" of the postwar period was not the US-Soviet confrontation, but the global revolution against foreign domination that swept the Third World.[45] Kolko argues that US resistance to revolution cannot be understood simply in terms of anti-Communism: American policy repeatedly came into conflict with nationalist movements and regimes that were non-Communist, but whose goals clashed with America's vision of a world economy open to American business.[46]

Much of the historiographic debate between orthodoxy and revisionism has addressed the question of apportioning relative responsibility to the two superpowers for the onset of the Cold War—that is, put crudely, who's more to blame, the Americans or the Soviets. Chomsky makes it clear that he believes the blame lies principally with the United States, but the bulk of his critique of US foreign policy has centered not on Europe, where the Cold War began, but on the Third World.

To assess Chomsky's view that American business interests have been the paramount drivers of US policy, we need to look at three broad approaches to explaining US Cold War foreign policy. The first approach focuses on economic variables; the second, on ideology; and the third, on geopolitics. Broadly speaking, revisionist historians emphasize the first of these three approaches, while their orthodox colleagues instead employ some combination of the other two. I will argue that some combination of all three is necessary for a fully satisfactory explanation of US foreign policy during the Cold War. Indeed, the three approaches overlap; while it is useful to distinguish them, the boundaries separating them at times become blurry.

Economic expansionism. Revisionist historians make a strong case that economic concerns have been a long-standing critical driver of US foreign policy. At least since the 1880s American statesmen and business leaders have repeatedly expressed the view that overseas economic opportunities were critical to the health and vibrancy of the US economy. One outgrowth of that view was America's debut as a formally imperialist power with the acquisition of Hawaii and, following the victory over Spain, of the Philippines, Guam, and Puerto Rico. But soon American leaders determined that open markets, rather than ownership of foreign lands, were the best route to ensuring opportunities for US firms. Secretary of State John Hay's "Open Door" notes of 1899 and 1900, asserting America's interest in maintaining equal rights for all foreign powers in an open Chinese market, were emblematic. The pursuit of open markets became a lodestone objective of American diplomacy.[47] According to William Appleman Williams, a historian widely viewed as the pioneer of the revisionist outlook, "the history of the Open Door Notes became the history of American foreign relations."[48] Thus, the United States opposed European powers' efforts to gain exclusive spheres of influence in China around the turn of the century, just as it sought to restrain Japanese expansionist ambitions in the 1920s and 1930s and to contain the Soviets' extension of their dominion after World War II.

Already during World War II, American officials began planning to ensure an open international marketplace in a post war world. According to Assistant Secretary of State Dean Acheson, American democratic capitalism required foreign markets if it was to survive without unacceptably altering itself. Testifying to a congressional committee in 1944, Acheson declared that "no group which has studied this problem . . . has ever believed that our domestic markets could absorb our entire production under our present system. You must look to foreign markets." The alternative, he warned, would require that we "completely change our Constitution, our relations to property, human liberty, our very conceptions of law."[49]

Acheson, formerly a Wall Street lawyer, was an archetypical representative of the elite that shaped US foreign policy during and after World War II. By background and experience, these men naturally brought to their work in government an abiding concern for advancing the interests of American business.[50] The planning not only of postwar international economic institutions but of a global US military presence reflected a worldview centered on the anticipated American leadership of the world economy: a global network of military bases was designed not merely to protect the homeland but to protect American overseas business and financial interests.[51]

For William Appleman Williams, economic interest was not a simple, direct determinant of US foreign policy; instead, it served as the underpinning of a broader ideological outlook in which overseas economic opportunities were viewed as a guarantor not only of prosperity at home but also of stability and democracy. Economic and political liberty were thus seen as inextricably linked. The pursuit of an Open Door world accordingly meant the pursuit of a world that was congenial to American democratic values. Adopting this perspective, Americans believed that "expanding the marketplace enlarged the area of freedom. Expanding the area of freedom enlarged the marketplace."[52] Williams thus was not a strict economic determinist; he believed that economic interests affected policy through the mediation of a broad ideological framework that was more than a simple outgrowth of economic interest. In this perspective, crude economic motivations need not always be operative in important foreign policy decisions. But the belief that economic expansion was key to preserving the American way of life led naturally to an assertive foreign policy that broadly sought to influence the international political and economic environment in ways that were congenial to US economic interests.

Ideology. Apart from Open Door ideology, with its identifiably economic moorings, two sets of beliefs largely independent of economic concerns played an important role in the way Americans viewed foreign policy in the postwar world. These two mindsets—nationalism and anti-Communism—melded together into a Cold War ideology, labeled "American nationalist globalism" by the historian John Fousek, that supported and indeed demanded an aggressive US role in fighting Communism worldwide.[53]

American nationalism centers on a widely and deeply entrenched belief in national greatness, on beliefs in this country's special role in the world as a carrier of universal values of liberty and democracy. Popular themes of American chosenness, mission, and destiny (eventually including Manifest Destiny) run through American history, dating back as far as the Puritan settlers in seventeenth-century New England.[54] American nationalism is intense. It was noted by the famous French observer of American mores, Alexis de Tocqueville, with both admiration and annoyance: "Democratic institutions generally give men a lofty notion of their country, and of themselves" but also "it is impossible to conceive of a more troublesome and garrulous patriotism."[55] Another famous chronicler of American mores, Herbert Croly, wrote in 1909, "The faith of Americans in their country is religious, if not in its intensity, at any rate in its almost absolute and universal authority. It pervades the air we breathe."[56]

Americans tend to believe that their country is not only unique, but superior to other countries—a belief that is generally not typical of other peoples of the world. Thus, a 1999 poll showed that six in ten Americans believed that "our culture is superior to others"–compared to only three in ten of the reputedly chauvinistic French. The same poll found that 72 percent of Americans reported that they were proud of their country; just 53 percent of British citizens, and 35 percent of French, made the same claim. These results closely tracked those of a poll taken fifteen years earlier.[57]

Anti-Communism became a pervasive theme of American public life after World War II. This development was in large part the product of a combustible mixture of traditional American nationalism, the United States' emerging frictions with its erstwhile Communist ally, and partisan political competition. American nationalism had received a tremendous boost from the war. Victory against evil had provided a dramatic, fresh confirmation of American greatness. A sense of American power and triumph was widespread in the popular press and cartoons, incorporating a new vision of American global supremacy and, with it, global responsibility.[58] But that heady vision ran up against the emerging conflict between the United States and the Soviet Union over the post war dispensation in Europe. The perception that a former ally had replaced the old enemy it had helped defeat grew during 1946 as revelations surfaced of wartime Soviet spying on the United States, and Britain's Winston Churchill announced the fall of an "iron curtain" across Europe. Sensing political opportunity, Republican politicians attacked the Truman administration for its alleged weakness in dealing with America's new adversary. Prominent Republicans like Senators Robert Taft and Arthur Vandenberg took the lead in making anti-Communism for the first time a major issue in American partisan politics. It proved to be a potent issue, and one widely believed to have contributed to the overwhelming Republican victory in the 1946 congressional elections.[59]

The Truman administration in turn steadily escalated its own use of anti-Communist rhetoric after 1946, both to neutralize Republican charges and to win support for its new policy of containment of the Soviet Union. The Truman administration was keenly sensitive to lingering isolationist sentiments. Consistent with Vandenberg's advice to "scare hell out of the American people" in order to counter Soviet power, administration policymakers adopted unrestrained rhetoric to dramatize the new threats the nation faced.[60] The Truman Doctrine, with its pledge of support for people resisting totalitarian (read: Soviet-inspired or sponsored) subversion anywhere in the world, magnified the Soviet threat and fueled the emerging anti-Communist consensus.[61] Administration spokesmen, in public speeches and congressional hearings, promoted anti-Soviet views, while the famous article by "X," an anonymous administration official (later revealed to be George Kennan) warned of a long-term struggle with Soviet expansionism. "X" described Soviet ambitions as essentially unlimited, and downplayed the possibility of constructive diplomacy with the new Cold War enemy.[62]

The administration's increasingly tough posture toward the perceived threat of Communism both at home and abroad facilitated the formation of a bipartisan foreign policy consensus that effectively kept foreign policy out of the 1948 presidential election. Truman's surprise victory in that contest came as shock to the Republicans, who concluded that foreign policy bipartisanship hadn't paid off. Their reaction was to move back to the hawkish stance that had helped them win in 1946. The switch was to serve them well, helping them win crucial victories at the polls in 1950 and 1952.[63] Truman, for his part, also adopted a frequently strident anti-Communism in his public pronouncements. By 1950, he was denouncing the Soviet Union as "a modern tyranny led by a small group who have abandoned their faith in God," and expressed confidence that the United States would win its struggle because it had God on its side.[64]

In sum, by 1950 competing anti-Communist rhetoric by both political parties, abetted by media that were by and large enthusiastically anti-Communist, had infused American political culture with a widely shared, militant anti-Communism. Combined with a strong nationalistic conviction in American rectitude and responsibility for world leadership, the new anti-Communism formed a consensus around a Cold War ideology that mandated vigorous opposition across the globe to the perceived threat of Soviet power. In the coming decades, Cold War ideology influenced US policy both directly and indirectly. The ideology influenced policymakers directly because they generally shared its basic assumptions. The indirect influence on policy operated through the mechanism of partisan politics, whose competitive exigencies led politicians of both parties to emphasize toughness in dealing with an implacable foreign enemy. The historians Campbell Craig and Fredrik Logevall describe this climate: "To an extent not seen elsewhere in the Western world, crusading anti-communism became intimately bound up with practical politics. Candidates for office learned quickly that opposing radicals and the Soviet Union was the sine qua non of effective campaigning, that there were few votes to be gained and many to be lost by preaching conciliation in East-West relations. The range of acceptable political debate narrowed sharply."[65] Once in office, politicians were constrained by their own rhetorical commitments and by their sense of vulnerability to partisan attack if they strayed too far from anti-Communist dogma. In famously lamenting Americans' "inordinate fear of communism," President Jimmy Carter was by no means overstating the issue; anti-Communism had indeed become something of a secular American religion in the three decades preceding his presidency.

Geopolitics. In *Politics among Nations,* Hans J. Morgenthau writes, "International politics, like all politics, is a struggle for power. Whatever the ultimate aims of international politics, power is always the immediate aim. . . . Whenever [statesmen and peoples] strive to realize their goal by means of international politics, they do so by striving for power."[66]

This statement pithily summarizes a typical "realist" perspective on international politics, but the view that power concerns are continually at the forefront in nation-states' foreign policy strategies is widely shared by historians and political scientists. Morgenthau is on solid ground in claiming that history bears out his assumption that statesmen habitually think and act in terms of interest defined as power.[67] In this view, much of international politics can be understood in terms of the interactions of nation-states seeking to safeguard or improve their power positions relative to others; nation-states thus seek power practically as an end in itself. Since power in international politics is exerted across geographic space, this perspective is called "geopolitics."

From a geopolitical perspective, a competitive, if not hostile, relationship between the United States and the Soviet Union was practically inevitable in the post–World War II world. With the war's end the United States and the Soviet Union were the only true great powers in the world. As one historian has put it, "As geopolitical great powers, the United States and the Soviet Union couldn't avoid looking on each other with the suspicions countries have always had for other countries capable of doing them serious harm. To each, the other was a strategic threat, and what augmented the military, economic or political power of one necessarily jeopardized the physical security of the other."[68]

A one-sided variant of this view is that the United States was constrained to take on the task of "balancing" the Soviet Union's predominant power position in Europe. In George Kennan's words,

> It [is] essential to us, as it was [historically] to Britain, that no single Continental land power should come to dominate the entire Eurasian landmass. Our interest has lain rather in the maintenance of some sort of stable balance among the powers of the interior, in order that none of them should effect the subjugation of the others . . . and enter . . . on an overseas expansion hostile to ourselves and supported by the immense resources of the interior of Europe and Asia.[69]

The Cold War originally centered on the European continent, but geopolitics helps explain how it spread to other areas of the globe, as each country sought opportunities to increase its power relative to the other, in turn creating threats that the other felt obliged to counter.

The historian Melvyn Leffler has made a strong case for the salience of geopolitical concerns to US policymakers during and after World War II. Leffler points out that already during the 1930s and 1940s, "in a world beleaguered by totalitarian regimes and ravished by global conflict, power became a central organizing concept for understanding behavior in the international system."[70] Geopolitical thinking became a commonplace among journalists, economists, and philosophers, as well as international relations experts and government officials.

The Nazi onslaught made concrete the nightmare possibility of a hostile power acquiring control of Europe. At the end of the war, a blue-ribbon panel of experts assembled by the Brookings Institution warned that it was essential to American security to prevent any one power or coalition of powers from gaining control of Eurasia. US policymakers knew that the Soviets, devastated by the war, were in no immediate position to pose such a threat, but Leffler shows that American policy planning was heavily oriented toward the long-term possibility that the Soviets could eventually come to dominate the Eurasian heartland and its resources, thus acquiring a war-making capability that would threaten US security.

Soviet expansionism at the war's end was limited to Eastern Europe, which was not of vital strategic interest to the United States. But, according to the Joint Chiefs of Staff, "control over strategic points [within Eastern Europe] and over their resources would represent a significant addition to the war potential of an adjacent great power."[71] In 1948 a National Security Council report in 1948 warned that "Soviet domination of the potential power of Eurasia, whether achieved by armed aggression or by political and subversive means, would be strategically and politically unacceptable to the United States."[72] Similarly, a CIA report advised that the task of American policymakers was to keep "the still widely dispersed power resources of Europe and Asia from being drawn into a single Soviet power structure with a uniformly Communist social organization."[73] To guard against these long-term perils, it became US policy to seek and maintain a decisive strategic superiority—a "preponderance of power"—over the Soviets.

CONCLUSION: PUTTING IT ALL TOGETHER

Each one of these three analytic approaches could in principle be pursued independently of the other. One could argue on geopolitical grounds that the United States and the Soviet Union would have come into conflict after World War II even if they had had perfectly compatible ideologies, or that the United States would have sought to impose its Open Door vision on the world economy regardless of any perceived configuration of geopolitical or ideological threats from abroad. In practice, the three approaches tend to overlap. As we have seen, advocates of an economic approach often see Open Door thinking as a component of a broader set of ideological beliefs about the American democratic way of life. Relative economic strength is a major determinant of international power relationships, so geopolitical strategy mandates attention to economic interests. And geopolitical concerns about Soviet power easily merge with ideological anti-Communism. It is useful to think of the three analytic approaches as strands of explanation that are in principle separately identifiable but in practice inextricably entangled.

The entanglement becomes knottier still when we consider a fourth factor—the military-industrial complex. As we have seen, Chomsky views the military-industrial complex as an important factor in the domestic US economy. The dependence of thousands of firms and the communities in which they were located throughout the country on military contracts—and the responsiveness of politicians to that dependence—ensured a broad base of vested interests in maintaining the Cold War, since it was Cold War "needs" that justified high levels of military spending. There was no comparable structure of organized interests on behalf of peace. The military-industrial complex almost certainly reinforced the other factors and helped perpetuate the Cold War, but it was a product, not an independent, originating driver of American foreign policy in the same way as the others.

Surprisingly, no scholar as yet has achieved a grand synthesis that fully takes into account all three approaches to explaining the Cold War. Leffler comes close: in according primacy to geopolitics, he clearly recognizes American leaders' interest in creating an international economy hospitable to US business, and he notes that partisan politics also hardened attitudes toward the Soviets and solidified anti-Communist sentiment.[74] Craig and Logevall stress geopolitical factors in the origins of the Cold War, while emphasizing US partisan politics (the refractor of ideology) in the Cold War's prolongation, but they downplay the importance of economic interests.[75] The political scientist Christopher Layne utilizes both economic and geopolitical arguments in explaining US grand strategy before, during and after the Cold War, but pays little attention to domestic partisan politics.[76]

Chomsky's explanatory approach to US foreign policy, focusing on a narrow set of economic causes, is more reductionist than most: American foreign policy sought to organize the world economy in the interests of American business. Where it encountered resistance to that objective, it reacted ruthlessly, promoting Third World fascism to thwart independent national paths to development that were inconsistent with the needs of American capitalism. Chomsky is dismissive of geopolitical approaches to foreign policy analysis and apparently has little interest in US partisan politics or ideology.

In one of his early books, Chomsky explicitly rejects power motives as an independent explanation of foreign policy, asserting that "the normal workings of state capitalism" provide a readier and simpler explanation for state behavior than some obscure, "deeper" drive for power.[77] But this seems to misunderstand geopolitical thinking, which relies not merely on murky psychological assumptions but on observations of hundreds of years of behavior of nation-states in the international system.

Somewhat similarly, Chomsky challenges Melvyn Leffler's finding that national security concerns weighed heavily in the formulation of US foreign policy in the immediate post war years. He correctly notes Leffler's observation that American policymakers developed a highly expansive notion of national security, positing relatively remote threats as justification for an aggressive foreign policy that actually aimed for preponderance. A definition of security needs that is practically limitless makes dubious the whole concept of security as a foreign policy motivator. Chomsky notes wryly that "By similar logic, any other state has a right to control global society for reasons of 'national security.'"[78] This is a reasonable point, but it fails to negate Leffler's convincing demonstration that American leaders, reasonably or not, really did think and talk in terms of actual and potentially changing power relationships between the United States and the Soviet Union. Chomsky in different contexts has remarked on the ability of public officials to deceive themselves about their "real" interests and motives, but it is hard to dismiss as mere self-deception a theme that continually informs internal government deliberations over a period of years. Chomsky denies the possibility that the enhancement of national power (in this case defined in terms of arguably inflated national security needs) can be effectively an end in itself. But the documentary record shows that while American leaders' strategic motivations certainly had a major economic component, geopolitical considerations were important in their own right.

If Chomsky underrates geopolitics as a factor in foreign policy making, he pays no attention whatever to the role of partisan politics in the United States in intensifying the Cold War. Chomsky's writings show no recognition that partisan political considerations repeatedly played an important role in crucial Cold War decisions. The hardening of the Truman administration's stance toward the Soviet Union in 1946–1948; the escalation of the Korean War in the fall of 1950; the deepening commitment to war in Indochina in the 1960s; the troubles of détente in the 1970s; and congressional Democrats' inhibitions in confronting Reagan's Central America policies in the 1980s—all of these and other foreign policy developments can be attributed at least in part to the pressures of domestic political competition in the United States.[79]

While Chomsky generally ignores partisan politics as a driver of US policy, he is hardly more inclined to attribute any independent significance to ideology. As we have seen (in Chapter 1), he did cite nationalism as a force influencing people to overlook their country's misdeeds in Vietnam but he almost never alludes to nationalism in his later writings. Chomsky's treatment of ideology, particularly anti-Communism, changed similarly over time. In *Mandarins,* Chomsky explicitly recognized the independent force of anti-Communist ideology, even while stressing its origins in concrete interests:

> Ideology can have a life of its own, contributing to the design and implementation of policy in a way that may, on occasion, even conflict with the interests from which it arose. The postwar American anti-Communist paranoia provides many examples. . . . In part it no doubt functioned as an almost independent basis for specific policy decisions.[80]

This recognition is largely missing in Chomsky's later writings, in which he tends to treat anti-Communism as hardly more than a rationale constructed by elites to justify their pursuit of corporate class interests: "The fear of communism was always a total fraud."[81]

Chomsky thus is unable to recognize that the Cold War was a real, not a phony, conflict between the two great powers—a conflict with geopolitical and ideological as well as economic causes. US policymakers took that conflict seriously and accordingly sought to counter what they perceived as potential advances in Soviet power anywhere in the world. There is abundant historical research that leaves no doubt that American leaders did indeed see the Third World as a critical battleground in a long US struggle with Soviet power.[82] American perceptions of Soviet threats were often exaggerated, but they weren't completely paranoid. The growth of nationalism in the Third World did offer the Soviet adversary opportunities for exploitation. The Soviet regime in the 1950s and 1960s was widely viewed as a model of rapid economic development: in little more than a generation it had transformed a largely agrarian society into one capable of defeating the Nazi war machine. Third World nationalist movements, seeking first political and then economic independence from the capitalist West, often attracted the support of domestic Communists, not to mention the opportunistic interest of the Kremlin.

But while the worldwide competition with Soviet Union was inarguably a constant preoccupation of US leaders, there is little evidence that economic concerns had a similar salience. Chomsky points to a National Security Council report that he says talks about the need to maintain a climate conducive to investment in the Third World, permitting the repatriation of profits and other benefits: "Language like that is repeated year after year in top-level U.S. planning documents . . . and that's what we do around the world."[83] But Chomsky is cherry-picking: the three documents he cites to support his assertion all relate to Latin America, and none is dated later than 1956. Economic concerns are among the many subjects discussed, but they are far from being predominant in any of these documents. One could just as easily cite NSC documents in the same volumes to illustrate US policymakers' concerns about Communist influence in Latin America and elsewhere and its threat to US security interests.[84] Indeed, according to William LeoGrande, with the progressive declassification of US government documents, "there is little evidence, especially after 1961, that US officials thought about Cold War policy in terms of defending U.S. economic interests, either in particular or in general."[85] The historian Odd Arne Westad, drawing on his extensive study of US and Soviet behavior in the Third World, basically agrees.[86]

The narrowness of Chomsky's focus on business interests as drivers of US foreign policy shows up in his analysis of the causes of the Vietnam War. Chomsky is right that Vietnam was not an aberration but a logical outgrowth of broad US policy objectives. He is also right to see the origins of the US commitment to Indochina in American leaders' concern to ensure that Southeast Asian markets and raw materials would be available to support Japan's economic recovery. That view, controversial when Chomsky (following the historian Walter LaFeber) first advanced it, has received strong confirmation from subsequent research.[87] But American leaders' concern to aid Japan's economic recovery represented more than simply the "long-term effort to reduce Eastern Asia and much of the rest of the world to part of the American-dominated economic system." (See Chapter 2.) John Foster Dulles and other American policymakers saw Japan and India as vulnerable to Soviet penetration, making Southeast Asia a critical battleground in the Cold War competition with the Soviet Union.[88] US involvement in Vietnam also reflected the sensitivity of US leaders to domestic partisan political considerations. The Democrats' burden of having "lost China" in the late 1940s played a major role in Democratic administrations' reluctance to "abandon" South Vietnam in the 1960s.[89]

The US role in promoting "Third World fascism," then, needs to be understood in the context of America's struggle with its Soviet adversary. In seeking allies in the Third World, the US government naturally gravitated toward the most reliable anti-Communists. These tended to be conservative elites who had little use for democracy. More often than not, they were happy to bolster their alliance with American power by accommodating American business interests.

For their part, US policymakers often saw US business as a tool of American political power and influence abroad, rather than vice versa. As Westad puts it: "During the Cold War the [US] government always wanted private companies to increase their investments abroad—in order to create influence and 'development'—but with limited success."[90] The government's use of private firms as instruments of US foreign policy objectives was not a new phenomenon. As early as the first decade of the twentieth century, the State Department, seeking to extend American influence in China, pushed for the formation of an international bankers' consortium, headed by the House of Morgan, to pursue Chinese business. The bankers obliged, though with more than a little chafing at government manipulation.[91] But if American business was seen as an extension of American power, it was natural to see challenges to American business privileges as challenges to American power—challenges that could not be ignored (cf. Guatemala 1954). Again, we can see the difficulty of unraveling the different strands of explanation—in this case, the economic from the geopolitical.

Undoubtedly, economic interests were a constant backdrop to US foreign policy during the Cold War. After discounting the specific role of business interests in US foreign policy decision making, Westad continues: "But this is in no way to say that the capitalist market has played a negligible part in the formation of American foreign affairs. In a way, the Marxists seem to be right in arguing for a *systemic* role for business interests: throughout its existence, the American elite has argued—though in very diverse ways—for the promotion of free market exchanges as being at the core of US 'national interest' abroad."[92] The expansion of American economic power abroad was, indeed a continuing objective of American foreign policy throughout the Cold War. American leaders did believe that the maintenance of prosperity and democratic capitalism in the United States depended on the maintenance of an open world economy managed by the United States. But that broad orientation did not entail the single-minded and consistent servitude to business interests that Chomsky posits. American Third World interventions were seldom a simple reaction to threats to US business interests, but more often a reflection of broad Cold War assumptions and objectives. Economic, geopolitical, and ideological objectives interacted and reinforced each other in driving American policy during the Cold War.

CHAPTER 4

Ideology, Illusion, and the Media

> Those who have a dominant position in the domestic economy command substantial means to influence public opinion. It would be surprising indeed if this power were not reflected in the mass media, themselves major corporations—and the schools and universities: if it did not, in short, shape the prevailing ideology to a considerable extent.
> —Noam Chomsky, 1982

As CHOMSKY SEES IT, the need to "shape the prevailing ideology" is the natural consequence of the combination of elite dominance and procedural democracy that exists in the United States and most advanced countries.¹ In the United States, according to Chomsky, "perhaps more than anywhere else in the world, the citizen is free from state coercion—at least, the citizen who is relatively privileged and of the right color, a substantial part of the population."² In such a democracy, the acceptance by the majority of citizens of privilege and inequality is not unproblematic. Democracy represents a potential challenge to corporate class dominance; it gives ordinary people the opportunity to associate with their peers and organize to advance their common interests.

In part, the challenge is met by keeping much of social and economic life out of the political arena, where corporate dominance could be contested. As noted in the last chapter, Chomsky argues that control over fundamental aspects of daily life—employment, workplace conditions and practices, and the very location of economic activity—is kept in private hands, and thus is controlled by structures of authority that are not easily challenged by individuals lacking substantial economic resources.

Corporate dominance is also protected by popular culture, which serves to immunize much of the population from "dangerous" ideas. Chomsky explains with characteristic sarcasm:

> The "stupid and ignorant masses" . . . must be kept that way, diverted with emotionally potent oversimplifications, marginalized, and isolated.³ Ideally, each person should be alone in front of the television screen watching sports, soap operas, or comedies, deprived of organizational structures that permit individuals lacking resources to discover what they think and believe in interaction with others, to formulate their own concerns and programs, and to act to realize them. They can then

be permitted, even encouraged, to ratify the decisions of their betters in periodic elections.[4]

The idea that popular culture and declining participation in organizations tend to weaken the conditions for a vibrant and meaningful democracy has a long history in American social criticism and political analysis, including such classics of the 1950s as Mills's *The Power Elite* and David Riesman's *The Lonely Crowd* and more recent works by the political scientists Robert Putnam and Theda Skocpol.[5] Chomsky, though, doesn't seek to elaborate on this perspective. His fragmentary writings along these lines are basically variations on the passage just quoted.

How, then, does the dominant corporate class "shape the prevailing ideology" to ensure acquiescence in its rule? One might expect Chomsky to answer this question with a discussion of the value system of democratic capitalism and the means by which system-supporting values are passed on to nonmembers as well as members of the corporate class. Marxists, for example, have often discussed the lack of a revolutionary anticapitalist consciousness among workers as indicative of the ruling class's ideological hegemony—its success in diffusing values and beliefs that legitimate its rule among the broad population, whose interests are presumptively inconsistent with that rule. Chomsky, though he repeatedly remarks on the narrowness of political debate in the United States and the tendency of people to conform to prevailing values, makes no effort to elaborate on a broad explanation of political acquiescence under capitalism.

Chomsky instead focuses more narrowly on what he calls the "doctrinal system," which is aimed primarily at the upper-middle classes on whom the corporate class must call for active and informed allegiance. As he explains:

> The problem of indoctrination is a bit different for those expected to take part in serious decision-making and control:—the business, state, and cultural managers, and articulate sectors generally. They must internalize the values of the system and share the necessary illusions that permit it to function in the interests of concentrated power and privilege—or at least be cynical enough to pretend that they do, an art that not many can master.[6]

The doctrinal system, according to Chomsky, is extraordinarily effective—arguably more effective than the system of coercion characteristic of totalitarian societies. The effectiveness of the doctrinal system in a formally free society is actually enhanced, rather than diminished, by the absence of official restrictions on free expression. The apparently lively and sometimes contentious public debate over a wide range of issues that characterizes the system cloaks a more important reality: the very limited range of assumptions within which debate takes place. By limiting debate to the prevailing range of acceptable assumptions, the system gives the appearance of tolerating and even encouraging dissent, when in fact it is promoting *con*sent: "The more vigorous the debate, the better the system of propaganda is served, since the tacit, unspoken assumptions are more forcefully implanted.... It is far more effective to constrain all possible thought within a framework of tacit assumption than to try to impose a particular explicit belief with a bludgeon."[7] The unspoken assumptions Chomsky is referring to generally center on the image of America as the world's beacon of democracy, freedom, and human rights; America's enemies—Communists, terrorists, and their sympathizers—by definition are always the antithesis of those values.

According to Chomsky, the mass media play a critical role in maintaining the doctrinal system. They function "to inculcate individuals with the values, beliefs, and codes of behavior that will integrate them into the institutional structures of the larger society."[8] He also attributes an important supporting role to American intellectuals in the maintenance of the doctrinal system. Chomsky's interest in the system-supporting roles of both the mass media and of intellectuals has been a recurrent theme in practically all his writings. Beginning with his earliest critiques of the war in Vietnam, Chomsky's accounts of American foreign policy have almost invariably been accompanied by observations about the complicity of the media and of intellectuals in the perpetuation of illusions in the service of power.

Many of Chomsky's early observations on ideology, illusion, and conformism have a simple, commonsense quality to them. As an explanation of the subservience of media and intellectuals to prevailing assumptions, he offers the following:

> To ask serious questions about the nature and behavior of one's own society is often difficult and unpleasant: difficult because the answers are generally concealed, and unpleasant because the answers are often not only ugly... but also painful....
> The easy way is to succumb to the demands of the powerful, to avoid searching questions, and to accept the doctrine that is hammered home incessantly by the propaganda system. This is, no doubt, the main reason for the easy victory of dominant ideologies, for the general tendency to remain silent or to keep fairly close to official doctrine with respect to the behavior of one's own state... while lining up to condemn the real or alleged crimes of its enemies.[9]

In the 1980s, Chomsky, working with Edward S. Herman, more systematically formulated his ideas on the maintenance of the doctrinal system. Chomsky and Herman developed a comprehensive analysis of the role of the American media. They called their analysis the "Propaganda Model."

The Propaganda Model: The Framework

The Propaganda Model, laid out in Chomsky and Herman's book *Manufacturing Consent,* is a conceptual framework for explaining and predicting the US mass media's treatment of news issues. Its central proposition is that the media "serve to mobilize support for the special interests that dominate the state and private activity, and that their choices, emphases, and omissions can often be understood best... by analyzing them in such terms."[10] Chomsky and Herman nowhere specifically define the "special interests that dominate the state and private activity," but we can assume they are the interests of the corporate class and its presumptive servants, the political elite. According to Chomsky and Herman, major media communications systematically exclude messages—whether in the form of "news" or "opinion"—that tend to call into question fundamental corporate values. The media's selection of events that are considered newsworthy, and of opinions that are worthy of serious consideration, reflects parameters defined by core corporate interests. Media bias is pervasive, systematic, and highly effective: "The difference between a society with official censorship (e.g., the Soviet Union) and one without (the United States) is real and significant, but the extent and especially the policy consequences of such differences are often overrated. There is a corresponding tendency to underestimate the significance of self-censorship and the strength of the underlying factors that make for unified mass media support for foreign policy."[11]

Chomsky and Herman emphasize that their view of the media is not a conspiracy theory: they do not claim to show massive collusion among media outlets or conscious control or direction of media content by corporate or government interests. Indeed, the beauty of the system is that such conspiratorial activity is unnecessary: the system works, instead, as if guided by an invisible hand. Desired outcomes are the product of structural or situational factors, which Chomsky and Herman call "filters," that operate seemingly naturally, much like market forces. The filters ensure that only acceptable messages get through to the public by shaping the incentives, resources, and worldviews of the people who report the news. The result is that mainstream media leaders and reporters tend to see the world through similar lenses as the political and economic elites, and report accordingly.

Chomsky and Herman acknowledge that the filters operate imperfectly; sometimes discordant messages do get through. They also recognize that the media are far from monolithic—they often present a considerable range of views, thus giving the appearance of vigorous, open debate.[12] But that appearance merely reflects the fact that the elite itself is not monolithic: "Where the powerful are in disagreement, there will be a certain diversity of tactical judgments on how to attain generally shared aims, reflected in media debate. But views that challenge fundamental premises . . . will be excluded from the mass media even when elite controversy over tactics rages fiercely."[13]

Chomsky and Herman describe five filters that serve to ensure the mass media's subservience to corporate interests. The first, and perhaps most important filter, in Chomsky and Herman's view, has to do with the very structure of the media industries: "the size, concentrated ownership, owner wealth, and profit orientation of the dominant mass-media firms."[14] Chomsky and Herman cite various studies documenting the increasing concentration of the media in the United States and elsewhere. Concentration is a reflection of market realities—the large investments required to enter and the continuing costs of operating in the media market ensure that the business of reporting and analyzing the news is mostly big business.

The concentration of the media entails the marginalization of the mostly small information outlets that are not profit-oriented and therefore more likely to carry messages that challenge corporate interests. Because media organizations are typically big businesses—i.e., large corporations—they are closely integrated into the corporate economy, linked by ties of ownership, financing, and overlapping board memberships with other large corporations. The leading media are owned and managed by members of the corporate class, who can be expected to advance their class interests along with their business interests. And, while not all media outlets are giant corporations, the major media that define the news agenda and supply much of the news to the lower tiers are owned by corporate giants—the one to two dozen companies that own the three television networks, the major cable systems, the leading newspaper chains, and the largest news and general-interest magazines.

The second filter, closely linked to the first, is advertising—specifically, the dependence of media on advertising revenues. Historically, advertising played an important role in the concentration of the media industry, because newspapers lacking in advertising revenues were competitively disadvantaged and tended to become marginalized.[15] Advertising revenue dependence also shapes the political orientation of the media directly, in two ways. First, because advertisers are naturally interested most in customers with buying power, the media are most interested in attracting affluent audiences; accordingly they gear their messages to the values and preferences of the affluent. Second, media dependence on advertising means that advertisers acquire influence over media content. Advertisers in top-tier media are mostly large corporations; they would tend not be attracted to radical, anticapitalist media even if these had sizable audiences. In addition, media content is responsive to subtle, and sometimes not so subtle, advertiser pressure. Chomsky and Herman cite instances in which advertisers have turned away from sponsoring documentary programming that carried messages critical of corporate values.[16] More often, they suggest, overt advertiser pressure is unnecessary: programming executives know what kinds of programs can be sold to advertisers and what cannot.

The third filter on the news is the media's reliance on sources.[17] Chomsky and Herman observe that even the biggest media organizations cannot have reporters everywhere that news is likely to break—resources are too limited. Reporters must therefore cultivate reliable sources of newsworthy information. One obvious source of news is government: most major news organizations have reporters on regular "beats" at the White House, the State Department, the Pentagon, and Congress. Large corporations, with their well-endowed public affairs and media departments, and business associations, including the US Chamber of Commerce and thousands of local chambers and industry trade associations, also have tremendous information resources, which are willingly tapped by reporters. Government and corporate sources have the great advantage of being recognized as credible by virtue of their status and prestige. Information obtained from them is presumed to be authoritative, and can be presented as "news" with relatively little fear of accusations of bias. Symbiotic relationships thus develop: news organizations maintain access to steady suppliers of news, while the government and corporate information sources they rely on obtain the opportunity to shape the news in conformity with their interests.

Reporters' need to maintain access to steady information sources naturally entails a reluctance to offend those sources: "It is very difficult to call authorities on whom one depends for daily news liars, even if they tell whoppers."[18] At the same time, reporters will tend to avoid less authoritative sources that may offer information and perspectives that clash with those of more established sources, to avoid offending the latter and because the information provided lacks the imprimatur of respectability that a major government agency or corporation can provide. (If Amnesty International says that the government is not reporting the full story of atrocities in Central America, whose version of reality is likely to get more play in the media?)

Another important source of information, mainly in the form of opinion and analysis, is expertise. Washington is the home of numerous think tanks, many of them financed by corporate sources, who can furnish a ready supply of "expert" commentary on news events. The experts on whom the media rely tend invariably to be upholders of prevailing perspectives. Chomsky and Herman cite Henry Kissinger, who defines the expert's "constituency" as "those who have a vested interest in commonly held opinions; elaborating and defining its consensus at a very high level has, after all, made him an expert."[19] In short, information is power, and the considerable information resources at the disposal of government and corporate America help ensure that the media report news and opinion that is generally in line with the parameters of acceptable debate as defined by the dominant corporate and political elites.

The fourth filter on news information is what Chomsky and Herman call "flak."[20] Flak consists of negative reactions to media content. If produced on a large scale by individuals or organized groups, flak can be uncomfortable and costly to media organizations. It is something they naturally prefer to avoid. Flak became an important factor in the US media world in the 1970s and 1980s, as wealthy individuals and corporations funded a variety of media "watchdog" groups charged with policing media content to deter departures from prevailing orthodoxies. Their targets generally are messages that they deem unpatriotic or hostile to the business point of view. Groups organized during this period specifically for the purpose of producing flak include the American Legal Foundation, the Capital Legal Foundation, the Media Institute, the Center for Media and Public Affairs, and Accuracy in Media. These organizations, all right of center in political orientation, use a variety of means—including lawsuits, conferences, and the sponsorship of books and periodicals—to harass the mainstream media. Despite these groups' frequently harsh criticisms, they generally get a respectful hearing from the mainstream media, reflecting the power of the groups' sponsors, who often have ties to the corporate media's owners and managers. Government, too, is a major producer of source of flak, often assailing, threatening, and "correcting" the media to punish or forestall unfavorable coverage. The Nixon and Reagan administrations were particularly adept in this area.

The fifth and last filter identified in the Propaganda Model is an ideology: anti-Communism.[21] The pervasiveness and quasi-religious intensity of anti-Communist ideology in the United States exerted a tremendous pull on the media during the Cold War, particularly in their treatment of international affairs. The media's framing of foreign policy issues generally reflected a Manichaean world in which Communist bad guys were continually arrayed against anti-Communist good guys. It was entirely natural for the media to root for "our" side; the possibility that "we" might sometimes be the bad guys was generally unthinkable.

In summary, Chomsky and Herman's Propaganda Model offers a fairly comprehensive explanatory framework for understanding the media in the United States. Chomsky and Herman's basic claim is that multiple mechanisms operate to filter out of media content messages that might challenge the core interests of the American elite. "Acceptable" messages pass through. The model's five filters represent a variety of determinants of media behavior, including economic interests and market forces (filters 1 and 2); institutional needs (filter 3); and the ideological environment in which the media must operate (filters 4 and 5).

A model should help explain, and therefore predict, actual behavior. Chomsky and Herman contend that theirs does so with great accuracy, and have marshaled evidence to prove that it does. We turn next to Chomsky and Herman's proof.

Case Studies

The bulk of *Manufacturing Consent* is devoted to five case studies of mass media treatment of issues related to US foreign policy. Chomsky and Herman's case studies all purport to show that the American mass media demonstrate a consistent and systematic bias toward presenting facts and opinions that tend to validate the currently prevailing assumptions of US foreign policy, ignoring or downplaying events and opinions that call those assumptions into question.

The focus on foreign policy might seem surprising. Chomsky and Herman nowhere define the Propaganda Model narrowly as a tool for the analysis of media treatment of foreign policy. In the introduction added to the book in 2002, Chomsky points to a few instances of media coverage of domestic matters that he says support the Propaganda Model, but the authors' initial, systematic attempt to demonstrate the applicability of their model is entirely limited to foreign affairs. Chomsky and Herman don't explain why they limit their testing of the model to foreign affairs. Implicitly, they seem to assume that the demonstration of the model's validity in the foreign policy realm would prove their larger point about the media's subservience to "the special interests that dominate the state and private activity."

There are two problems with this assumption, however. First, it could well be that certain factors that operate in the foreign policy arena are either absent or less effective in the domestic arena. Most obviously, the anti-Communist filter would operate more effectively for foreign news than for domestic. A demonstration of media subservience to elite preferences and interests in foreign policy, then, would still fall short of a comprehensive demonstration of media subservience. Second, Chomsky and Herman take it for granted that the main lines of US foreign policy are determined by the interests of the corporate class; for them, to demonstrate the media's servitude to US foreign policy is equivalent to demonstrating its servitude to the corporate class. In Chapter 3, however, I argued that US foreign policy is not a simple expression of business interests—that it has to be understood in terms of a complex interplay of economic, ideological, and geopolitical factors. Assuming this argument is correct, even a successful demonstration of media subservience to US foreign policy would not confirm Chomsky and Herman's broader argument about the media's servitude to corporate class interests.

The way around these problems is simply to redefine the Propaganda Model for present purposes as a framework for understanding the mass media's role in the "manufacture of consent" to US foreign policy.[22] Of Chomsky and Herman's five case studies, the first two concern Central America; the third, Vietnam; the fourth, an incident of international terrorism; and the fifth, Laos and Cambodia. I think that the first three of these provide the clearest tests of Chomsky and Herman's model, and so this chapter will examine just those three.

CENTRAL AMERICA AND POLAND: WORTHY AND UNWORTHY VICTIMS

In October 1984 Jerzy Popieluszko, a Polish priest, was murdered by the Polish police. The murder took place in the context of a stubborn, mounting challenge to Communist rule by the workers' Solidarity movement. The US mass media treated the Popieluszko murder as a sensation. Both print and broadcast reports stressed the brutality of the crime and the widespread outrage it elicited in Poland. The murder was portrayed as an atrocity typical of a police state, and editorials and commentaries pointedly raised questions as to the possible involvement of the Communist authorities in the slaying. By contrast, the media's handling of the March 1980 murder of El Salvador's Archbishop Oscar Romero (see Chapter 2) was very limited and low-key. Romero's death got nowhere near the amount of media attention accorded to Popieluszko's, and commentaries avoided speculating about official involvement in the crime, even though evidence soon surfaced that state security forces were probably responsible. Romero, in fact, was among several dozen church people who were victims of official violence in El Salvador between the mid-1960s and mid-1980s, including four American women in December 1980. The Popieluszko murder received considerably more attention from major US media than all the Salvadoran murders *combined*.[23]

How is this stark disparity explained? According to Chomsky and Herman, the Polish priest was a "worthy victim"; worthy, that is of American attention and sympathy. The Salvadorans were "unworthy victims."[24] "Worthiness" is a function of the supportiveness of the narrative of victimhood to prevailing assumptions and themes of US foreign policy. Anti-Communism of course had been the dominant theme of US foreign policy for decades, and had gotten a new boost with President Reagan's denunciation of the "evil empire." Evidence of the perfidy of a Communist regime supports this theme very nicely, and so Popieluszko was a "worthy" victim. On the other hand, the Salvadoran murders were potentially embarrassing to the United States. American policymakers were not eager to call attention to atrocities committed by agents of regimes enjoying US patronage. The US media accordingly treated those atrocities with restraint. Chomsky and Herman's designation of the Salvadoran victims as "unworthy" is of course sarcastic. The media didn't consciously regard them as unworthy; they simply didn't see them as meriting the same attention as a victim of Communism.[25] A victim of official violence in an enemy state is "naturally" big news; a victim of official violence in a friendly state, much less so.[26]

Chomsky and Herman present overwhelming quantitative evidence of the media's asymmetrical treatment of the Polish and Salvadoran murders. Surveying the eighteen-month period following each murder, Chomsky and Herman count seventy-eight articles in the *New York Times* on the Popieluszko murder, compared to only sixteen articles on Romero. During the same periods, *Time* and *Newsweek* devoted a total of sixteen articles to Popieluszko and a mere three to Romero. CBS News coverage was similarly lopsided. The sensational murder of four US churchwomen in December 1980 got more US media attention than did the Romero murder, presumably because of the women's American citizenship. Still, their murders got only about one-third the coverage as Popieluszko's in the three print media surveyed by Chomsky and Herman, and less than one-half of the attention by CBS News.[27]

Chomsky and Herman supplement their quantitative content analysis of leading US media outlets with descriptions of biased reporting. The context in which the media placed the Romero murder was one of increasing violence in El Salvador by both the Left and the Right—violence that the government was trying to contain but with little success. Readers of Chapter 2 will recognize this picture as badly distorted by false balance: violence against noncombatants came overwhelmingly from the political right, utilizing not only private death squads (whose existence was acknowledged by the US media) but also allies in the army and state security forces. The government's efforts to combat this violence were more cosmetic than real. Romero himself repeatedly called attention to these realities, but his views got no notice (or in some cases were actually misrepresented) in the leading US media. Chomsky and Herman point out that there was plenty of evidence that could have been investigated by an inquiring media: "The linkages between the army and the death squads were close: there was at least some degree of common command, shared operation and mutual protection. Could the killer have been a member of the armed forces? Given the links of the army to the paramilitary forces, wasn't it likely that they knew who killed Romero? The U.S. media did not *raise*, let alone press, these questions."[28]

The media were hardly more interested in the possibility of official involvement in the December 1980 murder of the four US churchwomen. Thus, one story by the reporter John Dinges cited a good deal of circumstantial evidence that the murders were planned within the armed forces. Dinges's report was carried by the *Washington Post,* the *Los Angeles Times,* and fifteen other newspapers, "but not a word of it found its way into the *New York Times, Time, Newsweek,* or CBS News, and *its leads were not pursued* by any media."[29] The preferred narrative was the official Salvadoran line that the murderers were rogue National Guardsmen acting alone. By contrast, the US media were persistent in raising questions of possible official involvement in the Popieluszko murder. No fewer than eighteen articles in the *New York Times* alone raised the question of how high in the official Polish hierarchy responsibility for the murder might be lodged.

Chomsky and Herman point to numerous other instances of asymmetry in the treatment of worthy and unworthy victims, and extend their investigation to Guatemala, where, as we have seen, state terror in the 1980s was even more widespread and deadly than in El Salvador. Human rights groups produced abundant evidence of the nature and extent of the slaughter, evidence that was overwhelmingly confirmed in truth commission investigations years later. Yet the US mass media paid little attention to the human rights groups' reports, relying instead on perennial State Department claims that the human rights situation was improving, and that most deaths were the tragic but inevitable products of civil war rather than one-sided assaults on noncombatants by the forces of the state. Using a selection of ten major reports on Guatemala produced by Amnesty International and Human Rights Watch between 1981 and 1987, Chomsky and Herman report that they could find *mention* of only four of those reports in their media sample.[30] None of those four was on a front page or the subject of an editorial.[31] Chomsky and Herman explain the inattention to the human rights groups partly as a response to US government flak. The Reagan administration consistently sought to discredit Americas Watch and Amnesty as biased and left-wing.

Was there an objective basis for the media's disparate treatment of victims of official violence in Central America and Poland? Is there any plausible explanation for the discrepancy, other than media bias? One Chomsky critic, Eli Lehrer, points out that ten million Americans of Polish ancestry lived in the United States, and that Chicago had almost as many Polish residents as Warsaw. "Thus, other things being equal, events in Poland will have far more relevance from a media point of view than events in El Salvador and Guatemala."[32] There are two problems with this claim: first, Lehrer offers no evidence that Poland actually did get more media attention than El Salvador during the relevant time periods; in fact, as we shall soon see, it apparently did not. Second, "other things" arguably were not quite equal. Popieluszko was a well-known Solidarity activist whose sermons had been broadcast widely in Poland by Radio Free Europe, but he was a rank-and-file priest. Romero, an outspoken critic of his country's traditional oligarchy, was an archbishop and the leader of the Catholic Church in El Salvador. Just weeks before his death he had sent an impassioned letter to President Carter asking the president to desist from sending further aid to the Salvadoran military. His sermons had been attended by the American ambassador to his country.

Lehrer also claims that the Polish priest's death got more attention because it was more consequential: it was "pivotal in turning the tide of Polish and world opinion against the Soviet occupation," while the Central American deaths, tragic as they were, were unremarkable, occurring in a region "where violence dominates the political landscape and where such atrocities are all too common."[33] But Lehrer's argument suffers from obvious circularity: the Polish murder affected world opinion in part *because* of the media attention it got, while the Central American murders were less consequential—and the violent context considered unremarkable—*because* of the relatively low-key media treatment routinely accorded official violence in US-friendly countries.

The noted journalist Nicholas Lemann offered another response to Chomsky and Herman's account of disparate media treatment: "Father Popieluszko . . . was killed when the U.S. press was most focused on Poland. Archbishop Romero was killed before the press had really focused on El Salvador. Popieluszko's murder wasn't more important; the discrepancy can be explained by saying the press tends to focus on only a few things at a time."[34] Lemann didn't offer any evidence to support his claim, however, and Chomsky effectively demolished it; he cited, as an indicator of relative media coverage of El Salvador and Poland, the columns devoted to the two countries in the *New York Times Index* for the relative twelve-month periods.[35] Coverage of the two countries was almost identical; slightly higher, in fact, for El Salvador. This finding also effectively refutes Lehrer's assertion that it was natural for Poland to receive more media attention than El Salvador.

Which was more newsworthy: the Popieluszko or the Romero murder? One can perhaps make a reasonable argument for either case, or for the view that they were of roughly equal newsworthiness. But there is certainly no reasonable basis for any argument that the Polish case was obviously and vastly more newsworthy than the Salvadoran. Chomsky and Herman's argument withstands any attempt at refutation: the huge imbalance in US media attention in favor of the Pole can only be explained by a systematic bias. An event that fits conveniently with the prevailing assumptions undergirding US foreign policy (America and its allies stand for democracy and the rule of law against an evil Communist empire) gets attention. Events that raise awkward questions about those assumptions (Can the government and security forces of a close US ally be engaged in the cold-blooded murder of their own citizens?) tend to get short shrift.

The media's treatment of the clerical murders in Poland and El Salvador serves as a nearly perfect illustration of what Chomsky and Herman call "dichotomization": the media's application of double standards in depicting the behavior of the United States and its allies as opposed to the behavior of their perceived enemies.[36] Dichotomization is also prominent in the comparative coverage of elections in Central America, to which we now turn.

CENTRAL AMERICA: PUTTING ELECTIONS IN CONTEXT (OR NOT)

In the early and mid-1980s important national elections were held in three Central American countries—El Salvador, Guatemala, and Nicaragua—that had had limited historical experience with democracy. Two of those countries—El Salvador and Guatemala—were traditional US client states; their regimes continued to enjoy the warm if occasionally qualified support of the administration in Washington. The Reagan administration hailed the elections in these two countries as evidence of new beginnings toward democratic governance; El Salvador and Guatemala could now be regarded as "fledgling democracies." Nicaragua, on the other hand, was targeted as an enemy by its giant northern neighbor—an agent of international Communism in the Western Hemisphere. Washington dismissed the Nicaraguan elections as a pseudo-democratic sham staged to hide the true totalitarian nature of the Nicaraguan regime from its people and from the rest of the world.

Chomsky and Herman aim to show that the US mass media's treatment of the elections in the three countries was broadly congruent with the narrative put out by official Washington. That congruence was particularly remarkable, in their view, because Washington's narrative turned the truth upside down. The Guatemalan and Salvadoran elections were practically meaningless "demonstration" elections, while the Nicaraguan elections, though imperfect, represented a genuinely democratic achievement.

To assess Chomsky and Herman's arguments, we need to consider the conditions that go into the making of fair, democratic elections. The most obvious set of conditions relate to procedural correctness: all eligible voters should be able to get to the polls and to vote by secret ballot, free of any efforts at coercion by contending parties. Procedural correctness also requires that votes be counted and reported honestly. The elections in question took place in El Salvador in 1982 for a provisional president and constituent assembly, in 1984 for president, and in 1985 for the national legislature; in Nicaragua in 1984 for the national legislature; and in Guatemala in 1984 and 1985, for a constituent assembly and president. International observers attested that all of these elections generally satisfied most conditions of procedural fairness. The major exception was the Salvadoran elections of 1982, in which significant irregularities in the vote-counting occurred.[37]

Hardly less important than procedural correctness is the political context in which elections are held. As Chomsky and Herman point out, ostensibly free elections can in fact be much less than free if critical contextual conditions are not met; notably: (1) freedom of speech and assembly; (2) freedom of the press; (3) freedom to organize and to maintain intermediate economic, social, and political groups, such as unions, peasant organizations, and political clubs; (4) freedom to form political parties and to mount partisan campaigns free of fear of violence; and (5) absence of state terror and a climate of fear among the public.[38] Chomsky and Herman concede that many of these conditions were only imperfectly met in Nicaragua. Arguably, they do not concede enough—as noted in Chapter 2, Chomsky is less than completely forthcoming in his discussion of Sandinista abuses of human rights. Still, Chomsky and Herman document convincingly that *all* of the contextual requirements for democratic elections were more nearly met in Nicaragua than in El Salvador and Guatemala. Often, the comparison isn't even close.

The common thread running through Chomsky and Herman's comparisons is the simple reality that Guatemala and El Salvador were indeed "terror states," while Nicaragua, for all its human rights infractions, was not. On freedom of the press, for example, they point out that the *only* Salvadoran newspapers critical of the government had been closed down in July 1980 and January 1981, "the first because its top editor and two employees were murdered and mutilated by the security forces, the second because the army arrested its personnel and destroyed its plant."[39] The church paper and radio station were repeatedly shut down by bombing attacks. In all, over thirty journalists were murdered in El Salvador in the early 1980s; none of the killers was ever prosecuted. In Guatemala, forty-eight journalists were murdered between 1978 and 1985, and many others kidnapped and threatened; again, there were no prosecutions or even apprehensions.

In Nicaragua, on the other hand, there were no reported deaths of journalists through state violence. And, while *La Prensa,* Nicaragua's leading opposition newspaper, was constantly harassed and frequently censored, it was at least allowed to operate through most of the 1980s; typically it was vociferous in its criticism of the regime, openly expressing sympathy with the invading contras. No comparable opposition paper was allowed to operate in either Guatemala or El Salvador during the early 1980s.[40]

The freedom for political parties to organize and mount effective campaigns also varied greatly among the three Central American countries. In El Salvador in November 1980, five leaders of the principal left opposition coalition, the Democratic Revolutionary Front (FDR), were kidnapped, tortured, and murdered. In October 1982, heavily armed men in civilian clothes seized another seventeen labor leaders and politicians affiliated with parties in the FDR coalition. Two days later, the armed forces announced that they were holding eight of the missing men; the rest were never heard from again.[41] Understandably fearful for their own lives, the surviving FDR leadership declined to contest either the 1982 or 1984 election. Both elections were fought out between the US-supported Christian Democrats and the far right.

The possibilities for independent political action were even more restricted in Guatemala than in El Salvador. "Illicit associations," which in practice meant any organizations potentially to the left of the Christian Democratic Party, were proscribed by law, and an elaborate state surveillance system ensured that none could develop. Chomsky and Herman quote two bishops, representing the Roman Catholic Bishops' Conferences of Scotland and England-Wales, who reported on their 1984 visit to Guatemala: "The civilian population is under almost total control by a heavy army and police presence throughout the country. . . . Much of Guatemala resembles a country under military occupation."[42]

In Nicaragua, on the other hand, the elections were contested by a full spectrum of political parties, ranging from the Sandinistas on the left to solid conservative parties on the right. No political party leaders were ever murdered or kidnapped, and the opposition parties were able to campaign freely without fear. Chomsky and Herman quote the Latin American Studies Association's observer group on the Nicaraguan elections: "It seems clear that the FSLN [Sandinistas] took substantial advantage of its incumbent position and, in some ways, abused it. However, . . . neither the nature of the abuses nor their frequency was such as to cripple the opposition parties' campaigns or to cast doubt on the fundamental validity of the electoral process."[43] The LASA observers added that the Sandinistas did somewhat less than ruling parties in other Latin American countries have done to exploit the advantages of incumbency.[44]

A major candidate did drop out of the running—Arturo Cruz, a respected banker and former Sandinista ambassador to the United States. The circumstances of Cruz's exit are a bit murky, but ultimately, pressure by the United States seems to have been decisive. The Americans feared that Cruz's participation would legitimate the Nicaraguan electoral process.[45]

Were the elections in El Salvador and Guatemala free and meaningful? Chomsky and Herman make a powerful argument that they were not. The notion that democratic elections can take place in an atmosphere of widespread terror has to be regarded as dubious at best. Certainly, the effective exclusion of all parties to the left of center—by means of murder, intimidation, and crippling restrictions on freedom of organization—would disqualify the elections from any strict definition of "free." The elections were not completely meaningless, however. The differences between the Christian Democratic parties in both countries and their extreme right opponents were significant, and the Christian Democratic victories in both countries in 1984–1985 did lay the basis for limited domestic reforms, for some degree of civilian government autonomy from military domination, and even for foreign policy initiatives that showed stirrings of independence from Washington.[46]

Were the elections in Nicaragua free and meaningful? Inarguably, they fell short of meeting a democratic ideal. But they did help to preserve a degree of political pluralism under a revolutionary mass mobilization regime that had authoritarian tendencies. Retrospectively, we know that, like the elections in Guatemala and El Salvador, the Nicaraguan elections set a precedent that eventually saw a peaceful transfer of national power. Most important of all, the general political atmosphere in Nicaragua was far less threatening to the opposition: Nicaraguans opposed to their government (or presumed friendly to the opposition) didn't get murdered, unlike tens of thousands of Salvadorans and Guatemalans.

Chomsky and Herman are surely correct: for all their shortcomings, the Nicaraguan elections were by any reasonable standard freer than their counterparts in the other two countries. Certainly, any claim that the Guatemalan and Salvadoran elections were freer or more meaningful than those in Nicaragua should be dismissed as partisan nonsense. That however, is precisely what the Reagan administration effectively did claim; the US media, according to Chomsky and Herman, accommodated that claim.

As in their comparison of worthy and unworthy victims, Chomsky and Herman use both qualitative and quantitative content analysis of the US media to support their arguments. The quantitative analysis is much more limited than in the previous case, however—it examines only *New York Times* coverage of the Nicaraguan and Salvadoran elections of 1984.

Chomsky and Herman show that the *Times*' coverage of the two elections differed in its much closer and more consistent concern with relevant contextual factors in the case of Nicaragua than in the case of El Salvador. Since both elections seemed generally acceptable from a procedural point of view, consideration of context was important to put the elections and their results in a more realistically critical perspective. The *Times*' much greater emphasis on context in covering the Nicaraguan elections thus fell in with Washington's desire to delegitimate the Nicaraguan elections while hailing the Salvadoran ones. Thus, not one of twenty-eight articles on the Salvadoran elections in the *Times* mentioned the absence of a free press or restrictions on organizational freedom as factors conditioning the election. On the other hand, twelve of twenty-nine articles covering the Nicaraguan election mentioned limited press freedom in Nicaragua. Only one article on El Salvador mentioned limitations on free speech and assembly, and none mentioned any limitations on the ability of candidates to qualify and campaign. (The *Times* correspondents presumably did not consider the high risk of getting murdered a limitation on a candidate's ability to campaign.) On the other hand, ten of twenty-nine Nicaraguan articles mentioned impediments to free speech and assembly, and sixteen cited inhibitions on the candidates' ability to qualify and campaign freely. Only three articles on El Salvador cited state violence or a climate of fear; an equal number cited similar concerns with regard to Nicaragua.[47]

In countries undergoing major internal warfare, another condition potentially affecting election outcomes is rebel activity. More than half of the articles in the *Times* mentioned rebel efforts in El Salvador to disrupt the elections, even though there were no reports of violence at any polling stations. In Nicaragua, on the other hand, the contras physically attacked several polling stations and threatened election workers, in addition to issuing radio appeals for abstentions. Not one of the *Times* articles on the Nicaraguan elections mentioned contra attempts to disrupt them. (The contrast between Nicaragua and El Salvador on this score is less dramatic than painted by Chomsky and Herman. While the Salvadoran rebels did not attack polling stations, they did make other violent efforts to disrupt the vote: for example, mining roads, disrupting electric power, and turning people back from trips to polling stations.[48] Still, the disparity in the *Times*' coverage of this question is striking.)

In short, a citizen whose only source of information on the elections in the two countries was the *New York Times* would surely have regarded the Nicaraguan elections with great skepticism; he would have had little basis for a similar view of the Salvadoran elections.

Probably because of the magnitude of the methodological task, Chomsky and

Herman did not apply the same quantitative content analysis to the rest of their media sample as they did to the *Times*. (In the comparison of worthy vs. unworthy victims, the quantitative analysis involved simple counting. In the elections coverage study, it required the coding of media content—a far more complex procedure.) Chomsky and Herman instead extend their argument by citing additional examples of reporting and commentary by other major media—examples that indicate a bias paralleling that which they demonstrated for the *Times*.

Voter turnout, for example is often viewed as an indicator of the validity of an election, and Chomsky and Herman document differential media treatment of voter turnout in El Salvador and Nicaragua. Reporting the Salvadoran elections of 1982, the CBS News anchor Dan Rather proclaimed, "A triumph! A million people at the polls." [49] He did not mention, nor did any other reporter in Chomsky and Herman's media sample, that voting was a legal requirement in El Salvador, whose defense minister shortly before the balloting announced that nonvoting would be regarded as treasonous. Unmentioned also was the Salvadoran practice of stamping voters' ID cards at the voting places as proof of voting. Anyone stopped by police or security forces was obliged to show their ID, which would quickly indicate whether the individual had voted as required. On the other hand, voting was not a legal requirement in Nicaragua, and the authorities had no mechanism for determining whether an individual had voted or not. The seven hundred thousand Nicaraguan citizens who went to the polls in the 1984 elections represented a higher proportion than the million Salvadorans hailed by Rather. Needless to say, there was no praise for the Nicaraguan turnout in the US media surveyed by Chomsky and Herman; nor was there any discussion of the differences in the legal obligation to vote.

The secrecy of the ballot also distinguished voting procedures in Nicaragua and El Salvador. The Salvadoran election procedures retained a dubious tradition of having marked ballots placed in transparent vote boxes in full view of election judges (allegedly to counter ballot-stuffing but obviously opening up opportunities for intimidation). Soldiers or members of the security forces were often present.[50] *Time* and the *New York Times* each mentioned this procedure just once without acknowledging it as a possible breach of the secrecy of the ballot. *Newsweek* and CBS News never mentioned it at all.[51]

The US media would naturally be concerned about freedom of the press as a precondition for a free election in any country. The trials and tribulations of *La Prensa* got plenty of attention from the *New York Times*, *Time*, *Newsweek*, and CBS News during the Nicaraguan election campaign as well as at other times. But none of the US media giants in its election coverage "even mentioned the destruction by physical violence and murder of *La Crónica* and *El Independiente*, or the toll of murdered journalists."[52]

Chomsky and Herman observe that the media coverage of the Guatemalan elections was less extensive than of the other countries. They see it as slightly more balanced, but still overwhelmingly in conformity with a pro-US administration perspective. Media reporting on the Guatemalan elections relied overwhelmingly on US and Guatemalan government sources, Guatemalan candidates (i.e., those permitted to run), and generals. Predictably, these sources cast the elections in a positive light. Less predictable non-government sources were not consulted or reported. The Guatemalan Bishops Conference, for example, issued an important statement prior to the 1985 elections questioning whether the balloting could be meaningful in "a situation close to slavery and desperation": "In order that the longed-for results be obtained, there must be not only the freedom at the moment of casting one's vote, but also a whole series of particular social, political and economic conditions which are, unfortunately, not happening in Guatemala."[53] The bishops' statement was reported in none of the major media Chomsky and Herman surveyed.[54]

Overall, Chomsky and Herman make a strong case for US media bias in the reporting of Central American elections. Still, in the absence of a more comprehensive quantitative content analysis such as the one they performed for the *New York Times*, their analysis is less than fully conclusive. Chomsky and Herman justifiably view the *Times* as a leading indicator of media content, but it cannot be assumed that its reporting was representative of the media as a whole.

My own limited survey of several additional print media turned up a number of counterexamples that suggest a somewhat more diverse picture than the one Chomsky and Herman depict. The *Los Angeles Times*, for example, on the day of the Salvadoran elections of March 1984, printed an op-ed piece that cataloged official repression in El Salvador, decrying "the absence of even the most basic conditions for the exercise of effectual electoral politics."[55] An editorial shortly after the vote noted that the Reagan administration was straining its rhetoric in describing the result as a triumph for democracy.[56] During the week before the Salvadoran elections, the *Washington Post* printed two op-eds that essentially discounted the elections as hollow demonstrations, in view of the lack of essential preconditions for electoral democracy.[57] (The same op-ed pages also contained commentaries that largely supported Reagan administration thinking.) A *Post* editorial as the elections were underway balanced admiration for the Salvadorans' achievement with a warning that the elections were not a cure-all, because El Salvador "is not a country ruled by law."[58] Even the *New York Times* published an op-ed by the leader of the Salvadoran left, Guillermo Ungo, denouncing the elections as a farce, held in an "atmosphere of repression, fear and death."[59]

On Nicaragua, the *Washington Post* published two front-page articles that challenged administration assumptions. The day before the election, the *Post* correspondent Robert McCartney quoted various sources as saying that the administration's successful efforts to induce Nicaraguan opposition parties to drop out of the electoral contest had hurt, rather than aided, the objective of fostering political pluralism in Nicaragua. The article broadly suggested that the Reaganites were more interested in delegitimating the Sandinistas than they were in furthering Nicaraguan democracy.[60] An article on election day quoted diplomats and other observers to the effect that the elections would be "neither the 'genuinely free' contest promised by the ruling Sandinistas nor the 'Soviet-style sham' suggested by the Reagan administration." The article went on to note that "even U.S. diplomats here acknowledged that the Sandinistas have allowed expression of a wide range of political views, including some that were harshly critical of the government."[61] Even the conservative *US News and World Report* told its readers that the United States would not be able to completely dismiss the elections as a sham. *US News* observed that the Sandinistas had given opposition parties access to state-run television and radio as well as public funds for election expenses. The Sandinistas, moreover, had made repeated concessions to Arturo Cruz and other potential candidates to obtain their participation in the contest.[62]

Chomsky and Herman are surely right that the prevailing tendency in the mass media was to celebrate the Salvadorans' and Guatemalans' elections and to dismiss the Nicaraguans,' but it seems that they overstate their case somewhat. The media didn't all sing to the administration's piper: there were discordant voices in the chorus. This does not, however, pose a critical problem for the Propaganda Model. As noted, Chomsky and Herman recognize that the media are not monolithic, and they will tend to reflect the diversity of views within the political elite.

There was indeed a clear diversity of views among the country's political elite on Central American policy during the 1980s. The Reagan administration's policies in Central America had encountered considerable pushback from public opinion and on Capitol Hill. Drawing on an extensive study of media coverage of Central America between 1979 and 1985, the political scientist Daniel Hallin found a surprising willingness to question administration factual claims and rationales. He attributes the media's relative independence to the often heated political contest under way in Washington over Central American policy. The challenge to administration policy—spearheaded by liberal Democrats—often went beyond mere tactical differences to question fundamental assumptions of US foreign policy, touching on this country's stance toward revolutions and the meaning and legacy of Vietnam, among other issues.[63] The Reagan administration, building on the president's overwhelming reelection victory in 1984, was ultimately able to contain and turn back the challenge. But the fact remains that the political elite was seriously divided over Central America in the early 1980s, and the media to some extent reflected that division. Chomsky and Herman fail to acknowledge the limited but noteworthy diversity within the media that resulted. That failure comports with Chomsky's general inclination to downplay the significance of differences between the two major political parties and their respective representatives in government.

THE VIETNAM WAR

The US media are widely credited with having played a major role in presenting to the American public an understanding of the Vietnam War that challenged official pronouncements. Some media critics even claimed that the media had taken on an adversarial role in its reporting of the war, presenting an unduly pessimistic view that ultimately weakened the American will to fight and thus contributed to the final defeat of the US effort.

Chomsky and Herman see it differently. In their view, the media were always supportive of the broad rationales US administrations offered to justify American involvement in Vietnam, from its origins in the 1950s through the escalations of the late 1960s and even beyond. The media did raise questions about the degree to which US objectives were being met, but such questions were basically about tactics. Media reporting and commentary almost never questioned the fundamental justice of this country's objectives in Vietnam. As the elite consensus favoring prosecution of the war began to crack in the late 1960s, the media increasingly gave voice to dissenting views, but still, these usually questioned the prospects for success, rather than the legitimacy, of American policy. In short, the media never did more than to reflect the range of elite views on the war.[64]

Two years before *Manufacturing Consent,* Daniel Hallin's pathbreaking study of media coverage of the war was published.[65] In their broad outlines, Hallin's arguments and findings are almost entirely supportive of those of Chomsky and Herman as just summarized. It is not a slight to Chomsky and Herman to observe that Hallin's book—which they frequently cite—is more comprehensive and systematic than is their chapter on Vietnam in *Manufacturing Consent.* Because Hallin has so conclusively made their case, I will limit my discussion of Chomsky and Herman to a few points where they go beyond Hallin's analysis.

Two major themes recur in Chomsky and Herman's critique of the media's handling of Vietnam. The first is the implicit, unquestioning adoption of the government's interpretative framework for understanding what was happening in that country. Their second recurring theme is the media's failure to convey adequately the impact of the war on the South Vietnamese people.

Chomsky and Herman begin their account of the media's Vietnam coverage with the Geneva Accords and their aftermath. This early period set a pattern: to the limited extent that Indochina was covered, the media relied overwhelmingly on official US government sources and reflected the official government line that Vietnam was on the front lines of a struggle between Communism and the free world. The US government's role after 1954 in undermining the Geneva Accords was practically unreported in the *New York Times* and the major newsweeklies. Communist charges that the United States was contravening the accords were occasionally reported, but relegated to the back pages and treated as propaganda. There were few clues in the American media as to the repressive nature of the Diem regime.[66] The *Times* in June 1956 remarkably described Vietnam as a country "divided into the Communist regime in the north and a democratic government in the south."[67]

Reporters' acceptance of Washington's definition of the issues at stake in Vietnam persisted as US involvement escalated to outright military intervention in the 1960s. Chomsky and Herman cite numerous examples of American war reporters' partisanship as reflected in the language they used. The American war effort was routinely described as a defense of democracy against Communist "aggression" and "subversion." The United States was fighting "international communism," rather than an indigenous revolution. The guerillas as well as the North Vietnamese troops were invariably described one-dimensionally as cruel, ruthless fanatics. That some guerillas might have been motivated by idealistic beliefs or anger at injustice escaped consideration. When reporters used the term "South Vietnamese," it was to refer to the South Vietnamese government and army, never to the South Vietnamese guerillas. American troops were said to be "protecting" or "defending" South Vietnamese villagers even as their shelling and bombardments produced enormous civilian casualties.[68]

The media's overwhelming inclination to accept the US government's interpretive framework for understanding Vietnam was vividly illustrated by the reporting of the Tonkin Gulf incidents. Chomsky and Herman cite Daniel Hallin's convincing demonstration that (in Hallin's words) "on virtually every important point, the reporting of the two Gulf of Tonkin incidents . . . was either misleading or simply false."[69] Chomsky and Herman point out that alternative interpretations of the incidents were available to the media to explore, but they simply chose not to. Questions raised by Senators Wayne Morse and Ernest Gruening were seldom noted, and when they were, it was only to dismiss them. North Vietnamese and Chinese plausible claims of provocation were similarly dismissed, even though *Time* had recently reported on recent US-South Vietnamese sabotage missions inside North Vietnam. Alternative possible explanations of the incidents were explored in the British and French press, as well as in the muckraking *I. F. Stone's Weekly* in the United States. The major US media, instead, treated the US government as the only legitimate source of information, and hence reported as fact the well-doctored official version of reality.[70]

Chomsky and Herman illustrate their second major theme, the failure of the media to convey the impact of the US war effort on the South Vietnamese people, with a number of instances of death and suffering caused by the US military but sparsely if at all reported in the US press. They cite reports that appeared in the Japanese but not the American press of gunboat and helicopter attacks on undefended Mekong Delta villages—attacks that apparently targeted civilians in the absence of any evident military targets. They point out that US war correspondents almost never interviewed the refugees that were streaming into camps and urban slums, who could have testified to the horrors inflicted by US firepower. All three TV networks had policies restricting the broadcast of excessively grisly images.[71]

But more than objecting to the media's failure to report horrors, Chomsky and Herman argue that when horrors were reported, the language used was typically devoid of any hint that what was reported was indeed a horror: "Reporters often did not conceal atrocities committed by the U.S. military forces, although they did not appear to perceive them as atrocities and surely did not express the horror and outrage that would have been manifest if others were the perpetrators, and the United States or its clients the victims."[72] This objection might seem to reflect a failure to understand and appreciate American journalists' commitment to objectivity—it seems to call for correspondents to editorialize, when they see their job as simply reporting "the facts." But a flat, matter-of-fact description of a grisly atrocity is arguably not objective: it suggests that what is being described is routine and unremarkable, unoffensive to our typical moral sensibilities. By suppressing any sense of outrage, a journalist helps convey the idea that the apparently horrible event being reported is perhaps, somehow, not so bad as it seems.

Chomsky and Herman devote a good deal of effort to refuting the claim, advanced in a widely cited study by Peter Braestrup, that the media adopted an adversarial stance toward the war in their reporting of the 1968 Tet offensive. Braestrup's argument, broadly, is that the media portrayed Tet as a defeat for the US war effort, when in fact it was a defeat for the Communists. This misrepresentation of the significance of Tet contributed significantly to a loss of American resolve that eventually led to defeat in the war.[73] Braestrup's thesis, of course, constitutes a serious, direct challenge to Chomsky and Herman's claims of media bias in favor of the war effort.

Hallin had dealt with the Braestrup thesis indirectly, pointing out that the media did accept the US government's claims that Tet was in fact a defeat for the Communists. Hallin argued that rather than marking a turning point in public and elite opinion, the dramatic coverage of Tet, especially on television, accelerated trends already underway.[74]

Chomsky and Herman confront Braestrup more directly and exhaustively than does Hallin. Expanding on a point made by Hallin, they show that the media's initial reporting of the offensive was if anything less pessimistic than the internal assessments underway in official Washington, which reacted to Tet with a mixture of shock and confusion. They demonstrate that the poll data Braestrup himself presents belie his claim that media coverage turned public opinion against the war. Chomsky and Herman also argue convincingly against Braestrup's claim that the media were decisive in turning decision makers against the war. Media reports could hardly have made a decisive impact on Washington's perceptions of the war, given the availability of military briefings, intelligence reports, and other abundant information sources available to the administration and its advisers.[75]

Chomsky and Herman thus effectively refute Braestrup's claim that an adversarial media undermined the American will to win in Vietnam. On the other hand, they have no trouble acknowledging that the media's reporting of the Tet offensive intensified a developing awareness in the broad American public of the intractable nature of the war America was fighting. But the media's portrayal of the obstacles to American victory never outpaced the political elite's own consciousness of those obstacles. The media mirrored the doubts and controversy that had already become a major part of the story of the American experience with Vietnam.

Even after Tet, Chomsky and Herman correctly insist, the media continued to accept the core assumptions legitimating US involvement in Vietnam. After Tet, questions were more often raised as to whether winning this righteous battle was worth the cost, and even whether victory was possible. But these were questions about the cost-effectiveness of the means chosen to achieve a set of ends whose rectitude continued to go essentially unquestioned.

The Propaganda Model in Perspective

The US media's coverage of foreign policy issues has been the subject of a considerable body of social scientific research over the course of the last three decades. This work overwhelmingly confirms Chomsky and Herman's basic proposition that the American mass media demonstrate a consistent and systematic bias toward presenting facts and opinions that validate the currently prevailing assumptions of US foreign policy. Perspectives opposed to current US foreign policy tend to inform media coverage only when such oppositional perspectives are to be found within the nation's political leadership—typically, in Congress.

EMPIRICAL FINDINGS

In a seminal article on press-state relations in the United States, the political scientist Lance Bennett in 1990 put forth an hypothesis that with modifications has been repeatedly validated by subsequent researchers. Bennett's hypothesis was that the major media in the United States "index" their news reporting and commentary on any given topic to accord with the range of views expressed by the country's political leadership. Thus, the range of perspectives to be found in the media reflects the spectrum of debate in official Washington. If a government policy has broad bipartisan support, it is extremely difficult to find reporting that would tend to call that policy into question.[76]

For an initial test of his hypothesis, Bennett chose a topic we already have some familiarity with—US policy toward Nicaragua, particularly the issue of the Reagan administration's effort to secure funding for the contras. His data sample consisted of all news articles and editorials indexed under "Nicaragua" in the *New York Times Index* for the period from January 1, 1983, to October 15, 1986—2,148 articles and editorials in total. Bennett found a remarkable correlation between congressional opposition to administration policy and opposition expressed in the op-ed pages of the *Times*. When congressional opponents of administration policy were active, opposing *Times* op-ed coverage went up; when congressional dissent abated, so did *Times* criticism. Most notably, after the administration in the spring of 1986 won a crucial contra funding vote in Congress, congressional opposition to the administration policy collapsed. The *Times*' news coverage of Nicaragua plummeted, as did expressions of opposition to administration policy on its editorial and op-ed pages. Bennett notes that opinion polls showed strong public opposition to contra funding throughout the period examined: public opinion, clearly, was not a criterion of newsworthiness.

Bennett and other scholars found a similar pattern in media coverage of the first Gulf War in 1990–1991. The Bush administration began to build its case for war against Iraq while Congress was on vacation in the summer of 1990, and congressional doubts were slow to develop. Media coverage of the crisis in its early stages was largely shaped by the administration's framing of the issues. Only as congressional skepticism began to surface during the course of the fall did reporting and commentary make room for alternative perspectives. Even then the media reflected the relatively narrow range of opinions debated, with a focus on issues of means rather than ends. When Congress in January 1991 approved a resolution supporting the administration's position, debate in Congress shut down, and debate in the media all but ended as well.[77]

The first Gulf War prompted an important elaboration of Bennett's indexing hypothesis. The political scientists Robert Entman and Benjamin Page noted that media attention to different perspectives on the war was calibrated according to perceptions of the degree of power exerted by supporters and critics of the war. When the administration seemed clearly to be prevailing, its views dominated the media more decisively than when congressional opponents seemed to have some chance of exerting an impact. Thus, journalists engaged in what media scholars have called "power indexing": they followed cues from appointed and elected public officials, but not all such public officials were equal. Those who seemed to be in a superior position to influence the course of events got more attention.[78]

A broader study of print and broadcast coverage of eight US military interventions abroad after Vietnam found a similar, consistent pattern. Interventions in which the Washington establishment was highly united (the bombing of Libya in 1986, the invasion of Panama in 1989, and the initial buildup to the first Gulf War) were covered with practically unanimous approbation by the media. Controversy within the political elite (over interventions in Grenada and Somalia, and, for a limited period, over the first Gulf War) was reflected in a still limited but much higher level of reporting of contrary facts and opinion.[79] Still another broad study of foreign policy crises between 1945 and 1991 concluded that the US media generally played the role of "government's little helper": "It is a truism that journalists find it difficult to report critically on government activity during foreign policy crises. They must contend not only with officials who strain to control the news, but with fear that tough reporting will undermine the government's ability to deal with the crisis. As a result, journalists often simply 'rally round the flag' and whatever policy the government favors."[80]

Where a solid foreign policy consensus was broadly shared by the American political elite, media reporting reflected a corresponding uniformity. A good example was the differential media treatment of two airline tragedies: the shooting down of a Korean Airlines (KAL) passenger plane in January 1983 by a Soviet warplane and the downing of an Iran Air passenger airliner in July 1988 by the US Navy. A Chomsky observation that the mass media applied a double standard to the two events was confirmed by the research of Robert Entman, who showed that the US mass media closely followed White House cues in its coverage of both incidents.[81] The Reagan administration seized the opportunity for a propaganda campaign against the Soviet enemy by denouncing the KAL shooting as a mass murder in the air. The administration stance was endorsed by a unanimous congressional resolution. The media followed suit, attributing to the Soviet government guilt for a deliberate atrocity. Almost no consideration was given to the possibility that the shooting was a mistake, which would have been a more than reasonable hypothesis given the lack of any rational motive for the Soviets to gratuitously murder hundreds of civilians. The context of the shooting—the fact that the KAL flight had wandered into an area housing highly sensitive military installations, around the time of a scheduled missile test and just after an American spy plane had entered the same area—was largely ignored. The Iran Air shooting, on the other hand, received far less attention in the US media, who generally took it for granted that the shooting was a mistake; news stories focused on human fallibility and the difficulties of forming quick and accurate assessments in militarily sensitive situations.

Objectively, there was no basis for a more forgiving view of the American shooting than of the Soviet. The differential coverage was another excellent illustration of Chomsky and Herman's idea of dichotomization. Chomsky and Herman also compare the media coverage of the KAL shooting to the much more benign treatment accorded the 1973 shooting of a Libyan airliner by Israel, an American ally.[82]

Evidence of the media's responsiveness to political elite opinion and particularly administration perspectives extends well beyond the Cold War. The Bush administration's propaganda buildup to the second Gulf War in 2002–2003 rested on claims about Saddam Hussein's possession of weapons of mass destruction and links to terrorism that were ultimately proved false. Those claims went largely unchallenged in the American media, even though there were plenty of leads available that journalists could have followed to explore alternative accounts.[83] Once the war got under way, US media were far more positive in their coverage than were their counterparts in Germany and the United Kingdom. [84]

Bennett and several colleagues used a power indexing framework to explain the marginalization of alternative story lines on Iraq. The media's perceptions of where the decision-making power lay were critical in shaping news coverage. Thus, Howard Kurtz of the *Washington Post* explained that his newspaper's editors had decided early on that war with Iraq was more or less inevitable, and discouraged journalists who found evidence that conflicted with the administration's rationales for war.[85] Bennett and his colleagues explain that in judging what is news, the media engage in an "ongoing, implicit calibration process" a weighting system based on perceptions of power, a system that determines what gets into the news, what prominence it receives, how long it gets covered, and who gets a voice in the stories. They metaphorically describe this process as the opening and closing of the news gates: "The press gatekeepers (that is, the news executives) open the gates wider or close them more tightly as they perceive potentially decisive challenges or a lack of challenges to the most powerful institutional players and their agendas." Accordingly, judgments about the importance and credibility of many dominant issues are based not so much on "whether [perspectives] are supported by available facts, but whether they have powerful champions, and whether they go unchallenged (or survive challenges) by other powerful players."[86]

EXPLANATIONS

Chomsky and Herman have explained US media behavior in terms of the operation of five filters, but they don't assign any order of importance to the filters; nor do they really explain interactions among the five filters. This absence of explanatory detail reflects an important limitation of the Propaganda Model: Chomsky and Herman treat the media like so many black boxes. They are mainly interested in what comes out of the boxes (media content) and comparing it to what goes in (raw facts, elite influences), but they have little to say about what happens inside, except to posit the operation of the five filters. Thus, they pay relatively little attention to what actually goes on at a newspaper or broadcast news channel—the practices of fact-gathering, writing and editing that govern how news is actually "worked up."[87](In this regard, they are not very different from many of the academic media scholars discussed in this chapter.) A more fully satisfactory explanation of media output would require greater attention to production processes.

Chomsky and Herman seem to place the most emphasis on the first filter, the concentration of corporate ownership of the media, but they don't claim that this filter alone—or this filter in combination with one or more of the others—is a sufficient explanation for the patterns of media content observed. Most media scholars have focused on the sourcing filter (though they don't use the term "filter") to explain media coverage of foreign policy issues. One of the most established findings of media research is that reporters rely heavily on public officials as sources of news stories and for framing the content of stories. The dominance of official, and particularly executive branch sources, has been particularly pronounced in foreign policy reporting.[88] The scholarly literature echoes many of Chomsky and Herman's explanations for this phenomenon, though with some differences in emphasis.

Media specialists frequently cite two sourcing-related factors pointed to by Chomsky and Herman: the economics of news gathering and the "principle of bureaucratic affinity."[89] Tapping into the vast overseas information resources of the federal government enables media to economize on their own information expenditures; the government, moreover, is organized efficiently to meet the needs of the media, which are themselves large bureaucracies with structurally predictable needs.[90] As Chomsky and Herman point out, reporters tend to be concentrated in places where foreign policy news is most likely to break—notably, the White House, the Pentagon, and the State Department. According to Timothy Cook, the resultant organization of reporting into regular "beats" redounds to the advantage of the executive branch over Congress as newsworthy sources. While reporters have highly regular interactions with executive branch officials, reporting on Capitol Hill is more freewheeling, attending as it does to 538 competing separate sources of information.[91]

Most media specialists place far more emphasis than Chomsky and Herman do on professional norms in explaining journalists' deference to government officials as sources of information. Daniel Hallin recounts the rise of an ethic of "objective journalism" that developed in the early decades of the twentieth century, displacing the practices of what was often a very openly partisan press.[92] "Objectivity" involved above all an avoidance of value judgments in reporting and a commitment to "the facts." But which facts? Whose facts? Objectivity required a reliance on the most generally accepted, authoritative sources of information, which, especially on foreign policy issues, meant first and foremost the federal government. The result was an implicit conflation of authority and political legitimacy with objectivity and fairness. A symbiotic relationship of mutual dependence developed in which journalists and officials each used the other side to promote their goals: as Hallin puts it, "Journalists were regularly taken into the confidence of government officials, for whom they were the primary means of communication with the public . . . [and] . . . came to rely on those officials as their primary source of information, to focus on their activities as the basic subject matter of news, to share their perspectives, and often to cooperate with them, though the principles of objectivity limited this more direct kind of relationship."[93]

Eventually symbiosis between officials and journalists developed into broader relationships as journalists took up regular and long-term career beats in Washington. Journalists became part of the Washington establishment and active participants in its political culture, most importantly, in its foreign policy consensus. Journalists and officials came to occupy the same social world, forming what Bennett and his colleagues describe as "a media-political system where the same people—journalists and politicians—attend the same social functions, send their children to the same private schools . . . , and attend the same parties. They also tend to live in the same communities."[94] A journalistic mind-set developed in which considerations of professional and even social acceptance tend to encourage conformity. According to one veteran journalist, challenging the political consensus of the moment "puts you out of step with 95 percent of your colleagues and . . . you feel left out . . . you stop getting invited to parties, and people say you're a crank and a weirdo. You're not part of the team anymore."[95] Clearly, this phenomenon is much more diffuse—and therefore powerful—in shaping media behavior than what is implied by talking simply of reporters' reliance on their sources. I will nevertheless continue to use the term "sourcing filter" to refer to the whole set of often informal relationships with sources that tend to promote reporters' conformism.

Even when journalists look outside of government for expert perspectives on foreign policy developments, they tend to rely disproportionately on experts whose views tend to be oriented toward government: former politicians and government officials and denizens of Washington think tanks.[96] Such individuals have natural inclinations and incentives to express views consistent with the prevailing foreign policy consensus—former government officials are often hopeful future government officials, and tend to align their views with those who might appoint them. Think tankers are often also former or aspiring government officials. Academic specialists, who tend to be on average more removed from the world of Washington, are less often sought after by journalists. Richard Mermin's study of post-Vietnam interventions counted 271 expert guests on PBS's respected

MacNeil/Lehrer Report. Thirty-five percent were former government officials and just 3 percent university academics.[97]

The sourcing filter seems to go very far in explaining mass media deference to political elite assumptions. What contribution, then, do Chomsky and Herman's other filters make to explaining media behavior? The first of their filters, the concentration of corporate ownership of the media, has gotten relatively little attention from academic media researchers, who seem to take it as a given. There is no particular reason to believe that concentrated corporate ownership would specifically affect foreign policy reporting; still, concentration of ownership cannot be dismissed as a contributor to media behavior. The very fact of media concentration by definition involves a reduction in the number, and therefore almost inevitably in the diversity, of news outlets. The range of perspectives available in the media is likely to be reduced accordingly. The fact that most mainstream media organizations are embedded in large corporations must also be consequential. Most journalists today ultimately report to organizations whose prime objectives are determined by profitability rather than by any commitment to public service. Regardless of their personal commitments, journalists may not achieve (if they indeed strive for) complete insulation from the larger corporate culture which, it can be assumed, does not place a particularly high value on journalistic ideals of independence and public service.[98]

Chomsky and Herman's anti-Communist filter was undoubtedly a major influence on the media during the Cold War. As Daniel Hallin explains, the Cold War perspective of a vast struggle between democracy and Communist totalitarianism

> dominated American thinking about international affairs so totally . . . that it became not merely dangerous but virtually impossible for most Americans to question or to step outside it. Americans simply knew no other language for thinking or for communicating about the world.
>
> The journalists were no exception. . . . The ideology of the Cold War was ideally suited to the reduction of . . . complexity: it related every crisis to a single, familiar axis of conflict; it enabled the journalist to explain to the news audience (and to him or herself), with minimum effort and, at least in appearance, great clarity, "what it all meant."[99]

As powerful as anti-Communism was in post–World War II America, it is surprising that Chomsky and Herman don't define the ideological filter more broadly to acknowledge the importance of nationalism. As I argued in Chapter 3, Cold War ideology was actually a blend of anti-Communism and nationalism. And, as we have seen, Chomsky himself attributed to nationalism the ability of some Americans to rationalize their country's brutal behavior in Vietnam. Not coincidentally, he was talking about journalists in particular. (See Chapter 1.) It can be assumed that even with the end of the Cold War and the obsolescence of the anti-Communist filter, the ideological filter in the form of nationalism remains an important variable in explaining journalists' perspectives. There is no reason to doubt that American reporters are like other Americans: they tend to believe that their country is a force for good in the world and resist evidence that contradicts that belief. Just as American reporters shied away from any suggestion that US military operations in Vietnam deliberately targeted civilians, American news stories forty years later were slow to employ the word "torture" in describing what had happened at Abu Ghraib.[100] Allegations of brutal, despicable behavior by their country clash with Americans' views of themselves as a nation; if it is impossible to look away entirely, reporters may nevertheless reach for ways to rationalize or minimize the significance of such behavior. Media in Canada and Europe were much less inhibited in reporting Abu Ghraib than were their American counterparts.[101]

Chomsky and Herman's remaining two filters—advertising and flak—are difficult to assess, but are almost surely less consequential than sourcing, concentration of ownership, and ideology. Chomsky and Herman give examples of advertisers or sponsors inhibiting news coverage of controversial foreign issues, and argue plausibly that the potential for similar advertisers' pushback would have a generally constraining influence on news coverage. Still, this kind of pressure would be most effective in inhibiting threats to specific corporate interests. It is less likely to be an important factor influencing foreign policy coverage of general interest issues.

Flak, like advertising, has the potential to influence news coverage mainly through prophylaxis. The possibility of incurring harsh criticism from media "watchdog" groups, and even sometimes from the federal government, may well have an inhibiting effect on media's coverage of certain issues. The threat of flak can be especially effective when charges of lack of patriotism (utilizing the ideological filter) can be lodged. But prophylaxis is a hard thing to demonstrate, much less measure: it is generally more difficult to show why someone *didn't* do or say something than to show why they *did* do something else, especially if the rejected option never came under explicit consideration. The watchdog groups Chomsky and Herman discuss do have some visibility in the US media world and are probably somewhat effective. It is hard to know how effective, but it seems unlikely that flak from watchdog groups is anywhere nearly as important as any of the first three filters.

The US government sometimes employs flak. A good illustration is the case of Raymond Bonner, a *New York Times* correspondent whose critical reporting on El Salvador in the early 1980s incurred the open displeasure of the State Department. Bonner was soon reassigned from his post and replaced by more administration-friendly reporters. It is not clear what if any direct role administration influence played in Bonner's reassignment. It was widely assumed among other reporters that official pressure had indeed forced Bonner out.[102] That assumption, correct or not, would constitute evidence of the potential effectiveness of official flak. Still, government use of flak is a relatively blunt instrument compared to the other news management techniques available to the executive branch. The ability of executive decision makers to set the news agenda, utilizing their positive, cooperative relationships with reporters, is undoubtedly a far more reliable and regularly utilized tool for shaping the news.

CONCLUSIONS

Manufacturing Consent is a major product of Chomsky's long-standing interest in media criticism. The evidence that Chomsky and Herman present of media acquiescence in the political elite's framing of foreign policy-related news is compelling, and has been confirmed repeatedly by other researchers.[103] Mainstream media scholars, often using power indexing analysis, do tend to be more interested than Chomsky and Herman in exploring the conditions under which the media may demonstrate independence from political elite narratives. These differences are more of emphasis than of fundamental assumptions or approach. Bennett and his colleagues, citing instances of media independence of the Bush administration's Iraq war policies, assert that their framework differs importantly from "some alternative models of press-government relations, particularly models that understand the news media to be little more than a closed-loop system for advancing government propaganda."[104] *Manufacturing Consent* is the lone example they cite of such alternative systems. But this attempt at differentiation from Chomsky and Herman is unconvincing. The instances Bennett et al. cite—of media attention to the dissenting views of the former White House counterterrorism czar Richard Clarke, the former Joint Chiefs chairman John Shakashvili, and the CIA analyst Paul Pillar—can easily fit within Chomsky and Herman's allowance for media diversity in the context of elite dissensus on mainly tactical issues.

A "closed-loop system for advancing government propaganda," moreover, is an unfairly simplistic description of the Chomsky and Herman framework. Chomsky and Herman's choice of terminology can certainly be criticized: a "propaganda model" does suggest a straightforward, one-way flow of officially sanctioned information. Chomsky has a penchant for provocative, overstated language that, in this case, belies the complexity of his analysis. But Bennett and his colleagues have characterized their own findings in terms of "a semi-independent press characterized by moments of relative independence within a more general pattern of compliance with government news management."[105] That sounds like a fairly closed loop, albeit one that occasionally gets untied. Another team of political scientists reach a fair conclusion: "While the propaganda model assumes a far larger circle of powerful elite influences on the news than the 'indexing' framework, when it comes to the nitty-gritty of reporting practices, the two are not incompatible."[106]

Manufacturing Consent, then, deserves to be recognized as a significant contribution—indeed, a pioneering contribution—to the voluminous literature on the American mass media's treatment of foreign policy. But recall that Chomsky and Herman do not frame their model narrowly as a device for the analysis of media coverage of foreign policy. What of the broader claims that Chomsky and Herman make for their Propaganda Model?

Chomsky and Herman maintain that their model shows how the media "serve to mobilize support for the special interests that dominate the state and private activity." This claim is a good deal harder to pin down—in social science jargon, to operationalize—than the more specific claim that the media will tend to reflect the elite foreign policy consensus. We can safely assume that the "special interests" referred to are those of the corporate class, but how do we define those interests? Chomsky and Herman, for example, cite benign media treatment of the chemical industry as an illustration of the Propaganda Model in action, but surely they would not claim that their model excludes the possibility of any and all media muckraking of corporate abuses.[107] Why, and under what conditions, do some industries get scrutinized while others escape scrutiny? Chomsky and Herman don't ask such questions, much less provide answers or guidance as to how to look for answers.

Chomsky and Herman's Propaganda Model is really something looser than a model—we can call it an analytic framework. Rather than offering predictions or explanations, it suggests relevant areas of inquiry. In its original, broad formulation, the Propaganda Model is most realistically viewed as a framework that focuses on the sensitivity of the mass media to corporate interests and on their disinclination to pursue lines of inquiry that raise questions about the nature and legitimacy of the capitalist system. Clearly, it is a framework inspired by a leftist ideological perspective that seeks to explore alternatives to the existing organization of economic life and distribution of political power. It is neither "right" nor "wrong." It has heuristic value for those who broadly share its authors' radical perspective; it is relevant and suggestive to researchers interested in investigating possibilities for major social change. It is naturally less interesting or useful for those who hold more centrist or conservative views.

The Role of Intellectuals

In 1982, Chomsky wrote, "In every society there will emerge a caste of propagandists who labor to disguise the obvious, to conceal the actual workings of power, and to spin a web of mythical goals and purposes, utterly benign, that allegedly guide national policy."[108] Nowhere, to my knowledge, does Chomsky cite Marx's famous dictum that the ruling ideas of every epoch are the ideas of its ruling class, but the foregoing quote points to something very similar. Those who hold political and economic power have the means to enlist in their service those who generate ideas. The dominant or ruling ideas of our time will therefore tend to be those that legitimate the existing structure of power and privilege and justify the policies pursued in its interests. But ideas must be developed and propagated. The propagation of the ruling ideas, particularly at the level of the mass public, is chiefly the function of the media. The articulation, refinement, and development of those ideas, and their dissemination to and utilization by the privileged strata and their servants, is the work of intellectuals.

But not all intellectuals. Chomsky accepts the distinction made by the establishment-oriented Trilateral Commission of the 1970s between "value-oriented intellectuals," who the trilateralists warned were prone to challenge authority and derogate established institutions, and the "technocratic and policy-oriented intellectuals," who, in the commission's view, were more inclined to be responsible and constructive contributors to society. It was the latter group, of course, on whom Chomsky focused in his critique of intellectuals' servitude to power. Most of them were social scientists: mainly political scientists, with economists, sociologists, anthropologists, and historians represented as well.[109]

Chomsky originated his critique of intellectuals in tandem with his critique of America's war in Vietnam. One of Chomsky's first significant publications outside his own field of linguistics was the essay I mentioned in the Introduction, "The Responsibility of Intellectuals." Troubled by so many Americans' apparent apathy in the face of the US government's brutalization of the people of Vietnam, Chomsky recalled a question posed two decades earlier by Dwight Macdonald on the responsibilities of peoples. To what extent, Macdonald had asked, were the German and Japanese peoples responsible for the atrocities committed by their governments? And, redirecting the question, Macdonald had also asked to what extent the American and British peoples were responsible for the massive terror bombings committed by their own governments against the civilian populations of the axis powers.

Chomsky might be expected to ask a similar question about Americans and Vietnam, but rather than pose the question with regard to the American people as a whole, he focuses specifically on America's intellectuals. He sees the "responsibility of peoples" as debatable, but the responsibility of intellectuals to seek and tell the truth is clear, because it is they whose training has given them the knowledge and ability to understand the actions of their government. It is the intellectuals who have a privileged opportunity, and therefore responsibility, "to expose the lies of governments, to analyze actions according to their causes and motives and often hidden intentions. . . . to seek the truth lying hidden behind the veil of distortion and misrepresentation, ideology, and class interest through which the events of current history are presented to us."[110] Instead, leading American intellectuals served as apologists for American foreign policy in general and its Vietnam War in particular. In a few cases—notably the political scientist McGeorge Bundy and the economist Walt Rostow—they actually served in government as leading planners of the war.

Much of Chomsky's early writings was devoted to exposing the biases prominent intellectuals displayed in their support for the war. He cites a Rostow memoir, for example, for its crudely one-sided and frequently distorted account of Cold War history and in particular of the origins of the Vietnam War. Another Chomsky target is the Harvard political scientist Samuel Huntington, who proclaimed the virtues of the "American-sponsored urban revolution" in Vietnam while eliding the fact that urbanization was largely the result of the flight of Vietnamese peasants from the Americans' bombardment of their villages and destruction of their farmlands.[111]

Chomsky is hardly gentler in his treatment of the eminent historian Arthur

Schlesinger Jr. After leaving the Kennedy White House, Schlesinger became skeptical of America's prospects for success in Vietnam. Still, Schlesinger refrained from any fundamental criticism of American objectives even as he became an advocate of a negotiated solution to the war. Chomsky points out that Schlesinger clearly understood the devastation the United States was wreaking on the Vietnamese people, yet he stoutly refused to cast doubt on the nobility of American motives; he reserved his moral outrage instead for the actions of the Viet Cong and North Vietnamese.[112] In criticizing the journalist Joseph Alsop, who was predicting American success in Vietnam, Schlesinger averred that "we all pray that Mr. Alsop will be right."[113]

Chomsky also has no trouble finding examples of intellectuals who did not directly serve the government but whose dedication to American foreign policy objectives reached grotesque extremes. Thus, the Reverend R. J. de Jaegher, regent of the Institute of Far Eastern Studies at Seton Hall University, explained that, like all people who live under Communism, the North Vietnamese "would be perfectly happy to be bombed to be free."[114] David Rowe, the director of international studies at Yale, proposed to a congressional committee that the United States engage in massive purchases and hoarding of wheat in order to produce mass starvation in China: "Mind you, I am not talking about this as a weapon against the Chinese people. It will be. But that is only incidental. The weapon will be a weapon against the Government because the internal stability of that country cannot be sustained by an unfriendly Government in the face of general starvation."[115]

Most of the intellectuals targeted by Chomsky had scholarly credentials—most typically, PhDs in political science—that enabled them to claim expertise in foreign policy. Chomsky, on the other hand, vigorously attacks what he calls the "cult of the expert"—the claim that only scholars with generally recognized credentials in national security affairs can be regarded as credible analysts of American foreign policy.[116] The pro-war "experts" used the language of the behavioral sciences to endow their views with the aura of objectivity. As Chomsky darkly observes, "Science, as everyone knows, is responsible, moderate, unsentimental and otherwise good."[117] Apologists for the war often sought to portray antiwar protesters as driven more by emotion than by realistic, well-informed, and objective analysis. Instead, they celebrated the image of the "tough-minded social scientist" who could understand the need to set aside traditional humanistic values in the pursuit of purportedly objective national interests. In practice, according to Chomsky, only a supporter of American foreign policy goals could win acclaim as a tough and realistic social scientist. Critics who raised more than purely tactical objections, questioning the morality of American policy, were dismissed as unreasonable, emotional ideologues.[118] It is apropos that the Kennedy administration—conspicuous for its utilization of first-class intellectual talent—nurtured a cult of toughness, effectively marginalizing allegedly soft-minded eggheads like Adlai Stevenson and Chester Bowles.[119]

Why were so many American intellectuals so ready to serve American foreign policy, even at its most brutal? Part of the answer, according to Chomsky, is that intellectuals had become a privileged group, and privilege tends to engender a benign attitude toward the established order. Up to a point, Chomsky follows the analysis of the sociologist Daniel Bell. Bell argued that in postindustrial society, intellectuals—historically exponents of radical ideologies—have come to share in a broad consensus that radical social transformation is no longer necessary, and that all major social and economic problems are susceptible to solution within the context of the modern welfare state. But even while large ideological controversies (most importantly, capitalism vs. socialism) are no longer in play, the welfare state poses innumerable specific policy issues whose solution requires careful, expert analysis that can only be provided by a trained technocratic intelligentsia. Chomsky cites Bell's belief that, with the increasing importance of specialized knowledge in running modern society, "the entire complex of social prestige and social status, will be rooted in the intellectual and scientific communities."[120] (Note again: the cult of the expert.) But, Chomsky adds, Bell fails to note that the new consensus of the intellectuals is self-serving: intellectuals have lost interest in transforming society because they play an increasingly important role in running the existing one. The analog of the welfare state in domestic policy is the national security state in foreign policy, and here too, intellectuals played an increasingly important role both as foreign affairs advisers and as advocates for government policy.[121]

Chomsky saw the privileged position of intellectuals—in particular the "technocratic and policy-oriented" types—as due in no small part to the increasingly active role of the federal government in the life of the university, where most intellectuals earned their livelihood. Not only did the government offer professors employment and consulting opportunities, but it became an important source of funding for research. A structure of incentives thus developed that subtly shaped the parameters within which scholars conducted their research. Academics didn't need explicit cues to understand that it was advantageous to develop and pursue research projects that tended to legitimate rather than challenge prevailing orthodoxies.

> Like the media, academic scholarship in general cautiously refrains from analytic investigation of U.S. foreign policy and its roots in domestic power.... Young scholars who might wish to undertake a systematic and rational analysis of the nature and exercise of U.S. power and its domestic determinants are steered in other directions, made to understand that there is little future in this direction. A network of pressures, including grants, promotions, access to external (state and private) power, class interest, the comforts, prestige and privilege that are natural concomitants of what Hans Morgenthau once called "our conformist subservience to those in power"—all these factors and others combine to provide an intellectual milieu in which few serious questions will be raised about sensitive issues.[122]

Academic servitude to power is evident, according to Chomsky, in avoidance of research subjects that might call into question the well-intentioned benevolence of American foreign policy. As specific examples, Chomsky decries the failure of political scientists and contemporary historians to study the role of US corporations in influencing US foreign policy, or to seek the root causes of the Vietnam War in postwar American grand strategy for Asia. Such investigations, which Chomsky believed would reveal the linkages between US business interests and foreign policy choices, are missing from the mainstream literature, and must be sought in the works of unconventional scholars—often dismissed by their professional peers—like William Appleman Williams or Gabriel Kolko.[123]

According to Chomsky, scholars of international relations tended implicitly to accept core legitimating assumptions of US foreign policy. As an example, he devotes several pages to an analysis of a 1965 history of the recent US-Thai relationship by the political scientist (and former CIA official) Frank Darling.[124] (Chomsky and Herman later relied extensively on Darling's book in their discussion of Thailand in *The Washington Connection and Third World Fascism*.) Darling gives what Chomsky considers a fair and accurate account of America's close involvement in the development and maintenance of a corrupt and brutal Thai dictatorship. But, though he clearly regards the whole situation as unpleasant, Darling rejects any alternative to continuing current US policy. To push for political and economic reforms, for example, would risk US relations with Thailand and other allies; besides, Darling writes that "extensive interference in the domestic affairs of other nations, no matter how well-intentioned, is contrary to American traditions."[125] Chomsky is cuttingly sarcastic in citing this last quote, which flies in the face of practically everything Darling himself had written about the history of the US-Thai relationship (not to mention the US relationship with nearby Vietnam). But the dogma of American benevolence must always be asserted, even in the teeth of contrary evidence.

Another academic who draws Chomsky's barbs is Norman Graebner, despite Chomsky's description of Graebner as "an excellent historian, a critic of Cold War idiocies."[126] Commenting on the historian's analysis of American foreign policy during the first fifteen years of the Cold War, Chomsky quotes Graebner's observation: "It was ironic that this nation generally ignored the principles of self-determination in Asia and Africa where it had some chance of success and promoted it behind the Iron and Bamboo curtains where it had no chance of success at all."[127] Chomsky, instead, finds it ironic that Graebner is unable to confront the obvious conclusion of his own findings: that American support for self-determination was hypocritical, a weapon to be used or discarded as convenient. Thus, even a first-rate scholar who deviated somewhat from Cold War orthodoxy could not free himself completely from the prevailing dogmatic belief in American good intentions.[128]

I WAS AN UNDERGRADUATE and then a graduate student of political science during the 1960s and 1970s. I'm not sure when I first read "The Responsibility of Intellectuals": whether when it was first published in the *New York Review of Books* in 1967 or when it was reprinted in *American Power and the New Mandarins* two years later. (I have used my first-owned copy of *Mandarins* in writing this book. Its pages are yellow with age and I use a rubber band to hold them together.) That essay, and others in *Mandarins,* came to me practically as revealed truths—truths that I had already perceived somewhat dimly but were now being articulated powerfully and clearly by a leading public intellectual.[129] More than forty years later, my view of those early Chomsky writings is more qualified but not fundamentally changed.

My disappointment was palpable when, in the spring of 1965, a forceful anti-Vietnam War petition was published in the *New York Times* with the signatures of professors from many universities, including my own Columbia, but no Columbia political scientists. That disappointment was hardly assuaged when, shortly thereafter, a milder petition statement, more deferential toward US government claims, was published and included one or two Columbia political science signatories, out of a department of several dozen members.

Chomsky was basically right. Political science—and, to a lesser extent, other social sciences—were deeply committed to Cold War definitions of reality in the 1950s and 1960s. There was little in a political science education at Columbia to equip a student with the tools to question the basic belief that a beneficent America was engaged in a mortal struggle to save the world from a deadly Communist enemy. And, while Cold War concerns did not explicitly inform the approach to the study of the US political system, they were not far in the background of a dominant paradigm that celebrated American pluralist democracy.

Chomsky's attack on the cult of the expert also struck home. Those of us who were outraged by America's onslaught on Vietnam did have to contend with the valid claim that most of the experts were indeed on the side of the government. The experts, at least initially, mostly agreed that the United States had to stand tough against the Communists in Indochina and the soft-minded intellectuals and ideologues at home. As Chomsky explains, strictly tactical objections were admissible, but morally principled ones were not. One Columbia economist with whom I spoke objected to the "moralistic" tone of that first antiwar petition. Not stuff for tough-minded social scientists.

There were, of course, exceptions. The political scientists Hans Morgenthau at Chicago and Stanley Hoffmann at Harvard and the Asia historian George McT. Kahin at Cornell all opposed the war. While they stressed pragmatic considerations, their opposition went beyond the practical to include moral concerns. Notable as they were, these men were atypical. There is no relevant survey data, but there can be little doubt that supporters of the war's legitimacy—people like Zbigniew Brzezinski and Roger Hilsman at Columbia, Ithiel de Sola Pool at MIT, and David Rowe at Yale—were by far more representative of the community of foreign policy intellectuals. Chomsky cites a 1967 pro-war manifesto by fourteen leading political scientists and historians of US Asian policy.[130] In contrast, the fervently antiwar Committee of Concerned Asian Scholars, formed in 1968, was for the most part peopled by junior members of their disciplines.

Why were the experts mostly on the side of the government? The burgeoning of federal funding for social science and especially foreign policy-related research during the Cold War years has been well documented. MIT's Center for International Studies was practically a CIA subsidiary during the 1950s, according to one scholar, and it had many imitators. The Russian research centers at both Columbia and Harvard and Princeton's Center for International Social Programs all had extensive State Department and CIA links.[131] By the end of the 1960s, federal agencies were spending about $40 million per year (roughly $260 million in 2009 dollars) on foreign affairs contract research, one-third of it for the Defense Department.[132] Samuel Huntington in 1967 reported that well over 90 percent of social science work on Vietnam was being conducted under the auspices of the US government.[133]

There is no way to prove that federal patronage decisively shaped academic intellectuals' worldviews; it is even possible to point to instances where federally funded researchers told their paymasters things that they presumably didn't expect or want to hear.[134] Still, it would require an act of faith to believe that the national security state had no significant impact on the academic disciplines it patronized. Vendors, after all, like to keep their customers happy, which means anticipating their needs, empathizing with their concerns, and—yes, if possible—telling them what they want to hear. The availability of federal dollars determined many research agendas. Especially in the fields of development studies, area studies, communication research, and operations research, the government-university nexus was highly influential in the development of the respective disciplines: in establishing the leading research institutes, shaping the texts and methodologies, and defining the critical bodies of knowledge.[135]

Much has changed since Chomsky wrote his early essays on the intellectuals. As noted in Chapter 3, the Vietnam War critically fractured the Cold War foreign policy consensus and helped form a new generation of scholars, including social scientists, many of whom saw the world very differently from their predecessors. The change was perhaps earliest and most evident in the field of the history of American foreign policy. By the mid 1960s, a new school of "revisionist" historians was challenging orthodox interpretations that absolved the United States of most responsibility for starting and maintaining the Cold War. The antiwar tumult on campuses also had the effect of pushing most government-sponsored social science research out of the university, to be taken up by lower-profile contractors like the Rand Corporation, Abt Associates, and Mitre. By the first decade of the twentieth century, federal funding of the academic social sciences had largely evaporated.

Social scientists, for their part, have become wary of doing work for the government. According to the political scientist Alan Wolfe, "Work for any government agency, particularly the Central Intelligence Agency, and your chances of getting tenure will diminish with more than deliberate speed."[136] The changes in political science are evident in the widespread opposition of international relations specialists to the US invasion of Iraq—a marked contrast to the general acceptance of the Vietnam intervention forty years earlier. Even in the analysis of

US domestic politics, as noted earlier, the 1950s scholarly consensus celebrating democratic pluralism has yielded to a more critical questioning of the nature and sources of political inequality.

Chomsky recognizes that big changes took place in American society as a result of the 1960s. That includes academia: "The universities have changed because the people in them have changed." Still, writing in 1996, Chomsky insisted that intellectuals have not essentially changed because "the *public intellectuals,* people who are in the public arena and who make profound statements about the world and so on—I do not think they have changed a great deal." Chomsky gave no examples or argument to support this assertion; instead he simply reaffirmed his belief that "in any society, the respectable intellectuals, those who will be recognized as serious intellectuals, will overwhelmingly tend to be those who are subordinated to power."[137] Whether or not Chomsky is correct to emphasize continuity over change, many of his original observations remain valid: Intellectuals are ultimately not altogether different from ordinary worldly human beings. They, too, are vulnerable to the lures of status and power. And, if university intellectuals have become less available to government and business elites, a partial functional substitute has arisen in the form of a panoply of think tanks that generate ideas and analysis that is invariably congenial to their corporate funders.[138]

CHOMSKY'S POLEMICS AGAINST LEADING intellectuals of his day did not always go unanswered. Two of Chomsky's antagonists—Arthur Schlesinger Jr. and Samuel Huntington—succeeded in raising some troubling questions about Chomsky's concept of the intellectual's obligation to tell the truth.

Schlesinger wrote a counterattacking review of *Mandarins* published in March 1969.[139] While much of the review engaged specific arguments that Chomsky had advanced, Schlesinger also took the opportunity to question Chomsky's integrity. Chomsky, making a point about US postwar imperial objectives, had quoted a speech by President Truman as follows: "All freedom is dependent on freedom of enterprise. . . . The whole world should adopt the American system. . . . The American system can survive in the world only if it becomes a world system."[140] Schlesinger, with obvious relish, pointed out that Truman in fact had never said those things. The second and third sentences "quoted" are from a book whose author, J. P. Warburg, was giving his own explanation of Truman's thinking, while the first seemed to be a distorted paraphrase of another passage in the Truman speech. Chomsky responded in the pages of *Commentary* magazine with an acknowledgment that he had mistakenly attributed to Truman some remarks by Warburg and a historian who cited him, and that he had compounded the error by garbling one quote. There followed an acrimonious and seemingly endless exchange between Chomsky and Schlesinger in which Chomsky, among other things, claimed that his misquotation nevertheless represented an accurate paraphrase of sections of Truman's speech. Schlesinger argued that it did not.[141] The polemics covered a number of issues. On the narrow question of Chomsky's accuracy in representing Truman's views, the exchange in my judgment came out roughly a draw, with perhaps a slight edge to Schlesinger.[142] The incident would hardly be worth recounting except insofar as it portended what was to be a more than occasional problem in Chomsky's writings: it was not to be the last time that Chomsky misquoted a source in making a point.

A more significant dispute embroiled Chomsky with Samuel Huntington. In July 1968 Huntington wrote an article for *Foreign Affairs* magazine in which he argued that, given the entrenchment of the Viet Cong in much of the Vietnamese countryside, some kind of political accommodation would be necessary between the United States and its South Vietnamese allies on the one hand and the National Liberation Front on the other. He proposed a "bottoms up" settlement which would leave much of the countryside effectively and indefinitely in the hands of the National Liberation Front. This was a significant proposal coming as it was from a long-time supporter of American objectives in Vietnam. A key passage in the Huntington article read as follows:

> With half the population still in the countryside, the Viet Cong will remain a powerful force which cannot be dislodged from its constituency so long as the constituency continues to exist. Peace in the immediate future must hence be based on accommodation.[143]

Chomsky quotes Huntington as follows:

> Writing in *Foreign Affairs,* [Huntington] explains that the Viet Cong is a "powerful force which cannot be dislodged from its constituency so long as the constituency continues to exist." The conclusion is obvious, and he does not shrink from it. We can ensure that the constituency ceases to exist by "direct application of mechanical and conventional power . . . on such a massive scale as to produce a massive migration from countryside to city."[144]

Note how Chomsky not only excises Huntington's last sentence ("Peace in the immediate future . . ."), completely changing the meaning and implication of the passage, but how he goes further, replacing the sentence with his own "paraphrase" of Huntington, which is not a paraphrase at all, but a false attribution. As Huntington noted in response, "It would be difficult to conceive of a more blatantly dishonest instance of picking words out of context so as to give them a meaning directly opposite to that which the author intended." Huntington further pointed out that the phrase "the direct application of mechanical and conventional power" was not his, but a quote of another writer that appeared earlier in his article.[145] Apparently assuming that the only defense of the indefensible is a resounding offense, Chomsky replied with a broadside against Huntington and the war.[146] There was of course no way to refute the inarguable fact that he had misrepresented Huntington's views.

Chomsky here committed a clear act of intellectual dishonesty. Huntington was an appropriate target of criticism for his support for the war. Still, in the

Foreign Affairs article Chomsky quoted, Huntington was not advocating further terror-bombing of the Vietnamese countryside, but rather a major change in US policy. Evidently, Huntington's change of mind did not suit Chomsky's polemical purposes, so he simply ignored what Huntington had said and implied that he had said something different. It was not an admirable performance from an intellectual who had proclaimed that intellectuals have a responsibility to tell the truth.

CHAPTER 5

America in the Post–Cold War World

THE COLD WAR CAME TO AN END around 1990: America's Soviet adversary first freed its empire and then essentially dissolved itself. The threat of international Communism—the dominant theme of American foreign policy practically since the end of World War II—had collapsed. This transformation in the international political scene might presumably have spurred dramatic changes in US foreign policy. For Chomsky, however, the essential continuity in American foreign policy objectives was far more striking than the inevitable but relatively minor changes occasioned by the new international realities. Chomsky's assessment is consistent with his understanding of what the Cold War was really all about. As we saw in Chapter 2, Chomsky regarded the Cold War as basically a smokescreen. It served both superpowers as an excuse to consolidate their control over their respective empires. In Chomsky's view, the disappearance of the United States' Cold War adversary thus created both an opportunity and a challenge for US leaders.

The opportunity lay in the exhilarating possibility of further expanding the reach of US power across the world. Whatever its motives, the Soviet Union had stood in the way of American global ambitions; it functioned as a deterrent, albeit not always effective, to American imperialism. With the Soviets out of the way, the United States could pursue its aggressive international agenda undeterred by concerns of colliding with a dangerous foe.

The challenge lay in finding new justifications for the global primacy of American power in the absence of the ostensible Soviet threat. Accordingly, US leaders contrived new pretexts to substitute for the anti-Communist crusade in justification of an aggressive foreign policy. Three themes in particular proved to be serviceable: the need to counter the threat to international peace and security by "rogue states" and their leaders; a new justification for military interventionism as a response to possible humanitarian catastrophes; and the international war against terrorism. Often, two or all three of the themes were invoked to justify one exercise of American power or another.

In Chomsky's account, US leaders' continued assertion of America's global primacy repeatedly demonstrated an arrogance and brutality that compare with the worst American behavior during the Cold War. The arrogance was reflected in the assumption—sometimes implicit, sometimes openly proclaimed—that the United States was uniquely entitled to pursue its overseas objectives without regard to the constraints of international law and world opinion observed by ordinary countries. The brutality was reflected in its readiness to utilize lethal force to achieve desired outcomes and in its continued complicity in the crimes of client regimes that willingly slaughtered large numbers of their own people when necessary to maintain political control.

Chomsky's critique of post–Cold War American foreign policy, like much of his earlier work, is almost invariably skewed to point to the immorality of American power. His use of evidence is typically selective, and his consideration of counterarguments superficial at best. Sometimes he makes factual assertions that simply don't follow from any evidence he presents. Occasionally, he makes himself look silly in his determination to paint the blackest possible picture of the motives and consequences of American policy. Obviously, these are serious shortcomings. Still, his arguments often have substantial merit, credibly challenging official claims and the narratives that support them.

Empire Redux

According to Chomsky, the second Bush administration's 2003 invasion of Iraq was emblematic of "the declared intention of the most powerful state in history to maintain its hegemony through the threat or use of military force."[1] This is not an extreme claim. That the Bush administration was seeking—or should be seeking—something akin to international hegemony is an argument that has been advanced by both critics and supporters of an aggressive US push for world leadership.[2] Chomsky quotes the Princeton political scientist John Ikenberry, who describes the Bush administration's "grand strategy [that] begins with a fundamental commitment to maintaining a unipolar world in which the United States has no peer competitor . . . a world order in which [the United States] runs the show."[3] In his post–Cold War writings, Chomsky more often uses the term "hegemony" than "empire" to describe the worldwide reach of American power, but the change in terminology does not signal any change in his perspective.

Chomsky nowhere specifically defines what he means by "hegemony"; he clearly recognizes that global hegemony falls well short of actual domination—he repeatedly points out that the US often doesn't get its way at the United Nations, for example. Probably Ikenberry's "a world order in which [the United States] runs the show" is a fair statement of Chomsky's concept of American hegemony: a position of power that is less than absolute, but still incomparably greater than that of any other nation, combined with a willingness on the part of American leaders to compel other countries to acquiesce in American global objectives. Other analysts use terms like "primacy," "ascendancy," "leadership," "empire," and "predominance" to characterize the international position of the United States since the mid-twentieth century and especially since the end of the Cold War. Whatever the precise definition and term employed, it is probably impossible to find any reputable analyst of international relations who would challenge Chomsky's claim that the United States, even after the Cold War, showed a consistent determination to maintain its leading position among nations.[4] Chomsky's use of "hegemony" has fairly wide acceptance, and I will continue to use it here.

Unlike many analysts, Chomsky doesn't see the second Bush administration's aggressive foreign policy as a dramatic departure from historical US international behavior, but as an expression of long-standing objectives and strategies, albeit taken to a reckless extreme. American elites even before the end of World War II had planned for a world economy dominated by US business interests. Successive administrations in Washington had sought to realize that grand strategic objective, extending the reach of US political and military power throughout the globe and utilizing the Soviet menace as their pretext. The end of the Cold War in no way led to a reduction in the United States' global ambitions. Chomsky points to the Clinton administration's insistence on expanding NATO as an early sign of the continuation of US hegemonic objectives. The collapse of the Soviet enemy might have been expected to render NATO—whose ostensible main purpose was defense against that enemy—obsolete. But NATO had historically served the objective of keeping Europe tied to American power. The expansion of NATO, which violated informal pledges made to Soviet leader Mikhail Gorbachev, enabled the United States to strengthen its control over NATO by bringing into the alliance small Eastern European countries with more reliably pro-American inclinations than the countries of "Old Europe."[5]

AN EXCEPTIONAL HEGEMON?

As Chomsky sees it, US leaders have continued as always to cloak their pursuit of global hegemony with the noblest of objectives: America seeks to promote freedom, democracy, and human rights throughout the world. The rationale for American power-seeking sometimes takes the form of "American exceptionalism": the doctrine holding that the United States has a unique role to play in the world as a carrier of universal values. Chomsky is relentless in his attack on what he regards as the myths of American essential goodness and benevolence, which are at the core of American exceptionalism: American ideals, always invoked, are readily violated in practice when interests so dictate.

Exceptionalism, Chomsky points out, is nothing new—one or another version of that doctrine has repeatedly been invoked by imperial powers to justify their domination of others. Thus, even such an admirable figure as John Stuart Mill could fall for imperial Britain's own version of exceptionalism: Chomsky recounts Mill's argument that Britain should not shrink from the exercise of its power, even though other countries would accuse it of base motives. England's critics could not understand that England is "a novelty in the world," selflessly bearing the costs of intervention, whose benefits would be widely shared among countries. In contrast, Chomsky quotes US founding father John Adams, who harbored no such illusions: "Power always thinks it has a great soul and vast views beyond the comprehension of the weak."[6]

Long before the end of the Cold War, American exceptionalism, though seldom invoked explicitly, served to rationalize the assumption that the United States was uniquely entitled to pursue its overseas objectives without regard to the constraints observed by "ordinary" countries. That arrogant presumption, as

Chomsky sees it, is possible because of America's unique power position: "The most powerful state in the world is not going to accept international authority. No other state would accept it, either, if it could get away with it."[7] Indifference to if not dismissiveness of world opinion and international law was frequently reflected in US behavior at the United Nations: Chomsky points out that beginning in the 1960s the United States was by far the most frequent user of the veto in the Security Council, with Britain in second place and France and the Soviet Union far behind. Chomsky also cites American official reaction to the World Court decision in 1985 faulting the United States for its not-so-covert war against Nicaragua and ordering the aggressor to cease and desist and pay reparations. The United States dismissed the court's decision, with the State Department using language suggesting that the American attack on Nicaragua was a domestic US matter over which the court had no jurisdiction. A Security Council resolution affirming the court's decision met with a US veto. Then, the United States stood practically alone, joined only by Israel and El Salvador, in voting against a General Assembly resolution calling for compliance with the court's decision.[8] The United States has been similarly indifferent to world opinion in pursuing its long-standing vendetta against Cuba. In 2006, for the fifteenth year in a row, the United States opposed a General Assembly resolution calling for an end to the US embargo of Cuba. The vote tally, similar to earlier years, was 183 to 4.[9]

Chomsky sees America's imperial arrogance also in the routine expectation that the United States is entitled to special treatment in all manner of international agreements. Chomsky points out that the United States often refuses to ratify human rights conventions; when it does, it invariably insists on exclusions for itself. The United States has also stood in the way of important international disarmament initiatives. In the mid-1990s NATO under US leadership turned down a Russian proposal (offered jointly with Belarus and the Ukraine) for a nuclear weapons–free zone (NWFZ) from the Arctic to the Black Sea, encompassing Central Europe. In response, Russia withdrew the policy of no first use of nuclear weapons that it had adopted under Gorbachev.[10] Instead of a nuclear-free zone, the United States under the second Bush administration sought missile defense installations in Eastern Europe. Chomsky finds Russia's disquiet over US intentions entirely reasonable.[11] He quotes the Rand Corporation and other military analysts who approvingly characterize missile defense as basically offensive in nature—as "not a *shield* but an *enabler* of U.S. action" aimed at "preserving America's ability to wield power abroad."[12]

Consistent with its insistence on moving ahead with missile defense, the Bush administration repeatedly thwarted arms control initiatives by the international community that would have placed limits on American power. Chomsky points to two UN Disarmament Committee resolutions in October 2002 that passed unanimously with just two abstentions: the United States and Israel. One of these called for stronger measures to prevent the militarization of outer space; the other reaffirmed the 1925 Geneva Protocol prohibiting chemical and biological warfare. (The Clinton administration, too, had balked at UN efforts to close outer space to military uses.)[13] The administration also defied world opinion in opposing a fissile material cutoff treaty (FISSBAN). In 2004, the UN Committee on Disarmament voted in favor of a verifiable FISSBAN, which would place international controls on the production and processing of weapons-usable nuclear materials. The vote was 147 to 1, with two abstentions (Britain and Israel). The following year, the full General Assembly voted in favor of FISSBAN. The same two dependable US allies abstained, but this time, Chomsky notes ironically, the United States was joined by Palau in voting nay.[14]

In sum, Chomsky makes a strong case that the United States has behaved consistently as if it is entitled to act as the world's hegemon, exempt from the rules and constraints that the international community has sought to place on individual members in the interest of advancing peace and stability. Indeed, Chomsky could be criticized for understating his case, since there are examples of American unilateralism that he hardly mentions or neglects entirely: during the post–Cold War period, the US government opposed or sought to weaken a succession of landmark treaties supported by most of the international community, including agreements to control or ban landmines and small arms sales; the comprehensive test ban and antiballistic missile treaties; and the agreement for an International Criminal Court.[15] These omissions may reflect the style of presentation that characterizes many (though not all) of Chomsky's writings, particularly in the post–Cold War period. Often, he doesn't try to set forth a tightly argued, systematic, and comprehensive indictment of American policy. Instead, he discusses a select number of cases with which he is familiar, linking them to broader subjects and moving among related themes in a style that suggests a stream of consciousness.

ECONOMIC HEGEMONY: NEOLIBERALISM AND THE WASHINGTON CONSENSUS

A global hegemon will naturally seek to shape the world economy according to the interests of its own ruling groups. Since World War II, as Chomsky sees it, the United States has sought actively, with considerable success, to construct a global economic order that serves the interests of American capitalism. The end of the Cold War enabled the United States to further extend the reach of American economic power as a large part of the world economy was now removed from the barriers that Communist rule had erected against the penetration of capitalist markets.

America has maintained its global economic dominance through the creation of an array of international institutions and practices, principles often described as "neoliberal," and frequently referred to, tellingly, as the Washington Consensus. Chomsky summarizes the rules of the Washington Consensus: "liberalize trade and finance, let markets set price ('get prices right'), and inflation ('macroeconomic stability'), privatize. The government should 'get out of the way'—hence the population too, insofar as the government is democratic, though the conclusion remains implicit."[16] Chomsky identifies the principal architects of the Washington Consensus as none other than the corporate class that dominates decision making in the American capital and who, out of self-interest, have taken on responsibility for the welfare of the world capitalist system—a responsibility that naturally rests in the first place with the world's most powerful country. Unfortunately, the welfare of the world capitalist system, as seen from Washington, is not necessarily congruent with the welfare of the world's peoples. Chomsky marshals a considerable amount of evidence and argument to show that, indeed, the Washington Consensus in much of the world has worked to thwart national sovereignty and democracy and stymie poorer countries' efforts to achieve economic development.

In Chomsky's account, "consensus" is something of a euphemism as a description of Washington's neoliberal world economic order. To a large extent, it is a "consensus" imposed by American power, exerted through international economic institutions that the United States largely controls as well as through so-called free-trade agreements whose terms generally reflect Washington's preferences. The international institutions include the World Trade Organization, the organization representing many of the world's countries that seeks to regulate the principles governing world trade, generally pushing in the direction of freer access to international markets. Chomsky cites a WTO agreement on telecommunications that he sees as designed to enable the United States to demand changes in the regulatory practices of the seventy countries who signed the agreement, enabling foreigners (read: American companies) to penetrate their markets.[17]

The WTO telecommunications pact is one of several examples Chomsky cites of "free trade agreements" (Chomsky often puts that phrase in quotation marks) that do far more than dismantle barriers to trade. Free trade agreements—much like IMF and World Bank loan agreements—typically incorporate standard neoliberal requirements for reducing state control over foreign investment and economic conditions affecting foreign investment. They thus undermine sovereignty by removing major areas of public policy from the purview of government. Sovereignty, in turn, is a prerequisite for democracy, since democratic self-government is impossible if critical policy choices are imposed on a country's people from outside. Moreover, the neoliberal demand for privatization—for reducing the role of the state in the economy—impedes democracy by transferring control over economic activities out of the public arena and into the private sector, where they are less subject to democratic accountability.[18]

As an example of an infringement on sovereignty, Chomsky cites a 1990 attempt by the Ontario provincial government to set up a universal single-payer no-fault auto insurance plan, similar to Canada's health insurance program. The insurance industry charged that the plan violated Canada's Free Trade Agreement (the predecessor of the North American Free Trade Agreement) with the United States, creating a "government monopoly" that would have an "adverse effect" on US insurance companies operating in the province "tantamount to an expropriation."[19] Unwilling to face the legal and other costs of contesting the companies' demand for billions of dollars in compensation, the provincial government withdrew its proposal.[20]

Chomsky believes that the neoliberalism imposed by the Washington Consensus, in addition to impeding sovereignty and democracy, has also impeded economic development prospects for the world's poor countries. Chomsky sees a close linkage among democracy, sovereignty, and development: Democracy and development "have a common enemy: loss of sovereignty. . . . [which] can entail decline of democracy, and decline in ability to conduct social and economic policy and to integrate on one's own terms into international markets. That in turn harms development." Chomsky qualifies this argument with the point that reliably useful knowledge of the causes of economic development remains elusive, since "the economy—particularly the international economy—is so poorly understood and involves so many variables that even when close correlations are found, one cannot be confident about whether there are causal relations, or if so in which direction."[21] This qualification notwithstanding, it is clear that Chomsky believes that active state intervention in the economy, including many policies typically labeled "protectionist," is generally necessary for a poor country to spur its economic development. Indeed, practically all of Chomsky's writings on economics are directed at refuting the neoclassical notion that markets best serve the general welfare when unhindered by state (i.e., government) intervention.

Chomsky invokes comparisons among world regions to make a case for state intervention, contrasting the outstanding economic development record of much of East Asia with the lackluster performance of Latin America. Japan, South Korea, and Taiwan all achieved their economic miracles by consistently violating free market orthodoxy. They relied on active state guidance of the economy, often utilizing trade barriers to nurture infant industries not yet ready for international competition. Latin America, by contrast, generally followed a more orthodox path, in accord with the Washington Consensus. Foreign investment was encouraged and enjoyed relatively light regulation, and domestic markets were generally open to the international economy. Not coincidentally, Latin America's development performance doesn't approach that of the Asian countries: "Latin America has the world's worst record for inequality, East Asia among the best. The same holds for education, health, and social welfare generally."[22]

Chomsky also points out that the advanced industrial countries often utilized—and indeed still utilize—a variety of subsidies, trade barriers, and other forms of state intervention to spur the development of their own industrial economies. England adopted its free trade agenda only in the middle of the nineteenth century, "after a century of intense protectionism and state intervention had left it so far in the lead in industrialization that competition seemed relatively safe." The United States, for its part, was "the mother country and bastion of protectionism" until the 1920s. Thus, both the United States and Britain advocated free trade for the rest of the world after their own leadership was secure, in a pattern sometimes called "kicking away the ladder": "First we violate the rules to climb to the top, then we kick away the ladder so that you cannot follow us, and we righteously proclaim: 'Let's play fair, on a level playing field.'"[23]

Even into the late twentieth century, the United States has continued to utilize state intervention to develop its economic capabilities while preaching free market fundamentalism to the rest of the world. Chomsky points particularly to the defense sector as a means by which the US government has critically supported the development of the modern high-tech economy, including computers and electronics generally, telecommunications and the Internet, automation, lasers, the commercial aviation industry, and much else. "It is hardly an exaggeration to say that the much-praised 'New Economy' is in large part a creation of the state sector." Chomsky takes evident glee in poking fun at fabled Federal Reserve chief Alan Greenspan, who, "in one of his orations on the miracles of the market," cited the Internet and advances in computers, information processing, lasers, satellites, and transistors. Chomsky comments, "The list is interesting: these are textbook examples of creativity and production taking place substantially in the public sector, mostly the Pentagon, in some cases for decades."[24] So, as Chomsky sees it, American advocacy of free market fundamentalism to the rest of the world constitutes a stance of "Do as I say, not as I do."

In arguing the benefits of state intervention in the economy, Chomsky applauds important features of the international economic regime constructed by the United States as World War II was coming to an end. The system based on capital controls and regulated currencies designed in Bretton Woods, New Hampshire, protected economic sovereignty. It enabled state intervention and thus made possible the widespread institution of social democratic policies. Beginning in the 1970s, the Bretton Woods system was gradually superseded by neoliberal principles. The result, unsurprising to Chomsky, was a slowdown in economic growth combined with increasing poverty and inequality in much of the world. The major exceptions to this pattern were China and its neighbors who resisted the turn toward orthodoxy.[25]

To summarize: Chomsky argues that the United States has used its economic power and its dominance of international economic organizations to impose on much of the world a version of global economic order that subordinates the interests of democracy and development to the interests of American capitalism. The neoliberalism of the Washington Consensus imposed an economic regimen of open markets and government nonintervention that favored the interests of foreign investors—with American business frequently in the forefront—over the interests of peoples who could have benefited from pursuing their own independent economic policies and development strategies.

Chomsky is certainly correct that the United States has played a leading role—indeed, a "hegemonic" one—in shaping the global economic order since World War II. Chomsky is also undoubtedly correct that in exercising global economic hegemony, American motives have not been strictly un-self-interested. As the Princeton political scientist Robert O. Keohane has observed, "Powerful states seek to construct international political economies that suit their interests and ideologies."[26]

Chomsky's critique of the Washington Consensus finds support in the views of scholars and activists ranging in orientation from Marxists on the left to what might be called social democrats on the center left.[27] On the social democratic end of that range, the Nobel prizewinner Joseph Stiglitz has developed a critique of American international economic policies that parallels Chomsky's in many ways. Stiglitz focuses on globalization, the increasingly free flow of economic activity across international borders. Like Chomsky, Stiglitz argues broadly that the globalization process has been managed by the advanced countries, led by the United States, in their own interests, particularly in the interests of their multinational corporations. As a result, the developing countries have often been deprived of their sovereignty and forced to adopt policies that actually damage their economic growth prospects. Stiglitz challenges the orthodox belief that the trade liberalization that facilitates globalization offers benefits to all concerned. He points to the usually unbalanced nature of free trade agreements that disadvantage poorer countries and argues that various protectionist measures are often necessary to nurture the growth of infant economies. Stiglitz presents numerous case studies of the devastating impact that IMF-imposed neoliberal policies have had on the economies of less developed countries, often creating instability and exacerbating problems of unemployment and inequality while failing to deliver on promises of economic growth. Like Chomsky, Stiglitz compares Chinese and East Asian economic development successes with Latin America's experience, and finds the contrast to be a strong refutation of the Washington Consensus.[28]

As striking as are the parallels between Stiglitz's and Chomsky's views of the international economy, there are noteworthy differences in emphasis. Even while stressing the need for an active state, Stiglitz makes clear that markets have a central role in economic development. Stiglitz isn't against capitalism; just unregulated capitalism. We might infer that that is Chomsky's view as well—after all, he is full of praise for East Asian economies which, despite active state intervention, are based on private property and markets. Still, Chomsky nowhere actually says anything good about markets; his discussion is entirely focused on their limitations. (Apparently, Chomsky does believe that poor countries can use a large dose of capitalism in their striving for economic development; he just can't quite bring himself to say so explicitly.) Similarly, while Chomsky inveighs against privatization, he nowhere allows that in some cases it might be correct and necessary. Stiglitz, by contrast, while warning against inappropriate or over-hasty privatization, avers that there are plenty of activities—like running steel mills—that governments typically do not perform well and should stay out of.[29]

In the end, then, Chomsky's discussion of international economics has clear limitations: he advances a number of often very compelling arguments, but these are unconnected to any comprehensive analysis of the determinants of economic development and prosperity. Chomsky is certainly right to argue that the United States has sought to fashion a global economic order in the interests and image of American capitalism. More controversial, but still very defensible, is his claim that the hegemonic role the United States has successfully asserted in the world economy has had baneful consequences for much of the world. Chomsky's defense of that claim is reasonable as far as it goes, but that isn't very far. Chomsky effectively highlights the inadequacies and disadvantages of neoliberalism, but his omission of any acknowledgment of a positive role for capitalism and free trade makes his discussion look like a partisan brief, rather than a probing, balanced analysis. His arguments would be more compelling in the context of a more comprehensive discussion of the development process and its requirements for success.

Interventions: Assets Turned Rogue

Despite the fall of the Soviet Union, there is still evil in the world, including rulers who threaten the peace and security of their own people and of others. Sometimes, the United States has no choice but to take forceful action against evil. This has been a trope of American foreign policy since the end of the Cold War. In Chomsky's view, it has served as a rationale for objectives both more traditional and less noble than those proclaimed by America's leaders. It has served to justify a world hegemonic role for America.

NORIEGA: AN OLD-FASHIONED THUG

According to Chomsky, the United States' first major post–Cold War assertion of its global hegemony occurred in December 1989. The United States invaded Panama, displacing the ruling strongman Manuel Noriega, a former loyal US ally. Chomsky regards this intervention as exceptional because Washington didn't invoke the Soviet threat as justification, as it did, for example, in the US attacks on Nicaragua and Grenada earlier in the decade. It was thus a "post"–Cold War intervention even though the Cold War had not yet ended. A global hegemon needs to be a credible hegemon in its own backyard; the invasion of Panama was a relatively cheap and easy demonstration of US power in its traditional Caribbean sphere of influence.

Chomsky sees the US invasion as a clear violation of international law, and has little trouble disposing of the pretexts Washington proffered for its action. The claim that American lives were endangered was flimsy, especially given the administration's apparent indifference to threats to American lives in neighboring El Salvador and Guatemala. No more credible was Washington's claim to be protecting Panamanian democracy after Noriega's rigging of the 1989 presidential election: Noriega did, indeed, steal the election, but he had also stolen his 1984 election, with no complaints from Washington (on the contrary: he had been praised for advancing democracy). American officials also pointed to Noriega's notorious corruption and drug trafficking, but again, this was nothing new; Washington had long tolerated these activities as long as Noriega had been a reliable friend of the United States.[30]

The real reason Washington decided to get rid of Noriega, according to Chomsky, was that he had lost his usefulness to the United States. He had demonstrated unwelcome signs of independence from his longtime patron, giving support to the Contadora peace process for Central America and allowing Cuba and Nicaragua to use the open Panamanian economy to evade American sanctions. The growth of opposition to Noriega's corrupt and brutal rule among Panama's more affluent classes spurred Washington's newfound interest in replacing him. Chomsky summarizes the situation:

> Noriega's career fits a standard pattern. Typically, the thugs and gangsters whom the US backs reach a point in their careers when they become too independent and too grasping, outliving their usefulness. Instead of just robbing the poor and safeguarding the business climate, they begin to interfere with Washington's natural allies, the local business elite and oligarchy, or even US interests directly. At that point, Washington begins to vacillate; we hear of human rights violations that were cheerfully ignored in the past, and sometimes the US government acts to remove them.[31]

The US media, following the pattern Chomsky and Herman had described in *Manufacturing Consent*, generally acted as cheerleaders for the invasion, offering almost no critical perspective. The media generally accepted the US government's low estimates of Panamanian casualties in the hundreds, while Chomsky cites credible reports by human rights organizations putting Panamanian deaths in the thousands. He contrasts the rosy post-invasion picture of Panama painted by the *New York Times*' reporter on the scene with far grimmer images appearing in the Mexican and Spanish-language US press.[32] But, from the standpoint of the United States, the invasion was a success, effectively returning to power the traditional local oligarchy that had always served US interests while at the same time demonstrating a willingness to deploy military power in the lawless pursuit of US interests. Noriega was brought to the United States, tried, and imprisoned.

WAS CHOMSKY RIGHT? WAS THE INVASION of Panama a more or less crude US power play in the service of global hegemony? Hegemony begins at or near home, and the 1989 invasion of Panama certainly had many of the earmarks of a traditional US assertion of dominance of its small neighbors in the Caribbean. Chomsky is very likely correct that the invasion violated international law: it was condemned both by the United Nations and the Organization of American States. The fact that the corrupt and murderous Noriega had until recently been a dependable servant of US interests deserves all the emphasis that Chomsky gives it. (Noriega started receiving CIA money in the early 1970s and was on the CIA payroll as late as 1987.)[33] Chomsky is also surely correct that the stated rationales for the invasion were weak. The U.S intervention can be regarded as legitimate only on the premise—which, indeed, is widely, implicitly held in the United States— that the United States has the right and responsibility to dominate the affairs of countries in its Caribbean sphere of influence. He points out that Noriega was sentenced to prison by an American court for crimes mostly committed while he was on the CIA payroll.[34] No CIA employees were indicted.

Chomsky makes a strong case that the US media were selective in reporting on events in Panama. The media, he argues convincingly, generally conformed to the familiar pattern of following Washington's lead in reporting events, underplaying the long prehistory of Noriega's servitude to the CIA; the apparent illegality of the invasion under international law; its general condemnation in Latin America, and indeed, in much of the rest of the world; and the significant civilian casualties inflicted in Panama. He points out that while the violence and fraud accompanying the 1989 elections were extensively reported in the US media, the equally fraudulent and perhaps even more violent elections of 1984 were hardly covered, an omission that undoubtedly reflects Noriega's status at the time as a favored son of Washington. He contrasts the increasingly sensational media attention to violence against Americans in Panama with comparable or worse incidents in US client states El Salvador and Guatemala, and in Nicaragua at the hands of the US-backed contras, which got little media notice. Departures from the pattern of media support were exceptional.[35] Even the *Wall Street Journal* acknowledged that the four television networks in reporting the Panama invasion gave "the home team's version of the story."[36]

Outside of the United States, media coverage of the American intervention in Panama was nowhere nearly as favorable. Chomsky cites a leading Canadian newspaper's criticism of "the shallow, boosterish U.S. media" with their "chilling indifference to the fate of innocent Panamanians" killed during the invasion.[37] A columnist in the same newspaper criticized the "mood of jingoism" fostered by the media, and the "peculiar jingoism so evident to foreigners but almost invisible for most Americans. . . . Reporters seeking alternative comments on the invasion typically have to go to the fringe of U.S. society merely to gather opinions on the invasion that would be common in other countries."[38] The widespread foreign opposition to the invasion was little noted in the US media.

In short, on Panama, Chomsky does a good job of reporting the other side of the story that the administration in Washington preferred not be told—and in critiquing the media for their servitude to Washington's agenda. Still, Chomsky's own version of the story—essentially that the United States got rid of Noriega mainly because he was no longer a reliable lackey of Washington and the local business elite—is too simple.

Chomsky's account of the history leading up to the invasion is selective. It ignores or downplays a series of events and developments in the immediately preceding years that had heightened awareness in the United States of Noriega's depredations and spurred significant domestic political demands for the United States to take action against him. The events included the 1985 murder of a former Noriega colleague, Hugo Spadafora, who had threatened to reveal damning evidence of Noriega's drug trafficking and arms smuggling; sensational revelations of Noriega's activities by his deputy, Roberto Diaz Herrera, in 1987; and Noriega's indictment on drug charges by two federal grand juries in Florida in 1988. The blatantly rigged elections of 1989 were followed by mass protests during which the opposition presidential candidate and his running mates were brutally beaten by Noriega's henchmen in a scene broadcast repeatedly on American television.[39]

Chomsky's account also largely ignores the domestic US political context of the Panama intervention. George H. W. Bush was elected president of the United States in November 1988 on a platform that had made the war on drugs a major theme, a theme that resonated with an American public that in polls was ranking illicit drugs as the country's leading domestic problem. Bush publicly took a much stronger anti-Noriega stance than did his predecessor, Reagan, but like Reagan, he hoped that the United States's Noriega problem would be resolved by a coup within Panama. A coup did materialize in October 1989 but failed as the United States did little more than look on. The Bush administration was subjected to a torrent of criticism in Washington, some of it from Bush's own party. Bush responded with intensified covert operations against the Noriega regime. In December, the Noriega regime declared that a state of war existed with the United States; there followed several well-publicized incidents of violence against American citizens in Panama. Bush, apparently sensitive to charges of indecisive leadership and under a compulsion to fulfill his campaign pledge to take strong action against drugs, decided to invade.[40]

The invasion of Panama, then, took place in the context of a set of domestic political pressures that President Bush, given his particular commitments and vulnerabilities, found difficult to resist. (His predecessor did resist calls from within and outside of his administration for military intervention.) Those pressures, nevertheless, might never have become so powerful had there not developed in the preceding years a consensus in Washington that Noriega had become a hindrance to US interests. The new Washington consensus encouraged greater media attention to Noriega's crimes, which in turn helped fan the public outrage and build the political pressure to which Bush ultimately chose to respond. Chomsky's account neglects an important development leading to Noriega's ouster—domestic political pressure, strengthened by a particularly high level of concern by Americans about illicit drugs. Still, Chomsky makes a plausible argument that increasing US hostility toward Noriega to a significant extent reflected his transformation from an asset to a liability for the United States. Counterfactual speculation is always problematic, but it is reasonable to suppose that Noriega might never have been ousted by US force of arms if he had continued in his familiar role as a dependable US ally. His crimes, like those of his counterparts in Honduras, Guatemala, and El Salvador, might well have been overlooked.

SADDAM HUSSEIN: A PERFECT VILLAIN

Washington's success in Panama was soon followed by a much larger US military action: the Gulf War of 1991. In August 1990 Iraq invaded Kuwait, its small, oil-rich neighbor. The United States, supported by UN Security Council resolutions, responded with demands for Iraq's immediate, unconditional withdrawal. After several months of diplomatic maneuvering failed to resolve the crisis, a US-dominated coalition in January 1991 initiated a large-scale bombing campaign that targeted Iraq's civilian infrastructure as well as its military capabilities. A ground campaign followed in February, soon compelling Iraq's retreat from Kuwait.

From Chomsky's perspective, the first Gulf War of 1990–1991 initiated a relentless American campaign to bring Iraq into line with the United States' project for global hegemony, a project whose success depended critically on American dominance of the strategically critical oil-rich Persian Gulf region. During the course of that campaign, the United States inflicted massive suffering and death on the people of Iraq and repeatedly demonstrated its contempt for international law and world opinion.

Chomsky acknowledges that the United States had plausible pretexts for the 1991 attack on Iraq: the Iraqi invasion of Kuwait the previous August was indeed an act of aggression, and the Iraqi dictator Saddam Hussein was indeed a vicious tyrant.[41] But, he argues, Washington's pose as an upholder of international law against a monstrous aggressor was blatantly hypocritical. The United States had demonstrated its own willingness to violate international law in its recent aggression against Panama and Nicaragua. Moreover, Saddam's viciousness had long been apparent, yet Washington had never been moved to take action against him. Chomsky repeatedly points out that the United States' hard-line response to Iraq's invasion of Kuwait was a sharp reversal from its previous policy of lavishing aid on Iraq, which it had regarded effectively as an ally in the Persian Gulf. The United States supported Saddam in his aggressive war against Iran. When Iraqi missiles struck a US destroyer in 1987, killing thirty-seven Americans, Saddam got no more than a slap on the wrist from the United States. The United States was similarly restrained in its reaction to Saddam's use of chemical weapons in 1988 to quell a revolt among Iraqi Kurds, killing tens of thousands.[42]

Saddam's brutalization of his own people and his aggression aren't what offended Washington, according to Chomsky; the Iraqi dictator's offense was to demonstrate an independent nationalism that threatened American interests in the oil-rich Gulf region. Having concluded that Saddam could no longer be trusted, the Bush administration was determined to crush him militarily. Contrasting Washington's tough stance toward Iraq with its soft posture of "constructive engagement" with the apartheid regime in South Africa, Chomsky cites repeated refusals by the US government to consider diplomatic solutions in the months following Iraq's invasion of Kuwait. The United States was more interested in a show of its military might than in defusing the crisis peacefully: "Thus, anything short of a total victory for US force [was] unacceptable, even if it [meant] a catastrophic war, with unpredictable consequences."[43] The war wasn't catastrophic for the United States, whose forces suffered negligible casualties, but it was catastrophic for the Iraqi people, who were to suffer for years to come from the deliberate, systematic devastation inflicted on Iraq's infrastructure, including its water, power, and sewage systems.

Chomsky points out that when popular revolts against Saddam flared up in the aftermath of the war, the United States did nothing to stop Saddam from crushing them. Washington was hoping for a military coup to overthrow the unreliable dictator, but given the choice between Saddam and a popular revolt leading to a possibly independent-minded regime, Washington preferred Saddam.[44] Subsequently, Washington sought to remove Saddam through a regime of sanctions, imposed by the United Nations at the United States' insistence. The sanctions, which crippled Baghdad's ability to recover from the destruction of the war, caused the deaths of hundreds of thousands of Iraqis (mostly very old and very young) from disease and malnutrition as badly degraded health care, food distribution, and sanitary systems were deprived of the means to respond to a burgeoning humanitarian catastrophe. An early and vociferous critic of the sanctions, Chomsky recounts that they prompted the resignations in protest of two successive UN humanitarian coordinators; one of them, Denis Halliday, described the sanctions as "genocidal" in character.[45]

Even while they inflicted terrible suffering on the Iraqi people, the sanctions failed to dislodge Saddam Hussein. The United States finally moved decisively to do so in 2003 under President George W. Bush. Chomsky was a vehement critic of the Bush administration's plans to invade Iraq, and continued in his criticism throughout the war. Chomsky's case against the war included three lines of argument: the war was illegal; it was counterproductive; and none of the administration's rationales for war could withstand scrutiny.

Always a strong advocate of international law, Chomsky launches his critique of America's 2003 invasion of Iraq with the simple observation that it was illegal. It was an attack on a sovereign national that had neither done nor threatened harm to the United States. In making this argument, Chomsky points to the important distinction between preventive and preemptive war. Preemptive war—action to forestall an imminent threat—constitutes a legitimate defensive action, generally recognized by international law. Preventive war—aimed at an alleged threat in the uncertain future—is not recognized as legitimate. The administration's principal justification for invading Iraq—that it posed a future threat to its neighbors and even to the United States—was an argument for preventive war, and therefore illegitimate.[46]

But the war was not just illegal, according to Chomsky; it was counterproductive, at least if we are to take Bush administration claims at face value. The invasion of Iraq actually aggravated the problems it was supposedly intended to ameliorate: the threats of international terrorism and nuclear proliferation. While the Bush administration generally framed its Iraq plans as part of its war on terror, the attack on Iraq was actually a gift to Osama bin Laden: it aggravated the terrorist threat to the United States and the rest of the world by enhancing the jihadists' appeal and thus spurring al-Qaeda's recruitment efforts.[47] The US invasion of Iraq also had the perverse effect of encouraging nuclear proliferation. Chomsky cites the view of several respected analysts of international relations that the "lesson" of Iraq, for potential American adversaries, would be that only nuclear weapons (which Saddam, to his misfortune, did not possess) could deter American aggressiveness.[48]

In any case, the "threats" posed by Saddam Hussein were essentially conjured up by an administration bent on justifying war. Saddam, in Chomsky's view, was not much of a threat to anyone except his own people. The threat scenario repeatedly cited by administration spokesmen involved Saddam Hussein giving weapons of mass destruction (WMD) to a terrorist group, which would then use them to strike at the United States. This scenario was particularly potent with an American public still reeling from the 9/11 attacks. But, Chomsky argues, Saddam Hussein was "a brutal tyrant, but a rational one."[49] If he had chemical and biological weapons, he would not risk putting them in the hands of the Osama bin Ladens of the world, who despised Saddam's secular regime.[50]

The administration also portrayed Saddam as a threat to his neighbors, but as Chomsky points out, there was no particular pressure from Iraq's Arab neighbors for the United States to do anything radical about Saddam—they had been mending fences with him for some years, and knew that Iraq, its wealth and military power devastated by war and sanctions, posed no threat to anyone in the region, much less to the United States.[51]

The Bush administration's main justification for invading Iraq—that an aggressive-minded Saddam Hussein possessed or was developing WMD—became increasingly untenable as the invading Americans proved unable to find any WMD in Iraq, or even evidence that such weapons had been under development. Accordingly, the administration spokesmen shifted, giving new emphasis to what had been a decidedly minor theme in their rationale for invading Iraq—replacing a tyrannical regime with democracy. A newly democratized Iraq, they argued, was not only a noble objective in itself: it would become a model for the rest of the Arab world, with a potential for initiating an unprecedented flowering of democracy in a region of traditional autocracy. Chomsky points to the obvious opportunism in the switch in rationales for war: skepticism is naturally in order when new visions are produced to replace pretexts that have collapsed.[52]

Besides, the Bush administration simply wasn't credible in the role of idealistic promoter of democracy abroad. Emblematic, for Chomsky, was Deputy Secretary of Defense Paul Wolfowitz, the administration figure most closely identified with the objective of democracy promotion in the Middle East. Wolfowitz's alleged passion for democracy was hardly consistent with his record of "strong support for some of the most corrupt and appalling murderers, torturers and aggressors of the late twentieth century."[53] One of the last of President Reagan's advisers to turn against the Philippine dictator Marcos, Wolfowitz had also been a strong supporter, both in government and afterward, of Indonesia's murderous dictator Suharto. Wolfowitz's contempt for democracy was evident as well in his harsh criticism of Turkey's government for abiding by the wishes of its people when it withheld logistic support for the US invasion of Iraq. According to Chomsky, the United States was interested only in an Iraqi democracy that it could control. Thus, the 2005 Iraqi elections, which Chomsky lauds as an important advance, had been resisted by the United States, which instead had sought a system of indirect electoral procedures more amenable to manipulation by the Americans.[54]

Chomsky was not indifferent to the Bush administration's stated goal of overthrowing Saddam Hussein. Chomsky repeatedly describes Saddam as a tyrant and has no trouble acknowledging that his overthrow was a good thing. But a legitimate approach to democracy promotion in Iraq would have been to give the Iraqi people a chance themselves to overthrow their tyrant. That would have required radically revising the sanctions that were devastating Iraqi society, directing them strictly at preventing weapons programs: "Unless the population is given the opportunity to overthrow a brutal tyrant . . . there is no justification for outside force to do so."[55]

If neither weapons of mass destruction, nor terrorism, nor democracy promotion provided a plausible justification for war, why *did* the Bush administration invade Iraq? Chomsky deals with that question in an article he entitles, "Who Is to Run the World and How?"[56] The invasion, in Chomsky's view, reflected the Bush administration's determined quest for world hegemony. Iraq would serve that goal as a newly created US client state and host to US military bases in a geostrategically critical world region. Its newly acquired power position at the heart of the world's energy reserves would give the United States critical leverage over European and Asian rivals in global competition.

CHOMSKY'S NARRATIVE OF US POLICY toward Iraq skewers official claims and rationales. Far from being a disinterested enforcer of international law, security, and decency, America in its lengthy crusade against Saddam Hussein demonstrated a brutal and arrogant determination to assert its role as global hegemon. Chomsky's arguments are generally cogent and well grounded in evidence. He does indulge in occasional flights of fantastic hyperbole and rhetorical excess. These more or less gratuitous digressions don't weaken his fundamental arguments, but they do naturally raise questions about his judgment and, hence, his credibility.

Chomsky is certainly right to point to the record of US support for Saddam Hussein during the 1980s. In light of that record, it is entirely reasonable to dismiss as hypocritical the two Bush administrations' efforts to justify both the first and second Gulf Wars by pointing to Saddam Hussein's various previous crimes. Some of the worst of those crimes were committed with the complaisance of the United States. Unfortunately, pointing to American tolerance for Saddam's crimes isn't enough for Chomsky, who seems unable to resist the temptation to fancifully overstate America's role in those crimes. Thus, Chomsky observes that Saddam's use of chemical weapons in his mass murder of Kurds in 1988 cost Iraq a loss of productive land. Soon afterward, the United States increased food exports to Iraq. This, to Chomsky, is evidence that the United States meant to help Saddam gas the Kurds: "[The United States] had to come to [Saddam's] rescue, to help out with this project of gassing Kurds in the north. And we did, by increasing the subsidized agricultural exports to Iraq, essentially for that reason."[57] Chomsky's comments would make sense only if Saddam had secured a promise of increased food aid from the United States before gassing the Kurds, while indicating that that was his intention. Chomsky doesn't make that wild claim explicitly; does he nevertheless want us to believe it? It is hard to characterize this kind of innuendo; it would seem to be an attempt to induce the reader to construe as fact a completely fanciful construction of events.

Chomsky's critique of the first Gulf War as an assertion of America's world hegemonic role in the Middle East is certainly debatable, but entirely reasonable. In demanding an immediate and unconditional Iraqi withdrawal from Kuwait, the United States was in effect denying any legitimate role for Iraq as a regional power in the Middle East. In the months following Iraq's August 1990 invasion, the United States rejected or ignored proposals for a negotiated settlement advanced by Jordan, Morocco, Algeria, France, the Soviet Union, and Iraq itself.[58] Indeed, as the former national security adviser Zbigniew Brzezinski remarked, US diplomacy during the crisis seemed dedicated to the prevention of a diplomatic solution.[59] The Bush administration also rejected reliance on countermeasures short of war, such as the UN sanctions applied shortly after the Iraqi invasion (which, the evidence suggested, quickly started taking a severe toll on Iraq's economy). A considerable constituency existed in the United States for giving the sanctions a chance to work; Democrats advocating that course very nearly succeeded in January 1991 in denying the Bush administration congressional authorization to wage war in Iraq. It is very hard to argue with Chomsky's contention that the Bush administration wanted war. A peaceful resolution of the crisis was simply not the objective of US policy; a show of American power was.

The Bush administration's inflexible and aggressive determination in its approach to the Gulf crisis is consistent with that of a great power bent on constructing a new world order under its hegemonic role. Of course, supporters of the United States's Gulf War intervention can point out that the United States did ultimately succeed in assembling a UN coalition that legitimated American military intervention under international law. But that does not refute Chomsky's basic point, that the United States in the Gulf War was displaying its world hegemonic drive. A hegemon, after all, should normally be able to expect preponderant support in the international community.

Chomsky bolsters his claim that US intentions in the Gulf were less than altruistic with observations about the American response to the internal turbulence that beset Iraq shortly after the end of the war in late February 1991. Chomsky is on solid ground in suggesting that Washington would have been pleased to see an army coup replace Saddam with an equally repressive, but more pro-American, ruler. The Bush administration was indeed nervous about the possibility of a breakdown in central authority in Baghdad, with the danger of turmoil and instability spreading beyond Iraq's borders.[60] After urging the Iraqi people to rise against their ruler, the United States did nothing to prevent Saddam's bloody suppression of revolts against his rule, first among Shiites mainly in southern Iraq, then among Kurds in the north.

Chomsky does not, however, merely criticize Washington for its inaction in the face of Saddam's post war repression. At different times he claims that the Bush administration authorized Saddam to crush the two revolts, or that he "tacitly" or "effectively" did so; the United States thereby "essentially returned to support for its favorite murderer, as he again carried out really atrocious and vicious acts."[61]

The claim that Washington authorized Saddam to crush the revolts against his rule is literally false: there was no such communication from Washington to Baghdad. Even Chomsky's more qualified claim that Washington "tacitly" or "effectively" authorized Saddam's brutality is a highly tendentious reading of a complex situation. The UN mandate of the US-dominated forces in the Gulf War was to force Iraq's withdrawal from Kuwait. There was a widespread, reasonable suspicion that the Bush administration had much more ambitious objectives in mind, and there was intense opposition within the United Nations by the Soviet Union, China, and several Arab countries, among others, to any interpretation of the UN resolutions that extended to removing Saddam from power. The administration was also under domestic pressure to keep the Gulf War limited. Fearful of a Vietnam-type quagmire, the Bush administration viewed any US involvement in Iraqi internal conflicts as risky.[62] To claim that Washington in its inaction "authorized" Saddam's repression, even "implicitly" or "effectively," ignores this important context.

Chomsky suggests that the United States need not have actively intervened to support the anti-Saddam rebels; it could have just given them access to the captured Iraqi equipment they were seeking. But Chomsky gives no consideration to the implications of such an action: Would it not have violated the United Nations' limited mandate? Would it have given the rebels a real chance to succeed, or merely ensured an even bloodier response by Saddam? Would it not have led inexorably to deeper US involvement in supporting the revolts? Chomsky reduces a problematically complex situation to a straightforward illustration of unambiguously evil US motives.

Chomsky is far more justified in his condemnation of the US role in maintaining the brutal twelve-year regime of UN sanctions on Iraq. The first Gulf War crippled Iraq's economy and radically degraded Iraq's agriculture and its facilities and systems for water treatment, sanitation, health care, and food distribution. The sanctions effectively prevented Iraq from importing a wide range of goods needed to rebuild the country. By most estimates, the excess morbidity in Iraq over the twelve years of sanctions was at least five hundred thousand, largely accounted for by waterborne diseases and malnutrition among children under five.[63]

Chomsky rightly disparages the constantly repeated American claim that Saddam Hussein was somehow to blame for the massive suffering and death inflicted by the sanctions. As the meticulous, exhaustive research of Joy Gordon has convincingly demonstrated, the extended humanitarian catastrophe was primarily due to the fact that Iraq was not allowed to import items critical to its reconstruction, not to Saddam's use of oil revenues to build palaces or to other Iraqi regime pathologies. The responsibility for the sanctions' devastation fell squarely on the United States and its partner Great Britain, who maintained effective control of the relevant UN machinery, often flouting the will of a clear majority of UN General Assembly and Security Council members and staff. US policy under all three presidents—Bush I, Clinton, and Bush II—was to inflict the most extreme possible economic damage on Iraq. The human costs of that policy were ignored: US officials responsible for Iraq policy literally gave no consideration to humanitarian concerns. Worse still, the Americans consistently denigrated the continuing flow of UN reports that documented the humanitarian catastrophe their actions were causing.[64]

The twelve-year regime of sanctions against Iraq must certainly rank among the worst atrocities by American leaders in the history of US foreign policy. US policymakers were evidently willing to expend the lives of countless Iraqi civilians—literally countless, because no Americans in authority were counting—in the pursuit of a political goal, the removal of Saddam Hussein. To that end, the objective of inflicting maximum damage on Iraq was built into the US policy-making bureaucracy at a very early point in time. There was no place in the policy-making machinery for any concern with the collateral damage entailed in this effort—its cost in human life.

A phrase that Chomsky has proposed on various occasions—"intentional ignorance"—is a very appropriate description of the stance on Iraqi sanctions adopted by US policymakers.[65] They weren't aware of the human costs of their actions—or they were only dimly aware—because they didn't want to know. But while this stance is morally reprehensible, it does not quite amount to a deliberate act of mass murder: there was never a conscious decision anywhere in the US government to kill up to x thousands of Iraqis. Chomsky, however, is not content to point to US policymakers' intentional ignorance of the consequences of their actions. Speculating on American motives for the Iraqi sanctions, Chomsky notes that the United States would not want to completely wipe out Iraq because it has oil:

> But you can wipe out its population. In fact it's in a way beneficial to do that. If you look at the history of oil production around the world, you find that it mostly takes place in areas where there aren't many people. Then there's little pressure to stop the profits from going to the people who really should have them: Western oil companies and the US Treasury. So, if the population of Iraq were reduced or marginalized, maybe even reduced to such a level that they're barely functional, then when the time comes—and it will—to bring Iraqi production back on line, they'll be less of an impediment. Iraq will be more like, say, Saudi Arabia, where there's a lot of oil but not many people around pressing for economic development and educational facilities and so on.[66]

Once again, Chomsky has crafted a remarkable piece of innuendo: he does not actually assert that the United States was engaged in a deliberate policy of depopulating Iraq, but he clearly would like the reader to consider the possibility (likelihood?) that this was the US goal. With roughly the same population but only one-fifth the land area of Saudi Arabia, Iraq would need to undergo the largest genocide in world history to become significantly "more like" Saudi Arabia. Chomsky would apparently have us believe that this might, indeed, have been the aim of US policy.

Chomsky's critique of the second Gulf War, on the other hand, is not only trenchantly argued, but also free of wild speculation or hyperbole. Most of his arguments, as summarized in this chapter, can be found in the antiwar critiques of established commentators, several of whom Chomsky cites in developing his own case. Chomsky does go beyond most mainstream commentary in his dismissal of democracy promotion as a motive for the Bush administration's invasion of Iraq. Many war critics took seriously the administration's claim to be seeking democracy for Iraq and the wider Middle East. Chomsky, on the other hand, doesn't believe for a minute that the Bush administration was genuinely interested in promoting democracy in Iraq or its neighbors. Chomsky's cynicism is well founded. The biographies of the major policymakers in the drive to war—not only Wolfowitz, but also Cheney and Rumsfeld—show no particular interest in democracy promotion except as a weapon against Communism. The administration didn't advance democracy promotion as a major argument for invading Iraq until after the principal argument—weapons of mass destruction—had collapsed. (Chomsky could have observed that "democracy" did not occur once among the more than one thousand words Bush devoted to Iraq in his 2003 State of the Union address.) Chomsky is also right to point out that once Iraq was under US occupation, the administration actually did its best to resist allowing completely free elections.

In sum, Chomsky makes a strong case that US policy toward Iraq from the late 1980s forward reflected the arrogance and brutality of a great power determined to seek and maintain global hegemony. He effectively skewers American leaders' claims of noble intent in rationalizing their global ambitions. Unfortunately, Chomsky now and again indulges in fantastic claims and innuendo in his determination to cast American motives in the worst possible light.

Interventions: Humanitarianism and Kosovo

In the 1990s the United States and its allies asserted a new right to intervene in the internal affairs of other countries—a right based on the alleged need to prevent humanitarian catastrophes. In Chomsky's view, the right of humanitarian intervention was little more than a cloak for older, less altruistic motives for the use of military force. Humanitarian intervention provided a new rationale for the presumption that great powers have a right to impose their will on smaller, weaker countries, and it helped justify the United States' continuing quest for worldwide hegemony. Chomsky's Exhibit A in his case against so-called humanitarian intervention was the use of force by the United States and its NATO allies in 1999 in the Serbian province of Kosovo.

During the course of the 1990s, the idea of humanitarian intervention acquired increasing legitimacy in elite opinion in the West. The idea is that regimes that employ violence against their own people should not enjoy the immunity from outside interference traditionally accorded sovereign nation-states in the conduct of their internal affairs. When faced with massive threats to the lives of innocent people because of the actions (or inaction) of their governments, the world community is obliged to act, employing military force as necessary. This was a relatively novel idea. The prevalent assumption had been that crimes committed by governments against their own people, however deplorable, were not the business of the international community. Thus, when in Rwanda in early 1994 a civil war culminated in a killing spree that extinguished eight hundred thousand lives over the course of a few months, the matter barely registered with US policymakers; the possibility of some kind of counteraction by the United States was never considered.[67]

Shock and outrage over the Rwandan horror helped to spur a developing discourse over humanitarian intervention, which got added impetus from events in the Balkans. In the midst of a civil war, Serbian forces in July 1995 took control of the Bosnian town of Srebrenica and, separating the men and boys from the women, took just one week to slaughter over seven thousand Muslims in cold blood. It was the largest massacre in Europe since World War II. Srebrenica evoked unprecedented pressure on the administration of President Bill Clinton to adopt a more aggressive posture toward the Balkans. An early administration response was a three-week NATO bombing campaign that laid the basis for a settlement of the Bosnian civil war reached in Dayton, Ohio.

By the late 1990s, the main locus of intercommunal violence in the Balkans had shifted to Kosovo, a region within Serb-dominated Yugoslavia whose predominant population of ethnic Albanian Muslims was seeking independence. Serb forces were locked in a continuing, brutal struggle with a guerilla insurgency, the Kosovo Liberation Army (KLA). After an American-brokered truce in October 1998 collapsed, another two rounds of peace negotiations ended in failure on March 18, 1999. On March 24, NATO initiated an intense bombing campaign aimed at crushing the Serb army and bringing the Serbian leader, Slobodan Milosevic, to terms. During the bombing campaign, Milosevic engineered a massive "ethnic cleansing" of Kosovo; massacres and expulsions forced most of the Muslim population—upwards of one million people—to leave their homes for refuge in neighboring countries. Thousands of Kosovars were killed by Serb forces. Seventy-eight days of relentless bombing, however, finally forced Milosevic to yield. The Serbian leader submitted to a peace agreement that provided for substantial autonomy for Kosovo.

NATO's action in Kosovo was widely credited with having forestalled the likelihood of future large-scale atrocities by the Serb forces against the Muslim minority. It was also acclaimed as a breakthrough for the principle of humanitarian intervention—a breakthrough for which the Clinton administration happily claimed credit. As the president announced after the Serbs' surrender over Kosovo, "If somebody comes after innocent civilians and tries to kill them en masse because of their race, their ethnic background or their religion, and it's within our power to stop it, we will stop it. . . . There are times when looking away simply is not an option. . . . We can't respond to every tragedy in every corner of the world, [but that doesn't mean that] we should do nothing for no one."[68]

Chomsky doesn't believe it. He doesn't believe that the United States' intervention in Kosovo was motivated by humanitarian concern. Its principal motivation, instead, was to assert American power. The bombing campaign served NATO's post–Cold War need to justify its continued existence. Since NATO was the principal instrument of American power and influence in Europe, the intervention was ultimately an assertion of American power—a demonstration of Washington's willingness to use military force as it pleased. It thus reaffirmed the United States' intention to maintain its world hegemonic role. According to Chomsky, "'Credibility of NATO' means credibility of US power: the 'disorderly' elements of the world must understand the price they will pay if they do not heed the orders of the master in Washington."[69]

Chomsky points out that outside of NATO, the Kosovo intervention was widely condemned around the world—a fact that went largely underreported in the US media. The defense of state sovereignty was a matter of concern to smaller and weaker countries whose historic experience of colonization and exploitation by the West left them leery of new rationales for the exercise of force by the powerful over the weak.[70]

Chomsky advances several lines of argument for his claim that Kosovo was not a genuine humanitarian intervention. First, he points to various instances of massive human rights violations around the world in which the United States and its allies were unmoved by humanitarian considerations. America's self-righteous claim to have acted on humanitarian objectives in Kosovo is hardly credible given US indifference to humanitarian concerns elsewhere. Second, the intervention in Kosovo actually aggravated the situation—the Serbs' massive expulsions of Kosovars from their homes occurred only after the commencement of the bombing campaign, and this was predictable: the United States and its allies understood that NATO military action would give the Serbs a pretext for ethnic cleansing and mass murder. They went ahead anyway, unconcerned about the human costs of their action. Third, the NATO allies did not exhaust the possibilities for resolving the Kosovo problem through diplomacy. It was clear that NATO was itching for a fight. The means (an exercise of military force) was clearly more important than the alleged end (protection of the people of Kosovo). Finally, Chomsky believes that circumstances point to other, nonhumanitarian motivations for the Kosovo intervention.

ANALYSIS: CHOMSKY'S LINES OF ARGUMENT

The United States is not credible as an agent of humanitarian values. Chomsky argues that in several instances more or less contemporaneous with the Kosovo crisis, the United States forfeited any claim to being in pursuit of a humanitarian foreign policy. The two cases he cites the most frequently involve formal or informal allies of the United States engaged in internal repression: Turkey's treatment of its Kurdish minority, and Indonesia's renewed suppression of East Timor's drive for independence. I will be examining each of these cases in some detail later in this chapter. For present purposes, I will simply make the point that it is certainly true that in each case, American action or inaction did indeed facilitate serious human rights abuses by its allies. Chomsky, however, goes further than that: he asserts that in each case, the United States actively supported and even instigated those abuses.

The distinction between merely ignoring or even facilitating human rights abuses, and actually instigating them, is critical. Implicitly, Chomsky seems to recognize that merely to demonstrate that the United States does act consistently on humanitarian concerns would not be sufficient in and of itself to prove that the Kosovo intervention could not have been motivated by humanitarian considerations. Any foreign policy decision is likely to reflect a variety of considerations. Even if humanitarian concerns are consistently taken into consideration, it may be that in some cases, other interests override them. Those other interests might well include a desire not to offend a valued ally. The argument can be made that in Turkey and East Timor and Colombia, such other interests were in play; in Kosovo, they were not, so humanitarian concerns were able to rise to the top. We could criticize the subordination of humanitarian concerns to other interests, but we can't prove that they were ignored completely. This argument loses some force, however, if it can be demonstrated that the United States didn't merely ignore humanitarian values in the other cases, but actively trampled on them. A repeat active violator of human rights is not a credible defender of human rights. This is precisely Chomsky's argument—he stresses repeatedly that the United States did not merely "look away" from its allies' crimes, but actively participated in them.[71]

As I will show later, Chomsky's contention that the United States was not a mere facilitator but an active instigator of terrible human rights abuses by its client states, Turkey and Indonesia, is untenable. But for now, let us posit that Chomsky is entirely correct. Even under that premise, his argument that Kosovo could not have been a humanitarian intervention is at best inconclusive, for two reasons.

The first is a simple one: people are inconsistent. A person's inconsistency in upholding a particular principle gives us reasonable grounds for doubting his sincerity, but it is not conclusive proof of insincerity. Even a brutal murderer may be capable of compassion—if not for his victims, perhaps for others. As the political psychologist Robert Jervis observes, neighbors are often stunned when serial murderers are caught: "He seemed like such a nice man; he always looked after my cats when he was away."[72] Even if we grant that Bill Clinton and Tony Blair showed a callous disregard for the lives of the East Timorese, it does not follow inexorably that they could not have been moved by the plight of the Kosovars.

The second reason is only a bit less simple. Whatever their personal motivations and inclinations, national policymakers are compelled to respond to a variety of pressures. By the late 1990s, there had been a tremendous buildup of pressure on the US government to do something about the Serbs' repeated serious human rights violations. The pressure came from the US Congress, where Bob Dole, the Senate majority leader and Clinton's 1996 challenger for the presidency, had long been pressing for a more vigorous US action against Serb abuses; from journalists and human rights organizations; and from America's European allies.[73] As the journalist Tim Judah noted, after nearly a decade of repeated human rights violations by the Serbs, the "spectre of the past" hung heavily over Western policymakers. In particular, the failure to forestall Srebrenica had been a serious embarrassment for NATO. A constant fear persisted that another enormous massacre might take place, again exposing the United States and its allies to criticism for inaction in the face of atrocity.[74] Whatever the personal motivations of Bill Clinton and Tony Blair in deciding for intervention in Kosovo, their choice needs to be understood in the broader political context of a groundswell of genuine humanitarian concern for the fate of the Kosovars. The two leaders may or may not have been truly principled humanitarians, but to the extent that their action in Kosovo responded to pressure inspired by humanitarian concerns, it can be considered a humanitarian intervention.

The NATO bombing campaign actually precipitated a tremendous escalation of atrocities, and this outcome was reasonably predictable. Chomsky is certainly correct that the Serbs used NATO's bombing campaign as a cover and a pretext for a systematic, massive campaign of ethnic cleansing in Kosovo. He cites various sources indicating that the number of people who had become refugees stood at around two hundred thousand in March 1999, when the bombing campaign began. By the end of the campaign in early June, an estimated 670,000 refugees had fled Yugoslavia, with the total number of displaced people estimated at over one million.[75] And, while about five hundred Albanians had been killed in the year before the bombing, the total by war's end passed ten thousand.[76] Chomsky observes wryly that during the bombing campaign NATO supporters often pointed to the ongoing Serb atrocities as justification for NATO's action, while it was NATO's action that evidently precipitated those very atrocities.[77] Chomsky also points out that the war's death toll included Serbian civilians killed as NATO extended its bombing campaign beyond military targets in Kosovo into Serbia proper.[78] Chomsky doesn't cite numbers, but later estimates indicated that Serbian civilians killed by NATO's bombs numbered between five hundred and two thousand. Even the lower number roughly equals the number of Kosovars killed by Serbian forces before the bombing started.[79]

Chomsky adds that the end of the bombing campaign didn't mean the end of atrocities in Kosovo, though the identity of the main perpetrators changed. Now it was the Kosovar Liberation Army, operating with NATO's complaisance, that engaged in ethnic cleansing and terror. The scale of atrocities was small compared with the Serbs' crimes during the bombing, but it was still significant. Most Serbs were effectively driven out of Kosovo, as were most Roma. Chomsky cites an Amnesty International report of dramatic increases in violence directed against not only Serbs and Roma, but also moderate Albanians resisting the KLA's determination to extract harsh vengeance.[80] Samantha Power, a leading advocate of humanitarian intervention, acknowledges that while NATO troops patrolled Kosovo, Albanian extremists expelled more than 100,000 Serbs and killed 1,500.

Prominent media outlets published the names of prominent Serbian "war criminals," who were often gunned down.[81]

It is clear, then, that the human costs of intervention in Kosovo were very high—certainly higher than anything that preceded the bombing campaign. The only way to claim that the intervention was a humanitarian success would be to argue that it had prevented a still worse evil. This is precisely what Samantha Power asserts: "As high as the death toll was, it was far lower than if NATO had not acted at all. After years of avoiding confrontation, the United States and its allies likely saved hundreds of thousands of lives."[82] This is an important but rather extravagant claim; Power offers no evidence or argument to support it.[83] If she could show a sharply increasing rate of Serb crimes in the months before the bombing, then she might have a point, but she does not and cannot. As Chomsky observes, there was no clear upward curve of Serb crimes during the run-up to the NATO bombing campaign.[84] It was, in fact, the KLA that had first violated the truce brokered in October 1998, provoking a renewed offensive by the Serbian security forces. There was, it is true, a massacre of forty-five people in a Kosovo village in January, an atrocity that received sensational media attention and prompted the allies to insist on new peace negotiations. But a massacre by the Serb forces of forty-five people, horrible as it is, is scant basis for a forecast of hundreds of thousands (or tens of thousands or even thousands) of imminent deaths. Western intelligence did have reports of Serb plans for large-scale ethnic cleansing in Kosovo, but as Chomsky points out, countries often make plans for a broad range of contingencies; the existence of Serb plans for ethnic cleansing is by no means proof that they would have been carried out in the absence of NATO's attack, which gave the Serbs cover and pretext.[85]

Any effort to justify a demonstrable present evil with the claim that it prevents a speculative future evil should be regarded skeptically. We know that the rate and scale of massacres and ethnic cleansing by the Serbs increased dramatically *after* the bombing began. We cannot know what would have happened without the bombing. What reason was there to expect an equally dramatic increase—much less an even greater increase—if there had been no bombing campaign? Power elsewhere points out that the allies did not expect Milosevic to react so viciously to the bombing. This miscalculation, she suggests, made the decision to bomb an easier one.[86] But if the allies didn't expect Milosevic to act with such criminality while being bombed, what basis was there to expect even worse criminality if he wasn't bombed? Power tries to have it both ways—the bombing was justified by the likelihood that even greater crimes would have occurred in its absence, but it was also justified in part because no one thought even Milosevic capable of such terrible crimes.

Chomsky, then, is almost surely correct that the bombing worsened the immediate humanitarian situation. But Chomsky is not just arguing that the intervention was unsuccessful; he goes further, claiming that the allies knew well that the bombing would very likely aggravate rather than improve the situation. Milosevic's response to the bombing campaign was unsurprising, according to Chomsky.[87] Obviously, then, the bombing could not have had humanitarian objectives; NATO knew that they would probably be inciting, rather than preventing, a humanitarian catastrophe.

The evidence for this argument is shaky. Chomsky cites a statement by General Wesley Clark, the NATO commander, four days after the bombing started, that the increase in Serb terror and violence "was entirely predictable."[88] Obviously, though, Clark could not be aware of the full extent of the coming humanitarian disaster just four days into the bombing campaign; moreover, his claim has the ring of a public figure denying that he was surprised by events his own actions had set in motion. More relevantly, Chomsky cites a warning by Italy's prime minister to President Clinton in early March 1999 that a large refugee flow could result from NATO action.[89] He also quotes the US House Intelligence chair, who stated that the intelligence community had been warning for months that bombing would precipitate "a virtual explosion of refugees."[90] The chair of the Joint Chiefs of Staff, Hugh Shelton, had similarly warned President Clinton that air strikes might provoke the Serbs into greater acts of butchery.[91]

On the other hand, as we have already noted, Samantha Power reports that the allies were genuinely surprised by the ferocity of Milosevic's response. Moreover, there is overwhelming evidence that NATO planners, from Clinton on down, expected Milosevic to capitulate quickly. He had done so previously in the face of military force, over Bosnia; now, many analysts believed, he needed only to make a show of resistance for domestic political purposes, after which he would willingly fold. Pentagon officials and Clinton cabinet members predicted that no more than a week of bombing would be needed to bring Milosevic to terms.[92] Obviously, if Western leaders believed the bombing campaign would be very short, they could not have anticipated the magnitude of terror and ethnic cleansing that the Serbs were able to perpetrate over the course of seventy-eight days. Even an "explosion" of refugees would be quite limited if confined to a short time frame.

In sum, the Kosovo experience should serve as a reminder that war almost invariably has unintended consequences; ostensibly humanitarian war is no exception. Chomsky is certainly right to insist that the death and human suffering occasioned by NATO's intervention in Kosovo far exceeded anything that had preceded intervention. If NATO had indeed fully anticipated the consequences of its Kosovo intervention, Chomsky could clinch his argument that NATO's action was not motivated by genuinely humanitarian concerns. The balance of evidence, however, suggests otherwise. Western leaders were aware that Milosevic might use a bombing campaign as an opportunity for atrocities. They did not, however, foresee the eventual magnitude of those atrocities, if only because they expected to bring Milosevic down before he had a chance to do as much damage as he might have wanted.

NATO wasn't interested in a peaceful resolution of the Kosovo dispute. Military force should normally be a last resort in an international dispute. Instead, according to

Chomsky, NATO didn't seriously consider alternatives to force. Following the US lead, NATO actively sought war.

The main alternative to war is diplomacy, but the Americans had no interest in engaging with the Serbs in genuine diplomacy. As Chomsky sees it, the so-called peace conference launched in February 1999 in Rambouillet, France, amounted to little more than the presentation of a series of mostly nonnegotiable demands to the Serbs that they could hardly be expected to accept. The Serbs were willing to entertain much of the Western proposal, which called for substantial autonomy for Kosovo during a three-year interim period during which a final settlement would be negotiated. But they were adamantly opposed to the provision for a NATO force to maintain the peace during the interim period. Suspicious of NATO, they would have been more amenable to what they could have regarded as a more neutral international presence, overseen perhaps by the United Nations, or by the Organization for Security and Cooperation in Europe (OSCE), which was less subject to US control than NATO was. And, critically, the Rambouillet proposal included a provision that would have allowed the NATO force essentially unlimited freedom to operate anywhere in Serbia. This was a "killer clause" apparently designed to ensure rejection; no country could accept such a blatant infringement on its sovereignty.[93] The Serbs' alternative proposal, presented on March 15 in Paris after a two-week adjournment of the Rambouillet talks and endorsed by the Serb parliament on March 23, was not given serious consideration.[94]

Is Chomsky right? Were the United States and its allies more interested in fighting a war than in finding a peaceful solution to the Kosovo crisis? The evidence is mixed.

Some of Chomsky's arguments, though reasonable at the time he made them, can now be discounted: most notably, the claim that the NATO occupation force provision was a "killer clause" designed to elicit rejection. According to one recent account, both Secretary of State Madeleine Albright (in a telephone call) and US ambassador Christopher R. Hill (in a face-to-face meeting) personally assured Milosevic that the clause was negotiable, but he refused any discussion.[95] Also, Chomsky's observation that the Serbs' late alternative proposal wasn't seriously considered by the West is accurate, but not very compelling. Having refused to negotiate the Rambouillet draft, the Serbs at the eleventh hour came up with a completely new proposal that would have given the Kosovars less autonomy than the Serbs had previously indicated would be acceptable to them.[96] It was reasonable to doubt the good faith of this counterproposal. Western diplomats nevertheless made last ditch efforts to avert war. US assistant secretary of state Richard Holbrooke and German foreign minister Joschka Fischer made direct appeals to Milosevic during the week following the final breakdown of talks and preceding the commencement of bombing.

Still, there is no question that NATO took an extremely tough, inflexible stance toward the Serbs at Rambouillet and afterward. The Serbs effectively were presented with an ultimatum to agree to NATO's terms or be bombed.[97] One US administration figure reportedly told media in an off-the-record briefing, "We intentionally set the bar too high for the Serbs to comply. They need some bombing, and that's what they are going to get."[98] John Gilbert, the UK's defense ministry chief of intelligence during the Kosovo war, later told Parliament that "I think certain people were spoiling for a fight in NATO at that time; . . . we were at a point when some people felt that something had to be done [against Serbia] so you just provoked a fight. . . . The terms put to Milosevic at Rambouillet were absolutely intolerable: How could he possibly accept them[?]"[99] No less an advocate of American power than Henry Kissinger wrote shortly after the adjournment in Rambouillet that the terms presented to the Serbs amounted to an intolerable diktat.[100] The West's insistence on a peacekeeping force under NATO command was close to a dealbreaker for Milosevic; a determined effort to avoid war could have included a proposal for an international force under UN auspices. Also, NATO never tried seriously to involve Russia, Serbia's traditional ally, in developing the Rambouillet proposal. A role for Russia would have provided some reassurance to the Serbs and possibly helped soften their stance.

How can we make sense of this conflicting evidence? Was NATO interested in avoiding war, or was it spoiling for a fight? It may be helpful to recall that governments, and certainly therefore coalitions of governments like NATO, are not unitary actors with consistent and unambiguous objectives. So, while there is evidence of an interest in avoiding war, it is clear that the desire to avoid war was highly qualified by other interests: nothing less than fairly complete capitulation by the Serbs would be acceptable, and solutions involving Russia or the United Nations or the OCSE were not to be considered. This was to be NATO's affair. Here, again, it is relevant that Western leaders generally expected the bombing campaign to be short, with a fairly quick Serb surrender in prospect. The avoidance of war would presumably have been a higher priority had NATO leaders been able to foresee a bombing campaign lasting seventy-eight days, with all its unintended consequences. But NATO clearly was more than ready, if not eager, for a fight.

There were other motivations for armed intervention. The real reason for the Kosovo intervention, according to Chomsky, was to assert US power, through NATO. Serbia-dominated Yugoslavia was a European holdout—in contrast to most of the rest of Eastern Europe, which undertook a fairly rapid transition to capitalism, Yugoslavia basically clung to its Communist-era economic system. Thus, Chomsky describes Serbia with his trademark sarcasm as "one of those disorderly miscreants that impede the institution of the U.S.-dominated global system."[101]

Little Serbia—an impediment to US world domination? It sounds far-fetched, but Chomsky goes on to explain that "Serbia was an annoyance, an unwelcome impediment to Washington's efforts to complete its substantial takeover of Europe. Although the resources of the Balkans are of no great interest, their strategic location is, not only with regard to Europe, West and East, but also the Middle East."[102] This is not altogether fanciful. The Balkans don't have quite the same geopolitical importance as Greece, with its location on sea lanes leading directly to the Middle East, but no one would completely discount the Balkans' strategic value. The Kosovo intervention did in fact lead to the establishment of a US base, Camp Bondsteel, in the Balkans, enhancing the already substantial US presence in southeastern Europe. The region was the site of a major planned energy project: Corridor 8, financed by the International Monetary Fund, was to pass along a route through Macedonia and Albania.[103] So, even if Serbia wasn't a particularly formidable obstacle to American power in Europe, Serbia's misbehavior did provide a pretext for an expanded American military presence in a region of some geostrategic interest.

On the other hand, there is scant evidence that energy or even broader economic concerns played a major role in the thinking of allied leaders in their approach to Kosovo. The historian David Gibbs suggests that economic concerns did play a major role, citing remarks by President Clinton in March 1999: "We need a Europe that is safe, secure, free, united, a good partner with us for trading; . . . if we're going to have a strong economic relationship that includes our ability to sell around the world, Europe has got to be a key. . . . *Now that's what this Kosovo thing is all about*" (emphasis added).[104] The thrust of Clinton's remarks, however, was to emphasize the economic importance to the United States of a stable, secure Europe. Turmoil in the Balkans, with its historically proved potential for spreading to neighboring countries, would surely threaten that objective.

Still, Chomsky makes a plausible argument that the Kosovo intervention served to affirm the United States' continued hegemonic role in Europe, which in turn was key to America's continued quest for global hegemony. Chomsky cites multiple statements by American and other Western leaders to show that the need to maintain NATO's credibility was a major factor motivating the tough stance the allies adopted toward the Serbs over Kosovo.[105] Chomsky's assertion that "credibility of NATO" means "credibility of US power" is an oversimplification, but it contains a large element of truth.[106] NATO was the primary organizational instrument through which the United States had historically pursued its leadership role in Europe.[107]

Europe during the 1990s had moved along a number of fronts to establish unified financial, foreign, and military policies that portended increased autonomy from American leadership. The United States had sought to react to this threat in a number of ways; among these ways was strengthening NATO—a particularly challenging objective during a period in which the disappearance of the Soviet adversary had robbed NATO of its original raison d'être. Intervention to prevent destabilizing civil wars or humanitarian catastrophes in or near its borders provided a useful rationale for affirming NATO's continued relevance.[108] Kosovo was a good opportunity for such an affirmation, and a number of fortuitous circumstances had enabled the United States to seize the initiative on Kosovo from its European partners, some of whom had resisted the hard-line stance favored by the Americans.[109] As Chomsky and others have pointed out, the approach of NATO's fiftieth anniversary in April 1999 lent an added impetus to decisive action over Kosovo.[110] The anniversary observances were planned as a powerful affirmation of NATO's relevance in a post–Cold War world; a resolution of Kosovo's future had to be achieved beforehand.

In sum, Chomsky's argument that the Kosovo intervention served important American geostrategic interests seems credible. An essentially similar explanation of American behavior toward Kosovo—let's call it the "geostrategic" explanation, as opposed to the "humanitarian" one—has been advanced by the political scientists Christopher Layne and Andrew Bacevich, among others.[111] It has been developed most thoroughly by David Gibbs.

Gibbs's account suggests that the United States by the end of 1998 had adopted a partisan anti-Milosevic stance that demonstrated more concern for a tough assertion of a US role in the Balkans than for saving lives. American and other Western officials had generally recognized the KLA as a terrorist organization that pursued a deliberate strategy of provoking Serb reprisals. But, instead of seeking to restrain the Kosovar insurgency, the Americans actually drew closer to the guerillas, providing them with various forms of covert assistance. While it is indisputable that it was the KLA, and not Milosevic, that initially undermined the October 1998 truce, the United States one-sidedly blamed Milosevic. It is hard to reconcile this behavior with humanitarian intent. It was, however, consistent with the US record in the Balkans during the 1990s, which was to assert an American role even at the cost of jeopardizing opportunities for peacemaking.[112] Thus, the United States actively encouraged intransigence by the Bosnian Serbs in their independence struggle in 1992–1993 and effectively undermined the peace plan proposed by former US secretary of state Cyrus Vance and former British foreign secretary David Owen. The Vance-Owen plan, while promising, was not stamped "made in America." The 1995 Dayton Accords, which were so stamped, were widely seen as an affirmation of American leadership and a setback for the European Union's efforts to forge an independent foreign policy.[113] Gibbs, like Chomsky, Layne, and Bacevich, sees humanitarianism as a pretext, not a motivation, for NATO's action in Kosovo.

While compelling, the geostrategic explanation is not quite fully adequate. In particular, it cannot easily account for what is known about the bureaucratic infighting over Kosovo policy within the Clinton administration. By all accounts, Secretary of State Madeleine Albright, based on her experience of the previous decade, genuinely and passionately believed that Milosevic was evil and must be stopped to ensure against a new humanitarian catastrophe in the Balkans. An early and unrelenting advocate of threatening force to restrain the Serbs, Albright encountered stiff resistance from Secretary of Defense William Cohen, who expressed skepticism of the practicality of humanitarian intervention. His views reflected those of the Joint Chiefs of Staff, who believed that there were no major US strategic interests at stake in Kosovo.[114] Thus, the Pentagon—the major bureaucratic power center whose institutional interests most clearly lay with the projection of American military might around the globe—rejected the logic that Chomsky and Gibbs believe motivated American policy. The reluctance of the Pentagon to contemplate forceful action in Kosovo is hard to square with the view that the Kosovo intervention was mainly about expanding the reach of American power.

Another problem with the geostrategic explanation is that the "credibility of NATO" repeatedly invoked by administration figures is not quite as simply a smokescreen for American power as Chomsky contends. Europeans could hardly be indifferent to the prospect of major turmoil in the Balkans, Europe's historic tinderbox. It is entirely natural that a political-military alliance of European countries would want to avert a humanitarian catastrophe in Kosovo or a civil war sending hundreds of thousands of refugees into neighboring countries. Failure to avert such a catastrophe would indeed call into question Europeans' ability to work together to meet common security needs.

Finally, an exclusively geostrategic explanation of the Kosovo intervention fails to consider that whatever the motivations of the American leaders in driving the NATO response to the Kosovo crisis, their decisions were taken in a context of pressure. As noted earlier, a genuine and increasingly influential humanitarian lobby had developed by the late 1990s that made it exigent for the United States and its allies to *do something* to ensure against another Srebrenica in Kosovo. This context has to be recognized as part of the explanation for why NATO acted as it did. Even if humanitarianism was a mere pretext for action, there had been a genuine buildup of political pressure that created the possibility for the pretext. Even if the Kosovo intervention was significantly motivated by the need to preserve NATO's credibility, it was humanitarian concerns that sharpened the perceived threat to NATO's credibility. The fact that Kosovo could not be ignored is in itself significant testimony to the growth of humanitarian influence on American foreign policy. The geostrategic explanation has undeniable merits: the US insistence on NATO acting alone, the extremely inflexible stance taken at Rambouillet, and the evident anxiety to "wrap up" Kosovo before the NATO anniversary celebrations—all suggest strongly that humanitarian considerations were not alone in the decision to intervene. Still, it is impossible to dismiss the evidence that humanitarian concerns played a significant role.

SUMMARY AND CONCLUSIONS:
CHOMSKY ON HUMANITARIAN INTERVENTION

Chomsky's critique of the Kosovo intervention contains valid and important observations. Chomsky's argument that NATO's intervention made things worse in Kosovo is convincing; it cannot be refuted without resorting to dubious, counterfactual speculation. And, even if Chomsky's geostrategic explanation of US motives falls short, it is nevertheless relevant: at the very least, a forceful demonstration of NATO power in Kosovo was consistent with broader US strategic objectives in the 1990s, and that fact needs to be taken into account in any general explanation of the Kosovo intervention. Chomsky is certainly right, too, to dismiss the notion that humanitarian concerns were a consistent, driving force of US foreign policy.

Still, Chomsky's arguments are too absolute. He does not allow even for the possibility that humanitarian considerations may have been in play along with other drivers of policy: "You can think [military intervention] was good or bad, but there was no humanitarian element. Zero. It had some other purpose."[115] He poses the right question: "Is [intervention] guided by power interests, or by humanitarian concern?"[116] He mistakenly assumes that the answer must strictly be either/or.

Varieties of Terrorism

With the attacks of 9/11, Americans for the first time became victims of international terrorism in their own country. The attacks led the Bush administration to declare a "war on terror," which in turn served as a justification of the US invasion of Iraq in 2003.

Chomsky was unambiguous in his condemnation of the 9/11 attacks, which he called "a horrible atrocity."[117] Chomsky dealt more broadly with the consequences and implications of the attacks in two ways. First, he warned repeatedly that the proper response to the threat of international terrorism was not an escalation of violence by the United States. Second, he sought to promote an alternative discourse on terrorism—one that recognized a critical role of the United States not as the victim but as the perpetrator of acts of terror.

FIGHTING INTERNATIONAL TERRORISM

Chomsky has repeatedly argued that an effective campaign against terrorism must be based on an understanding of its causes. Those causes may well include legitimate grievances harbored by the terrorists and their supporters. To recognize as much is not to justify or apologize for terrorist acts; it is simply a prerequisite to the understanding that is necessary for effectively combating terrorism: "If you're serious about trying to prevent further atrocities, you try to find out what their roots are. And almost any crime, a crime in the streets, a war, whatever it may be, there's usually something behind it that has elements of legitimacy, and you have to consider those elements."[118] Thus, Chomsky believes that while terrorist networks can and should be fought by collaborative international police work, it is necessary to address the economic, social, and political grievances of the larger Muslim community from which the terrorists draw their support. Chomsky approvingly quotes a commentator who asserts that the key to weakening al-Qaeda lies in eroding its support base—in weaning away its supporters and potential supporters.[119]

Chomsky identifies three causes of Muslim anger that feed terrorism: US support for Israel in its dispute with the Palestinians, the murderous US-UK sanctions inflicted on Iraq, and the long-standing alliance between the United States and corrupt and repressive regimes in the Middle East. The terrorists are able to exploit these issues as they pursue their broader goal of establishing extremist Islamic regimes in the Muslim world.[120] The implications of this analysis are clear: the United States must end the sanctions on Iraq, and presumably make some amends for the damage done (the sanctions did in fact end with the overthrow of

Saddam); it must end its one-sided partisanship for Israel and advance an equitable solution of the Israel-Palestine conflict; and it must withdraw its support for Middle Eastern autocracy.

In an early comment on 9/11, Chomsky warned that "if the United States chooses to respond by escalating the cycle of violence, which is most likely what bin Laden and his associates hope for, then the consequences could be awesome."[121] Of course, the Bush administration did resort to violence in both Afghanistan and Iraq, waving the banner of the war on terror. As we have seen, a major theme of Chomsky's anti-Iraq War critique was that the American attack on a major Muslim country would actually strengthen the terrorists, spurring the recruitment of jihadists around the globe. That prediction, as Chomsky later pointed out, proved to be accurate.[122] It is very likely that the post-9/11 bombing of Afghanistan also helped to spur Muslim resentment against the United States, boosting the recruitment of jihadists.

Chomsky opposed the American bombing and invasion of Afghanistan. The rationale for the attack, of course, was Washington's belief that the Afghan Taliban regime was sheltering Osama bin Laden and other al-Qaeda leaders who were responsible for the 9/11 attacks. Writing shortly afterward, Chomsky claimed that (1) the administration had not proved al-Qaeda's complicity in 9/11, (2) Washington had rebuffed feelers from the Afghan Taliban rulers to discuss extradition of Osama bin Laden, (3) the bombing of Afghanistan was killing large numbers of innocent people, and (4) other, less violent ways were available to achieve the removal of the Taliban from power.[123]

The first of these assertions had some merit at the time; in retrospect, it was clearly off target. Chomsky's observation that the administration had spurned Taliban feelers to turn over bin Laden to a third country was correct, and his argument that no one could know whether an agreement with the Taliban would have been possible seems plausible. It ignores, however, that the United States had already been in discussions with the Taliban for three years prior to 9/11 over US requests for bin Laden's extradition. Those discussions had achieved no progress; according to US negotiators, the Taliban had shown no real interest in an agreement.[124] Chomsky's third claim, that the US bombing campaign was killing large numbers of innocent Afghans, was indisputably correct. It was certainly a point worth making, given the relatively little concern the issue of Afghan civilian casualties has generated in the United States.[125] But Chomsky's claim that other means could have been found to remove the Taliban from power was weak. As evidence, he offered no more than a vague statement to that effect by a large gathering of Afghan opposition leaders in late October 2001.[126]

In short, Chomsky's indictment of the war in Afghanistan was far less compelling than his arguments against the subsequent invasion of Iraq, discussed earlier. Chomsky charged that the bombing "was undertaken without credible pretext, as later quietly conceded."[127] Apart from the fact that Chomsky does not tell us who allegedly "quietly conceded" his point, his remarkable claim ignores the very credible grounds that the United States had for the attack.

THE UNITED STATES AS TERRORIST

Alongside his counsel of a nonviolent and enlightened response to Muslim grievances, Chomsky consistently advanced a parallel theme in his response to the 9/11 attacks. The theme was that the United States had suffered an example of the type of horror that this country had long inflicted on other countries. The United States, newly a direct victim of terrorism on its own shores, had long been a perpetrator of comparable crimes. Indeed, "the United States is a leading terrorist state." [128]

Assuming, for the moment, that this claim was defensible, why make it, as Chomsky hastened to do, in the immediate aftermath of 9/11? One commentator suggested that Chomsky in an early post-9/11 interview adopted a "weirdly dispassionate tone" in reaction to the terror attacks, betraying his "inability to connect to the emotional reality of American suffering."[129] This may well be a valid observation, but I'm more interested in the validity and relevance of the content of Chomsky's statement than its tone or psychological underpinnings. Chomsky's evident objective, in making his claim, was to use 9/11 as an opportunity to renew arguments that he had been making for many years about US foreign policy. He was trying to turn the prevailing discussion, about US innocent victimhood, into one about US victimization of others. His comments show a clear concern that the theme of victimhood and its attendant self-righteousness would be used to rationalize aggressive behavior by the United States—a concern that turned out to be well founded. Chomsky's effort to change the subject may or may not have been politically or psychologically astute; what I want to explore here is whether and to what extent his arguments had substantive merit.

Chomsky begins by challenging conventional notions of terrorism that would tend to exclude the possibility that the US government could ever be considered to engage in terrorism. He approvingly quotes a political scientist who points out that "by convention—and it must be emphasized only by convention—great power use and the threat of the use of force is normally described as coercive diplomacy and not as a form of terrorism."[130] This is so, even though great powers sometimes engage in actions that would be described as terroristic if performed by guerilla or jihadists or other nonstate actors. Chomsky goes on to quote the official US government definition of terrorism: "Any activity that (A) involves a violent act or an act dangerous to human life that is a violation of the criminal laws of the United States or any State . . . and (B) appears to be intended (i) to intimidate or coerce a civilian population; (ii) to influence the policy of a government by intimidation or coercion; or (iii) to affect the conduct of a government by assassination or kidnapping."[131] Chomsky views this definition as quite reasonable and proposes it as a standard against which to assess the actions of the US government.

In part, Chomsky's indictment of the United States as a leading terrorist state consists of a recitation of past crimes by the US government, including its complicity in state terror by client states, particularly in Central America, and its sponsorship of the Nicaraguan contras, who liberally employed terror.[132] As we saw in Chapter 2, there is substantial merit in these accusations, even if Chomsky tends to overstate the directness of US responsibility for the crimes of its clients. Chomsky also cites the US covert campaign of sabotage against Cuba, including numerous assassination attempts on the life of its leader. This is an old story, but Chomsky reasonably points to the continuing gentle treatment by the United States of the anti-Cuban terrorists Orlando Bosch and Luis Posada Carriles as indicative of a willingness to tolerate the "right kind" of terrorism.[133] However valid, most of these accusations are either too old or too small-scale to lend more than marginal support to Chomsky's claim that the United States was a leading terrorist state as of the turn of the twenty-first century. His brief against US terrorism does, however, include a number of more contemporary and very grave charges. These include an alleged willingness to cause mass starvation in Afghanistan following 9/11, the US bombing of a Sudanese pharmaceutical plant in 1998, and allegedly active participation in state terror by allies—most notably, Turkey and Indonesia. We will examine each of these accusations in turn.

Starving Afghanistan. This is the least meritorious of Chomsky's attributions of terrorist behavior to the United States in the 9/11 era. It has been well covered elsewhere, so my discussion will be brief.[134] In an October 2001 speech Chomsky charged that the United States, initiating its intervention in Afghanistan, was engaged in a "silent genocide" by demanding that Pakistan eliminate truck convoys that were carrying food supplies critical to the survival of millions of Afghans. With some modifications, he repeated the claim in his books *9-11* and *Hegemony or Survival*.[135] Chomsky's accusation, based on inferences from news reports, was easily refuted soon afterward. All the available evidence indicates that American intervention actually facilitated the delivery of food supplies to Afghanistan. In fact, no mass starvation occurred. Chomsky's original accusation might be defended as a somewhat reckless but well-intended effort to raise an issue of important humanitarian concern. His subsequent iterations of the charge suggest both an unwillingness to admit error and a resolute determination to ascribe the worst possible motives and consequences to US policy.

The al-Shifa bombing. In August 1998 US cruise missiles struck and destroyed the al-Shifa factory in Khartoum North, Sudan. American spokesmen justified the attack on the grounds that the factory, ostensibly a manufacturer of pharmaceuticals, was involved in the production of chemical weapons and that the plant had ties with the al-Qaeda terrorist network, which US intelligence had linked to recent bombings of American embassies in Kenya and Tanzania. Subsequent independent investigations demonstrated quite conclusively that the al-Shifa plant was not involved in the manufacture of chemical weapons, but the US government never admitted as much. Nor did it ever offer any apology, much less compensation, for the damage caused.[136]

In an interview soon after 9/11, Chomsky called the attacks on the United States a major atrocity, but stated that "in terms of number of victims they do not reach the level of many others, for example, Clinton's bombing of the Sudan with no credible pretext, destroying half its pharmaceutical supplies and probably killing tens of thousands of people (no one knows, because the US blocked an inquiry at the UN and no one cares to pursue it)."[137] The tens of thousands dead would result from a lack of essential lifesaving antibiotics and antimalarial and antituberculosis medicines. Chomsky's statement elicited strong reactions from the essayist Christopher Hitchens and others, who challenged Chomsky's claim that the two attacks—9/11 and al-Shifa—were morally comparable.[138]

One immediate problem with Chomsky's comparison of the two attacks was pinpointed by Hitchens: the manifest purpose of the 9/11 assault was to kill very large numbers of innocent people. The same cannot be said of the al-Shifa bombing, which was carried out at night to minimize casualties. (The only casualty was a night watchman who was killed.) Whatever the consequences of the al-Shifa bombing, it cannot "be characterized as directly homicidal in the same way."[139] Moreover, Chomsky's claim that the factory bombing had "no credible pretext" was something of an overstatement: however unjustified, based as it was on weak intelligence, the bombing was at least ostensibly a reaction to the bombings of American embassies in which over two hundred people were killed. That bombing was credibly linked to al-Qaeda, whose leader, Osama bin Laden, had been sheltered by the Sudanese regime.

If the two crimes were not comparable qualitatively, how comparable were they quantitatively? Was the al-Shifa bombing likely to result in the deaths of large numbers of people? Chomsky's claim that it probably was was based on credible sources. In its support Chomsky cited Jonathan Belke, the regional program manager for a respected NGO, and Werner Daum, West Germany's former ambassador to the Sudan, in addition to journalists' reports.[140] (On the other hand, Chomsky's unsupported assertion that Human Rights Watch had also arrived at a similar assessment was repudiated by an HRW spokesperson, who reported that HRW had not investigated the issue.)[141]

The validity of these assessments was challenged by the political activist and essayist Leo Casey. Casey took particular aim at the contention that the destruction of the factory had created a critical shortage of medicines that the Sudanese government would be unable to remedy. While acknowledging that the loss of medicines was significant, Casey argued that the Sudanese government did indeed have the means to remedy the shortage through imports, in which case Chomsky's presumptive causal relationship between the bombing and a possible increase in Sudanese mortality collapses.[142] Casey also pointed out that in the three years following the al-Shifa bombing there were in fact no reports of a significant health crisis traceable to a shortage of medicines. Chomsky's retort to Casey, that the available data on Sudan was too unreliable to make any definite assessments, can hardly be regarded as strong support for his case; it can even be turned against him, as an argument against making unverifiable claims of increased mortality.[143]

Casey had somewhat the better of the argument, but, in fairness to Chomsky, it needs to be acknowledged that Casey's argument was, after all, post-9/11; Chomsky's comments as of that date reflected his knowledge of estimates by credible sources that, up to that point, had not been rigorously challenged. Arguably, Chomsky should have treated those estimates more skeptically, given their lack of hard evidence and given the gravity of the charge of comparability with 9/11. Still, his belief as of that date that the factory bombing had probably resulted in significant suffering and death in the Sudan cannot be dismissed as completely unreasonable. (It is also worth asking whether the internal US government debate leading to the al-Shifa bombing decision considered the humanitarian implications of bombing a pharmaceutical factory. The full internal record is not available, but it seems unlikely that it did.)

The bombing of al-Shifa certainly lacked legal or moral justification. It could very well fit the US government's definition of "terrorism" quoted earlier. Al-Shifa can reasonably be regarded as a callous and reckless act of imperial arrogance. It supports Chomsky's broad argument that the US government has repeatedly acted as if it presumes itself to be above international law and accepted standards of behavior. But al-Shifa fails to measure up to the 9/11 attacks as an act of terrorism. It was clearly different both in its intent and in its immediate consequences, while its long-term consequences were at worst unclear. Chomsky's comparison of the two crimes was therefore dubious at best.

Chomsky's invocation of the al-Shifa bombing in the immediate aftermath of 9/11 is all the more curious because he could have cited a much better, ongoing example of US violence: Iraqi sanctions. The sanctions were in fact a widely expressed grievance among Islamists, and bin Laden himself cited them as proof of US hypocrisy in its claims to value human life. Chomsky, of course, had condemned the sanctions in the past and would do so in the future. They fit most definitions of terrorism, including certainly the official US definition that Chomsky made his own. Perhaps Chomsky felt the need to pinpoint a single dramatic act—a bombing—as an analog to 9/11. The sanctions imposed on Iraq by the United States and Britain, while far more deadly than the 9/11 attacks, killed more slowly, and invisibly.

Turkey and its Kurds. Turkey, a US NATO ally, has long resisted the demands of its Kurdish minority for linguistic freedom and regional autonomy, if not independence. Turkey's repression of its Kurds escalated brutally during the 1990s, with a counterinsurgency campaign that resulted in thousands of deaths and generated millions of refugees. The US government, according to Chomsky, not only supported a campaign of ethnic cleansing and terror that Turkey waged on its Kurds; it actively instigated that campaign.

Citing a variety of credible sources, Chomsky argues convincingly that Turkey was, indeed, a massive human rights violator during the 1990s. Employing the familiar counterinsurgency strategy of depriving insurgents of their rural base of support, Turkish forces destroyed some 3,500 Kurdish villages, forcing some 2.5 million Kurds to become refugees by 1996. The internal war produced tens of thousands of casualties. The Turkish government enjoyed diplomatic support and abundant military assistance from the United States all through this period. Indeed, in 1994, as atrocities peaked, Turkey became the biggest single importer of American military hardware and thus the world's largest arms purchaser. That same year, the US State Department's annual human rights report for Turkey was little better than a whitewash of the atrocities. Chomsky points out that while Turkey's human rights record was a serious obstacle to its application for European Union membership, it posed no problem for the United States, which strongly supported Turkey's application. American military aid to Turkey declined only toward the end of the decade, as "successful state terror and ethnic cleansing . . . reduced the level of necessary atrocities below that of the mid-1990s."[144]

Chomsky is certainly correct to point to American leaders' apparent indifference to Turkey's human rights abuses as a reason for skepticism about America's attachment to humanitarian values in its foreign policy. Turkey did employ terror in its counterinsurgency campaign, and this practice elicited no strong opposition from the United States, which indeed equipped the Turks for their dirty work. Still, Chomsky's account grossly overstates the United States' role in Turkey's internal war.

Chomsky doesn't merely assert that the United States supplied Turkey with military hardware that it used in its internal repression; he claims that the United States actually pressured its Turkish client to employ maximum violence. Thus, he says that in 1993 the United States "intervened decisively to escalate the atrocities," and that the Turkish government's turn away from possible negotiated solutions to its Kurdish problem reflected the preferences of the United States, "which rushed sophisticated equipment to the Turkish military . . . so that it could escalate the ethnic cleansing and terror."[145] Chomsky offers no evidence whatsoever for his claim that the United States pushed for Turkey's escalation of violence. Nor does he suggest any reason as to why the United States would have preferred a violent to a peaceful solution. It is, indeed, hard to imagine why the United States would have taken such a stance. Chomsky's claim thus lacks plausibility as well as supporting evidence.

There was in fact some official American pressure—albeit too limited to be effective—for Turkey to curtail its human rights abuses. In 1993 John Shattuck, a former head of the American Civil Liberties Union, became assistant secretary of state for human rights. Shattuck made two trips to Turkey in 1994, meeting with human rights groups and dissidents and incurring bitter criticisms from nationalistic Turks. Turkish indignation was also spurred by a US congressional panel's investigations into human rights abuses, which led to the cancellation of sales of cluster bombs and Cobra helicopters to Turkey.[146] Chomsky alludes to the Clinton administration's success in evading congressional restrictions on aid to Turkey, but otherwise doesn't tell his readers any of this.[147]

Washington's willingness to provide arms to Turkey undoubtedly reflected Turkey's status as a valued US NATO ally, as Chomsky argues. Arms sales were also a source of profits for US businesses and jobs for their employees. Notably, the steady supply to Turkey of Black Hawk helicopters, manufactured in Connecticut, reflected the considerable influence of Connecticut's Senator Christopher Dodd. In a claim for which he offers no evidence, Chomsky tells us that the United States was the only country willing to supply Turkey with weapons for its terror campaign.[148] But the political scientist John Tirman, in a book Chomsky repeatedly cites, explains that the arms sales business was internationally competitive: French, German, and Russian firms were ready and eager to sell to the Turks any weapons they couldn't get from Americans.[149]

Chomsky's claim of US responsibility for Turkish repression obliterates the important distinction between agency and complicity. A reasonable argument can be made that the US government, in its failure to apply meaningful counterpressure on an ally guilty of atrocities, was complicit in those atrocities. But Chomsky's contention that the United States was not merely complicit, but was a driving force in Turkey's internal repression, is baseless.

East Timor, again. American policymakers also looked away while Indonesian army and paramilitary units engaged in mass murder and terror in 1999 in response to East Timor's move toward independence from Indonesia. As background to the 1999 crisis, Chomsky provides a good overview of East Timor's ordeal beginning with Indonesia's quasi-genocidal crushing of the East Timor independence struggle in the late 1970s.[150] (See Chapter 2.) He observes that the United States never had the slightest compunction about developing and expanding warm relations with Suharto's blood-soaked regime—including, particularly, extensive military cooperation. Suharto fell out of US favor only in the late 1990s, as a result of his economic mismanagement, his resistance to harsh IMF-proposed economic programs, and domestic political troubles. He was thus "abandoned" by the United States, "in the usual pattern of criminals who have lost their usefulness or become disobedient: Trujillo, Somoza, Marcos, Noriega, Saddam Hussein, Mobutu, Ceausescu, and many others."[151]

Suharto's departure in May 1998 opened up new possibilities for Timorese independence. The following year, a UN-sponsored referendum on autonomy was scheduled for late summer. Powerful groups within Indonesia, however, remained adamantly opposed to giving up Indonesia's colony. Even before the referendum was announced, a network of paramilitary organizations, or militias, mobilized for violence to thwart Timorese independence. Between February and July 1999 between three thousand and five thousand Timorese were murdered by militia terrorists, presumably as a warning of more bloodshed to come if the Timorese chose independence. Chomsky cites abundant, convincing evidence from the United Nations, Australian intelligence, the Australian government, and other sources documenting that the official Indonesian army (the TNI) was heavily involved in supporting the militias.

In turn, the Indonesian military was the client of extensive US training programs, which had continued officially through 1997 and more discreetly afterward to evade congressional restrictions. A principal recipient of US training programs was Kopassus, a special forces unit that had a long record of human rights violations. Chomsky cites a British newspaper report that noted that Kopassus's American-provided training focused on "military expertise that could only be used internally against civilians, such as urban guerilla warfare, surveillance, counter-intelligence, sniper marksmanship, and 'psychological operations.'"[152] Chomsky also points out that in April 1999, a few days after a militia massacre of as many as two hundred Timoreans in church, Admiral Dennis Blair, the US Pacific commander, met with the head of the Indonesian army, assuring him of US support and assistance and proposing a new US training mission.[153]

The East Timorese did vote overwhelmingly (80 percent) for independence in the August 30 referendum, provoking a renewed wave of terror by the militias. Hundreds of thousands of people fled their homes. Now the international community, led by the Australian media and public opinion, took notice, and demands mounted for an international peacekeeping force to put an end to the violence. In September, after initially expressing confidence in Jakarta's ability to end the bloodshed, the Clinton administration threatened sanctions, characterized by Chomsky as "some timid gestures, threats to veto loans and cancellation of military cooperation."[154] These limited threats were enough to induce the Indonesian generals within three days to drop their opposition to an international presence in Timor. An Australian-led UN force entered the territory on September 20.

Chomsky argues plausibly that the alacrity with which the Indonesian military responded to modest US pressure demonstrates that an earlier American decision to take action could have saved large numbers of lives. The post-referendum explosion of militia terror could have been anticipated, yet the Clinton administration sidestepped Australian and other countries' suggestions for preventive action. Even after the referendum, the administration acted only after an intense buildup of international and domestic pressure. Why did it delay? The answer to that question is hardly obscure. Chomsky cites an analysis by *New York Times* correspondents: the Clinton administration "has made the calculation that the United States must put its relationship with Indonesia, a mineral-rich nation of more than 200 million people, ahead of its concern over the political fate of East Timor, a tiny impoverished territory of 800,000 people."[155] Or, as an anonymous US diplomat quoted by Chomsky put it, "Indonesia matters and East Timor doesn't."[156]

The East Timor crisis was almost contemporaneous with the Kosovo crisis. As Chomsky repeatedly points out, the Clinton administration's inaction with regard to East Timor stands in stark contrast to its claims of humanitarian concern for the people of Kosovo. Certainly, measured by body count, the humanitarian toll in East Timor in the months preceding the referendum far exceeded that in Kosovo prior to Western intervention there in March 1999. As I have argued, US inaction on East Timor does not constitute proof that humanitarian concerns were absent in the Western intervention in Kosovo. It is clear, however, that US policy toward East Timor assigned little importance to humanitarian concerns.

Is there anything to mitigate the harsh conclusion that US policy toward East Timor was at best characterized by callous indifference? Chomsky cites no mitigating circumstances, but he gives no sign of having looked for any. A more balanced analysis would acknowledge that American policy toward Indonesia and East Timor in 1999 reflected conflicting impulses. As early as February 1999, the US assistant secretary of state for Far Eastern Affairs was suggesting to reluctant Australian diplomats that an international peacekeeping force would be necessary to assure a peaceful transition in East Timor.[157] But while elements of the State Department—both in Washington and in the Jakarta embassy—advocated a tougher line with the Indonesian military, Pentagon officials resisted. When Admiral Blair in April 1999 assured the Indonesian military of continued US assistance, he actually had instructions, which he flouted, to tell the Indonesians to shut down the militias. Given what were at worst mixed signals from Washington, the Indonesian military felt no need to change course.[158]

Effectively, then, the thrust of US policy was indeed to "look away" from the depredations of the Indonesian military. That, essentially, was Chomsky's assessment in his first major commentary on the East Timor events of 1999. Chomsky posited three possible responses by outsiders to a developing humanitarian catastrophe: (1) act to escalate the catastrophe; (2) do nothing; and (3) try to mitigate the catastrophe. He placed East Timor in the second category.[159] Subsequently, he observed that the agents of criminal violence, the Indonesian military, were "armed, trained, funded and supported by the U.S. and its allies."[160] The word "supported" is arguable—what kind of support, for what specific activities?—but otherwise Chomsky's assertion is correct. There was no real effort to curtail longstanding policies of assistance to the Indonesian military, including training and funding.

Later, however, Chomsky goes further, claiming that the US government was hoping to achieve plausible deniability by "subcontracting terror" to the Indonesian military and militias, which the United States was "organizing, arming, and directing."[161] Chomsky offers no evidence for his fantastic assertion that the United States was organizing and directing Indonesian official violence. His claim, in fact, is completely baseless. The US military, loath to disturb its close relationship with its Indonesian counterparts, chose not to interfere with their atrocities. But noninterference is very far from "organizing" and "directing." Chomsky for some reason evidently decided that his earlier accusation of US complicity in atrocity did not go far enough. It was not sufficient to say that the United States was complicit in evil; it must be *the source* of the evil. Once again, Chomsky has conflated complicity in atrocity—which should be bad enough—with agency.

Hegemony and Its Discontents

Few analysts of international affairs would argue with Chomsky's contention that even before the George W. Bush administration brought unilateralism to new levels, much of the world had come to view the United States as an arrogant "hyperpower" (in the words of the French foreign minister Hubert Vedrine) presuming its own immunity from international law and world opinion.[162] A more controversial question would be: "Has US hegemony been good for the world?" Chomsky doesn't pose that question directly and explicitly, but the overwhelming thrust of his writings is to ask it and to answer it firmly in the negative.

For the post–Cold War period, Chomsky's indictment of US policy can be summarized under three themes: the United States has been the perpetrator, instigator, and facilitator of large-scale violence in other countries, causing or contributing to the deaths of hundreds of thousands of people; the United States has constantly raised obstacles to the extension and strengthening of international law and cooperation; and the United States has imposed policies on less developed countries that have reduced those countries' chances of overcoming economic backwardness and poverty.

The people of Iraq have constituted the most numerous victims of direct US violence. It is possible that the reversal of Saddam Hussein's 1990 aggression against Kuwait would have required military force in any case, but the United States clearly was uninterested in any solution that eschewed force. The war that followed, combined with the sanctions imposed by the United States and its British allies, killed hundreds of thousands of Iraqi civilians. The 2003 invasion of Iraq added many more hundreds of thousands to the civilian death toll.[163] And, while the United States was not the instigator of crimes committed by such allied governments as Turkey and Indonesia, as Chomsky contends, US actions or inaction did facilitate violence by those governments' armed forces' against innocent noncombatants. Chomsky has raised very credible doubts about claims that US-led interventions in the Balkans saved large numbers of lives. It is quite possible that a more restrained Western handling of Kosovo in 1999 would have resulted in less human suffering and death than what eventually occurred.

The second category of Chomskian charges against American policy is that the United States has repeatedly opposed efforts to strengthen international law and cooperation when such moves clashed with American hegemonic objectives. The extension of NATO, the perseverance with missile defense, and the opposition to a wide range of arms control efforts all reflected US determination to resist limits on its hegemonic power, and all raised obstacles to the goal of creating a more stable and secure international order. These claims are compelling. Nor is it easy to dismiss Chomsky's argument that the imposition of a US-inspired neoliberal global economic order has inflicted great damage on many countries' prospects for sovereignty, democracy, and economic growth.

In short, there is a great deal of merit in Chomsky's view of US hegemony as an arrogant, brutal, disruptive, and exploitative force in the world. Can US hegemony be justified? Chomsky certainly doesn't think so; indeed, if Chomsky thinks that the US government plays any positive role in the world at all, he never tells us so—his accounts of the exercise of American power are consistently, uniformly negative. But there are reasonable counterarguments that seldom come into consideration in Chomsky's worldview.

Most scholarly analysts of international relations take a more benign view of American power. A substantial school of thought views the existence of a single hegemonic power as an important if not essential condition for world order—the hegemon provides a framework of formal and informal rules and institutions that facilitate cooperation among nations and thus make war less likely.[164] A variant of this perspective is that a clear preponderance of power in the hands of one essentially unchallengeable country forestalls the great power rivalries that cause war.[165] The hegemonic power typically enjoys numerous advantages—including economic advantages—over other countries, and a peaceful, stable world enables it to exploit those advantages. A hegemonic power thus has the means as well as the incentive to encourage international cooperation and peace. And, even if it uses its power position to extract some advantage for itself, the hegemon cannot rule by brute force: it must demonstrate that its primacy benefits the other major countries in the international system. Thus, Robert Keohane argues that a successful economic hegemon, like the United States, achieves and maintains its position by building a structure of international cooperation—a genuine consensus—that serves to convince the leaders of less powerful countries that they, too, benefit from the international economic order created by the hegemon.

The single benefit to the international system that analysts most often credit to a hegemonic power is stability, which is often understood to mean peace. Charles Kupchan, a critic of the unilateralism of the George W. Bush administration, asserts that "the United States has been either minding the store or putting out fires in virtually every quarter of the globe. American forces preserve the uneasy peace in East Asia, guarding South Korea from the regime to the north, keeping the lid on tensions between China and Japan, and trying to support Taiwan's de facto independence without inciting Beijing. America still maintains a sizable troop presence in Europe to help ensure stability on the Continent."[166] Kupchan goes on to praise globalization—managed and underwritten by the United States—as a force for international stability, and to commend US-led efforts, however flawed, at humanitarian intervention. Another critic of Bush foreign policy, Zbigniew Brzezinski, is less laudatory of globalization than Kupchan, but otherwise agrees that American world leadership is indispensable to global security: "global chaos" would ensue should the United States suddenly withdraw from its international responsibilities.[167]

The United States is often credited not only with providing stability, but with spreading democracy around the world. As Kupchan sees it, "democracy is flourishing in much of the world at least in part because the world's only superpower is a democracy—and a fanatic proselytizer at that."[168] Chomsky's old antagonist Samuel Huntington summed up the case for American hegemony: "A world without U.S. primacy will be a world with more violence and disorder and less democracy and economic growth than a world where the United States continues to have more influence than any other country in shaping global affairs."[169]

So, we have two dramatically contrasting pictures. One is of the essentially predatory hegemon according to Chomsky: the United States engages in or promotes violence as it pleases, undermines international law and stability, subverts democracy and succors tyrants, and impedes poorer countries in their search for economic growth and justice. The other is of the essentially benign hegemon according to Brzezinski, Huntington, Kupchan, and many others: the United States promotes peace and stability, democracy, and prosperity around the globe. In fairness, most mainstream advocates of the "essentially benign hegemon" perspective (including the trio just cited) acknowledge abuses of American power, and thus present a somewhat more nuanced picture than does Chomsky, who sees no good whatsoever coming out of Washington.[170] Brzezinski, for example, observes that neoliberal globalization has been far from uniformly benign, while Huntington eventually came to warn American leaders to "abandon the benign hegemon illusion that a natural congruity exists between their interests and values and those of the rest of the world. It does not. At times, American actions may promote public goods and serve more widely accepted ends. But often they will not."[171]

Still, the contrast between Chomsky's views and those of the mainstream analysts is stark. The latter generally believe that whatever its faults, American power has on balance been good for the world. Some see the likelihood of a declining American global hegemony as a problem for world order, and worry that unilateralist excesses by the United States might speed its loss of hegemonic position. Chomsky views with equanimity, if not satisfaction, the inevitable relative decline in American power; he commends countries like Venezuela, Bolivia, and Ecuador that have challenged the hegemon in its own hemisphere.

I am not going to ask, much less attempt to determine, which of the two perspectives—the predatory vs. the benign hegemon—is more accurate. However one answers that question, Chomsky's writings are useful if only for posing it, since others so seldom do. Even the moderate mainstream analysts tend to present an exceedingly optimistic picture of the motivations and consequences of American power. The optimism is most obvious in the ready assumption that US-led globalization has been good for the world. As we have seen, that assumption runs into the considerable evidence that the Washington Consensus has wrought havoc on the economy of many poorer countries. Is US hegemonic power a force for peace and stability in the world? Kupchan says that the United States has been "minding the store" in much of the world, but many of the instances he cites could well use asterisks supplied by Chomsky. For example, is the United States helping to preserve an uneasy peace between the two Koreas? Perhaps, but the Bush administration deliberately torpedoed the efforts of one South Korean government to explore accommodation with its northern neighbor; Chomsky's account of the United States' confrontational posture toward North Korea, and its failure to honor its agreements with that country, provides a useful corrective to prevailing accounts that focus only on North Korean culpability.[172] Has the sizable American military presence in Europe helped ensure stability on the continent, or has it merely served to maintain American influence there? The US insistence on NATO expansion created a permanent source of friction with Russia—exacerbated by plans for missile defense deployments—while American policymakers have discouraged the Europeans' development of an independent defense capability.[173]

Another major tenet of the benevolent hegemon model—that the United

States is a force for democracy in the world—is also problematic. American policymakers have traditionally invoked democracy and freedom as core values of this country's foreign policy, but as we have seen (in Chapter 2), during the Cold War the United States often subverted democratic governments and nurtured oppressive, autocratic regimes when it suited American interests. Has the end of the Cold War made any difference? It almost certainly has, to some extent. The US government has not undertaken actively to overthrow any of the left-leaning governments that took power in Latin America beginning in the 1990s. Indeed, pressure by the Clinton administration may have been instrumental in forestalling threatened coups against democratic governments in Guatemala, Ecuador, and Paraguay, and in mitigating some of the antidemocratic excesses of Alberto Fujimori of Peru.[174] Even the Reagan administration, despite its earlier open embrace of "authoritarian" (as opposed to "totalitarian") anti-Communist regimes, sought during the late 1980s to apply some modest pressure on its authoritarian allies in Latin America to move toward democratic governance.[175]

It seems, then, that the long-standing rhetorical commitment to democracy by US policymakers began to take on increasing substance with the end of the Cold War. Partly, this reflected the disappearance of the perceived Communist threat, which could so often be invoked to justify antidemocratic behavior. In part, it undoubtedly reflected a natural strain toward consistency. As the democracy promotion expert Thomas Carothers explains:

> Once senior officials state particular goals, even if only for rhetorical purposes, they will find that they are held to them. Critics and commentators in the public, as well as other agencies and branches of the government, will begin asking what the government is actually doing to achieve the stated goals. Faced with such inquiries, senior officials tend to respond by telling their subordinates to start doing something in pursuit of the goals, if only to give the impression that they are serious about them.[176]

By the turn of the twenty-first century, Carothers notes, democracy promotion objectives had been institutionalized in the US foreign policy bureaucracies.[177]

Chomsky shows no recognition of these changes. Instead, he emphasizes that the United States supports democracy only when it coincides with US strategic and economic interests. Chomsky's perception is selective, but he has a point. Boosters of America's democratic mission in the world would be hard put to cite instances in which the US government has promoted democratization even in the expectation that it would likely produce governments adverse to American interests. In countries with low levels of organization and mobilization of lower-income groups, the trappings of formal democracy can serve as useful cover for domination by oligarchies friendly to the United States. Chomsky cites Carothers's observation that in Latin America, the United States encouraged "limited, top-down forms of democratic change that did not risk upsetting the traditional structures of power with which the United States has long been allied [in] quite undemocratic societies."[178] And, while the United States has freely used the ideology of democracy against nations viewed as enemies—such as Iran, Saddam's Iraq, and Syria—American leaders have demonstrated high comfort levels in working closely with a wide variety of authoritarian regimes in North Africa, the Persian Gulf, and Central Asia. A brief effusion of democracy promotion gestures following the 2003 invasion of Iraq was soon curtailed by the Bush administration in deference to the sensitivities of America's autocratic friends.

In sum, we need not totally accept Chomsky's predatory hegemon model to recognize that the alternative and much more common benign hegemon perspective is credible only with the use of numerous elisions. American power may be a force for peace, stability, prosperity, and democracy in some parts of the world, but it has often worked effectively against those values. Chomsky's indictment of American foreign policy, one-sided as it is, helps us fill in a good many blanks.

Summary and Conclusions

How Chomsky Has Been Right

It should be clear by now that I believe Noam Chomsky has been right about a great many important issues during the course of his long career as a public intellectual. He was right to condemn America's war in Vietnam not merely as a disastrous mistake but as a moral catastrophe: it was a war that inflicted massive violence on a noncombatant population the United States claimed to be protecting in order to maintain a Vietnamese government that served US foreign policy objectives.[1] He was right, too, to point to America's alliance with repressive regimes throughout the Third World, some of them owing their very existence to US sponsorship. Widespread and sometimes staggering human rights abuses in what Chomsky called the American empire were often abetted—sometimes actively and directly, more often indirectly—by American power. Chomsky has been a persistent and productive muckraker of American foreign policy for nearly half a century.

Chomsky's critique of the limitations of American democracy—of the concentration of political power in the holders of corporate wealth, and the relative powerlessness and alienation of much of the citizenry—is more relevant than ever in an era of widening economic and political inequality. Whatever the limitations of his analysis, he deserves credit for his relatively early identification of problems that eluded recognition by mainstream pundits and academics alike.

Chomsky has also been mostly on target in his criticisms of the US mass media for their servitude to the prevailing orthodoxies of American foreign policy. From his early writings on Vietnam through his discussions of post–Cold War foreign policy, Chomsky has been adept at exposing journalists' implicit and largely unconscious adoption of Washington-centered values and assumptions. The main findings of Chomsky's most important work of media analysis, *Manufacturing Consent*, have been largely confirmed by subsequent academic scholarship, even though some of the academics resist acknowledging the kinship between their work and Chomsky's.

Chomsky has also been correct that America's leaders have continued to pursue global hegemony since the end of Cold War. He was on solid ground in analyzing the 2003 US invasion of Iraq in the context of the Bush-Cheney administration's world hegemonic ambitions, and his arguments against that misadventure were incisive. More broadly, Chomsky makes a strong case that America's striving for world hegemony has undermined international law and infringed on the sovereignty of poor countries seeking independent paths to development.

Chomsky has repeatedly taken up themes that were mostly neglected in the American public arena; for example, the consistently benign attitude taken by US policymakers toward the Suharto regime in Indonesia, especially during the massive bloodletting of the initial Suharto coup period and during its brutal suppression of the East Timorese struggle for independence. Similarly, few Americans were aware that during the 1990s the United States' Turkish ally was engaged in a counterinsurgency campaign that displaced millions of people, or that American-imposed sanctions were causing the deaths of hundreds of thousands of innocent Iraqis.

At other times, Chomsky has spoken out on controversies that were very much in the public arena, but his critiques usefully challenged the boundaries of existing debate. Congressional Democrats generally opposed the Reagan administration on Central America because they did not want to risk embroilment in open-ended wars, but few Democrats were willing to call our Guatemalan and Salvadoran clients "terror states" as Chomsky quite reasonably did; few were willing to stress that the contra army sponsored by the United States in Nicaragua engaged in terrorism, or to acknowledge the very real achievements of the Sandinista regime in addressing the needs of the poor. "Responsible" critics of American policy were generally loath to argue, as Chomsky plausibly argued, that Sandinista Nicaragua was more nearly a democracy than were the United States' Central America's client states—those proclaimed repeatedly as "fledgling democracies." And, on Iraq, while others criticized the second Bush administration for naive expectations of promoting democracy in the Middle East, Chomsky cast more than reasonable doubt on whether the administration was genuine in its proclamations of democratic intent.

Chomsky is a prodigious researcher, drawing on an incredibly wide range of both primary and secondary sources, both in the United States and abroad. Often, he brings to a larger audience the work of human rights and other nongovernmental organizations, as well as the writings of radical scholars and journalists and sundry other muckrakers, that otherwise tend to get little or no attention from mainstream American journalists and scholars. The endnotes for the first chapter of *Turning the Tide*, for example, include citations of reports by the Latin American Studies Association, the Institute for Food and Development Policy, Americas Watch, the World Council of Churches, the Institute for Policy Studies, the British *New Statesman*, the *Melbourne Sun*, the BBC, and several Israeli publications, as well as of articles from the *New York Times*, the *Boston Globe*, the *St. Louis Post Dispatch*, and the *Wall Street Journal*.[2]

Chomsky's contributions to our understanding of American politics and foreign policy can be summarized in terms of three related themes that have recurred in his writings since his 1960s debut as a public intellectual: his critique of the general assumption that America's role in the world is invariably motivated by good intentions; his skewering of the double standards and doublethink that

Americans have used to justify their country's behavior; and his willingness to espouse unpopular, even outrageous, positions in defiance of prevailing beliefs.

THE CRITIQUE OF "GOOD INTENTIONS"

Chomsky's indictment of America's war in Vietnam was perhaps as much concerned with how Americans—particularly intellectuals and other influentials—thought about the war as it was with the war itself. Even as disillusionment with the war mounted, and even in the postwar assessments stressing the failures of vision and understanding that underpinned America's march to war, influential commentators continued to stress the essentially decent motivations driving American policy. So powerful was the belief in American benevolence that even most critics of the war couldn't bring themselves to view it as morally wrong. As Chomsky put it at the time, this "unshakable belief in American goodwill and generosity... stultifies political thinking and debases political discourse."[3]

A quarter century later, Chomsky reiterated that point, quoting a reputable historian, Paul Kattenburg, who believed that the United States in going to war in Vietnam was pursuing its superpower role "devoid of artifice or deception" and with "the mind set of an emancipator."[4] Chomsky goes on to quote Kattenburg, who had opposed the Vietnam War, as follows: "It will help us understand America's performance and psychology as a superpower... if we bear in mind this analogy of the American performance in the superpower role with that of the benevolent but clearly egocentric professor, dispensing emancipation through knowledge of both righteousness and the right way to the deprived students of the world."[5] Chomsky acidly remarks, "This is not intended as irony or caricature, but is presented seriously, taken seriously, and is not untypical of what we find in the literature—not at the lunatic fringe, but at the respectable and moderately dissident end of the mainstream spectrum."[6] Chomsky similarly chides the liberal *New York Times* op-ed columnist Tom Wicker. Wicker criticized the Reagan administration's campaign against the Sandinista regime in Nicaragua partly on the grounds that "the United States has no historic or God-given right to bring democracy to other nations."[7] Chomsky derides the naiveté of Wicker's assumption that the Reaganites' hostility to the Sandinistas was significantly motivated by a desire to bring democracy to Nicaragua.

Chomsky is certainly right that an implicit, practically unquestioning faith in American good intentions is widely held even among sophisticated critics of American foreign policy, not to mention its staunch defenders. Not long after Chomsky's criticisms of Kattenburg and Wicker appeared, the political scientist Tony Smith—who was to become a harsh critic of George W. Bush's foreign policies—published a book proclaiming America's historic mission to have been the worldwide promotion of democracy.[8] A decade later, the former Reagan administration official Clyde Prestowitz mounted compelling evidence of the arrogance and presumption of US unilateralism in a book entitled *Rogue Nation*. He nevertheless reassured readers with its subtitle, which bemoans "the failure of good intentions," that he too, could not conceive of American malevolence.[9]

Chomsky doesn't cite the cliché about the paving on the road to hell. Clearly, his skepticism about good intentions is based on his well-documented observations that American policymakers have repeatedly acted in violation of the American ideals of freedom and democracy that supposedly underlay their good intentions. But his critique aims mainly to demonstrate the irrelevance, rather than malevolence, of intentions: American leaders may sincerely believe that they are acting consistently with noble ideals; people in general are not self-consciously evil and they naturally want to believe, and do believe, that they are doing good. Chomsky observes that "the chairman of the board may sincerely believe that his every waking moment is dedicated to serving human needs. Were he to act on these delusions instead of pursuing profit and market share, he would no longer be chairman of the board. It is probable that the most inhuman monsters, even the Himmlers and the Mengeles, convince themselves that they are engaged in noble and courageous acts."[10] Beautifully illustrating this point, Chomsky quotes Japanese emperor Hirohito's surrender declaration in August 1945: "We declared war on America and Britain out of Our sincere desire to ensure Japan's self-preservation and the stabilization of East Asia, it being far from Our thought either to infringe upon the sovereignty of other nations or to embark upon territorial aggrandizement."[11]

Was Hirohito sincere? Does it matter? Compare Hirohito's statement to Robert McNamara's reflections on the decisions that brought America into Vietnam: "I truly believe that we made an error not of values and intentions but of judgment and capabilities."[12] Many Americans undoubtedly would be as sympathetic to McNamara's expression of good intentions as they would be dismissive of Hirohito's.

It may not matter what Americans think of Hirohito's intentions, but it does matter what they think of McNamara's and those of other American leaders. McNamara acknowledges that people may regard his expression of good intentions with cynicism, which would be unfortunate, because "it is cynicism that makes Americans reluctant to support their leaders in the actions necessary to confront and solve our problems at home and abroad."[13] From a Chomskian perspective, the cynicism McNamara decries would actually be a salutary realism—a refusal to adopt a default assumption of American good intentions. That assumption accords policymakers benefits of the doubt that are not justified by the historical record; it effectively exempts American foreign policy from moral scrutiny. Chomsky refuses to grant any such exemption.

SKEWERING DOUBLE STANDARDS, DOUBLETHINK, AND DOUBLETALK

The reflexive belief in American good intentions is part of the bundle of beliefs and attitudes that has come to be called "American exceptionalism." The conviction that the United States is an exceptionally virtuous, beneficent actor in world affairs with a unique global mission is particularly emphatic and explicit among neoconservatives and the American political right more generally. In more implicit and sophisticated formulations, however, it pervades American political culture, leading naturally to the view that the standards that restrain the behavior of "ordinary" nations need not and should not apply to the United States. The assumption that the United States is entitled to substantial immunity from the constraints of international law and opinion has been repeatedly manifest in the words and actions of American leaders. It also informs the broader public discourse, producing a kind of doublethink in which the very language and concepts used in describing the behavior of the United States are different from usage in connection with other countries. Chomsky is constantly challenging Americans to recognize these double standards for what they are, and to apply to their own country the standards that they would routinely use in assessing the behavior of others.

The US government's campaign of subversion against Castro's Cuba, revealed in Senate Committee investigations in the 1970s, is a frequent theme of Chomsky's:

> Suppose that Fidel Castro had organized or participated in at least eight assassination attempts against the various presidents of the United States since 1959. It is safe to conclude that the *New York Times*, CBS News, and the mass media in general would have portrayed him as an international gangster and assassin, who must be excluded from the community of civilized nations. But when it is revealed that the United States has made or participated in that many attempts on Castro's life, it's just "one of those things that governments do." . . .
>
> Suppose further that Fidel Castro had arranged for his agents in the United States to disperse various disease carriers in agricultural regions in an attempt to poison and destroy livestock and crops. Can one imagine the hysteria of the *Wall Street Journal* and *Times* on the depths to which barbarian evil can sink under Communism?[14]

Chomsky doesn't mention that the Senate committee revelations did trigger harsh criticisms—and new legislative restrictions—on US government overseas behavior, but he is certainly correct that the reaction was mild compared to the outrage that would be ignited by similar behavior by a US adversary.

Chomsky also points to the double standards Americans applied in evaluating the Cuban missile crisis of 1962. Nikita Khrushchev's introduction of missiles into Cuba was universally regarded as a reckless and provocative act in the United States, a view dramatically represented by US ambassador to the United Nations Adlai Stevenson when he displayed a photograph of a Soviet missile site in Cuba. But what about the US missiles introduced into Turkey not long before? Suppose a Martian observer, "free from earthly systems of doctrine and ideology," had descended to observe global developments in 1961–1962:

> [The] Martian would surely note that there is no "Khrushchev moment" in history: no moment at which Soviet Premier Nikita Khrushchev or his UN ambas-

sador dramatically unveiled photographs of the Jupiter missiles placed in Turkey in 1961–62, or of the provocative transfer of the missiles to the Turkish military with "ceremonial fanfare." ... And he might observe that there was no Russian threat to invade Turkey, nor any large-scale Russian terrorist campaign or economic warfare against Turkey.[15]

There was no "Khrushchev moment" in the United States because Americans took it for granted that the United States had a right to project military power into the Soviet back yard, but the Soviets had no such reciprocal right. The Kennedy administration historian Arthur Schlesinger Jr., among others, condemned Khrushchev's move as an unacceptable attempt to alter the global balance of power, but a less one-sided perspective would have viewed it as a step toward redressing the global *imbalance* of power that strongly favored the United States. From Schlesinger's perspective, which was the perspective of the dominant superpower, imbalance was balance.

As another striking example of double standards, Chomsky cites the differing official handling and public perception of two airplane tragedies in the 1980s. When the Soviets shot down the Korean airliner KAL 007 in September 1983 the Reagan administration treated the event as a deliberate mass murder, and the US media and Congress fell into line with that portrayal. When, however, the US warship *Vincennes* shot down an Iranian civilian airliner off the coast of Iran in July 1988, the event "was dismissed as an unfortunate error in difficult circumstances"; Iranian protests were "occasionally noted and dismissed [in the US media] with derision as 'boilerplate attacks on the United States.'"[16] As we have seen (in Chapter 4), there was no objective basis for the radically different standards of judgment applied to the two tragedies.

Chomsky has said that there is no direct relationship between his work as a linguist and his political work, but the latter shows a consistent, keen attention to the uses and abuses of language in political discourse, very much in the spirit of George Orwell's classic "Politics and the English Language." Chomsky often points out that the language Americans use in discussing foreign policy embodies implicit double standards. Thus, "The category of 'American aggression' cannot exist as a matter of doctrinal faith."[17] Nor are terms like "terror" and "invasion" normally applied to acts of US foreign policy, even when quite appropriate. Chomsky notes, for example, that American commentators universally and appropriately characterize the Soviet military intervention into Afghanistan in 1979 as an invasion. But the American intervention in Vietnam almost never is called an invasion. The Soviets, like the Americans in Vietnam, could claim to have been "invited" into Afghanistan by a friendly government—really, by a regime created by Soviet power, much as South Vietnam had been created by the United States. But the extenuating circumstances that somehow permit the United States not to call its action in Vietnam an invasion are never applied to the Soviets in Afghanistan.[18]

Probably the terms cited most often by Chomsky as embodying unacknowledged double standards are "terror" and "terrorism." Chomsky repeatedly points out that typically, "terror" is associated almost exclusively with the actions of insurgent movements and dissidents, but "the term 'terrorism' never includes a bombardier on a B-52 mission over Indochina wiping out entire villages . . . nor the higher authorities ultimately responsible for such attacks."[19] "Terror" is almost never attributed to the actions of national governments, unless a government is considered hostile to the United States, like Saddam Hussein's after 1990. This usage facilitates US support for regimes that utilize torture and mass murder (but not "terror") in repressing dissent. Among other examples, Chomsky cites a scholarly study that discusses Communist terror in South Vietnam during the 1950s and 1960s but makes no mention of Diem's terror that preceded it.[20] Another term whose usage Chomsky sees as reflecting a pro-American double standard is "deterrence." It was widely assumed during the Cold War that the United States needed to deter Soviet aggression. But while Soviet power also served to restrain American aggressiveness during the Cold War (for example, with regard to Cuba), the concept of the Soviets' deterring the United States was foreign to American thinking.[21]

Henry Kissinger, in Chomsky's account, is particularly adept at the Orwellian use of apparently neutral language to justify America's quest for global supremacy. Thus, Kissinger uses words like "equilibrium" and "stability" as codes for the maintenance of dominant American power positions. Noting Kissinger's acknowledgment at one point that equilibrium usually requires "siding with the weaker to deter the stronger," Chomsky observes wryly that Kissinger's belief in promoting international equilibrium somehow did not lead him to the natural conclusion that the USSR should have sided with Cuba and Vietnam against the United States.[22]

Kissinger is a natural target, but Chomsky seems to take special satisfaction in showing that even presumptively more liberal commentators on US foreign policy betray tendencies toward doublethink. Thus, he quotes Robert Pastor, a former Carter administration official who was critical of the Reaganites' policies in Central America: "The United States did not want to control Nicaragua or the other nations in the region, but it also did not want to allow developments to get out of control. It wanted Nicaraguans to act independently, *except* when doing so would affect US interests adversely." (emphasis in the original).[23] Chomsky comments aptly, "In short, Nicaragua and other countries should be free—free to do what we want them to do."[24] As another example of doublethink, Chomsky cites a discussion of Chile by James Chace, a former editor of the prestigious establishment journal *Foreign Affairs*, who asserted in effect that instability is stability, as long as it is generated by the United States:

> "We were determined to seek stability," Chace asserts, and as an illustration—literally—he offers "our efforts to destabilize a freely elected Marxist government in Chile." Even a direct self-contradiction in successive sentences does not suffice to raise a question about "our own motivations."[25]

Double standards apply to American allies as well as adversaries when the allies go astray, as France did in threatening to veto a UN Security Council authorization for the United States' planned war on Iraq. Chomsky quotes a Columbia University scholar, Edward Luck, who warns that "if lesser powers contrive to turn the council into a forum for counter-balancing American power with votes, words, and public appeals, they will further erode its legitimacy and credibility."[26] Luck's presumption is that that the United States is entitled to use the UN Security Council as an instrument of American power and can do so without jeopardizing the UN's legitimacy. Other countries' challenges to that entitlement detract from the UN's legitimacy and credibility.[27]

CONTRARIANISM

Chomsky once stated, "Putting it a bit crudely, it is best to tell people that which they least want to hear, to take up the least popular causes, other things being equal."[28] Chomsky has never been reluctant to espouse unpopular, even outrageous, views in defiance of prevailing beliefs and official claims. On occasion, he has been very wrong, as in his challenge to the dominant and correct view of the Khmer Rouge regime in Cambodia. At other times, however, he has raised legitimate issues that would tend to be (and in fact usually are) excluded from debate. His heterodox view of the Cuban missile crisis—Khrushchev may have been unwise and reckless in introducing missiles into Cuba, but he had good reason and every right to do so—is one example. In this and in other cases, his contrarianism often involves apparently "taking sides" with an American adversary. Another example was his argument that the Soviet invasion of Afghanistan in 1979 was an essentially defensive move. The invasion was treated by the Carter administration and by most of the US foreign policy establishment as new evidence of Soviet aggressive expansionism. Chomsky cited plausible alternative interpretations suggesting that the invasion was an essentially conservative action in a border region of critical strategic importance to the Soviets, in a context of Soviet perceptions of insecurity and vulnerability.[29] Few Americans were amenable to arguments about extenuating circumstances in judging an "obviously" reprehensible act by the Communist enemy.

Another US enemy that Chomsky was willing to "defend" was North Korea. US government spokesmen and media commentators have generally portrayed the North Koreans as duplicitous and evasive of their commitments to accommodate reasonable American concerns about the Koreans' nuclear weapons programs. Chomsky, on the other hand, points to another side of the story: the United States reneged on pledges made to the North Koreans in the 1990s to provide fuel oil and take other steps to improve bilateral relations.[30] On occasion, even a bizarrely repressive regime like North Korea may have legitimate complaints to make against the United States. Mainstream commentators are seldom willing to say that; Chomsky has no such inhibitions.

Chomsky also played the part of contrarian when he pointed out that the evidence was far from clear-cut for Saddam Hussein's alleged assassination attempt on the first President Bush, which served as a pretext for a US retaliatory missile attack on Iraq in 1993. The US media mostly ignored the circumstantial nature of the evidence, perhaps reflecting a disinclination to be seen as defenders of an obvious villain like Saddam. Contrarian Chomsky raised an issue that deserved more scrutiny than it got. Chomsky also savaged the US media for their generally uncritical treatment of UN ambassador Madeleine Albright's justification of the attack under article 51 of the UN charter, which authorizes the self-defensive use of force by member states pending UN action. Chomsky was not grossly overstating when he argued that "to invoke Article 51 in bombing Baghdad two months after an alleged attempt to assassinate a former president scarcely rises to the level of absurdity."[31]

Sometimes Chomsky's contrarianism takes the form of deliberately provocative, apparently outrageous statements designed to challenge widely shared basic assumptions. For example, Chomsky's suggestion that America's client states in the Third World were collectively responsible for more and worse human rights abuses during the Cold War than were the Soviet Union's satellites was almost surely correct, but it would certainly have struck most Americans as outlandish. It clashes head-on with the fundamental Cold War dogma that "we" were essentially good and "they" were bad. Chomsky's contrarianism was on much shakier ground when he compared the 9/11 attacks with the US's al-Shifa bombing. This comparison was misconceived, but its objective was to provoke a rethinking of fundamental assumptions (e.g., the United States never engages in terror) with an outrageous hypothesis.

SUMMARY

Chomsky's attack on the dogma of American good intentions, his persistent exposure of double-think in foreign policy discourse, and his contrarianism are closely intertwined. To a significant extent, it is the myths of American innocence and good intentions that form the basis for the double standards and doublethink that enable Americans to exempt the United States from the constraining norms and expectations they assume appropriate for other countries. Those myths are so pervasive and implicit that they enable policymakers to propound, the media to transmit, and ordinary citizens to accept highly skewed understandings of reality. Anyone who contests those myths and those understandings perforce takes on the role of contrarian.

To suggest that American policymakers have been directly or indirectly responsible for horrible atrocities challenges Americans' credulity. Most Americans cannot believe such claims, because they "know" their country is good; its leaders may make mistakes, but they always mean well. Anyone making such charges must be some kind of eccentric—a borderline crackpot at best. But American foreign policy *has* been directly or indirectly responsible for terrible atrocities—in Indochina, Iraq, Central America, and elsewhere—as well as for many lesser offenses against democratic values and human rights. Chomsky has said so repeatedly, usually documenting his claims with extensive research. Certainly, he tends to overstate his case, but he has usually been at least partly right; often, he has been mostly right. He has been right, too, in his relentless effort to puncture the intellectual defenses against unpleasant truths that Americans would rather not accept and would prefer to reject as obviously farfetched.

Chomsky deserves credit as well for his insistence on outrage as the morally obligatory reaction to crimes of state and to the hypocrisy and indifference that make those crimes possible. It was outrage against American actions in Vietnam that brought Chomsky into the public arena in the 1960s, and outrage clearly has motivated his continued engagement in politics as a dissident public intellectual. In a post-9/11 interview, Chomsky recalls one of his early writings on Vietnam, a commentary on an article that appeared in the respected *Christian Science Monitor*:

> [The article I discussed] raised the question, in Vietnam, should we bomb dams or should we bomb trucks?
>
> And then it said, Well, bombing dams is much more satisfying because you see a big effect, and disaster, and lots of people starving, and so on. But despite the advantages it still makes more sense tactically to bomb trucks. . . . So, therefore, we should overcome our pleasure at bombing dams and instead bomb trucks. I don't even know how you comment on this. But what was striking about it was there was no reaction to it, absolutely no reaction.[32]

Chomsky was shocked by the "calm and analytic attitude" with which the war's planners and their apologists in the media and academia evaluated alternative modalities of mass killing.[33] After nearly fifty years, his shock at official amorality has worn off, but his outrage has continued. Often, it has been more than appropriate.

The Problems with Chomsky

A reviewer of Chomsky's first collection of political essays remarked with some wonderment, "In the entire book I do not recall a single act of American foreign policy of which he approves."[34] More than forty years and dozens of Chomsky books later, it is still difficult if not impossible to identify a single act of American foreign policy of which Chomsky has approved.[35]

In a famous essay, the political philosopher Isaiah Berlin distinguished between the hedgehog and the fox. The hedgehog knows one big thing—he sees the world through a confident, clearly defined, all-encompassing and relatively unchanging perspective. The fox, by contrast, takes a more eclectic view of worldly knowledge—he admits more readily to uncertainty and sees a multiplicity of factors, often not easily identifiable, influencing human behavior.[36] Chomsky is a hedgehog. He does, indeed know one big thing—let's call it "Chomsky's Truth"—which is that American imperialism, driven by capitalist greed, is responsible for much of the ills of the world. Chomsky has never explicitly formulated this Truth in so many words, but it clearly serves as the basic organizing principle of his political analysis. It is almost invariably his point of departure as well as his point of arrival.

As we have seen, Chomsky's Truth often leads him to uncover important truths: business elites certainly have been influential in US foreign policy making, and American power has indeed inflicted a considerable amount of suffering on the world. But much too often, Chomsky's Truth serves as an intellectual straitjacket, or a distorting lens with which he views the world. Evidence that contravenes The Truth is ignored or dismissed. Arguments and factual claims that support The Truth are advanced based on shaky and occasionally nonexistent evidence. As a result, Chomsky's political analysis is chronically marred by one-sidedness, overstatement, and oversimplification.

These problems were noted in a thoughtful discussion by the economist and popular blogger Brad DeLong. DeLong explains his "allergy" to Chomsky by describing his reaction to a 1992 Chomsky book, *What Uncle Sam Really Wants*. The early pages of the book are devoted to a description of American behavior during and immediately after World War II. DeLong found in those pages a relentlessly one-dimensional account of American perfidy. Chomsky assails US cooperation with former fascists without any discussion of the circumstances that might have made those alliances opportune in the war with the Nazis. Chomsky chronicles US hostility to leftist forces in Greece, Italy, and Korea without any consideration of the possible nature of the Communist-dominated regimes that would have come to power in the event of leftist victories. And, DeLong finds, Chomsky's account of American aggressiveness toward the Communist world is divorced from any consideration of Soviet behavior and the mutuality of the escalating tensions between the two great powers. DeLong also notes what he calls a number of "casual lies" in Chomsky's narrative—for example, the claim that (doomed) postwar partisans trying to fight guerrilla wars against Soviet rule in the Ukraine, Belarus, Poland, and elsewhere were "armies that had been established by Hitler."

After seventeen short pages, the exasperated DeLong stopped reading. He stresses that he might well have been receptive to a significant part of the case that Chomsky was making, if Chomsky had demonstrated serious consideration of all relevant evidence. But, he explains,

> What I object to is that Chomsky tears up the trail markers that might lead to conclusions different from his. He makes it next to impossible for people unversed in the issues to understand what the live and much-debated points of contention might be.... What I object to is the lack of background, to the lack of context.... Chomsky ruthlessly suppresses half the story of the Cold War—the story of the other side of the Iron Curtain.... You can't show only half (or less than half) the picture. That's an act of intellectual authoritarianism, ... an attempt to keep people from knowing things that are not "good" for them—an intellectual foul.[37]

Having read a badly skewed Chomsky account of an historical period that DeLong happens to know something about, DeLong reasonably enough feels compelled to wonder: "Whenever we reach an issue that I do not know deeply, what things that I would like to know is Chomsky going to try to keep me from noticing?"

DeLong made a poor choice of reading: *What Uncle Sam Really Wants* is hardly more than a pamphlet; it represents Chomsky more or less at his polemical, schematic worst. (DeLong would have done much better to read *Deterring Democracy*, published just a year earlier.) Still, DeLong makes a valid point. The reader can never take for granted that Chomsky is presenting a reasonably balanced account of whatever subject he is dealing with. The reader may well be getting an important and underreported side of the story but must assume that it is just one side of the story. The possibility must always be considered that Chomsky is withholding information that might, just might, not lead the reader to the conclusion—consistent with The Truth—that Chomsky is determined to lead him or her to.

Chomsky's attachment to his Truth leads him to reductionism: the explanation of complex phenomena in overly simple, practically monocausal terms. It leads him to a reckless misuse of sources of evidence. And, because The Truth is certain, it leads him to intellectual intolerance: an ever-readiness to accuse his critics of servitude to the evils that Chomsky exposes.

REDUCTIONISM

Chomsky's proclivity for explaining complex phenomena in simple monocausal terms is most evident in his explanation of American Cold War policy as a straightforward expression of US business interests. He dismisses the visceral anti-Communism that pervaded American society as little more than a ruse perpetuated by policymakers to veil their real motivations. Nor can he see international power politics as anything more than a competition for economic advantage.

Chomsky reduces the two major US political parties to one business party with two factions. Accordingly, he does not acknowledge the significant, differential consequences of Democratic vs. Republican stewardship of domestic affairs, and he ignores the important role of US partisan conflict as a driver of Cold War policy.[38] The latter failure is evident in his accounts of US Central American policy in the 1980s. The Reagan administration's determination to sponsor the contras in Nicaragua and to empower its client regime in El Salvador were the continuous subject of often bitter partisan battles in the US Congress for much of the decade. Liberal Democrats spearheaded the opposition, often in the face of vicious attacks on their patriotism by Republican colleagues.[39] A reader only of Chomsky's writings would know practically nothing of these conflicts. Almost invariably, when Chomsky does mention a specific action taken by Congress on Central America, it is to cite an example of congressional subservience to administration policy, with no discussion of the relevant history of often acrimonious debate and closely divided votes that were usually along partisan lines. An egregious example is his assertion that after the World Court found for Nicaragua in its claims against the United States, "the Democrat-controlled Congress reacted by instantly escalating the crimes."[40] Congress did renew aid to the contras soon after the court's decision, but Chomsky's statement is partly wrong and largely misleading. Only one of the two houses of Congress had a Democratic majority, and the overwhelming majority of Democrats in both houses voted against the renewed aid.[41]

In the post–Cold War era, Chomsky's reductionism was clearest in his interpretation of the Western intervention in Kosovo. Chomsky's explanation for the intervention in terms of US geostrategic objectives provides a useful corrective to a simple explanation solely in terms of humanitarian intent. But Chomsky insists on his own monocausal explanation: it isn't sufficient, for Chomsky, to show that other than humanitarian impulses helped explain the intervention; he insists that "there was no humanitarian element. Zero."[42] Also, in his explanation of the 1989 US intervention in Panama, Chomsky fails to consider a good deal of historical context that complicates his own simple explanation of US government motivations. Chomsky again ignores critical context in his repeated claim that the United States somehow authorized Saddam Hussein's suppression of revolts against his rule in the aftermath of the first Gulf War. Chomsky's claim rests on a highly tendentious and oversimplified reading of a complex situation.

A recurrent aspect of reductionism in Chomsky's writings is an unwarranted attribution of rationality and coherence to government organizations and their policies. For example, in his critique of the second Bush administration's war on Iraq, Chomsky makes a compelling argument that the effects of the war would be to increase the dangers of terrorism and nuclear proliferation, but he goes further than that, alleging that Bush administration launched the war *knowing* that these consequences would follow. As evidence for this claim, he cites analyses both within and outside of the government discussing the possibility or probability that the war would provoke increased terrorism and encourage nuclear proliferation.[43] But the processes by which information is utilized and acted on within governmental organizations are complex—occasionally near-byzantine—and human defenses against unwanted ideas can be formidable. The availability of insights about the war's consequences does not constitute evidence that these insights reached and were digested by top decision makers within the government. Chomsky assumes that Bush and Cheney must have been as smart and well informed as Chomsky himself in their assessment of the possible consequences of the war; they just had different objectives and priorities. That reasonable-seeming assumption reflects a naive understanding of how governmental organizations work.

Chomsky's unrealistic attribution of rationality and coherence to government policies also shows up in his accounts of US actions in Central America in the late 1970s and 1980s and with regard to East Timor in 1999. Another example, not treated in the preceding chapters, is Chomsky's discussion of US involvement in counterinsurgency in Colombia. US policy in Colombia officially has been motivated by the long-standing American preoccupation with the war on drugs, but Chomsky has argued repeatedly that the war on drugs in Colombia is nothing but a cover for the real reasons for American intervention in that country, which are to serve American economic and strategic interests in Latin America. Chomsky's argument rests on apparently unexceptionable logic: there is abundant evidence, confirmed and reconfirmed over the years, that the war on drugs, focusing on sources of supply, is futile. Instead, Chomsky says, it is well known that the most effective way to fight the drug problem in the United States is *in* the United States, through education and treatment. The obvious futility of the war

> reinforces the natural conclusion that the "drug war" . . . is pursued for reasons other than the announced goals.
> To determine the reasons, we may adopt a procedure familiar in the legal system, which takes predictable consequences to be evidence of intent, particularly when the consequences are so clear over a long period, along with the predictable failure to reach the announced purposes.[44]

The problem with this logic is that governments don't necessarily act logically and coherently. The "intent" that the legal system seeks to identify is the intent of a person or discrete group of persons. A government doesn't have the singularity of conscious intent attributable to a person, who is a unitary, more-or-less rational actor. If "the government" were a person, she might well accept Chomsky's logic and abandon the war on drugs for more effective antidrug programs. But "the government" is not a person; instead it represents a collection of sometimes conflicting interests and bureaucratic commitments that often elude the application of simple rationality. As one scholar has put it,

> over two decades the war on drugs has become institutionalized within the US government's policy process, an occurrence that necessitates continuous annual funding for US government agencies involved in antidrug efforts. The US war on drugs has taken on a life of its own, an inertial drive that will continue regardless of its success in actually reducing the amount of illegal drugs that enter the United States.[45]

This is not to say that Chomsky's critique of American policy in Colombia is entirely without merit; only that his assumption of coherent, rational action by government leads him to dismiss an important part of the explanation for policy, reducing his own explanation to an oversimplification.

Numerous other instances can be cited of Chomsky's dubious attribution of rationality to government leaders in their acquisition and processing of policy-relevant knowledge. For example, in criticizing the Truman administration's alarmist rhetoric in response to Soviet behavior in 1946–1947, Chomsky states that Secretary of State Acheson "presumably was . . . aware" that Stalin was urging restraint on Communist movements in Greece and Western Europe.[46] Chomsky's presumption that Acheson knew what Chomsky knew decades later is questionable. Similarly, discussing American aggressive reactions to increased Soviet influence in the Third World in the 1970s, Chomsky asserts that the emptiness of

Soviet gains was "obvious at the time." It may have been obvious to Chomsky, but by any reasonable reading of the historical record, it was not obvious to US policymakers.[47]

Occasionally, Chomsky goes beyond assuming that policymakers have full information and perspicacity, and credits them with something approaching clairvoyance. One example was Chomsky's argument that the NATO intervention in Kosovo could not have been motivated by humanitarian concerns because NATO leaders knew well that their intervention in March 1999 would very likely precipitate rather than forestall a humanitarian catastrophe. That likelihood, of course, is easy to pronounce with the benefit of hindsight; instead, as we saw, Western leaders, expecting a rapid triumph, did not foresee the tragic consequences of their bombing campaign. Chomsky's argument that they very probably did was based on fragmentary evidence that was less than compelling.

Another Chomskian attribution of near-clairvoyance to policymakers involved Cambodia. After pointing accurately to the staggering devastation US bombing inflicted on Cambodia in the early 1970s, Chomsky offers as one "reasonable explanation" for the level of US brutality the Americans' desire to maximize the brutality of the eventual victors, the Khmer Rouge. The Americans would then be able to reap a propaganda victory by pointing to the new regime's atrocities.[48] This "reasonable explanation" must assume that (1) the Americans actually expected a Khmer Rouge victory while still expending considerable resources in pretending to wage war against them; (2) a brutal Khmer regime was a natural and highly predictable outcome of the American bombing campaign, which in fact had ended about two years prior to the final Khmer victory; (3) the Americans did in fact foresee the probable brutality of the future new regime; and (4) the Americans actually wanted the new regime to engage in widespread cruelty out of a cynical, calculated desire to reap a propaganda victory. Every single one of these assumptions is highly problematic, to put it mildly. To even speculate that the coincidence of all four can constitute a "reasonable explanation" is utterly fanciful. Chomsky is sometimes wrongly accused of paranoia, but this speculation does bear some resemblance to paranoia in its readiness to ascribe supernormal powers—something approaching clairvoyance—to evil forces.

Chomsky's fantastic speculation about American motives in the bombing of Cambodia is an example of the effects that can follow from viewing the world through the distorting lens of Chomsky's Truth. We have seen other examples in Chomsky's repeated attribution of direct and indeed proactive US responsibility for the crimes of its allies when in fact the American role was one of varying levels of complicity. Chomsky casts all nuances cast aside in order to consistently portray American government criminality—often real enough—in the very worst possible light. In Central America in the 1980s, and in Turkish Kurdistan and East Timor in the 1990s, Chomsky without evidence accuses the United States of instigating—sometimes of actually organizing and directing—atrocities committed by client governments. These accusations can involve such absurd formulations as "Carter's war against the peasantry" in El Salvador.[49] No less absurd was the case (discussed in Chapter 5) in which Chomsky merely accused the US government of complicity: Saddam Hussein's use of chemical weapons against the Kurds in 1988. The American complicity, according to Chomsky, consisted in providing food aid to Iraq *after* the chemical weapons attack.

THE USE AND ABUSE OF SOURCES

Chomsky uses a great variety and quantity of information sources—newspapers, books, magazines, news services, the Internet—to develop his political analyses and support his arguments. Most of his books are exhaustively documented with extensive references—usually endnotes—citing the information sources he has used to establish the facts and support the arguments that he presents to his readers. Source citations of course are a critical tool of scholarship. They provide readers with assurance that the scholar/writer has evidence to support the assertions he is making—that he or she isn't just making things up. They also enable interested readers to explore further on their own—to go to the sources that have been cited in order to deepen their understanding of the subject and, possibly, to pursue follow-up research. Another function of source citations is to enable the scholar/writer to strengthen the credibility of his or her argument by demonstrating that the writer is not alone—that other reputable scholars or experts have made similar arguments.

The careful and honest use of sources is a sine qua non of responsible scholarship. When a writer misrepresents the evidence he or she purports to document, or omits consideration of obviously relevant evidence, his or her credibility and reliability as a reporter and analyst are subject to doubt. Chomsky's adherence to standard scholarly practice in his source citations is uneven. In some of his books, his use of references, at least in appearance, is beyond reproach. In other books, Chomsky's reference notes cite whole chapters of books, or whole books, without page numbers, which makes the reader's task of verifying and following up arduous if not impossible. This problem is sometimes compounded by Chomsky's frequent practice of citing his own works. The historian Thomas Nichols amusingly describes the travail that can result:

> Quite often, [Chomsky's] citations regarding a contentious point only lead the reader back self-referentially to another of Chomsky's own works in which he makes the same unsupported assertion. . . .
>
> For example, in *World Orders Old and New*, his first note in his chapter on the Middle East reads: "For sources where not given here, see *Deterring Democracy*, chap. 1; *Year 501*, chap. 2." An intrepid reader seeking to follow Chomsky's trail in this footnote will find that very little of the first chapter in Chomsky's own *Deterring Democracy* is actually about the Middle East. But when he does turn to a discussion of the region . . . in that book, his first footnote in the section reads: "For references and further discussion, see *Towards a New Cold War*." In other words, a reference in Chomsky's book points only to two more of his own books, which in turn leads to a citation that refers to yet another of his books, along with four

other books on the Middle East, all of which are cited *in their entirety*, without page references. Thus, to track Chomsky's sources in just one footnote, the reader must follow a trail of two more useless citations that lead only to a dead end in which Chomsky cites himself at length.[50]

The self-referential nature of many of Chomsky's citations reflects the fact that he has written many books, many of which overlap with earlier books in subject matter. When revisiting previously covered material, it is entirely reasonable for Chomsky to refer back to an earlier work rather than to reproduce the citations in that earlier work. In several instances I have followed trails similar to the one described by Nichols and found that the earlier Chomsky works cited did, indeed, apparently support the assertions in his later texts. But not always. For example, in *For Reasons of State*, Chomsky asserts bluntly that in the 1950s Japan was pressured (presumably by the United States) into breaking its trade relations with China, and cites his *At War with Asia* (chapter 1, no page reference) as a source.[51] *At War with Asia* does contain the assertion that "there is reason to believe that American pressure was a factor in the reduction of [Japan's] China trade," but the "reason to believe" he gives is nothing more than a statement by Secretary of State Dulles of the goal of developing markets for Japan in order to counteract the Communists' own efforts to develop their trade.[52] Thus, an essentially unsupported hypothesis (a "reason to believe") in the earlier text becomes the source for an unqualified assertion of fact in the later one.

Questions about Chomsky's use of sources arise particularly in his treatment of quotations. For Chomsky as for other writers on public affairs, the statements of other people are an important form of information. Sometimes, Chomsky quotes other people's words to point to examples of attitudes or opinions he means to criticize. Other times, he cites the views of journalists, academics, or other experts to demonstrate support for his own views. Occasionally—which is to say, too often—Chomsky makes dubious use of quotations. We have already seen (in Chapter 4) an early and blatant example of this in his misrepresentation of Samuel Huntington's views, when he omitted a critical sentence from his citation of a passage written by Huntington and instead substituted his own "paraphrase," which in fact had no relationship to Huntington's actual words.

Forty years later, Chomsky reprised this artifice. Commenting on reactions to the killing of bin Laden, Chomsky quoted another writer's comment on the killing as exemplifying "America's obsessive belief in capital punishment . . . [which] is reflected in its rejoicing at the manner of bin Laden's demise."[53] Chomsky went on to observe, "For example, *Nation* columnist Eric Alterman writes that 'The killing of Osama bin Laden was a just and necessary undertaking.'"[54] Alterman lost no time in pointing out that Chomsky's quote of him omitted the sentences that immediately followed the one Chomsky cited. Those sentences read: "But it should not be occasion for joy. The Talmud tells the story of angels dancing and singing as the waters of the Red Sea close over the heads of the Egyptian troops after the Israelites have safely crossed over, only to be rebuked by their God."[55]

Thus, Chomsky cited Alterman as an example of someone rejoicing at bin Laden's death, having just read Alterman's statement (which Chomsky withholds from his own readers) that there should be no rejoicing.

The Huntington and Alterman citations are instances of Chomsky's misrepresenting someone's words in order to fabricate examples of views that he finds noxious. Chomsky is also capable of misrepresenting a writer's words in order to claim support for Chomsky's own views. An example is a Chomsky citation of a work of the historian John Gaddis. Chomsky's quote of Gaddis, which appears in several of Chomsky's books, purports to show Gaddis's agreement with Chomsky's interpretation of American Cold War policy as an expression not of security concerns but of domestic economic interests. Chomsky quotes Gaddis as follows (the ellipsis points and interpolations in this instance are Chomsky's):

> To a remarkable degree, containment has been the product, not so much of what the Russians have done, or of what has happened elsewhere in the world, but of internal forces operating within the United States. . . . What is surprising is the *primacy* that has been accorded economic considerations [namely, state economic management] in shaping strategies of containment, *to the exclusion of other considerations* [Gaddis's emphasis].[56]

These are indeed Gaddis's words, but they don't mean what Chomsky represents them to mean. The two sentences that Chomsky has separated with ellipsis points appear about a page apart in Gaddis's book, and in reverse order. The use of an ellipsis to indicate the omission of words extraneous to the immediate point is of course a standard practice. It is somewhat dubious procedure to quote two sentences that appear far apart in the original text as if they constitute a single coherent thought, but it can be defended if the two sentences respectively introduce and then summarize the intervening material. To reverse the order of the sentences, however, is indefensible. In this case the passage Chomsky has constructed makes it appear that Gaddis is saying something he is not saying. Gaddis is discussing how partisan differences in approach to macroeconomic policy influenced the two American parties' respective approaches to foreign policy.[57] This discussion has no relevance to Chomsky's broad explanation of the roots of American Cold War policy. Gaddis's writing here is neither entirely lucid nor particularly cogent. Could Chomsky have misunderstood? That is conceivable, in which case it would constitute powerful evidence of how Chomsky's perception can be warped by his intellectual biases. But that interpretation seems rather charitable. Chomsky's manipulation of text, piecing together a quotation out of two such disparate sentences, is not only improper; it strongly suggests conscious misrepresentation.

Another dubious Chomskian use of quotations was identified by an implacable Chomsky critic, the British journalist Oliver Kamm. Chomsky cites Daniel Patrick Moynihan's memoirs on Moynihan's efforts as US ambassador to the United Nations to forestall UN measures against Indonesia's 1975 assault on East Timor. Kamm shows that Chomsky misrepresents passages from Moynihan's memoirs to imply that Moynihan took pride in facilitating Indonesian actions that resulted in the murder of sixty thousand people. As in the case of the Gaddis citation, Chomsky cited separate passages together and out of order as if they were sequential, this time in order to attribute the worst possible intent to them.[58] Moynihan did, indeed, report on his success in achieving American goals in the United Nations on East Timor and in Africa. Earlier, he had noted the tragic consequences of UN inaction in East Timor; he did not celebrate those consequences, as Chomsky implies. Kamm also points out that Chomsky attributes to Moynihan satisfaction at the disappearance of the Timor issue in media coverage; in fact, Moynihan noted the disappearance of the issue without indicating that that was his desired outcome.

Of course, it isn't necessary to quote a writer directly in order to misrepresent his views. Thus, Chomsky cites memos written by presidential adviser Arthur Schlesinger Jr. in support of Chomsky's assertion that "the fear of Communism was always a total fraud. We know that and have known it for years from the declassified internal record." Chomsky claims that the fraud was revealed in the analysis Schlesinger provided to President Kennedy.[59] In fact, the Schlesinger memos discuss Fidel Castro's appeal to Latin Americans and the various ways the United States might seek to counter it. There is nothing in those memos that can reasonably be interpreted as an analysis acknowledging the fraudulence of Americans' fear of Communism.[60]

Another example of a Chomskian misrepresentation of another writer's views occurs in his discussion of the historical background to the Kosovo intervention. Chomsky asserts that the respected journalist Tim Judah suggested "that the U.S. also gave a green light to the Serb attack on Srebrenica, which led to the slaughter of 7000 people, as part of a broader plan of population exchange. The U.S. 'did nothing to prevent' the attack though it was aware of Serb preparations for it."[61] Chomsky's implication is that Judah reported that the United States in effect preapproved the infamous Srebrenica massacre of July 1994. Chomsky doesn't tell his readers, however, that Judah at the same time observed that while the United States indeed was acquiescing in ethnic cleansing by the Serbs, no one had foreseen that the Serbs, after moving into Srebrenica, would engage in wholesale slaughter. Chomsky's use of language here is worth noting: the word "attack" surely connotes the whole of Serb actions in Srebrenica that summer—the occupation of the town and the subsequent massacre. To cite Judah's reporting on "the attack" without mentioning Judah's point about the Americans' unawareness of plans for mass murder is highly misleading: most readers would very likely infer from Chomsky that, according to Judah, the United States knew the Serbs would engage in mass murder and approved of it.

Chomsky's problem with source citations isn't limited to quotations: sometimes, the sources Chomsky cites don't provide the information he ascribes to them. For example, in *Manufacturing Consent*, Chomsky and Herman casually assert that the Salvadoran leader José Napoleón Duarte knew in advance about the plans to murder a group of American churchwomen in December 1980. This is a spectacular accusation, but it is not documented in the pertinent endnote. In the same book two pages later, Chomsky and Herman assert that US officials had "clear knowledge" of a cover-up of the murder, but the source cited only expresses skepticism about the seriousness of the Salvadoran official investigation—Chomsky and Herman thus transform suspicion into "clear knowledge."[62] Another Central American example, already discussed in Chapter 2: Chomsky's manipulation of source citations to imply that the Carter administration in 1980 utilized the services of the Argentine dictatorship to initiate a campaign of subversion against Sandinista Nicaragua.

Chomsky's most blatant misrepresentation of sources may have been his "reconstruction" of his own previous work on the Khmer Rouge regime in Cambodia. Recall that in *Manufacturing Consent*, he and coauthor Edward S. Herman wrote that in their original *Nation* article they had been "clear and explicit . . . that refugee reports left no doubt that the record of Khmer Rouge atrocities was 'substantial and often gruesome' and that . . . 'there is no difficulty in documenting major atrocities and oppression primarily from the reports of refugees.'"[63] As I indicated earlier (in "Indochina Afterword"), this is simply untrue.

I could cite additional instances of Chomsky's misuse of sources, but it would be tedious as well as superfluous. It is obvious that Chomsky's intellectual integrity is subject to serious question. From the reader's perspective, the problem is the classic cockroach problem: when you see one or two roaches, you tend to assume there are others around that you haven't seen. My main objective in this book has been to assess Chomsky's ideas and analysis, not to gauge the honesty of his scholarship. Accordingly, I have not spent much time investigating the accuracy of Chomsky's source citations. Some of the instances recounted in the preceding pages came to my attention because they were pointed out by others (Huntington, Alterman, Kamm). Some resulted from my own follow-up after reading a Chomsky claim or citation that looked suspicious (Gaddis, Judah, Argentina's role in relation to Nicaragua). But how many instances are there of twisted quotes or misleading references that don't immediately arouse suspicion and have therefore not been identified by me or by others?

INTELLECTUAL INTOLERANCE

In 1980 the political theorist Steven Lukes wrote an article criticizing Chomsky for intellectual irresponsibility in his writings on Cambodia. Chomsky's writings, according to Lukes, showed a loss of perspective, and had contributed to misinformation regarding the nature of the revolutionary Cambodian regime.[64] Chomsky subsequently assailed Lukes for neglecting the comparison Chomsky allegedly had made between roughly contemporaneous events in East Timor and Cambodia:

> By making no mention of the clear, unambiguous, and explicit comparison, [Lukes] is demonstrating himself to be an apologist for the crimes in Timor. That is elementary logic: if a comparison of Pol Pot to Timor is apologetics for Pol Pot, as Lukes

claims (by omission of the relevant context, which he could not fail to know), then it must be that the crimes in Timor were insignificant. Lukes, then, is an apologist for the worst slaughter relative to population since the Holocaust.[65]

Chomsky's response is misleading as well as convoluted.[66] My immediate concern, however, is with the nature of Chomsky's accusation, which insists that Lukes is not merely wrong, but that his criticism of Chomsky makes him an actual apologist for horrible crimes. Chomsky makes this argument through deflection: Lukes was talking about Cambodia, but Chomsky changes the subject to East Timor.

Chomsky utilizes deflection again in replying to a review of Chomsky's first book on Kosovo by the veteran civil liberties advocate Aryeh Neier.[67] Chomsky points out that the 1999 Western intervention in that Balkan country took place at around the same time as Western inaction in the face of renewed Indonesian atrocities in East Timor. According to Chomsky, Neier's failure to make that same comparison is evidence that he condones Western inaction in East Timor. Neier, according to Chomsky, is guilty of "easy tolerance of the refusal to lift a finger to mitigate ongoing genocide when the agent is a favored state."[68] But Neier wasn't writing about Indonesia and East Timor; Chomsky uses Neier's inattention to those countries in this particular context to make the unfounded accusation that Neier is tolerant of inaction in the face of Indonesian atrocities.

Chomsky similarly accused his opponents of reprehensible views in his polemics over the 1998 al-Shifa bombing. According to Chomsky, Christopher Hitchens's response to Chomsky's critique of the bombing expressed "racist contempt for African victims of a terrorist crime."[69] There was in fact nothing in Hitchens's piece that expressed racism; the only apparent basis for Chomsky's charge was the fact that Sudan, the site of the bombing, is an African country. Defending his use of the racist characterization, Chomsky later pointed out accurately that he had written that Hitchens "cannot mean what he is saying" and "cannot intend what his words imply." This wording shows, Chomsky says, that he did not accuse Hitchens of racism, and that he "unambiguously and explicitly said the precise opposite: that [Hitchens] is clearly not a racist, and therefore surely did not mean what his words imply."[70] In fact, Chomsky did not state "unambiguously and explicitly" that Hitchens was not a racist; at most, he may have implied as much, but his qualifier (Hitchens "cannot mean what he is saying") could well have been interpreted as a mere rhetorical ploy. Even if Chomsky sincerely meant to absolve Hitchens, his invocation of racism was an entirely unfounded effort to discredit the views of a critic. Chomsky was even harsher toward Leo Casey in responding to the latter's criticisms of Chomsky on al-Shifa (see Chapter 5). Chomsky absurdly charged that Casey was "laboring to conceal" terrible crimes.[71]

The issue here is not the substantive merits of the arguments Chomsky employed to refute his critics. It is, instead, his readiness to accuse them effectively of moral turpitude—of expressing repugnant views (racism, indifference to mass murder) or, worse, of apologetics for, and thus complicity in, state-sponsored criminality. Chomsky's propensity to hurl such accusations at his intellectual adversaries indicates an unwillingness to acknowledge that their opinions might be held in good faith, much less that they might, conceivably, be valid. This apparent rejection of civil, constructive debate is especially noteworthy in the four cases discussed here because all of these adversaries were at least moderate leftists with whom Chomsky should, presumably, hope to be able to find common ground. It suggests a disdain for viewpoints that differ more than slightly from his own. It represents a different but equally troubling side of the "intellectual authoritarianism" that Brad DeLong decried in explaining his allergy to Chomsky.

The Chomsky Conundrum

Noam Chomsky has produced important and valid insights into American politics and foreign policy. There has been no sharper critic of the implicit, often unconscious assumptions that pervade Americans' thinking about their country's behavior abroad—the beliefs that US government actions are always nobly intended and motivated by an underlying commitment to democracy and freedom. Chomsky has been a valuable contrarian on numerous important policy issues, challenging officially inspired narratives that tend to go unquestioned. At the same time, Chomsky's political writings are frequently marred by imbalance and oversimplification. He too readily makes claims and draws conclusions that are unsupported or inadequately supported by evidence. Occasionally, his dubious use of sources raises reasonable doubts about his intellectual honesty.[72]

How should readers deal with such a deeply contradictory figure? One option is simply to dismiss Chomsky. That, evidently, is the course favored by the Chomsky-allergic Brad DeLong. DeLong's stance is understandable, but unfortunate. The undeniable shortcomings of Chomsky's political writings should not lead us to overlook their considerable value.

A helpful perspective on Chomsky's contribution to political discourse can be gotten from a distinction formulated by the British historian Timothy Garton Ash.[73] Garton Ash contrasts "intellectuals" and "politicians." An intellectual has a responsibility to tell the truth. His professional obligation is to provide a full and balanced account of whatever subject matter he is investigating, and to follow the facts wherever they may lead him, even if they lead to conclusions that are not altogether to his liking. A politician, on the other hand, has no such obligation: "If a politician gives a partial, one-sided, indeed self-censored account of a particular issue, he is simply doing his job. . . . If an intellectual does that, he is not doing his job; he has failed in it." Garton Ash believes that both politicians and intellectuals play important roles in a liberal democracy, and that there is, indeed, a necessary and healthy division of labor between them. The give and take among opposed politicians' ideas is essential to free and lively debate of public issues. The careful, generally more nuanced and qualified pronouncements of intellectuals are less suited for that purpose: "On the one hand . . . but on the other hand . . ." is not an effective debating position; nor is it likely to crystallize interest in an issue. But the intellectual's scrupulous attention to evidence and logic can be critically useful to an informed and engaged citizenry in their efforts to sort out the truth from the cacophony of "he said . . . she said."

Garton Ash's distinction is suggestive, though his definitions, I think, are unduly restrictive. The concept of "politicians" can usefully be extended to encompass not only people who actually run for public office but more broadly people who consistently adopt positions of political advocacy. I would substitute "advocates" for "politicians," to convey the concept of people who may work to advance a political party's cause or to promote a particular point of view or ideology. Garton Ash's definition of "intellectual" also seems too narrow, since intellectuals—people who work with ideas—are often recognized as legitimate advocates for one or another point of view. I prefer the term "scholar" to signify the kind of commitment to objectivity that Garton Ash associates with the "intellectual."

Even the most ardent of Chomsky fans must acknowledge that Chomsky, in his political work, is not a scholar, but an advocate. Chomsky is not committed to following the facts wherever they may lead him; he mainly follows and presents facts that help confirm his Truth. But Chomsky's critics should be able to recognize that even a highly tendentious and skewed advocacy can make useful contributions to public discourse. We need muckrakers and intellectual provocateurs like Chomsky to tell us things we might otherwise not hear, and perhaps not want to hear.

Granted, even an advocate/provocateur should be held to minimal standards of intellectual honesty and balance—a responsibility to tell the truth with a small "t"—that Chomsky too often fails to meet. Those failures are all the more regrettable because however valid Chomsky's arguments may be, the credibility of his message is naturally limited by the credibility of the messenger. Chomsky's intellectual irresponsibility gives ammunition to his critics; it provides excuses for those who would prefer not to confront the radically critical perspective he represents.

Chomsky is often worth reading; both the scholarly specialist and the general interest reader can often utilize the insights and information that Chomsky has to offer. But caveat lector! The critical reader needs to understand, first of all, that practically anything Chomsky writes is likely to be unbalanced. Chomsky tells one side of the story. It is often a side that has gotten too little attention, and so may well be valuable as a corrective and supplement to the dominant narrative. But the reader should assume that a reasonably full understanding of the issue at hand will require reading more than what Chomsky has to say. He or she can be fairly sure that Chomsky's analysis omits consideration of significant counterarguments and evidence. A more than usual skepticism may also be in order with regard to some of Chomsky's assertions of fact. With that awareness, together with a willingness to explore further, the critical reader can often make constructive use of Chomsky's provocations.

Notes

ABBREVIATIONS

ATC	*After the Cataclysm, 1979* (with Edward S. Herman)
AWWA	*At War with Asia, 1969*
DD	*Deterring Democracy, 1991*
FROS	*For Reasons of State, 1970*
FS	*Failed States, 2006*
H&P	*Hopes and Prospects, 2010*
H/S	*Hegemony or Survival, 2003*
L&P	*Language and Politics, 1988* (edited by C. P. Otero)
Mandarins	*American Power and the New Mandarins, 1969*
MC	*Manufacturing Consent, 1988* (with Edward S. Herman)
New Generation	*A New Generation Draws the Line, 2000*
NI	*Necessary Illusions, 1989*
NMH	*The New Military Humanism, 1999*
P&T	*Power and Terror, 2003*
POP	*Profit over People, 1999*
TANCW	*Towards a New Cold War, 1982*
TTT	*Turning the Tide, 1985*
Washington Connection	*The Washington Connection and Third World Fascism, 1979* (with Edward S. Herman)
World Orders	*World Orders Old and New, 1994*
Year 501	*Year 501, 1993*

INTRODUCTION

1. Robert Barsky, *Noam Chomsky: A Life of Dissent* (Cambridge, MA: MIT Press, 1998), 1–46.
2. Allen J. Matusow, *The Unraveling of America: A History of Liberalism in the 1960s* (New York: Harper and Row, 1984); Maurice Isserman and Michael Kazin, *America Divided: The Civil War of the 1960s* (New York: Oxford University Press, 2008).
3. Noam Chomsky, "The Responsibility of Intellectuals," *New York Review of Books*, February 23, 1967; reprinted in Chomsky, *American Power and the New Mandarins* (New York: Vintage, 1969—hereinafter cited as *Mandarins*), 323–66. "The most important essay": Robert Buzzanco, *Vietnam and the Transformation of American Life* (Malden, MA: Blackwell, 1999), 97.

CHAPTER 1

1. Charles Kadushin, *The American Intellectual Elite* (Boston: Little, Brown, 1974), 188.
2. The literature on the history of the Vietnam War and its origins is vast. Two widely respected basic histories are George Herring's *America's Longest War: The United States and Vietnam, 1950–1975* (Boston: McGraw Hill, 2002) and Robert Schulzinger, *A Time for War: The United States and Vietnam, 1941–1975* (New York: Oxford University Press, 1997).
3. Herring, *America's Longest War*, 46.
4. John Prados, *Vietnam: The History of an Unwinnable War, 1945–1975* (Lawrence: University Press of Kansas, 2009), 35.
5. Ibid.
6. Schulzinger, *Time for War*, 71; also Carlyle A. Thayer, *War by Other Means: National Liberation and Revolution in Viet-Nam, 1954–1960* (Sydney: Allen and Unwin, 1989), 79.
7. John Foster Dulles, quoted in James M. Carter, *Inventing Vietnam: The United States and State-Building, 1954–1968* (Cambridge: Cambridge University Press, 2008), 25.
8. Kathryn C. Statler, *Replacing France: The Origins of America's Intervention in Vietnam* (Lexington:

University of Kentucky Press, 2007); see, for example, 117, 143, and 184.
9. William J. Duiker, *The Communist Road to Power in Vietnam*, 2nd ed. (Boulder, CO: Westview Press, 1996), 146.
10. Carter, *Inventing Vietnam*, 59.
11. Statler, *Replacing France*, 161–62, 173.
12. Thayer, *War*, 34–35, 47, 75–76.
13. Statler, *Replacing France*, 156–60.
14. Ibid., 69–70, 79.
15. Thayer, *War*, 17–18
16. Prados, *Vietnam*, 65.
17. Schulzinger, *Time for War*, 81; Prados, *Vietnam*, 65.
18. David L. Anderson, *Trapped by Success: The Eisenhower Administration and Vietnam, 1953-1961* (New York: Columbia University Press, 1991), 129.
19. Ibid., 131–32; Duiker, *Communist Road*, 15.
20. Eric M. Bergerud, *The Dynamics of Defeat: The Vietnam War in Hau Nghia Province* (Boulder, CO: Westview Press, 1991), 16–17; Prados, *Vietnam*, 58.
21. Bergerud, *Dynamics*, 14.
22. Prados, *Vietnam*, 57.
23. Duiker, 196. For additional estimates, see also Thayer, *War*, 116–17.
24. US Defense Department, quoted in Bergerud, *Dynamics*, 14.
25. Following common US practice, I will refer to the Vietnamese Workers Party as "the Communist Party," even though the word "Communist" doesn't appear in the official party name.
26. Ibid.; Duiker, *Communist Road*, 196.
27. Thayer, *War*, 139–41.
28. Duiker, *Communist Road*, 200–203; Bergerud, *Dynamics*, 20–21.
29. Robert K. Brigham, "Why the South Won the American War in Vietnam," in *Why the North Won the Vietnam War*, ed. Marc Jason Gilbert (New York: Palgrave, 2002), 98–105.
30. Prados, *Vietnam*, 66.
31. Bergerud, *Dynamics*, 31.
32. David L. Anderson, *The Vietnam War* (New York: Palgrave Macmillan, 1975), 38.
33. In the interests of impartiality I will use "NLF" and "Viet Cong" interchangeably hereinafter.
34. Marilyn B. Young, *The Vietnam Wars: 1945–1990* (New York: HarperCollins, 1991), 84–86.
35. Schulzinger, *Time for War*, 140.
36. Anderson, *Vietnam War*, 46.
37. Schulzinger, *Time for War*, 182.
38. Ibid., 189–91; Young, *Vietnam Wars*, 167–68.
39. Schulzinger, *Time for War*, 252–56; Prados, *Vietnam*, 209–10.
40. Rick Perlstein, *Nixonland: The Fracturing of America* (New York: Scribner, 2008), 228.
41. Ibid., 228, 230.
42. *Mandarins*, 231.
43. *TANCW*, 163.
44. Arthur Schlesinger Jr., quoted in Perlstein, *Nixonland*, 296.
45. A classic, seminal text in the realist tradition is Hans Morgenthau's *Politics among Nations: The Struggle for Power and Peace*, 5th ed. (New York: Knopf, 1973). Other basic works are Kenneth Waltz's *Theory of International Politics* (Reading, MA: Addison-Wesley, 1979) and John J. Mearsheimer's *The Tragedy of Great Power Politics* (New York: Norton, 2001).
46. Nicholas Spykman, quoted in Jack Donnelly, *Realism and International Relations* (Cambridge: Cambridge University Press, 2000), 162–63.
47. Donnelly, *Realism*, 166.
48. Ibid., 185–86. For other examples of realists hedging their claims, see Arnold Wolfers, *Discord and Collaboration* (Baltimore: Johns Hopkins University Press, 1962), 84–86.
49. Michael Walzer, *Just and Unjust Wars: A Moral Argument with Historical Illustrations*, 3rd ed. (New York: Basic Books, 2000), 21.
50. *Mandarins*, 243.
51. Duiker, *Communist Road*, 212–13. See also Thayer, *War*, 190–91, and Jeffrey Race, *War Comes to Long An: Revolutionary Conflict in a Vietnamese Province* (Berkeley: University of California Press, 1972), 105–7, 107n.
52. Final Declaration at Geneva, quoted in *Mandarins*, 241.
53. Constitution of South Vietnam (1967), quoted in *Mandarins*, 243.
54. *Mandarins*, 241, 243.
55. Noam Chomsky, *At War with Asia* (1969; Oakland, CA: AK Press, 2005—hereinafter cited as *AWWA*), 28.
56. Noam Chomsky, *For Reasons of State* (1970; New York: New Press, 2003—hereinafter cited as *FROS*), 240–41.
57. The Pentagon Papers, quoted in Noam Chomsky, *Towards a New Cold War* (1982; New York: New Press, 2003—hereinafter cited as *TANCW*), 398–99n. For an elaboration of the argument that the South Vietnamese state was an "invention" of the United States, see Carter, *Inventing Vietnam*.
58. *FROS*, 119, 240. For 1965 North Vietnamese troop strength, Chomsky, relying on information then available, actually mentions only a single battalion of four hundred to five hundred.
59. John Norton Moore, "The Lawfulness of Military Assistance to the Republic of Viet-Nam," in *The Vietnam War and International Law*, ed. Richard A. Falk (Princeton, NJ: Princeton University Press, 1968), 1:258–60.
60. Statler, *Replacing France*, 156–62.
61. US Department of State, Office of the Legal Adviser, "The Legality of the United States Participation in the Defense of Vietnam,"

in *From Nuremberg to My Lai*, ed. Jay Baird (Lexington, MA: D. C. Heath, 1972), 172.
62. *FROS*, 104; Carter, *Inventing Vietnam*, 25–26; Quincy Wright, "Legal Aspects of the Viet-Nam Situation," in Falk, *Vietnam War*, 273n.
63. Wright, "Legal Aspects," 280–81.
64. Moore, "Lawfulness," 238–41.
65. Ibid., 239.
66. *Mandarins*, 246–52.
67. *FROS*, 217.
68. Richard A. Falk, "International Law and the United States Role in the Vietnam War," in Baird, *From Nuremberg*, 173–78.
69. Ibid., 183.
70. Ibid., 179–80.
71. See, for example, Telford Taylor, "Aggressive War, Vietnam, and the Courts," in Baird, *From Nuremberg*, 195–98; and Wolfgang Friedmann, "Law and Politics in the Vietnamese War: A Comment," in Falk, *Vietnam War*, 301.
72. *Mandarins*, 252.
73. Quoted in *FROS*, 29–30.
74. Dean Acheson, quoted in *FROS*, 128.
75. US National Intelligence Estimate, quoted in Carter, *Inventing Vietnam*, 53.
76. *FROS*, 128.
77. Douglas Pike, *War, Peace and the Viet Cong* (Cambridge, MA: MIT Press, 1969), 6; cited by Chomsky in *FROS*, 250.
78. James Walker Trullinger Jr., *Village at War: An Account of Revolution in Vietnam* (New York: Longman, 1980), 79–80, 90–91.
79. David W. P. Elliott, *The Vietnamese War: Revolution and Social Change in the Mekong Delta, 1930–1975* (Armonk, NY: M. E. Sharpe, 2003), 526–29, 619–20.
80. Bergerud, *Dynamics*, 3, 4.
81. *Mandarins*, 227.
82. This did change by the late 1960s, largely as a consequence of the impact of the war on the countryside. Millions of peasants were driven from their homes, depriving the guerillas of the social base on which they depended. Under pressure, the Viet Cong in turn increased their demands on those who remained, more frequently using coercion and terror to ensure compliance. As a result, popular support for the guerillas fell. The declining support for the revolution thus reflected the devastation of Vietnamese society wrought by American firepower and the Communists' responses to it.
83. *Mandarins*, 260. Chomsky's idea of supporting Hanoi as a bulwark against China had been suggested at a Vietnam teach-in by Professor George McT. Kahin: Young, *Vietnam Wars*, 157.
84. *FROS*, 34.
85. Not even Michael Lind, who strives mightily to emphasize the unity of Hanoi with Moscow and Peking (in *Vietnam, the Necessary War* [New York: Free Press, 1999]), makes such a claim.
86. Elliott, *Vietnamese War*, 222.
87. Pike, *War*, 40.
88. Herring, *America's Longest War*, 178. See also George Herring, "Fighting without Allies," in Gilbert, *Why the North Won*, 85.
89. *FROS*, 229.
90. *AWWA*, 33.
91. *FROS*, 259.
92. Bernard Fall, "Vietnam Blitz," *New Republic*, October 9, 1965; cited in *FROS*, 4–5.
93. Earl H. Tilford Jr., "Air Power, Role in War," in *Encyclopedia of the Vietnam War: A Political, Social and Military History*, ed. Spencer Tucker (Santa Barbara, CA: ABC-CLIO, 1998), 1:13.
94. Gary Hess, *Vietnam: Explaining America's Lost War* (Malden, MA: Blackwell Publishing, 2009), 120; Young, *Vietnam Wars*, 177; Herring, *America's Longest War*, 197.
95. Ronald H. Spector, *After Tet: The Bloodiest Year in Vietnam* (New York: The Free Press, 1993), 209.
96. Bernd Greiner, *War without Fronts: The USA in Vietnam*, trans. Anne Wyburd with Victoria Fern (London: Bodley Head, 2009), 73.
97. GAO, quoted in Neil Sheehan, "Should We Have War Crimes Trials?" *New York Times Book Review*, March 28, 1971; reprinted in *The Vietnam War*, ed. Mark Lawrence (Chicago: Fitzroy Dearborn Publishers, 2001), 2:608.
98. Michael Sallah and Mitch Weiss, *Tiger Force: A True Story of Men and War* (New York: Little, Brown, 2006), 71–72.
99. William Corson, *The Betrayal* (New York: Norton, 1968), 68.
100. Guenter Lewy, *America in Vietnam* (Oxford: Oxford University Press, 1978), 229.
101. Ibid., 25.
102. Ibid., 25, 226.
103. William Westmoreland, quoted in Richard Critchfield, *The Long Charade: Political Subversion in the Vietnam War* (New York: Harcourt, Brace, 1968), 173. This passage is quoted in more abbreviated form in *FROS*, 5–6.
104. Westmoreland, quoted in Elliott, *Vietnamese War*, 1133.
105. Lewy, *America*, 65.
106. Ibid., 64–65, 110–11.
107. Corson, *Betrayal*, 69.
108. Ibid.
109. Westmoreland, quoted in Greiner, *War*, 155.
110. Greiner, *War*, 97.
111. Raymond Coffey, "The People beneath the War," *Nation*, January 17, 1966; reprinted in *In the Name of America*, ed. Seymour Melman (Annandale, VA: Turnpike Press, 1968), 181–82.

112. Jeffrey Race, *War Comes*, 233.
113. Lewy, *America*, 109.
114. Spector, *After Tet*, 208.
115. Jonathan and Orville Schell, quoted in *AWWA*, 226.
116. Richard A. Falk, Gabriel Kolko, and Robert J. Lifton, *Crimes of War* (New York: Random House, 1971); Melman, *In the Name*.
117. Neil Sheehan, "Rubble Depicts the Agony of a Town in Vietnam," *New York Times*, November 30, 1965.
118. Eric Norden, "American Atrocities in Vietnam," in Falk, Kolko, and Lifton, *Crimes*, 279.
119. Elliott, *Vietnamese War*, 1126.
120. Ibid., 1126, 1134.
121. The journalists' books are Deborah Nelson's *The War Behind: Vietnam Veterans Confront the Truth about U.S. War Crimes* (New York: Basic Books, 2008) and Sallah and Weiss's *Tiger Force*. The major exception among historians is Greiner (*War without Fronts*).
122. Nelson, *War Behind* (see, for example, 2–3). The terms "atrocities" and "war crimes" are often used almost interchangeably. I prefer "atrocities" since I don't want to enter into issues of legality. "War crimes" implies identifiable violations of international law, but as Telford Taylor has shown, it is possible to describe actions in war that most people would regard as heinous atrocities but which technically do not qualify as "war crimes." See Taylor, "War Crimes, Son My," in Baird, *From Nuremberg*, 262–63.
123. The letter is quoted in Greiner, *War*, 265, 272. Greiner noted, however, that the operation described by the sergeant lasted only six months, not twelve.
124. Lewy, *America*, 309.
125. Ibid.
126. Greiner, *War*, 87.
127. Lewy, *America*, 442–53.
128. Greiner, *War*, 30.
129. Edward S. Herman, *Atrocities in Vietnam: Myths and Realities* (Philadelphia: Pilgrim Press, 1970).
130. *Mandarins*, 284n; Lewy, *America*, 447.
131. Greiner, *War*, 73.
132. Ibid., 86–87.
133. Ibid., 96–100.
134. Sheehan, "War Crimes Trials?," 606.
135. *FROS*, 249–50n.
136. Sheehan, "War Crimes Trials?," 606.
137. *FROS*, 225.
138. Sheehan, "War Crimes Trials?," 605.
139. Jack Langguth, "The War in Vietnam," *New York Times Magazine*, September 19, 1965; reprinted in Melman, *In the Name*, 175.
140. See Lewy, *America*, 448–49.
141. Tucker, *Encyclopedia*, 95.
142. *TANCW*, chapter 7.
143. Lewy, *America*, 241–42.
144. Ibid., 231–32.
145. Walzer, *Just and Unjust Wars*, 195–96.
146. *TANCW*, 163.
147. Chomsky does acknowledge that US policy in Vietnam was not genocidal, and that Nazi Germany was sui generis: "One cannot compare American policy to that of Nazi Germany, as of 1942. It would be more difficult to argue that American policy is not comparable to that of fascist Japan, or of Germany prior to the 'final solution'" (*AWWA*, 236).
148. *AWWA*, 62.
149. *FROS*, 230.
150. *AWWA*, chapter 5.
151. Noam Chomsky and Edward S. Herman, *The Washington Connection and Third World Fascism* (vol. 1 of The Political Economy of Human Rights; Boston: South End Press, 1979—hereinafter cited as *Washington Connection*), 341–44.
152. Edwin Moise, *Land Reform in China and North Vietnam: Consolidating the Revolution at the Village Level* (Chapel Hill: University of North Carolina Press, 1983), 217–22; Balazs Szalontai, "Political and Economic Crisis in North Vietnam, 1955–56," *Cold War History* 5 (November 2005): 401.
153. *FROS*, 231; *TANCW*, 174; Lewy, *America*, 274; Prados, *Vietnam*, 240; Herring, *America's Longest War*, 231–32.
154. *Washington Connection*, 345–54.
155. *Mandarins*, 277n.
156. Ibid., 260.
157. Ibid., 10, 333.
158. Ibid., 254.
159. *Washington Post*, quoted in Noam Chomsky and Edward S. Herman, *After the Cataclysm: Postwar Indochina and the Reconstruction of Imperial Ideology* (vol. 2 of The Political Economy of Human Rights; Boston: South End Press, 1979—hereinafter cited as *ATC*), 14. Chomsky and Herman have authored several books together. I sometimes refer to the author of those books simply as "Chomsky." This usage intends no slight to Herman, but this after all is a book about Chomsky, and it is fair to assume that Chomsky shares equal responsibility for the contents of a work he coauthored.
160. Anthony Lewis, quoted in *ATC*, 15.
161. Richard Strout, quoted in *ATC*, 15.
162. *ATC*, 15.
163. *Mandarins*, 255.
164. *Washington Post*, quoted in *ATC*, 14.
165. Roger Hilsman, quoted in *Mandarins*, 256.
166. *FROS*, xxix–xxxi.
167. An excellent review of Vietnam War

historiography is Hess's *Vietnam: Explaining America's Lost War*.
168. Kendrick Oliver, "Toward a Moral History of the Vietnam War?" *Historical Journal* 47 (2004): 757–58.
169. Townsend Hoopes, "Legacy of the Cold War in Indochina," *Foreign Affairs* 48 (July 1970): 601.
170. The only academic historian to have made extensive use of these sources is Greiner (*War without Fronts*), a German.
171. Marilyn Young, "Introduction," in *The War that Never Ends: New Perspectives on the Vietnam War*, ed. David L. Anderson and John Ernst (Lexington: University of Kentucky Press, 2007), 7.
172. Patrick Hagopian, "Interchange . . . ," *Journal of American History* 93, no. 2 (September 2006): 457.

INDOCHINA AFTERWORD

1. Noam Chomsky and Edward S. Herman, "Distortions at Fourth Hand," *Nation*, June 25, 1977.
2. Ben Kiernan, *The Pol Pot Regime: Race, Power and Genocide in Cambodia under the Khmer Rouge, 1975–1979*, 3rd ed. (New Haven, CT: Yale University Press, 2008), 48–49.
3. Ibid., 269–71; David Chandler, *A History of Cambodia*, 4th ed. (Boulder, CO: Westview Press, 2008), 259.
4. George Hildebrand and Gareth Porter, *Cambodia: Starvation and Revolution* (New York: Monthly Review Press, 1976).
5. Francois Ponchaud, *Cambodia Year Zero*, trans. Nancy Amphoux (New York: Holt, Rinehart and Winston, 1978).
6. John Barron and Anthony Paul, *Murder of a Gentle Land* (New York: Thomas Y. Crowell, 1977).
7. Bruce Sharp, "Averaging Wrong Answers: Noam Chomsky and the Cambodia Controversy," *Cambodia: Beauty and Darkness*, last updated July 19, 2010, www.mekong.net.
8. Ibid.
9. Ponchaud, xv–xvi.
10. See, for example, Michael Vickery, *Cambodia, 1975–1982* (Boston: South End Press, 1984), 44.
11. See, for example, Lind, *Vietnam*, 146.
12. Sharp, "Averaging Wrong Answers"; Ponchaud, *Cambodia Year Zero*, 21, 50.
13. Ponchaud, *Cambodia Year Zero*, 6–7.
14. *ATC*, vii, 140.
15. Ibid., 274.
16. Ibid., xiv–xv, 136.
17. Ibid., 145, 150.
18. Ibid., 293.
19. Ben Kiernan, *Genocide and Resistance in Southeast Asia: Documentation, Denial and Justice in Cambodia and East Timor* (New Brunswick, NJ: Transaction Publishers, 2008), 209.
20. William Shawcross, "The Third Indochina War," *New York Review of Books*, April 25, 1978; Bruce Sharp, "Fun with Milton Bradley: A Reply to Josh Buermann," *Cambodia: Beauty and Darkness*, last updated July 19, 2010, www.mekong.net.
21. Chomsky, *Necessary Illusions* (1989; Toronto: Anansi Press, 2003—hereinafter cited as *NI*), 155–57.
22. Ibid., 156–57.
23. Chomsky, *Deterring Democracy* (New York: Hill and Wang, 1991—hereinafter cited as *DD*), 380. Putting the Cambodian death toll at about one hundred thousand, Chomsky and Herman had indeed asserted that the bloodbath in East Timor was comparable to that of Cambodia in absolute terms and many times greater relative to population (*Washington Connection*, 168, 130). But by 1991 Chomsky surely knew or should have known that the figure of only one hundred thousand Cambodian deaths was preposterously low. He must therefore have known or should have known that the Cambodian slaughter was many times greater in absolute terms (actually about ten times greater). Only relative to population was the bloodletting in tiny East Timor roughly comparable to that in Cambodia.
24. Edward S. Herman and Noam Chomsky, *Manufacturing Consent: The Political Economy of the Mass Media* (1988; New York: Pantheon, 2002—hereinafter cited as *MC*), 293. The self-quoted phrases come not from the *Nation* article, as Chomsky and Herman claim, but from the later discussion in *ATC* (135–36).
25. Sharp, "Averaging Wrong Answers," 30.

CHAPTER 2

1. Excellent surveys of Cold War historiography are provided in *Reviewing the Cold War: Approaches, Interpretations, Theory*, ed. Odd Arne Westad (London: Frank Cass, 2000), especially in the essays by Westad and Geir Lundestad. See also Anders Stephanson, "The United States," in *The Origins of the Cold War in Europe: International Perspectives*, ed. David Reynolds (New Haven, CT: Yale University Press, 1994), 23–52.
2. Chomsky's view of Cold War history is stated most succinctly in Chomsky, *World Orders Old and New* (New York: Columbia University Press, 1994—hereinafter cited as *World Orders*), 26–73. See also *DD*, 9–58.
3. *AWWA*, 4.
4. *FROS*, 31, 35, 37.
5. *DD*, 27.
6. *AWWA*, 2.
7. *Washington Connection*, 3–4.
8. Ibid. (see, for example, 42–49, 65); *TANCW*.

9. Chomsky nowhere formally defines "fascist" but rather applies the term—which he uses interchangeably with the term "subfascist"—loosely to authoritarian regimes that harshly repress opposition and rule in the interests of a relatively small elite. A distinctive ideology like that which characterized the European varieties of fascism that emerged in the 1920s and 1930s is not a necessary feature of fascism under this loose definition.
10. Amnesty International, *Report of an American International Mission to the Republic of the Philippines, 22 November–5 December 1975* (London: Amnesty International Publications, 1976); *World Orders*, 39–40.
11. *Washington Connection*, 1.
12. Ibid., 230–31.
13. "Philippines: A Government That Needs U.S. Business," *Business Week* 4 (November 1972); cited in *Washington Connection*, 53, 375n.
14. *Washington Connection*, 234–37.
15. Amy Blitz, *The Contested State: American Foreign Policy and Regime Change in the Philippines* (Lanham, MD: Rowman and Littlefield, 2000), 43.
16. For good overviews of Philippine political history, see Nathan Gilbert Quimpo, "Oligarchic Patrimonialism, Bossism, Electoral Clientelism, and Contested Democracy in the Philippines," *Comparative Politics* 37 (January 2005): 229–50, and Tony Smith, *America's Mission: The United States and the Worldwide Struggle for Democracy in the Twentieth Century* (Princeton, NJ: Princeton University Press, 1994), 54–55.
17. Raymond Bonner, *Waltzing with a Dictator: The Marcoses and the Making of American Foreign Policy* (New York: Vintage, 1988), 5–6, 99–100.
18. Blitz, *Contested State*, 108–10, 121.
19. Ibid., 131–35.
20. *DD*, 237–38.
21. Marcos had amassed a fortune estimated in the billions by the end of his reign.
22. Patricia Ann Paez, *The Bases Factor: Realpolitik of RP-US Relations* (Manila: Center for Strategic and International Studies of the Philippines, 1985), 111, 119.
23. Ibid., 128–60.
24. W. Scott Thompson, *Unequal Partners: Philippine and Thai Relations with the United States, 1965–1975* (Lexington, MA: D. C. Heath, 1975), 9–10.
25. Blitz (*Contested State*, 144) states flatly that the concern for keeping the bases was the main reason for the pro-Marcos stance by the US government; see also 133–34, 139, 154n. See also Scott Kaufman, *The Foreign Policy of the Carter Administration* (DeKalb: Northern Illinois University Press, 2008), 32–35.
26. For this section, see *Washington Connection*, 205–17, and Noam Chomsky, *Year 501: The Conquest Continues* (Boston: South End Press, 1993—hereinafter cited as *Year 501*), 121–32.
27. Robert Cribb, "Unresolved Problems in the Indonesian Killings of 1965-6," *Asian Survey* 42 (July/August 2002): 557–58
28. *Washington Connection*, 207–9; Henry Crouch, *The Army and Politics in Indonesia* (Ithaca, NY: Cornell University Press, 1978), 155–56. Some researchers have emphasized the role of pre-existing tensions, particularly religious in nature, in giving rise to widespread eruptions of anti-Communist violence that exceeded the intentions of the army. For a discussion, see Cribb, "Unresolved Problems," 553–57. While recognizing that the army in places may have lost control of the violence it unleashed, Crouch clearly identifies the army as the prime mover in the slaughter (135, 156), as does John Roosa, *Pretext for Mass Murder: The September 30th Movement and Suharto's Coup d'Etat in Indonesia* (Madison: University of Wisconsin Press, 2006), 28–29.
29. Cf. Roosa, *Pretext*, 177, 181–83.
30. *Year 501*, 123.
31. *Washington Connection*, 210–14.
32. Ibid., 205, 215. In a later book Chomsky describes the US reaction to the Indonesian bloodbath as "unrestrained euphoria": *A New Generation Draws the Line: East Timor and the Standards of the West* (New York: Verso, 2000—hereinafter cited as *New Generation*), 64.
33. *Year 501*, 124.
34. Antonie C. A. Dake, *The Sukarno File, 1965–1967* (Leiden, Netherlands: Koninklijke Brill, 2006), 263–82.
35. Bradley R. Simpson, *Economists with Guns* (Stanford, CA: Stanford University Press, 2008), 177.
36. Ibid., 184, 188.
37. Ibid., 18.
38. US Department of State, *Foreign Relations of the United States, 1964–1968, Vol. 36: Indonesia; Malaysia-Singapore; Philippines* (Washington, DC: US Government Printing Office, 2001—hereinafter cited as *FRUS 36*), 338–39.
39. Ibid., 361.
40. Helen-Louise Hunter, *Sukarno and the Indonesian Coup: The Untold Story* (Westport, CT: Praeger Security International, 2007), 112, 114.
41. Bradley R. Simpson, *Economists*, 186, 188.
42. Marshall Green, *Indonesia: Crisis and Transformation 1965–1968* (Washington, DC: Compass Press, 1990), 67–68.
43. Bradley R. Simpson, *Economists*, 185–86.
44. Ibid., 186–87.

45. Roger Kerson, "The Embassy's Hit List," *Columbia Journalism Review* 29 (November 1990); *FRUS* 36, 338–39.
46. *Year 501*, 123.
47. Bradley R. Simpson, *Economists*, 189.
48. Howard Federspiel, quoted in Bradley R. Simpson, *Economists*, 189.
49. Bradley R. Simpson, *Economists*, 190.
50. William Colby, the head of the Far Eastern division of the CIA's Directorate of Plans during the postcoup period, was asked in 1988 to comment on the apparent lack of criticism or objection within the US government to the mass killings. He acknowledged that he hadn't been aware of any such objection or criticism. Audrey R. Kahin and George McT. Kahin, *Subversion as Foreign Policy: The Eisenhower and Dulles Debacle in Indonesia* (New York: New Press, 1995), 230, 308n.
51. *Year 501*, 126–31.
52. Robert Kennedy, quoted in Roosa, *Pretext*, 26–27.
53. Green, *Indonesia*, 59–60, 75.
54. Kiernan, *Genocide and Resistance*, 135.
55. *Washington Connection*, 134.
56. Ibid., 155.
57. Richard Woolcott, quoted in *Washington Connection*, 157.
58. Henry Kissinger, quoted in the *Los Angeles Times*, July 12, 1975, which in turn is quoted in *Washington Connection*, 156.
59. *TANCW*, 389.
60. George H. Aldrich, quoted in *Washington Connection*, 158–61.
61. US State Department, quoted in *Washington Connection*, 200.
62. *Washington Connection*, 201.
63. US State Department, quoted in *TANCW*, 361.
64. Ibid., 502n.
65. Scott Sidel, "The United States and Genocide in East Timor," *Journal of Contemporary Asia*, 11 (1981): 48.
66. "Memorandum of Conversation between Presidents Ford and Suharto, 5 July 1975, 12:40 p.m.–2:00 p.m.," in *East Timor Revisited: Ford, Kissinger and the Indonesian Invasion, 1975-76* (National Security Archive Electronic Briefing Book No. 62), ed. William Burr and Michael L. Evans (Washington, DC: National Security Archive, George Washington University, 2001), doc. 1, www.gwu.edu/~nsarchiv/NSAEBB/NSAEBB62.
67. "Embassy Jakarta Telegram 1579 to Secretary State, 6 December 1975," in Burr and Evans, *East Timor Revisited*, doc. 4.
68. US State Department, quoted in Kiernan, *Genocide and Resistance*, 110.
69. Henry Kissinger, quoted in Kiernan, *Genocide and Resistance*, 110.
70. Brad Simpson, "'Illegally and Beautifully': The United States, the Indonesian Invasion of East Timor and the International Community, 1974–76," *Cold War History* 5, no. 3 (August 2005): 304–5.
71. Noam Chomsky, quoted in Milan Rai, *Chomsky's Politics* (London: Verso, 1995), 17.
72. Noam Chomsky, *Turning the Tide: U.S. Intervention in Central America and the Struggle for Peace* (1985; Boston: South End Press, 1987—hereinafter cited as *TTT*), 95.
73. Ibid., 98.
74. Ibid., 101. This is an example of the sketchiness of Chomsky's narrative: the reader is left wondering how neighboring countries could have intervened in El Salvador's elections. What happened is that the Salvadoran military's obvious electoral fraud occasioned widespread popular protests, which the military put down with help from Guatemalan and Nicaraguan forces.
75. Oscar Romero, quoted in *TTT*, 102.
76. *TTT*, 102–3.
77. Ibid., 102.
78. Ibid., 15.
79. Ibid., 105–7.
80. Ibid., 109.
81. Ibid., 117.
82. Ibid.
83. Ibid., 122–23.
84. *MC*, 49, 349 (notes 18, 19, and 23); *TANCW*, 39, 46.
85. John H. Coatsworth, *Central America and the United States: The Clients and the Colossus* (New York: Twayne, 1994), 97–103.
86. Ibid., 90-121; Walter LaFeber, *Inevitable Revolutions: The United States in Central America* (New York: Norton, 1993), 150–61.
87. William M. LeoGrande, *Our Own Backyard: The United States in Central America, 1977-1992* (Chapel Hill: University of North Carolina Press, 1998), 34.
88. See Coatsworth, *Central America*, 116, 232n38.
89. Michael McClintock, *The American Connection, Vol. 2: State Terror and Popular Resistance in Guatemala* (London: Zed, 1985), 184–86.
90. Ibid., 215–16.
91. Viron Vaky, quoted in William Stanley, *The Protection Racket State: Elite Politics, Military Extortion, and Civil War in El Salvador* (Philadelphia: Temple University Press, 1996), 129-30.
92. Raymond Bonner, *Weakness and Deceit: US Policy and El Salvador* (New York: Times Books, 1984), 164–67; Coatsworth, *Central America*, 147–52; LeoGrande, *Our Own Backyard*, 40–42; Stanley, *Protection Racket State*, 171–77.
93. Stanley, *Protection Racket State*, 1, 281n.
94. Americas Watch, *El Salvador's Decade of*

Terror: Human Rights Since the Assassination of Archbishop Romero (New Haven, CT: Yale University Press, 1991), 122; LeoGrande, *Our Own Backyard*, 59, 92-93.
95. *World Orders*, 50.
96. *TTT*, 102, 105.
97. Jesse Helms, quoted in Bonner, *Weakness*, 181, and in LeoGrande, *Our Own Backyard*, 59.
98. Stanley, *Protection Racket State*, 216-17; LeoGrande, *Our Own Backyard*, 51; Coatsworth, *Central America*, 156, 162.
99. Bonner, *Weakness*, 14.
100. Stanley, *Protection Racket State*, 213.
101. LeoGrande, *Our Own Backyard*, 57.
102. Gerry Studds, quoted in LeoGrande, *Our Own Backyard*, 156.
103. Americas Watch, *El Salvador's Decade*, 120-22.
104. US State Department, quoted in LeoGrande, *Our Own Backyard*, 227.
105. Bonner, *Weakness*, 13, 365.
106. Tommie Sue Montgomery, *Revolution in El Salvador: From Civil Strife to Civil Peace* (Boulder, CO: Westview Press, 1995), 152, 172-73; Michael McClintock, *The American Connection, Vol. 1: State Terror and Popular Resistance in El Salvador* (London: Zed, 1985), 305-7.
107. Robert D. Ramsey III, *Advising Indigenous Forces: American Advisors in Korea, Vietnam, and El Salvador* (Fort Leavenworth, KS: Combat Studies Institute Press, 2006), 83-84.
108. McClintock, *American Connection*, 1:337-40.
109. For example, see Noam Chomsky, *The Culture of Terrorism* (Boston: South End Press, 1988), 125, 154, 225-44; *NI*, 15, 51.
110. *TTT*, 117. "Atmosphere of terror and despair" is a quotation from a British parliamentary human rights group that had observed the elections.
111. Terry Karl, cited by Coatsworth, *Central America*, 174-75.
112. *TTT*, 52; *Washington Connection*, 274-76.
113. *DD*, 393.
114. Chomsky doesn't go into detail on the coup operation. A good concise account is in Stephen Kinzer, *Overthrow* (New York: Holt, 2006), chapter 6.
115. *Year 501*, 173. The accuracy of this number is very questionable. Chomsky cites Susanne Jonas's *The Battle for Guatemala: Rebels, Death Squads, and U.S. Power* (Boulder, CO: Westview Press, 1991) as his source, but Michael McClintock credibly estimates the death toll in the hundreds rather than in the thousands: cf. McClintock, *American Connection*, 2:29-30. Chomsky, who otherwise cites McClintock's book repeatedly, does not acknowledge the discrepancy.
116. *Year 501*, 173

117. Victoria Sanford, *Buried Secrets: Truth and Human Rights in Guatemala* (New York: Palgrave Macmillan, 2003), 14.
118. Jonas, *Battle*, 25.
119. Piero Gleijeses, *Shattered Hope: The Guatemalan Revolution and the United States, 1944-1954* (Princeton, NJ: Princeton University Press, 1991), 147-48.
120. Coatsworth, *Central America*, 86.
121. Richard H. Immerman, *The CIA in Guatemala: The Foreign Policy of Intervention* (Austin: University of Texas Press, 1982).
122. Ibid., 182-83.
123. Ibid., 88, 111-13, 182-83.
124. *TTT*, 55-56.
125. United Fruit's subsequent problems with the US Justice Department suggest that the company's influence within the federal government may in fact not have been so great. Despite heavy lobbying, United Fruit failed to persuade the department to drop an antitrust suit that severely affected the company's Guatemalan operations. In 1958, United Fruit accepted a consent decree requiring it to surrender some of its business and land to local companies.
126. Coatsworth, *Central America*, 88.
127. *Year 501*, 173-74.
128. There is some controversy as to whether the United States actually preapproved the coup. There is no doubt, however, that the US leadership was informed of the coming coup, did nothing to stop it, and quickly recognized the junta that emerged. See Stephen Schlesinger and Stephen Kinzer, *Bitter Fruit: The Story of the American Coup in Guatemala*, expanded ed. (Cambridge, MA: Harvard University Press, 1999), 243-44.
129. Coatsworth, *Central America*, 111-12, 119.
130. Jonas, *Battle*, 68-70; Coatsworth, *Central America*, 118-19.
131. McClintock, *American Connection*, 60-62.
132. Schlesinger and Kinzer, *Bitter Fruit*, 247; McClintock, *American Connection, Vol. 2*, 59-62, 84-86, 91-92, 102-3.
133. Viron Vaky, quoted in Joseph Gilbert, "What We Know and Should Know: Bringing Latin America More Meaningfully into Cold War Studies," in *In from the Cold: Latin America's New Encounter with the Cold War*, ed. Joseph Gilbert and Daniela Spenser (Durham, NC: Duke University Press, 2008), 25; Thomas S. Blanton, "Recovering the Memory of the Cold War: Forensic History and Latin America," in Gilbert and Spenser, *In from the Cold*, 55.
134. Jonas, *Battle*, 195-98; Coatsworth, *Central America*, 147.
135. Jonas, *Battle*, 149. Detailed accounts for one Guatemalan province, based on extensive

interviews with refugees in camps mostly in Mexico, are provided by the Jesuit priest and anthropologist Ricardo Falla in *Massacres in the Jungle: Ixcan, Guatemala, 1975-1982* (Boulder, CO: Westview Press, 1994).
136. Sanford, *Buried Secrets*, 14; Gabriel Aguilera Peralta, "The Hidden War: Guatemala's Counterinsurgency Campaign," in *Crisis in Central America: Regional Dynamics and U.S. Policy in the 1980s*, ed. Nora Hamilton, Jeffrey A. Frieden, Linda Fuller, and Manuel Pastor Jr. (Boulder, CO: Westview Press, 1988), 158.
137. Peralta, "Hidden War," 166; McClintock, *American Connection*, 2:198-99.
138. *TTT*, 108; *DD*, 393.
139. Jonas, *Battle*, 196-99; Sanford, *Buried Secrets*, 154-55, 203-5, 297n.
140. *Washington Connection*, 287.
141. Ibid., 292.
142. Ibid., 296.
143. Ibid.
144. *DD*, 313
145. *DD*, 311-13.
146. *TTT*, 13-14.
147. Ibid., 54-57, 129.
148. Ibid., 82-83.
149. Ibid., 235-36, 137-40.
150. Ibid., 73.
151. *NI*, 324-25.
152. *DD*, 295-97; *NI*, 89-93.
153. *DD*, 298-99.
154. Coatsworth, *Central America*, 52.
155. Todd Greentree, *Crossroads of Intervention: Insurgency and Counterinsurgency Lessons from Latin America* (Westport, CT: Praeger, 2008), 70.
156. Robert A. Pastor, *Condemned to Repetition*, 143.
157. LeoGrande, *Our Own Backyard*, 29-31.
158. Fidel Castro, quoted in Robert A. Pastor, *Condemned to Repetition*, 214.
159. Chomsky cites Brian Jenkins's *New Modes of Conflict* (Santa Monica: Rand Corporation, 1983) without giving a page number, quoting Jenkins's reference to Argentina acting as "a proxy for the United States." Jenkins (*New Modes*, 6), writing two and a half years after Carter left office, mentions the Argentine proxy role, but does not specify the time period he is referring to. Chomsky carefully phrases his language to imply, without actually saying, that the Carter administration collaborated with the Argentines: *DD*, 312-13, 329n17.
160. Ariel C. Armony, "Transnationalizing the Dirty War: Argentina in Central America," in Gilbert and Spenser, *In from the Cold*, 135, 154.
161. Robert A. Pastor, *Condemned to Repetition*, 216-17, 355n.

162. Coatsworth, *Central America*, 176-78; LeoGrande, *Our Own Backyard*, 581.
163. *TTT*, 139-40.
164. Arturo Cruz Sequeira, "The Origins of Sandinista Foreign Policy," in *Central America: Anatomy of Conflict*, ed. Robert S. Leiken (New York: Pergamon Press, 1984), 99.
165. Morris Rothenberg, "The Soviets and Central America," in Leiken, *Central America*, 133-35.
166. Coatsworth, *Central America*, 178-79.
167. Coatsworth, *Central America*, 180; Sequeira, "Origins," 95-96.
168. Nina H. Shea, "Human Rights in Nicaragua: The Sandinista Way of Repression," *New Republic*, September 1, 1986: 21-22.
169. For various assessments, see International League for Human Rights, *Report on Human Rights Defenders in Nicaragua* (mimeo, July 1986); Americas Watch, *Human Rights in Nicaragua: Reagan, Rhetoric and Reality* (New York: Americas Watch Committee, 1985); and Catholic Institute for Human Relations, *Right to Survive, Human Rights in Nicaragua* (London: CIIR, 1987). See also LeoGrande, *Our Own Backyard*, 413-16.
170. Coatsworth, *Central America*, 201; LeoGrande, *Our Own Backyard*, 582-83.
171. *Washington Connection*, ix.
172. Geir Lundestad, "Empire by Invitation? The United States and Western Europe, 1945-1952," *Journal of Peace Research* 23 (1986).
173. *Washington Connection*, 17.
174. Stephen Morris, "Chomsky on U.S. Foreign Policy," *Harvard International Review* (December-January 1981): 5

CHAPTER 3
1. *TANCW*, 98.
2. For examples: "ruling class," *TANCW*, 113; "dominant social groups," *FROS*, 64; "private business sector," *TANCW*, 5; "the powerful," *DD*, 359.
3. Chomsky also uses a variety of terms to refer to the broader alignment of the corporate class with its allies in government. He sometimes refers to the "government-corporate nexus," "the elite," "powerful societal interests," or simply "the powerful." It is not always clear whether Chomsky in any given instance is referring to the corporate class or to the broader government-corporate nexus. Where it seems to be the latter, I will generally use the term "the elite" in describing Chomsky's views.
4. *TANCW*, 5.
5. Noam Chomsky, *Understanding Power: The Indispensable Chomsky*, edited by Peter R. Mitchell and John Schoeffel (New York: New Press, 2002), 62.

6. Ibid., 63.
7. Noam Chomsky, *Language and Politics*, edited by C. P. Otero (Montreal: Black Rose Books, 1988—hereinafter cited as *L&P*), 168.
8. *L&P*, 144.
9. Cf. Fred Block, *Revising State Theory: Essays in Politics and Postindustrialism* (Philadelphia: Temple University Press, 1987), chapters 3 and 5.
10. *L&P*, 184.
11. *TTT*, 63. See also Alison Edgley, *The Social and Political Thought of Noam Chomsky* (London: Routledge, 2000), 87.
12. Edgley, *Social and Political Thought*, 113–14.
13. *DD*, 21–22, 49, 81.
14. *L&P*, 185.
15. *DD*, 253.
16. *DD*, 373.
17. *DD*, 59, 369, 375–76.
18. *TANCW*, 98.
19. *FROS*, 64.
20. C. Wright Mills, *The Power Elite* (London: Oxford University Press, 1956).
21. Robert Dahl, "A Critique of the Ruling Elite Model," in *C. Wright Mills and the Power Elite*, ed. G. William Domhoff and Hoyt B. Ballard (Boston: Beacon Press, 1968), 25–36.
22. E. E. Schattschneider, *The Semi-Sovereign People: A Realist's View of Democracy in America* (New York: Holt, Rinehart and Winston, 1960); William E. Connolly, ed., *The Bias of Pluralism* (New York: Atherton Press, 1969); G. William Domhoff, *Who Rules America?* (Englewood Cliffs, NJ: Prentice Hall, 1967). Domhoff subsequently published five revised and updated editions of his book, the latest in 2010.
23. Peter Bachrach and Morton S. Baratz, "Two Faces of Power," in Connolly, *Bias*, 51–66.
24. American Political Science Association Task Force on Inequality and American Democracy, "American Democracy in an Age of Rising Inequality," *Perspectives on Politics* 2 (2004); Lawrence R. Jacobs and Theda Skocpol, eds., *Inequality and American Democracy* (New York: Russell Sage Foundation, 2005).
25. Larry M. Bartels, *Unequal Democracy: The Political Economy of the New Gilded Age* (Princeton, NJ: Princeton University Press, 2008), chapters 9 and 10.
26. Martin Gilens, "Inequality and Democratic Responsiveness in the United States," Conference on the Comparative Politics of Inequality and Redistribution, Princeton University, May 11–12, 2007.
27. Jeffrey A. Winters and Benjamin I. Page, "Oligarchy in the United States?" *Perspectives on Politics* 7 (2009): 731–51.
28. Jacob S. Hacker and Paul Pierson, *Winner-Take-All Politics: How Washington Made the Rich Richer—and Turned Its Back on the Middle Class* (New York: Simon and Schuster, 2010); Winters and Page, "Oligarchy," 9–12. Chomsky does, however, attribute importance to campaign finance in American politics. On several occasions he cites the work of political scientist Thomas Ferguson, who argues that party elites' dependence on the financial contributions of major "investors" effectively restricts the range of policy alternatives that become the subject of partisan debate. See Thomas Ferguson, *Golden Rule: The Investment Theory of Party Competition and the Logic of Money-Driven Political Systems* (Chicago: University of Chicago Press, 1995).
29. Bartels, *Unequal Democracy*, 292–93.
30. *DD*, 85.
31. Charles Lindblom, *Politics and Markets: The World's Political-Economic Systems* (New York: Basic Books, 1977).
32. Ibid., 175.
33. Ibid., 185.
34. Two political scientists who have tried conclude that strictly speaking, the structural Marxist perspective can neither be proved nor disproved: Dennis P. Quinn and Robert Y. Shapiro, "Business Political Power: The Case of Taxation," *American Political Science Review* 85 (September 1991): 867–68.
35. Robert Reich, *Locked in the Cabinet* (New York: Vintage, 1997), 61–64.
36. It is problematic in any case for Marxists, structural or not, to attribute statesmen's concerns for natural resource availability to special solicitude for the interests of the corporate class. It can be assumed that the economy's need for resource availability is broadly shared across social classes—factory workers as well as their bosses need materials to work with, and the American economy would have roughly the same natural resource needs regardless of whether it was largely capitalist or socialist. There is no compelling reason to believe that a socialist America would be significantly more selfless or benevolent than capitalist America is in its dealings with overseas suppliers of natural resources.
37. *FROS*, 150n.
38. Melvyn P. Leffler, "New Approaches, Old Interpretations, and Prospective Reconfigurations," in *America in the World: The Historiography of American Foreign Relations since 1941*, ed. Michael J. Hogan (Cambridge: Cambridge University Press, 1995), 85–86.
39. Richard J. Barnet, *Roots of War* (Baltimore: Penguin, 1972), 49.
40. Gabriel Kolko, *The Roots of American Foreign Policy* (Boston: Beacon, 1969), 18–22.
41. See Philip H. Burch Jr., *Elites in American*

History, Volume 3: The New Deal to the Carter Administration (New York: Holmes and Meier: 1980), especially 372-84.
42. Lawrence R. Jacobs and Benjamin I. Page, "Who Influences US Foreign Policy?" *American Political Science Review* 99, no. 1 (February 2005).
43. An early "orthodox" treatment of the Cold War is Herbert Feis's *Churchill, Roosevelt, Stalin: The War They Waged and the Peace They Sought* (Princeton, NJ: Princeton University Press, 1957). An updated orthodox, or perhaps neo-orthodox, viewpoint is presented by John Lewis Gaddis in *The Cold War: A New History* (New York: Penguin, 2005).
44. A seminal statement of Cold War revisionism is William Appleman Williams's *The Tragedy of American Diplomacy* (New York: Norton, 1959). Other prominent revisionist historians include Walter LaFeber, Lloyd Gardner, and Thomas J. McCormick. See also Chapter 2, Note 1.
45. Gabriel Kolko and Joyce Kolko, *The Limits of Power: The World and United States Foreign Policy, 1945-1954* (New York: Harper and Row, 1972), 6-7.
46. Gabriel Kolko, *Confronting the Third World: United States Foreign Policy, 1945-1980* (New York: Pantheon, 1988), 97-98, 123.
47. That objective did not prevent the United States from seeking its own sphere of influence, buttressed by military intervention when necessary, in the Caribbean and Central America.
48. William Appleman Williams, quoted in Andrew J. Bacevich, *American Empire: The Realities and Consequences of U.S. Diplomacy* (Cambridge, MA: Harvard University Press, 2002), 26.
49. Dean Acheson, quoted in H. W. Brands, *The Devil We Knew: Americans and the Cold War* (New York: Oxford University Press, 1993), 10-11.
50. Lloyd Gardner, *Architects of Illusion* (Chicago: Quadrangle, 1970).
51. Christopher Layne, *The Peace of Illusions: American Grand Strategy from 1940 to the Present* (Ithaca, NY: Cornell University Press, 2006), 220n.
52. Williams, quoted in Bacevich, *American Empire*, 26.
53. John Fousek, *To Lead the Free World: American Nationalism and the Cultural Roots of the Cold War* (Chapel Hill: University of North Carolina Press, 2000).
54. Ibid., 5. See also Anatol Lieven, *America Right or Wrong: An Anatomy of American Nationalism* (Oxford: Oxford University Press, 2004); and Michael Hunt, *Ideology and U.S. Foreign Policy* (New Haven, CT: Yale University Press, 1987), especially chapter 2.
55. Alexis de Tocqueville, quoted in Lieven, *America Right or Wrong*, 21.
56. Herbert Croly, quoted in Lieven, *America Right or Wrong*, 22.
57. Lieven, *America Right or Wrong*, 19-20. A more recent poll, however, found only 38 percent of Americans believing that the United States "stands above all other countries in the world," while 53 percent would assert only that the United States was "one of the greatest countries in the world, along with some others." Belief in American superiority was strongest among self-identified Republicans and conservatives: Pew Research Center for the People and the Press, "U.S. Seen as among the Greatest of Nations, but Not Superior to All Others," June 30, 2011, www.people-press.org.
58. Fousek, *To Lead*, 46.
59. Julien E. Zelizer, *Arsenal of Democracy: The Politics of National Security—From World War II to the War on Terrorism* (New York: Basic Books, 2010), 65-66.
60. Campbell Craig and Fredrik Logevall, *America's Cold War: The Politics of Insecurity* (Cambridge, MA: Harvard University Press, 2009), 79. See also Melvyn P. Leffler, *A Preponderance of Power: National Security, the Truman Administration, and the Cold War* (Stanford, CA: Stanford University Press, 1992), 145.
61. Richard Freeland, *The Truman Doctrine and the Origins of McCarthyism* (New York: New York University Press, 1985), xvi, 99-100.
62. Leffler, *Preponderance of Power*, 179-81.
63. Zelizer, *Arsenal*, 80.
64. Harry S. Truman, quoted in Athan Theoharis, "The Rhetoric of Politics: Foreign Policy, Internal Security, and Domestic Politics in the Truman Era, 1945-1950," in *Politics and Policies of the Truman Administration*, ed. Barton J. Bernstein (Chicago: Quadrangle, 1970), 213.
65. Craig and Logevall, *America's Cold War*, 134-35.
66. Hans J. Morgenthau, *Politics among Nations: The Struggle for Power and Peace*, 7th ed. with revisions by Kenneth W. Thompson and W. David Clinton (New York: McGraw Hill, 2006), 29.
67. Ibid., 5. For a wealth of examples of the international struggle for power over time, see Paul Kennedy, *The Rise and Fall of the Great Powers* (New York: Vintage, 1989).
68. Brands, *Devil We Knew*, 4.
69. George Kennan, quoted in Lynn Eden, "The End of U.S. Cold War History? A Review Essay," *International Security* 18 (Summer 1993): 187.
70. Leffler, *Preponderance of Power*, 10.
71. Joint Chiefs of Staff, quoted in Leffler, *Preponderance of Power*, 50.
72. National Security Council, quoted in Leffler, *Preponderance of Power*, 12.

73. Central Intelligence Agency, National Security Council, quoted in Leffler, *Preponderance of Power*, 12.
74. Ibid., 14. In a later work, Leffler admits that on reconsideration he would have assigned greater importance to ideology: Leffler, "Bringing It All Together: The Parts and the Whole," in Westad, *Reviewing the Cold War*, 44-45.
75. Craig and Logevall, *America's Cold War*.
76. Layne, *Peace of Illusions*.
77. *FROS*, 57-58.
78. *World Orders*, 30.
79. LeoGrande, *Our Own Backyard*; Craig and Logevall, *America's Cold War*; Zelizer, *Arsenal*.
80. *Mandarins*, 297.
81. Noam Chomsky, *Power and Terror: Post-9/11 Talks and Interviews* (New York: Seven Stories Press, 2003—hereinafter cited as *P&T*), 123.
82. Chester J. Pach, "Introduction," in *The Eisenhower Administration, the Third World, and the Globalization of the Cold War*, ed. Kathryn C. Statler and Andrew L. Johns (Lanham, MD: Rowman and Littlefield, 2006); Stephen G. Rabe, *The Most Dangerous Area in the World: John F. Kennedy Confronts Communist Revolution in Latin America* (Chapel Hill: University of North Carolina Press, 1999); Odd Arne Westad, *The Global Cold War: Third World Interventions and the Making of Our Times* (Cambridge: Cambridge University Press, 2007).
83. Mitchell and Schoeffel, *Understanding Power*, 64.
84. The documents cited by Chomsky are NSC 144/1 and NSC 5432/1, in US Department of State, *Foreign Relations of the United States, 1952-1954, Vol. 4: The American Republics* (Washington, DC: US Government Printing Office, 1983); and NSC 5613/1, in US Department of State, *Foreign Relations of the United States, 1955-1957, Vol. 6: American Republics: Multilateral; Mexico; Caribbean* (Washington, DC: US Government Printing Office, 1987).
85. William M. LeoGrande, review of Gilbert and Spenser, *In from the Cold*, H-Diplo Roundtable Review 10, no. 23 (2009): 16-17, www.h-net.org.
86. Westad, *Global Cold War*, 28.
87. Andrew Rotter, *The Path to Vietnam: Origins of the American Commitment to Southeast Asia* (Ithaca, NY: Cornell University Press, 1987); Michael Schaller, *The American Occupation of Japan: The Origins of the Cold War in Asia* (New York: Oxford University Press, 1985).
88. Schaller, *American Occupation*, viii, 296.
89. Craig and Logevall, *America's Cold War*, 221-22; Zelizer, *Arsenal*, 176.
90. Westad, *Global Cold War*, 30.
91. Ron Chernow, *The House of Morgan: An American Banking Dynasty and the Rise of Modern Finance* (New York: Simon and Schuster, 1990), 132-33, 230-32.
92. Westad, *Global Cold War*, 29.

CHAPTER 4

1. *TANCW*, 5.
2. *DD*, 372.
3. "Stupid and ignorant masses": Chomsky here is paraphrasing the political scientist Harold Lasswell.
4. *DD*, 369-70.
5. David Riesman, with Nathan Glazer and Reuel Denney, *The Lonely Crowd: A Study of the Changing American Character* (New Haven, CT: Yale University Press, 1950); Robert D. Putnam, *Bowling Alone: The Collapse and Revival of American Community* (New York: Simon and Schuster, 2000); Theda Skocpol, *Diminished Democracy: From Membership to Management in American Civic Life* (Norman: University of Oklahoma Press, 2003).
6. *DD*, 370.
7. *TANCW*, 86-87.
8. *MC*, 5.
9. *TANCW*, 9-10.
10. *MC*, lix.
11. *Washington Connection*, 23-24.
12. *MC*, xii.
13. Ibid., lx.
14. Ibid., 2-14.
15. Ibid., 14-15.
16. Ibid., 16-17.
17. Ibid., 18-28.
18. Ibid., 22.
19. Kissinger, quoted in *MC*, 23.
20. Ibid., 26-28.
21. Ibid., 29-31.
22. Two authors of a strongly favorable article on the Propaganda Model treat it as simply a model of media handling of foreign policy, without acknowledging the broader claims Chomsky and Herman make. See Eric Herring and Piers Robinson, "Too Polemical or Too Critical? Chomsky on the Study of the News Media and US Foreign Policy," *Review of International Studies* 29 (2003): 553-68.
23. *MC*, 38-71.
24. Ibid., 37.
25. Bias need not be a matter of conscious preference or aversion; it may reflect a largely unconscious predisposition to perceive things in a certain way.
26. Chomsky and Herman explain the "naturalness" of the processes they describe in *MC*, lxii and 2.
27. *MC*, 40-41.
28. Ibid., 55.
29. Ibid., 66.
30. The sample consisted of the *New York Times*,

Time, *Newsweek*, and CBS News. It is a common practice among media researchers to limit their samples to a relatively small number of leading news outlets, on the reasonable assumption that their reporting is indicative of the media more broadly. Such sample lists almost invariably include the *New York Times*, *Time*, and/or *Newsweek*, and (if broadcast media are being studied) one or more of the broadcast network news shows.

31. *MC*, 77.
32. Eli Lehrer, "Chomsky and the Media: A Kept Press and a Manipulated People," in *The Anti-Chomsky Reader*, ed. Peter Collier and David Horowitz (San Francisco: Encounter Books, 2004), 80.
33. Ibid., 81.
34. Nicholas Lemann, quoted in *DD*, 146.
35. *DD*, 146–47, 382n.
36. *MC*, 31–35.
37. Tommie Sue Montgomery, *Revolution in El Salvador: From Civil Strife to Civil Peace* (Boulder, CO: Westview Press, 1995), 160.
38. *MC*, 89.
39. Ibid., 97.
40. Ibid., 97–98.
41. LeoGrande, *Our Own Backyard*, 178.
42. *MC*, 95.
43. The Latin American Studies Association (LASA) is the international association of scholars of Latin America.
44. LASA observers, quoted in *MC*, 104–5.
45. LaFeber, *Inevitable Revolutions*, 309.
46. Ibid., 252; Coatsworth, *Central America*, 174–75.
47. *MC*, 132–37.
48. Robert J. McCartney, "Disorganization, Rebel Raids, Disrupt Vote in El Salvador," *Washington Post*, March 25, 1984, A1.
49. *MC*, 108.
50. Coatsworth, *Central America*, 172.
51. *MC*, 120–21.
52. Ibid., 129.
53. Guatemalan Bishops Conference, quoted in *MC*, 113.
54. *MC*, 113.
55. Joseph T. Eldridge, "Hope vs. Reality in El Salvador," *Los Angeles Times*, March 27, 1984, C7.
56. "Democracy and Killing," *Los Angeles Times*, March 29, 1984, A10.
57. Edwin M. Yoder Jr., " . . . On a Bad Bet," *Washington Post*, March 23, 1984, A15; Donald E. Schultz, "Stacking the Deck?" *Washington Post*, March 25, 1984, C8.
58. "Elections in El Salvador," *Washington Post*, March 27, 1984, A22.
59. Guillermo Ungo, "Salvador's Election Farce," *New York Times*, March 22, 1984, A23.
60. Robert J. McCartney, "Vote Boycott Lamented," *Washington Post*, November 3, 1984, A1.
61. Robert J. McCartney, "Controversial Vote Set Today in Nicaragua," *Washington Post*, November 4, 1984, 1.
62. "Nicaragua's Rulers: Can They Survive?" *US News and World Report* 97 (November 5, 1984), 39–40.
63. Daniel C. Hallin, *We Keep America on Top of the World: Television and the Public Sphere* (London: Routledge, 1994), 13, 63, 73.
64. *MC*, chapter 5.
65. Daniel C. Hallin, *The Uncensored War: The Media and Vietnam* (New York: Oxford University Press, 1986).
66. Hallin, *Uncensored War*, 187.
67. "Vietminh Breaks Truce, US Holds," *New York Times*, June 2, 1956, quoted in *MC*, 187.
68. *MC*, 177, 185, 191, 205, 214, 220.
69. Hallin, *Uncensored War*, 16, quoted in *MC*, 208.
70. *MC*, 206–9.
71. Ibid., 177, 195–98, 200–201.
72. Ibid., 193.
73. Peter Braestrup, *Big Story: How the American Press and Television Reported and Interpreted the Crisis of Tet 1968 in Vietnam and Washington* (Boulder, CO: Westview Press, 1977).
74. Hallin, *Uncensored War*, 167–74.
75. *MC*, 211–28, 321–30.
76. W. Lance Bennett, "Toward a Theory of Press-State Relations in the United States," *Journal of Communications* 40 (Spring 1990), 103–24.
77. Robert Entman and Benjamin I. Page, "The News before the Storm," in *Taken by Storm: The Media, Public Opinion, and U.S. Foreign Policy in the Gulf War*, ed. W. Lance Bennett and David L. Paletz (Chicago: University of Chicago Press, 1994), 82–101; Timothy E. Cook, "Domesticating a Crisis," in Bennet and Paletz, *Taken by Storm*, 105–30; W. Lance Bennett and Jarol B. Manheim, "Taking the Public by Storm: Information, Cuing, and the Democratic Process in the Gulf Conflict," *Political Communication* 10 (1993): 331–51.
78. Entman and Page, "News," 93–101.
79. Jonathan Mermin, *Debating War and Peace: Media Coverage of U.S. Intervention in the Post-Vietnam Era* (Princeton, NJ: Princeton University Press, 1999), 101, 154–55. Mermin's findings, in my view, are at least as significant for showing the overall low level of critical coverage as for showing the difference between coverage of controversial vs. consensual interventions.
80. John Zaller and Dennis Chiu, "Government's Little Helper: US Press Coverage of Foreign Policy Crises, 1945–1991," *Political Communication* 13 (1996): 385.
81. *DD*, 379; Robert Entman, *Projections of Power:*

Framing News, Public Opinion, and U.S. Foreign Policy (Chicago: University of Chicago Press, 2004), 29–45.
82. *MC*, 32.
83. W. Lance Bennett, Regina G. Lawrence, and Steven Livingston, *When the Press Fails: Political Power and the News Media from Iraq to Katrina* (Chicago: University of Chicago Press, 2007), 13–45.
84. Ibid., 119.
85. Ibid., 34.
86. Ibid., 49–50.
87. Jeff Goodwin, "What's Right (and Wrong) about Left Media Criticism? Herman and Chomsky's Propaganda Model," *Sociological Forum* 9 (March 1994): 109–10.
88. W. Lance Bennett, "The Media and the Foreign Policy Process," in *The New Politics of American Foreign Policy*, ed. David Deese (New York: St. Martin's, 1994), 177; Zaller and Chiu, "Government's Little Helper," 385–86.
89. Mark Fishman, *Manufacturing the News* (Austin: University of Texas Press, 1980), 143, quoted in *MC*, 19.
90. Mermin, *Debating War*, 18.
91. Cook, "Domesticating a Crisis," 110, 124.
92. Hallin, *Uncensored War*, 68–69; Hallin, *We Keep America*, 24.
93. Hallin, *Uncensored War*, 69.
94. Bennett, Lawrence, and Livingston, *When the Press Fails*, 149.
95. Journalist quoted in Bennett, Lawrence, and Livingston, *When the Press Fails*, 149.
96. Mermin, *Debating War*, 29.
97. Ibid., 31.
98. Cf. Eric Alterman, *What Liberal Media?* (New York: Basic Books, 2003), 21–27.
99. Hallin, *Uncensored War*, 50.
100. Ibid., 150.
101. Bennett, Lawrence, and Livingston, *When the Press Fails*, 115–19.
102. Mark Hertsgaard, *On Bended Knee: The Press and the Reagan Presidency* (New York: Schocken Books, 1988), 196–97, 202.
103. See Herring and Robinson, "Too Polemical," 554–61. I agree with Herring and Robinson that academic media scholarship has tended wrongly to ignore or dismiss *Manufacturing Consent*, though I believe that their explanation for that phenomenon, focusing exclusively on scholars' aversion to Chomsky's radicalism, is a bit too simple.
104. Bennett, Lawrence, and Livingston, *When the Press Fails*, 155.
105. Ibid., 106.
106. Brigitte L. Nacos, Yaeli Bloch-Elkon, and Robert Y. Shapiro, *Selling Fear: Counterterrorism, the Media, and Public Opinion* (Chicago: University of Chicago Press, 2011), 12.
107. *MC*, xlvi–xlvii.
108. *TANCW*, 93.
109. Ibid., 74.
110. *Mandarins*, 324.
111. Ibid., 42.
112. Ibid., 299–301.
113. Schlesinger, quoted in *Mandarins*, 301.
114. R. J. de Jaegher, quoted in *Mandarins*, 338.
115. David Rowe, quoted in *Mandarins*, 337.
116. *Mandarins*, 342
117. *Mandarins*, 57.
118. Ibid., 349, 342–43.
119. Thomas Paterson, "Introduction," in *Kennedy's Quest for Victory* (New York: Oxford University Press, 1989), 14, 19.
120. Daniel Bell, quoted in *Mandarins*, 26.
121. *Mandarins*, 26–28, 343–49.
122. *Washington Connection*, 82.
123. *TANCW*, 108–12.
124. *Mandarins*, 61–68.
125. Frank Darling, quoted in *Mandarins*, 67.
126. *TANCW*, 118.
127. Norman Graebner, quoted in *TANCW*, 119.
128. *TANCW*, 118–19.
129. The political scientist Alan Wolfe similarly reports responding to these essays "as if visiting the oracle at Delphi": Alan Wolfe, "Academia (Kind of) Goes to War: Chomsky and His Children," *World Affairs*, Winter 2008, www.worldaffairsjournal.org.
130. *Mandarins*, 33.
131. Bruce Cummings, "Boundary Displacement: Area Studies and International Studies during and after the Cold War," in *Universities and Empire: Money and Politics in the Social Sciences during the Cold War*, ed. Christopher Simpson (New York: New Press, 1998), 165–73.
132. David C. Engerman, "Social Science in the Cold War," *Isis* 101 (2010): 398.
133. Irene L. Gendzier, "Play It Again, Sam: The Practice and Apology of Development," in Christopher Simpson, *Universities and Empire*, 86–87.
134. Engerman, "Social Science," 398–99.
135. Christopher Simpson, "Universities, Empire, and the Production of Knowledge: An Introduction," in *Universities and Empire*, xii–xiii.
136. Wolfe, "Academia."
137. Noam Chomsky, "The Cold War and the University," in Chomsky et al., *The Cold War and the University: Toward an Intellectual History of the Postwar Years* (New York: New Press, 1997), 187–89.
138. See, for example, Kim Phillips-Fein, *Invisible Hands: The Businessman's Crusade against the New Deal* (New York: Norton, 2009), especially

chapters 8 and 9, and Alterman, *What Liberal Media?*, chapter 6.
139. Arthur Schlesinger Jr., "Three Cheers for Professor Chomsky," *Chicago Tribune Book World*, March 23, 1969, P4.
140. Harry S. Truman, quoted in Noam Chomsky, *American Power and the New Mandarins* (New York: Pantheon, 1969), 268. (Schlesinger reviews and quotes from the Pantheon edition. The quoted passage is different in my Vintage edition, the one otherwise cited in this book—presumably a correction in response to the Schlesinger review.)
141. "Letters from Readers," *Commentary* 48 (October 1969): 22. Subsequent thrusts and counterthrusts between the two intellectuals appeared in *Commentary*'s "Letters" section in December 1969 and February, March, and June 1970. Most of this exchange is available on Paul Bogdanor's anti-Chomsky website, www.paulbogdanor.com.
142. Schlesinger was correct that Truman had said nothing approximating the alleged quote in the speech in question, but Truman as well as other members of his administration had said similar things on other occasions. I am accepting Chomsky's plea that his initial misquotation had been in honest error.
143. Samuel P. Huntington, "The Bases of Accommodation," *Foreign Affairs* 46 (July 1968): 653.
144. Noam Chomsky, "After Pinkville," *New York Review of Books* 14 (January 1, 1970).
145. Samuel P. Huntington, "A Frustrating Task" (Letter to the Editor), *New York Review of Books*, 14 (February 26, 1970).
146. "Noam Chomsky Replies," *New York Review of Books*, 14 (February 26, 1970).

CHAPTER 5

1. Noam Chomsky, *Hegemony or Survival: America's Quest for Global Dominance* (New York: Henry Holt, 2003, hereinafter cited as *H/S*), 11.
2. For critics, see among others Andrew Bacevich (*American Empire*) and Christopher Layne (*Peace of Illusions*). For supporters, see Niall Ferguson (*Colossus: The Rise and Fall of the American Empire* [New York: Penguin, 2005]) and Robert Kagan (*Dangerous Nation* [New York: Knopf, 2006]). A more moderate supporter of US hegemony is Zbigniew Brzezinski (*Choice: Global Domination or World Leadership* [New York: Basic Books, 2004]). Stephen Walt uses the weaker term "primacy" to characterize American global objectives, in *Taming American Power: The Global Response to US Primacy* (New York: Norton, 2005).
3. John Ikenberry in *Foreign Affairs*, September/October 2002; quoted in *H/S*, 11–12.
4. In addition to the sources cited in Note 1 of this chapter, see Robert O. Keohane, *After Hegemony: Cooperation and Discord in the World Political Economy* (Princeton, NJ: Princeton University Press, 2005), and Michael Hunt, *The American Ascendancy: How the United States Gained and Wielded Global Dominance* (Chapel Hill: University of North Carolina Press, 2007).
5. Noam Chomsky, *Hopes and Prospects* (Chicago: Haymarket Books, 2010—hereinafter cited as *H&P*), 173–74.
6. John Adams, quoted in Noam Chomsky, *Interventions* (San Francisco: City Lights Books, 2006), 215–16.
7. Noam Chomsky, *Power and Terror* (New York: Seven Stories Press, 2003—hereinafter cited as *P&T*), 34.
8. Noam Chomsky, *Profit over People* (New York: Seven Stories Press, 1999—hereinafter cited as *POP*), 73–75.
9. Chomsky, *Interventions*, 158–59.
10. *H&P*, 171.
11. Ibid., 136–37.
12. "Not a *shield* . . ." and "preserving America's ability . . .": Rand Corporation, quoted in *H&P*, 172 (emphases in the original).
13. *H/S*, 121, 231–32.
14. Chomsky, *Interventions*, 184.
15. See, for example, Clyde Prestowitz, *Rogue Nation: American Unilateralism and the Failure of Good Intentions* (New York: Basic Books, 2003), 47, 143–70.
16. *POP*, 19–20.
17. Ibid., 68–69.
18. Ibid., 132–33. For a broadly similar argument, see Paul Starr, "The Meaning of Privatization," *Yale Law and Policy Review* 6 (1988): 6–41.
19. Elaine Bernard, quoted in *World Orders*, 165.
20. *World Orders*, 165.
21. *H&P*, 75–76. Chomsky had similarly cited uncertainty of causes of economic development eleven years earlier: cf. *POP*, 25.
22. *POP*, 33.
23. *H&P*, 75–78. The "kicking away" metaphor is developed in Ha Joon Chang, *Kicking Away the Ladder: Development Policy in Historical Perspective* (London: Anthem, 2002).
24. *H&P*, 84–87.
25. Ibid., 82–83.
26. Keohane, *After Hegemony*, 136.
27. A Marxist view is advanced by William K. Tabb in *Economic Governance in the Age of Globalization* (New York: Columbia University Press, 2004). Sharing many similar views but not explicitly anchored in Marxist analysis are many of the essays in *Alternatives to Globalization:*

A Better World is Possible, ed. John Cavanaugh and Jerry Mander (San Francisco: International Forum on Globalization, 2004).
28. Joseph Stiglitz, *Making Globalization Work* (New York: Norton, 2006); Stiglitz, *Globalization and Its Discontents* (New York: Norton: 2002).
29. Stiglitz, *Globalization and Its Discontents*, 54.
30. *DD*, 144–53.
31. *DD*, 161.
32. Ibid., 164–66.
33. Eytan Gilboa, "The Panama Invasion Revisited: Lessons for the Use of Force in the Post Cold War Era," *Political Science Quarterly* 110 (Winter 1995-1996): 539–62.
34. *DD*, 153
35. *DD*, 149–51.
36. *Wall Street Journal*, quoted in *DD*, 146.
37. *Toronto Globe and Mail*, January 3, 1990, quoted in *DD*, 149.
38. Martin Mittelstaedt, quoted in *DD*, 149.
39. Gilboa, "Panama Invasion," 542–8.
40. Ibid., 551–54.
41. Ibid., 179, 185.
42. Noam Chomsky, "U.S. Iraq Policy: Motives and Consequences" in *Iraq under Siege: The Deadly Impact of Sanctions and War*, ed. Anthony Arnove (Cambridge, MA: South End Press, 2000), 48–50.
43. *DD*, 203–9.
44. *H/S*, 141.
45. Ibid., 126–28; Denis Halliday, quoted in *H/S*, 127.
46. *H/S*, 12–13.
47. Ibid., 42; Chomsky, *Interventions*, 135.
48. *H/S*, 37–38.
49. Ibid., 123.
50. Chomsky, *Interventions*, 15.
51. *H/S*, 41.
52. Ibid., 247.
53. *H/S*, 248.
54. Ibid., 140, 246–48; Chomsky, *Interventions*, 115–16.
55. *H/S*, 249.
56. Noam Chomsky, "Who Is to Run the World and How?," June 17, 2004 (distributed by the New York Times Syndicate); reprinted in *Interventions*, 85–88.
57. Chomsky, "U.S. Iraq Policy," 48.
58. Richard K. Herrmann, "US Policy in the Conflict," in *International Perspectives on the Gulf Conflict, 1990-1991*, ed. Alex Danchev and Dan Keohane (London: St. Martin's, 1994), 106–35.
59. Jo-Anne Hart, "American Objectives in the Crisis," in *Iraq, the Gulf Conflict, and the World Community*, ed. James Gow (London: Brassey's, 1993), 44.
60. Lawrence Freedman and Efraim Karsh, *The Gulf Conflict, 1990-1991: Diplomacy and War in the New World Order* (London: Faber and Faber, 1993), 414.
61. *P&T*, 132–33; Chomsky, "U.S. Iraq Policy," 51. Elsewhere, Chomsky says that Washington "effectively authorized" (*Interventions*, 9) or "tacitly authorized" (*NMH*, 20, 131) Saddam's action.
62. Lawrence Freedman, "The Theory of Limited War," in Danchev and Keohane, *International Perspectives*, 214; Freedman and Karsh, *Gulf Conflict*, 412–13, 417.
63. Joy Gordon, *Invisible War: The United States and the Iraq Sanctions* (Cambridge, MA: Harvard University Press, 2010), 37.
64. Gordon, *Invisible War*. The Americans and British enjoyed effective veto power in the relevant UN bodies.
65. *H/S*, 42–43.
66. Chomsky, "U.S. Iraq Policy," 52–53.
67. Stephen Wertheim, "A Solution from Hell: The United States and the Rise of Humanitarian Interventionism, 1991–2003," *Journal of Genocide Research* 12 (September–December 2010): 152–53.
68. Bill Clinton, quoted in *New Generation*, 2–3.
69. *New Generation*, 29–30.
70. *H/S*, 23–24.
71. Ibid., 21, 37–38, 117.
72. Robert Jervis, "International History and International Politics: Why Are They Studied Differently," in *Bridges and Boundaries: Historians, Political Scientists, and the Study of International Relations*, ed. Clinton Elman and Miriam Fendius Elman (Cambridge, MA: MIT Press, 2001), 397–98.
73. Samantha Power, *"A Problem from Hell": America and the Age of Genocide* (2002; New York: HarperPerennial, 2007), 421–42.
74. Tim Judah, *Kosovo: War and Revenge* (New Haven, CT: Yale University Press, 2000), 180–81.
75. Noam Chomsky, *The New Military Humanism: Lessons from Kosovo* (Monroe, ME: Common Courage Press, 1999—hereinafter cited as *NMH*), 16–17.
76. David N. Gibbs, *First Do No Harm: Humanitarian Intervention and the Destruction of Yugoslavia* (Nashville, TN: Vanderbilt University Press, 2009), 199.
77. *NMH*, 5, 16–17, 84; *New Generation*, 95–96, 100.
78. *NMH*, 34–35, 93; *New Generation*, 97–98, 134, 135–36.
79. Gibbs, *First Do No Harm*, 202.
80. *NMH*, 135–38.
81. Power, *Problem*, 463.
82. Ibid., 472.
83. Power may have had in mind the death toll of two hundred thousand or more in the Serbs' brutal suppression of the Bosnians' war for independence in 1992–1995. But it is

clearly dubious to assume that that experience would have been replicated, under different circumstances and years later, in Kosovo.
84. *New Generation*, 99, 103–8; *H/S*, 55–56.
85. *New Generation*, 33.
86. Power, *Problem*, 452.
87. *NMH*, 16, 21–22.
88. Wesley Clark, quoted in *NMH*, 20.
89. *NMH*, 21.
90. Porter Gross, quoted in *NMH*, 21.
91. Gibbs, *First Do No Harm*, 198.
92. Power, *Problem*, 451–52; Judah, *Kosovo*, 228–29.
93. *New Generation*, 124.
94. Ibid., 121–31.
95. James Gow, "The War in Kosovo," in *Confronting the Yugoslav Controversies: A Scholars' Initiative*, ed. Charles Ingrao and Thomas Emmert (West Lafayette, IN: Purdue University Press, 2009), 332. See also Tim Judah, *The Serbs: History, Myth and the Destruction of Yugoslavia*, 3rd ed. (New Haven: Yale University Press, 2009), 323–24.
96. Gow, "War," 329.
97. Christopher Layne, "Miscalculations and Blunders Lead to War," in *NATO's Empty Victory: A Postmortem on the Balkan War*, ed. Ted Galen Carpenter (Washington, DC: Cato Institute, 2000), 15–16.
98. Quoted in James George Jatras, "NATO's Myths and Bogus Justifications for Intervention," in Carpenter, *NATO's Empty Victory*, 24.
99. John Gilbert, quoted both in Gibbs, *First Do No Harm*, 190, and *New Generation*, 126.
100. Danilo Zolo, *Invoking Humanity: War, Law and Global Order* (London: Continuum, 2002), 29–30.
101. *NMH*, 13.
102. Ibid., 137.
103. Zolo, *Invoking Humanity*, 46; Gibbs, *First Do No Harm*, 203, 304n.
104. Bill Clinton, quoted in Gibbs, *First Do No Harm*, 174. The same remarks are cited in Layne, *Peace of Illusions*, 130–31. The fact that the same relatively obscure speech by Clinton is cited by two scholars making a similar argument suggests a paucity of other supporting evidence.
105. *NMH*, 134–36; *New Generation*, 124–27.
106. *NMH*, 134; *New Generation*, 107, 127.
107. Walt, *Taming American Power*, 45; Layne, *Peace of Illusions*, 104–13; Gibbs, *First Do No Harm*, 173–75.
108. Layne, *Peace of Illusions*, 112–17; Gibbs, *First Do No Harm*, 26–44.
109. Gibbs, *First Do No Harm*, 195–96.
110. *NMH*, 135. See also, for example, Gibbs, *First Do No Harm*, 174.
111. Layne, *Peace of Illusions*, 130–32; Bacevich, *American Empire*, 195–97. See also Lind, *Vietnam*, x–xi, 278–79.
112. Gibbs, *First Do No Harm*, 175, 184–87, 194.
113. Ibid., 108–12, 142–47, 168–70.
114. Stefano Recchia, "Limited Liability Multilateralism: The American Military, Armed Intervention, and IOs" (PhD dissertation, Columbia University, 2011), 303, 310–11.
115. *P&T*, 125.
116. *NMH*, 13.
117. *P&T*, 13
118. Ibid., 15.
119. *H/S*, 209–10.
120. Ibid., 211–14.
121. Noam Chomsky, *9-11* (New York: Seven Stories Press, 2001), 35.
122. Noam Chomsky, *Failed States* (New York: Holt, 2006), 18–24.
123. *H/S*, 199–201.
124. David Ottaway and Joe Stephens, "Diplomats Met with Taliban on Bin Laden," *Washington Post*, October 29, 2001, A1.
125. John Tirman, *The Deaths of Others: The Fate of Civilians in America's Wars* (Oxford: Oxford University Press, 2011), 277–81.
126. *H/S*, 201.
127. *H/S*, 241.
128. Chomsky, *9-11*, 16, 40.
129. Adam Schatz, "The Left and 9/11," *Nation*, September 5, 2002.
130. Michael Stohl, quoted in Chomsky, *9-11*, 16.
131. *US Code Congressional and Administrative News*, 98th Congress, Second Session (October 19, 1984), quoted in Chomsky, 9-11, 16.
132. Chomsky, *9/11*, 24–25, 43–44.
133. *H&P*, 50–51.
134. Michael Bérubé, *The Left at War* (New York: New York University Press, 2009), 75–81; David Horowitz and Ronald Radosh, "Chomsky and 9/11," in Collier and Horowitz, Anti-Chomsky Reader (see Chapter 4), 162–69.
135. Chomsky, *9/11*, 94–99; *H/S*, 128–29.
136. Timothy Noah, "Why Sudan Revisionism Is Unjustified," *Slate*, March 30, 2004, www.slate.com; Noah, "Khartoum Revisited, Part 2," *Slate*, March 31, 2004, www.slate.com.
137. Chomsky, "A Quick Reaction," *CounterPunch*, September 12, 2001, counterpunch.org; also available at www.chomsky.info.
138. An excellent analysis of the arguments on both sides is in Bérubé, *Left at War*, 48–60.
139. Christopher Hitchens, "A Rejoinder to Noam Chomsky," *Nation*, October 4, 2001, thenation.com.
140. Chomsky, *9-11*, 46–50.
141. Bérubé, *Left at War*, 50.
142. Leo Casey, "Let Us Not Inherit This Ill Wind: A Rejoinder to Chomsky's 'Reply to Casey' on Issues Emanating from the September 11 Mass Murders," *ZNet* [c. October 2001], zmag.org.

Accessed via *web.archive.org* on February 6, 2012.
143. Chomsky, "Noam Chomsky Replies to 'The Unbearable Whiteness of Chomsky's Arguments,'" [hereinafter "Chomsky Replies to Casey"] *The Struggle Site*, accessed on April 9, 2013, struggle.ws.
144. *NMH*, 52–57.
145. Ibid., 53.
146. John Tirman, *Spoils of War: The Human Cost of America's Arms Trade* (New York: Free Press, 1997), 224–29.
147. *NMH*, 55.
148. *P&T*, 18.
149. Tirman, *Spoils of War*, 202, 233, 237.
150. *NMH*, 43–48; *New Generation*, chapter 2.
151. *New Generation*, 84.
152. Quoted in *New Generation*, 69.
153. *New Generation*, 70–76.
154. Ibid., 49–50.
155. Elizabeth Becker and Philip Shenon, quoted in *New Generation*, 77.
156. Quoted in *New Generation*, 76.
157. Nicholas J. Wheeler and Tim Dunne, "East Timor and the New Humanitarian Intervention," *International Affairs* (2001): 813; Desmond Ball, "Silent Witness: Australian Intelligence and East Timor," in *Masters of Terror: Indonesia's Military and Violence in East Timor*, ed. Richard Tanter, Gerry van Klinken, and Desmond Ball (Lanham, MD: Rowman and Littlefield, 2006), 190–91.
158. Allan Nairn, "U.S. Support for the Indonesian Military: Congressional Testimony," September 30, 1999; reprinted in *Bitter Flowers, Sweet Flowers: East Timor, Indonesia and the World Community*, ed. Richard Tanter, Mark Selden and Stephen R. Shalom (Lanham, MD: Rowman and Littlefield, 2001), 165–66. Joseph Nevins, *A Not-So Distant Horror: Mass Violence in East Timor* (Ithaca, NY: Cornell University Press, 2005), 122.
159. *NMH*, 48.
160. *New Generation*, 61.
161. Chomsky, "Foreword," in Tanter, van Klinken, and Ball, *Bitter Flowers*, xi. Chomsky attributes the phrase "subcontracting terror" to Desmond Ball, but the phrase appears nowhere in Ball's contribution to this volume. Ball's chapter does not discuss US-Indonesian military relations ("Silent Witness," 177–201).
162. Samuel Huntington, "The Lonely Superpower," *Foreign Affairs* 78 (March/April 1999); Prestowitz, *Rogue Nation*.
163. There has been no convincing refutation of the methodologically rigorous but much-maligned Johns Hopkins/*Lancet* study, which estimated 655,000 civilian deaths during the first forty months of the war. See Tirman, *Deaths of Others*, 325–30, for a discussion of various death toll estimates.
164. See Keohane, *After Hegemony*, chapter 3.
165. Charles A. Kupchan, *The End of the American Era: U.S. Foreign Policy and the Geopolitics of the Twenty-First Century* (New York: Vintage, 2005), 57.
166. Kupchan, *American Era*, 58–59.
167. Brzezinski, *Choice*, viii, 8, 213.
168. Kupchan, *American Era*, 60.
169. Samuel Huntington, "Why International Primacy Matters," *International Security* 17 (Spring 1993): 83.
170. I distinguish "mainstream" analysts like Brzezinski, Huntington, and Kupchan from more aggressive, typically neoconservative advocates of American power whose views of the world are practically mirror images of Chomsky's—cf. Niall Ferguson, *Colossus*, and Kagan, *Dangerous Nation*.
171. Huntington, "Lonely Superpower," 48.
172. *H/P*, 137–39.
173. Kupchan (*End*, 14) acknowledges that the Russians were "justifiably apoplectic" over NATO expansion. Does apoplexy in the world's second largest nuclear power promote European stability?
174. Thomas Carothers, *Critical Mission: Essays on Democracy Promotion* (Washington, DC: Carnegie Endowment, 2004), 40, 47.
175. Thomas Carothers, *In the Name of Democracy: U.S. Policy toward Latin America during the Reagan Years* (Berkeley: University of California Press, 1991), 240. The authoritarian/totalitarian distinction was popularized by Jeane Kirkpatrick, who served as US ambassador to the United Nations in the Reagan administration: Kirkpatrick, "Dictatorships and Double Standards," *Commentary* 68 (November 1979), 3435.
176. Carothers, *In the Name*, 244.
177. Carothers, *Critical Mission*, 72.
178. Carothers, quoted in *H/P*, 46.

SUMMARY AND CONCLUSIONS
1. Chomsky wasn't sure, in fact, that the war was a mistake from the standpoint of the long-term objectives of American foreign policy. It may have helped to deter other Third World challenges to American power: *ATC*, 7–11. In this respect, he tends to agree with Michael Lind, a defender of the war's legitimacy (*Vietnam: A Necessary War*), but from an obviously very different value perspective.
2. *Turning the Tide* is in many ways an exasperating book, marked by many of the characteristic problems with Chomsky's work discussed in the next section. It is nevertheless essential reading for anyone interested in acquiring a thorough

understanding of the US impact on Central America in the 1980s.
3. Mandarins, 254
4. Paul Kattenburg, quoted in *DD*, 17.
5. Ibid.
6. *DD*, 18.
7. *NI*, 51.
8. Tony Smith, *America's Mission: the United States and the Worldwide Struggle for Democracy in the Twentieth Century* (Princeton, NJ: Princeton University Press, 1994). Smith's scholarship is impressive, but in making his case he bypasses many inconvenient topics. For example, his chapter titled "Reagan's Democratic Revolution" hardly mentions Central America; Indonesia also gets only passing mention in the book. Cf. David F. Schmitz, *Thank God They're on Our Side: The United States and Right-Wing Dictatorships, 1921-1965* (Chapel Hill: University of North Carolina Press, 1999) and Schmitz, *The United States and Right-Wing Dictatorships, 1965-1989* (Cambridge, MA: Cambridge University Press, 2006).
9. Prestowitz, *Rogue Nation: American Unilateralism and the Failure of Good Intentions* (see Chapter 5, Note 15).
10. *NI*, 19.
11. Hirohito, quoted in *H&P*, 49.
12. Robert S. McNamara, *In Retrospect: The Tragedy and Lessons of Vietnam* (New York: Random House, 1995), xvi.
13. Ibid., xvi–xvii.
14. *Washington Connection*, 69.
15. *H/S*, 75-76.
16. *DD*, 379.
17. *TANCW*, 12.
18. Ibid., 10-12.
19. *Washington Connection*, 92.
20. Ibid., 88.
21. Ibid., 28.
22. *TANCW*, 179-80.
23. Robert Pastor, quoted in *DD*, 261.
24. *DD*, 261-62.
25. *TANCW*, 118.
26. Edward Luck, quoted in *H/S*, 31.
27. *H/S*, 31-32.
28. *L&P*, 372
29. *TANCW*, 397n; *H/S*, 110-11.
30. *H&P*, 137.
31. *World Orders*, 17, 275n. See also Jim Lobne, "So, Did Saddam Hussein Try to Kill Bush's Dad?" *Inter Press Service*, October 19, 2004; available at www.commondreams.org.
32. *P&T*, 22.
33. *Mandarins*, 14
34. Thomas Lask, "Why Are We in Vietnam?" reprinted in Noam Chomsky, *Critical Assessments*, ed. Carlos Otero, vol. 3, book 1: 60.
35. The only exception I have found is Chomsky's positive comments on the Bretton Woods agreements (see Chapter 5).
36. Isaiah Berlin, *The Hedgehog and the Fox: An Essay on Tolstoy's View of History* (New York: Simon and Schuster, 1986).
37. Brad DeLong, "My Allergic Reaction to Noam Chomsky," October 23, 1998; accessed May 31, 2012, at econ161.berkeley.edu [J. Bradford DeLong homepage].
38. The policies of the second Bush administration did prompt a rare Chomsky acknowledgment of significant difference between the parties. For the 2004 election, he advised, "One of the two groups now contending for power is extremist and dangerous.... If you are in a swing state, you should vote to keep the worst guys out" (*Interventions*, 99-100).
39. LeoGrande, *Our Own Backyard* (see, for example, 240-46, 340-43, 422-26, and 469-473).
40. *POP*, 73.
41. LeoGrande, *Our Own Backyard*, 470-73.
42. *P&T*, 125.
43. *H/S*, 121-25; *H&P*, 27-28. 44. *H&P*, 60-61.
45. Russel Crandall, *Driven by Drugs: US Policy toward Colombia*, 2nd ed. (Boulder, CO: Lynne Rienner, 2008), 7.
46. *TANCW*, 209.
47. *DD*, 26. On US-Soviet competition in the Third World in the 1970s, see Westad, *Global Cold War*, especially chapters 7 and 8.
48. *ATC*, 218-19.
49. *TTT*, 105-7.
50. Thomas Nichols, "Chomsky and the Cold War," in Horowitz and Collier, *Anti-Chomsky Reader*, 48-49.
51. *FROS*, 45.
52. *AWWA*, 22.
53. Geoffrey Robertson, quoted in Noam Chomsky, "There Is Much More to Say," *ZNet*, May 20, 2011, www.zcommunications.org.
54. Eric Alterman, quoted in Chomsky, "There Is Much More."
55. Eric Alterman, "How Dishonest Is Noam Chomsky?" (blog entry), *Nation*, May 23, 2011, www.thenation.com.
56. *DD*, 23; also in *World Orders*, 34.
57. John Lewis Gaddis, *Strategies of Containment: A Critical Appraisal of Postwar American National Security Policy* (New York: Oxford University Press, 1982), 356-57.
58. Oliver Kamm, "'LM Was Probably Correct'– Chomsky," *Oliver Kamm* (blog), October 21, 2005, oliverkamm.typepad.com.
59. *P&T*, 73.
60. Chomsky's original reference, in *POP*, 78, provided an accurate short description of the Schlesinger memos. Cf. *The Foreign Relations of the United States, 1961-1963, vol. 12, American*

Republics (Washington, DC: US Government Printing Office, 1996), 13–14, 33, 9.
61. *NMH*, 32.
62. *MC*, 66, 68, 352n61, 352n67.
63. *MC*, 293.
64. Steven Lukes, "Chomsky's Betrayal of Truths," *Times Higher Education Supplement*, July 7, 1980: 31 (discussed in Barsky, *Noam Chomsky*, 187).
65. Noam Chomsky, letter to Robert F. Barsky (February 13, 1996), quoted in Barsky, *Noam Chomsky*, 188.
66. Chomsky implies that a comparison with East Timor was a salient feature of his writings on Cambodia. It was not. There was no mention of East Timor in the *Nation* article in which Chomsky and Herman first disparaged reports of large-scale atrocities in Cambodia. In *After the Cataclysm* and *Washington Connection*, Chomsky and Herman do point to differences in media coverage of Cambodia and Timor, but there is no comparative analysis of events in the two countries, just a brief (and partly incorrect) allusion to the comparative death tolls.
67. Aryeh Neier, "Inconvenient Facts" (review of *The New Military Humanism*), *Dissent*, Spring 2000.
68. Noam Chomsky, "On the Facts," *Dissent*, Summer 2000, *www.dissentmagazine.org*.
69. Noam Chomsky, "Reply to Hitchens," *Nation*, October 1, 2001, *www.thenation.com*.
70. Chomsky, "Chomsky Replies to Casey."
71. Ibid.
72. Chomsky's shortcomings are explored in Collier and Horowitz's polemical collection, *The Anti-Chomsky Reader*. Most of the essays in that volume, however, are hardly less selective in their consideration of evidence than the Chomsky works they criticize; they acknowledge little or no merit whatsoever in Chomsky's political writings.
73. Timothy Garton Ash, "Prague: Intellectuals and Politicians," *New York Review of Books* 42 (January 12, 1995): 35–36.

Index

Abrams, Creighton, 36
Abu Ghraib (prison, Iraq), 148
Acheson, Dean, 13, 22, 108, 111, 220
Adams, John, 162
advertising, 125, 148
Afghanistan
    famine in, 195
    invaded by Soviet Union, 212, 214
    US bombing and invasion of, 193
After the Cataclysm: Postwar Indochina and the Reconstruction of Imperial Ideology (Chomsky and Herman), 49–52
agrarian reform. *See* land reform
airline tragedies, 143–44, 212
Albright, Madeleine, 187, 190, 215
Alliance for Progress, 72, 84
Alsop, Joseph, 152
Alterman, Eric, 223–24
American exceptionalism, 2, 162–63
American Political Science Association (APSA), 104
Amnesty International, 56, 59, 130, 184
anti-Communism, 112–14, 118, 218
    in Propaganda Model, 127–29, 147
anti-Semitism, xi
Apodeti (East Timor), 67
Arbenz, Jacobo, 81
Arevalo, Juan Jose, 81, 83
Argentina, 87, 92, 226, 239n159
arms sales, 198–99
atrocities
    in Cambodia, 47, 50–52
    committed during Vietnam War, 32–37, 39
    by contras in Nicaragua, 88
    by dictatorships allied with US, 96
    in East Timor, 66, 68, 200, 201, 235n23
    in El Salvador, 72, 75–76, 78
    in Guatemala, 83–85
    in Guatemalan coup (1954), 80, 238n115
    in Indonesia, 62–66
    in Kosovo, 184–86
    against Kurds in Turkey, 197–98
    My Lai massacre as, 25–26, 31–32
    in Nicaragua, 87, 91
    in Philippines, 58–60
    in Rwanda, 181
    September 11th terrorist attacks as, 192
    in Srebrenica, 181
    Sudan factory bombing as, 195–96
    US participation in, 97, 215
    in Vietnam, media coverage of, 140–41
    war crimes distinguished from, 234n122

Bacevich, Andrew, 190
Ball, Desmond, 248n161
Ball, George, 64
Bao Dai (emperor, Vietnam), 7, 8, 22
Barron, John, 46–49
Belize (British Honduras), 85
Belke, Jonathan, 196
Bell, Daniel, 153
Bennett, Lance, 142, 143, 149
Bergerud, Eric, 9, 23
Berlin, Isaiah, 216
Bin Laden, Osama
    Afghanistan invasion and, 193
    death of, 223–24
    Iraq invasion and, 174
    on Iraqi sanctions, 197
    Sudan linked to, 196
Blair, Dennis, 200, 201
Blair, Tony, 184
Bonner, Raymond, 78, 148
Bosch, Orlando, 195
Bowles, Chester, 152
Braestrup, Peter, 141
Bretton Woods agreements, 167, 249n35
British Honduras (Belize), 85
Brzezinski, Zbigniew
    on First Gulf War, 177
    as supporter of Vietnam War, 155
    on US hegemony, 203, 204
Buddhists, 11
Bundy, McGeorge, 151
Bush, George H. W.
    alleged attempted assassination of, 214–15
    on Nicaragua, 91
    Panama invaded under, 172
Bush, George W.
    Chomsky on, 219
    Hussein and, 174
    on Iraq, 180
Bush administration (G. H. W. B.), 142–43
    Iraq and, 173, 177, 178
    Panama and, 172

Bush administration (G. W. B.), 144, 149
   Chomsky on, 248n38
   foreign policy of, 162
   Iraq invaded by, 161, 174–76, 180, 219
   September 11th terrorist attacks during, 192, 193

Cambodia
   Chomsky and Herman's book on, 49–52, 226
   Chomsky and Herman's *Nation* review on, 45–49
   history of, 44–45
   under Khmer Rouge, 214
   US bombing of, 221
   Vietnam War extended to, 14
Cambodia: Starvation and Revolution (Hildebrand and Porter), 46
Cambodia Year Zero (Ponchaud), 46
Cam Lo (Vietnam), 29–30
Canada, 165
capitalism, 104
   control over state in, 101
   expansion to foreign markets of, 111
   reforms under, 105
   Washington Consensus and, 164–69
Carothers, Thomas, 205–6
Carter, Jimmy
   disliked by Salvadorian right, 77
   El Salvador and, 75
   on fear of Communism, 114
   Philippines and, 60
   Romero and, 71, 130
   Somoza and, 87, 92
Carter administration
   aid to Indonesia by, 68
   El Salvador during, 71, 75–76
   Guatemala during, 85
   human rights policies of, 74–76
   Nicaragua during, 87, 91, 92
   Philippines during, 61
Casey, Leo, 196–97, 227
Castro, Fidel, 92, 211
Catholic Church
   in El Salvador, 74, 130
   in Guatemala, 137
   in Nicaragua, 89
   in Vietnam, 7, 8, 11
censorship, 124
Center for International Studies (MIT), 156
Central America, 70
   Alliance for Progress in, 72
   elections in El Salvador, Guatemala, and Nicaragua, 131–38
   Panama invaded by US, 169–72
   US aid to, 92
   worthy and unworthy victims in, 128–31
   See also El Salvador; Guatemala; Nicaragua
Central Intelligence Agency (CIA), 115
   in El Salvador, 71
   in Indonesia, 62–65
   Noriega and, 170
   research institutes funded by, 156
Chace, James, 213
Chamorro, Edgar, 88
Chamorro, Fernando, 90
Chamorro, Violeta, 90–91, 95
Cheney, Richard, 180, 219
Chile, 213
China
   Open Door trade policy with, 111
   Revolution in, 5
   trade between Japan and, 223
   US investments in, 119
   Vietnam War caused by expansionist policy of, 24–25
Christian Democratic Parties (El Salvador; Guatemala), 134
Churchill, Winston, 113
Clark, Wesley, 186
Clarke, Richard, 149
clientelism, 58
Clinton, Bill, 106
   on humanitarian intervention, 181
   on Kosovo, 184, 189
Clinton administration
   on East Timor, 200
   Kosovo during, 181, 190
   NATO and, 162
Cohen, William, 190
Colby, William, 35, 237n50
Cold War, 2
   business influence in origins of, 107
   Chomsky on origins of, 116–20, 217
   debate over origins of, 109–10
   economic expansionism in origins of, 110–12
   end of, 160
   exaggerations of Communist influence during, 82
   geopolitics in origins of, 114–15
   ideology in origins of, 112–14
   media during, 147
   US foreign policy during, 53–57
Colombia, 219–20
Committee of Concerned Asian Scholars, 155
Communism and Communists
   anti-Communism and, 112–13, 118
   in Cambodia, 45–46
   during Cold War, 55
   elections under, 23–24
   end of threat of, 160
   expansionism of, 24–25
   in Guatemala, 82
Communist Party (Guatemala), 81
Communist Party (Indonesia; PKI), 62–65
Communist Party (Vietnam; Vietnamese Workers Party), 9, 17, 232n25
   National Liberation Front (NLF) under control of, 10
   ties to China and Soviet Union of, 24–25

Cong An (Vietnamese police), 9
Congress, US
    aid to Central America passed by, 92
    on aid to El Salvador, 79
    Gulf of Tonkin Resolution of, 11
    human rights legislation of, 74, 77
    ignored by Chomsky, 102
    on Latin American policies, 218–19
    media coverage of, 145
    media coverage of international issues tied to, 142–44
Contadora countries, 90
Contadora Process, 90, 93
contrarianism, 214–15
contras (Nicaragua), 208
    election disrupted by, 135
    funded by US, 88, 92, 95, 218
    media coverage of, 142
Cook, Timothy, 145
corporate class (ruling class), 99–103
    control of natural resources by, 240n36
    ideology shaped by, 122–23
    influence over foreign policy by, 107–9
    media concentration in, 125
    Propaganda Model on control of media by, 128, 145, 147
    Washington Consensus under, 164–69
Corson, William, 29–30
Craig, Campbell, 114, 116
Croly, Herbert, 112
Cronkite, Walter, 13
Cruz, Arturo, 134, 138
Cuba, 21
    missile crisis in, 211–12, 214
    Nicaragua and, 92, 94
    US campaign against, 211
    US embargo of, 163
    US use of terrorism against, 195
Czechoslovakia, 56

Dahl, Robert, 103, 105
Darling, Frank, 154
Daum, Werner, 196
Dayton Accords (1995), 190
death squads
    in El Salvador, 71, 72, 75, 77–78
    in Guatemala, 84
    Romero murder by, 129
DeLong, Brad, 217–18, 228
democracy
    as goal of US foreign policy, 209–10
    sovereignty and development tied to, 166
    US as force for, 205–6
Democratic Party (US), 104
    on Latin American policy, 218–19
Democratic Republic of Vietnam (DRV). See Vietnam, Democratic Republic of
Democratic Revolutionary Front (FDR; El Salvador), 133

Derian, Patricia, 60
deterrence, 213
development, tied to sovereignty and democracy, 166
Devillers, Philippe, 17
Devine, Frank, 74, 76
Diaz Herrera, Roberto, 171
Diem, Ngo Dinh, 7–9, 22
    elections blocked by, 19
    insurgency against, 9–11
Dienbienphu (Vietnam), 6
Dinges, John, 130
disarmament, 163–64
doctrinal system, 2, 102, 122–23
Dodd, Christopher, 198
Dole, Bob, 183
Dominican Republic, 55
domino theory, 54
DRV (Democratic Republic of Vietnam). See Vietnam, Democratic Republic of
Duarte, Jose Napoleon, 71–72, 74–76, 225–26
Duchai (Vietnam), 31
Dulles, John Foster, 108
    on Asia during Cold War, 119
    United Fruit and, 82
    on Vietnam, 6

Eastern Europe, 54
    origins of Cold War in, 115
    under Soviet dominance, 96–97
East Timor, 51
    Cambodia compared with, 235n23
    Indonesian invasion of (1975), 66–70, 224–25
    Indonesian invasion of (1999), 199–201, 219, 227
Eisenhower, Dwight D., 101
Eisenhower administration, 80
elections
    campaign financing in, 240n28
    in Central America, 131–38
    Chomsky on, 102
    under Communism, 23–24
    in El Salvador, 237n74
    in El Salvador (1972), 71
    in El Salvador (1981), 72
    in El Salvador (1982 and 1984), 79
    in Guatemala (1944), 79
    in Guatemala (1985), 80
    in Nicaragua, 89, 94
    in Nicaragua (1990), 90–91, 95
    in Panama, 169, 171
    in US (1948), 113
    in US (1968), 13
    in US (1980), 77
    in Vietnam (1955; Diem's referendum), 8
    in Vietnam (1956; proposed), 6–8, 18, 19, 22
    in Vietnam (1967), 12–13
Elliott, David, 22–23, 31
El Salvador, 72–79
    Chomsky on, 70–72, 208
    elections in, 131–38

El Salvador, *continued*
   murder of American church women in, 225–26
   Nicaraguan Sandinistas and, 89
   Romero murder in, 128–31
   US aid to, 95
   US participation in atrocities in, 97
England. *See* Great Britain
Entman, Robert, 143
Esquipulas Process, 90, 93
Europe
   Eastern Europe, 54, 96–97
   nuclear weapons-free zone proposed for, 163
   origins of Cold War in, 115
   US interests in, 189
   US military presence in, 204

Falk, Richard, 20–21, 57
Fall, Bernard, 26
"fascist" states, 56, 236n9
   in Third World, 57, 98, 119
Faurisson, Robert, x–xi
FDR (Democratic Revolutionary Front; El Salvador), 133
Ferguson, Thomas, 240n28
First Gulf War. *See* Gulf War (First, 1990–1991)
Fischer, Joschka, 187
FISSBAN (fissile material cutoff treaty), 164
flak, 126–27, 148–49
Ford, Gerald
   East Timor and, 66
   meets with Suharto, 67–69
Ford administration, 68–69
foreign policy
   during Cold War, 53–57, 109–20
   corporate class interests in, 103
   economic consequences of, 106–7
   after end of Cold War, 161–62
   "good intentions" in, 209–10
   influence of elite groups over, 108–9
   media coverage of, tied to congressional debate, 142–44
   Propaganda Model on, 127–28
   Propaganda Model on media coverage of, 145–47
Forrestal, James, 108
Fousek, John, 112
France
   at Geneva Conference, 7
   on Iraq War, 214
   in war in Indochina, 5–6
free trade agreements, 165
French Indochina, 5. *See also* Cambodia; Vietnam
Fretilin (East Timor), 66–67, 69
Fujimori, Alberto, 205

Gaddis, John, 224
Galbraith, Francis, 65
Garton Ash, Timothy, 228–29
Geneva Accords, 18–20, 139

Geneva Conference (1954), 6
   elections promised by, 7–8
   on unified Vietnam, 18–20
genocide, 234n147. *See also* atrocities
geopolitics, in origins of Cold War, 114–17
Germany, 57, 234n147
Gibbs, David, 189, 190
Gilbert, John, 188
globalization, 168, 203, 204
God, 113
Gordon, Joy, 178
Graebner, Norman, 154
Great Britain
   in First Gulf War, 202
   free trade policies of, 166
   power exercised by, 162
   sanctions against Iraq by, 178
Green, Marshall, 64–66
Greenspan, Alan, 167
Greentree, Todd, 91
Gruening, Ernest, 140
Guam, 111
Guatemala, 55, 80–83, 96
   Chomsky on, 79–80, 208
   coup of 1954 in, 81–83, 238n115
   elections in, 131–38
   human rights violations in, 130
   interference in Salvadorian elections by, 71, 237n74
   US participation in atrocities in, 97
   US role in repression in, 83–86
Guatemalan Bishops Conference, 137
Gulf of Tonkin incident (1964), 11, 140
Gulf War (First, 1990–1991), 142–43, 172–73, 202
   Chomsky on, 177–78
Gulf War (Second, 2003). *See* Iraq War

Halliday, Denis, 174
Hallin, Daniel
   on Central America, 138
   on ethic of objective journalism, 145–46
   on media coverage of Vietnam War, 139–41
   on media during Cold War, 147
Harriman, Averell, 13, 108
Hawaii, 111
Hay, John, 111
hegemony, 161
   Chomsky on, 208
   economic, 164–69
   of US power, 201–6
Herman, Edward S., 2
   on Cambodia, 44–52
   on Central American elections, 132–38
   on media coverage of Vietnam War, 139–41
   on murder of American church women in El Salvador, 226
   on Philippines, 60
   on Propaganda Model, 123–28, 142, 144, 145, 147–50
   on Third World dictatorships, 55

on Vietnam War casualties, 34
on worthy and unworthy victims, 128–31
Hildebrand, George, 46, 47, 49, 50
Hill, Christopher R., 187
Hilsman, Roger, 42, 155
Hirohito (emperor, Japan), 210
historians
    on Cold War, 53, 109–20
    revisionist, 156
    on Vietnam War, 43
Hitchens, Christopher, 196, 227
Ho Chi Minh, 5, 24
Hoffman, Stanley, 155
Holbrooke, Richard, 187
Hoopes, Townsend, 43
Hoover, J. Edgar, 82
Hue (Vietnam), 40
humanitarian intervention, 180–82
    Chomsky on, 182–83, 191–92
human rights, 56
    Carter administration policies on, 60, 74–76, 85
    in East Timor, 68
    in Guatemala, 130
    humanitarian intervention and violations of, 182
    in Nicaragua, 94
    in Philippines, 59
    in Turkey, 197–98
    US legislation on, 74, 77, 78
Human Rights Watch, 130, 196
Huntington, Samuel
    dispute between Chomsky and, 157–59, 223
    on research on Vietnam, 156
    on US hegemony, 203, 204
    on Vietnam War, 151
Hussein, Saddam, 144, 172–78, 202, 219
    alleged assassination attempt on G. H. W. Bush by, 214–15
    chemical weapons used by, 222

ideology
    Chomsky on, 117–18
    in origins of Cold War, 112–14
    in Propaganda Model, 127
    shaped by corporate class, 122–23
I. F. Stone's Weekly, 140
Ikenberry, John, 161
Immerman, Richard, 82, 83
imperialism, 58, 111
Indochina
    French, 5
    media on, 139
    post-WW II, 54
    See also Cambodia; Vietnam
Indonesia
    Chomsky on, 61–62, 208
    coups and bloodbath in, 62–66
    East Timor and, 51, 66–70, 199–201, 224–25
    US participation in atrocities in, 97
instrumental Marxism, 101, 102, 107

intellectuals, 150–59, 228–29
Inter-American Development Bank, 88
interest groups, 103
international law
    on civilian deaths, 37
    Falk on, 21
    First Gulf War (1990–1991) and, 173
    Iraq War and, 174
    US hegemony and, 201, 202
    on war crimes, 234n122
International Monetary Fund (IMF), 189
    neoliberalism of, 165
    in Philippines, 59
Interstate Commerce Commission (ICC), 101
Iran, 55
Iran Air, 143–44, 212
Iraq
    in First Gulf War (1990–1991), 142–43
    under Hussein, 172–80
    US bombing of (1993), 215
    as victim of US violence, 202
Iraq War (2003)
    casualties of, 202, 248n163
    Chomsky on, 180, 193, 207, 219
    media on, 144
    US hegemony as cause of, 161
    US reasons for, 174–76
Israel, 144
Italy, 57

Jacobs, Lawrence, 108–9
Jaegher, R. J. de, 152
Japan
    French Indochina occupied by, 5
    post-WW II, 54
    trade between China and, 223
    WW II goals of, 210
Jenkins, Brian, 239n159
Jervis, Robert, 183
Johnson, Lyndon
    Gulf of Tonkin incident under, 11
    on Indonesia, 65
    Vietnam War under, 12–13
Johnson administration, 11–13, 39
Judah, Tim, 184, 225
just war theory, 16

Kahin, George McT., 17, 155, 213
Kamm, Oliver, 224–25
Kampuchea, Democratic (DK; Cambodia), 45, 47
Kampuchea, People's Republic of (Cambodia), 45
Kattenburg, Paul, 209
Kennan, George, 113, 115
Kennedy, John F., 72, 225
Kennedy, Robert, 66
Kennedy administration
    Guatemala and, 83, 238n128
    intellectuals in, 152
    Vietnam and, 10

Kenya, 195
Keohane, Robert O., 167, 203
Keynes, John Maynard, 101-2
Khmer Rouge, 45-52, 214, 221, 226
Khrushchev, Nikita, 211-12, 214
Kirkpatrick, Jeane, 248n175
Kissinger, Henry
    East Timor and, 67
    on equilibrium, 213
    on Kosovo, 188
    as media source, 126
    Suharto meets with, 66, 69
Kolko, Gabriel, 110, 154
Kopassus (Indonesian military unit), 200
Korea, 204
Korean Airlines (KAL), 143-44, 212
Korean War, 5, 117
Kosovo (Serbia), 180-82, 200, 202
    Chomsky on, 182-91, 219, 225
    NATO intervention in, 221
Kosovo Liberation Army (KLA), 181, 184, 185, 190
Kupchan, Charles, 203, 204
Kurds
    in Iraq, 173, 176, 177, 222
    in Turkey, 197-99
Kurtz, Howard, 144
Kuwait, 172, 173, 177, 178, 202
Ky, Nguyen Cao, 12-13, 22

Lacouture, Jean, 17
LaFeber, Walter, 119
land reform
    in Guatemala, 80, 82
    in Vietnam, 8-9
La Prensa (Nicaragua), 133, 136
Latin America
    Alliance for Progress in, 72
    Communist Parties banned in, 81
    Contradora and Esquipulas Processes in, 90
    economic policies in, 166
    military coups in, 55
    Panama invaded by US, 169-72
    recent US policies in, 205-6
    See also Central America; El Salvador; Guatemala; Nicaragua
Latin American Studies Association (LASA), 134
Layne, Christopher, 116, 190
Leffler, Melvyn, 107, 115-17
Lehrer, Eli, 130-31
Lemann, Nicholas, 131
LeoGrande, William, 118-19
Lewis, Anthony, 41
Lewy, Guenter, 28-30, 33-35, 37-38
Libya, 144
Lind, Michael, 233n85
Lindblom, Charles, 105-6
Lodge, Henry Cabot, 36
Logevall, Fredrik, 114, 116

The Lonely Crowd (Riesman), 122
Los Angeles Times, 137
Lowell, Robert, 1
Luck, Edward, 214
Lukes, Steven, 226-27

Macdonald, Dwight, 151
Mailer, Norman, 1
Majano, Adolfo, 90
Managua (Nicaragua), 87
Manufacturing Consent (Chomsky and Herman), 149, 244n103
    on Cambodia, 226
    on media, 170, 207
    on media coverage of Vietnam War, 139
    on Propaganda Model, 123
Marcos, Ferdinand, 59-61, 96, 97, 175
Marx, Karl, 100-101, 150
Marxism and Marxists, 100, 120, 122
    instrumental and structural, 101, 106, 107, 240n34
mass media, 2
    on Cambodia, 50-51
    Chomsky on, 207
    coverage of international issues tied to congressional debate, 142-44
    on elections in El Salvador, Guatemala, and Nicaragua, 132, 135-38
    on Panama invasion, 170-71
    on Popieluszko murder, 128-29
    Propaganda Model on, 123-27, 145-49
    during Tet Offensive, 13
    on Vietnam War, 41-42, 138-42
matanza massacre (El Salvador, 1932), 70
McCarthy, Eugene, 13
McCarthy, Mary, 1
McCartney, Robert, 137
McCloy, John J., 108
McNamara, Robert, 36, 60, 210
media. *See* mass media
Melchor, Alejandro, 60
Mendez Montenegro, Julio, 83-84
Mermin, Jonathan, 146-47, 243n79
military-industrial complex, 102
    Eisenhower on, 101
    in origins of Cold War, 116
Mill, John Stuart, 162
Mills, C. Wright, 102, 103, 122
Milosevic, Slobodan, 181, 185-88, 190
Minh, Duong Van, 12
Mondale, Walter, 68
Moorer, Thomas, 60
morality, in Chomsky's opposition to Vietnam War, 15-16
Morgenthau, Hans J.
    on comfort of intellectuals, 153
    as realist theorist, 16, 114
    on Vietnam War, 1, 155
Morse, Wayne, 140

Moynihan, Daniel Patrick, 224–25
Murder of a Gentle Land (Barron and Paul), 46–47
Muslims, 192–93
Mussolini, Benito, 57
My Lai massacre, 25–26, 31–32

nationalism, 112, 117–18, 147–48
National Liberation Front (FLN; Nicaragua), 93
National Liberation Front (NLF; Vietnam), 57
    in agreement between North Vietnam and US, 14
    anti-Diem insurgency of, 10–11
    attacks on civilian populations by, 34
    autonomy of, 39
    Huntington on, 158
    North Vietnam's aid to, 21
    Pentagon Papers on, 42
    popularity of, 22–23, 233n82
    Tet Offensive of, 13
NATO (North Atlantic Treaty Organization), 162
    expansion of, 204
    intervention in Kosovo by, 221
    Serbia bombed by, 181–91
    Turkey in, 198
natural resources, 107, 240n36
Neier, Aryeh, 227
neoliberalism, 164–69, 202
news, 125–26
    development of objectivity in, 145–46
    See also mass media
New York Review of Books, 1
New York Times
    anti-Vietnam War petition published in, 155
    on Central America elections, 135–37
    on East Timor, 200
    on El Salvador and Poland, 131
    on Nicaragua, 142
    on Panama invasion, 170
    on Popieluszko and Romero murders, 129
    on Vietnam War, 139
Ngo Dinh Diem. *See* Diem, Ngo Dinh
Ngo Dinh Nhu, 7, 11
Nicaragua, 91–95
    Chomsky on, 86–91, 208, 213
    contras in, 218
    elections in, 131–38
    interference into Salvadorian elections by, 71, 237n74
    media coverage of, 142
    World Court decision on, 163, 218–19
Nichols, Thomas, 222–23
Nixon, Richard M.
    Cambodia invaded under, 44–45
    Marcos and, 60, 96
    Vietnam War under, 14
Noriega, Manuel, 169–72
North Korea, 204, 214
North Vietnam. *See* Vietnam, Democratic Republic of

objectivity, 145–46
oil
    corporate interests of, 101
    in Indonesia, 65
    in Iraq, 179
Ontario (Canada), 165
Open Door trade policy, 111, 116
Operation Cedar Falls, 29
Operation Rolling Thunder, 11–12, 39
Operation Speedy Express, 32
ORDEN (El Salvador), 71
Ortega, Daniel, 90
Orwell, George, 212
Owen, David, 190

Page, Benjamin, 108–9, 143
Pakistan, 195
Panama, 169–72, 219
Pastor, Robert, 213
Paul, Anthony, 46–49
Peers, William, 32
Peers Commission, 32, 43
Pentagon Papers, 18–19, 42, 107
Peru, 205
Philippines, 59–61, 96, 111
    Chomsky on, 58–59
    US participation in atrocities in, 97
Phnom Penh (Cambodia), 45, 46, 48, 50
Pike, Douglas, 22
Pillar, Paul, 149
pluralism, 103
Poland, 128–31
political parties
    in Central America, 133–34
    Chomsky on, 104, 218, 248n38
political science, 155
politicians, 228–29
Pol Pot, 45, 51, 226–27
Ponchaud, Francois, 46–50
Popieluszko, Jerzy, 128–31
popular culture, 121–22
Porter, Gareth
    on Cambodia, 46, 47, 49, 50
    on Hue massacre, 40
Portugal, 66
Posada Carriles, Luis, 195
Power, Samantha, 184–85
power elite, 103
The Power Elite (Mills), 103, 122
power indexing, 143, 144
press freedom, in Central American elections, 132, 136
Prestowitz, Clyde, 209
privatization, 168
Propaganda Model, 123–27
    on Central American elections, 131–38
    empirical findings on, 142–44
    explanations of, 145–49

Propaganda Model, *continued*
  intellectuals in, 150–59
  on Vietnam War, 138–42
  worthy and unworthy victims in, 128–31
Puerto Rico, 111
Putnam, Robert, 122

al-Qaeda, 174, 192, 193, 196
Quangngai Province (Vietnam), 30–31

Race, Jeffrey, 30
Rambouillet (France), 187, 188
Rather, Dan, 136
Reagan, Ronald, 56
  El Salvador and, 77, 78
  on evil empire, 129
  Guatemala and, 85
  Nicaragua and, 88
  on Noriega, 172
  on Sandinistas, 93
Reagan administration
  contras supported by, 92, 218
  on elections in El Salvador, Guatemala, and Nicaragua, 132, 134, 137–38
  El Salvador during, 72, 79
  Guatemala during, 85
  human rights groups discredited by, 130
  human rights policies of, 78
  Latin American policies of, 205
  Nicaragua during, 88
  Philippines during, 61
  on Sandinistas, 89, 90, 95, 209
  on shooting down of Korean Airlines (KAL) plane, 143
realist school of international relations, 15–16
reductionism, 218–22
refugees
  Cambodian, 45–48, 226
  Guatemalan, 85
  Salvadorian, 72
  of Vietnam War, 26–31
  Yugoslavian, 184
Republican Party (US), 104, 113
"The Responsibility of Intellectuals" (essay, Chomsky), 1, 151, 154–55
Reston, James, 64
revisionist historians, 109–11, 156
Riesman, David, 122
Romero, Oscar, 71, 128–31
Rostow, Walt, 151
Rowe, David, 152, 155
ruling class. *See* corporate class
Rumsfeld, Donald, 180
Russia
  NATO expansion and, 204
  nuclear weapons–free zone proposed by, 163
  See also Soviet Union
Rwanda, 181

Sandinistas (Nicaragua), 87–95
  Chomsky on, 208
  in Nicaraguan elections, 132, 134, 137–38
  Reagan on, 209
Schell, Jonathan, 30–31
Schell, Orville, 30–31
Schlesinger, Arthur, Jr.
  on anti-Communism, 225
  on Cuban missile crisis, 212
  dispute between Chomsky and, 157–58, 245n142
  on Vietnam War, 15, 107, 152
Second Gulf War (2003). *See* Iraq War
self-determination
  hypocritical US support for, 154
  for South Vietnam, 21–24
Senate, US
  economic influence over, 104
  on US campaign against Cuba, 211
  See also Congress
September 11th terrorist attacks, 192–94
  Sudan bombing compared with, 196, 215
Serbia, 181–92
Shakashvili, John, 149
Sharp, Bruce, 52
Shattuck, John, 198
Sheehan, Neil, 31, 35–36
al-Shifa (factory, Sudan), 195–97, 215, 227
Sihanouk, Norodom (prince, Cambodia), 44
Simpson, Bradley, 65
Skocpol, Theda, 122
Smith, Bedell, 6
Smith, Tony, 209, 249n8
social sciences, 156
Sola Pool, Ithiel de, 155
Somoza, Anastazio, 87, 91, 92, 96, 97
Somoza family (Nicaragua), 86–87, 91
Sontag, Susan, 1
sources (in media), 125–26, 145–47
Southeast Asia
  during Cold War, 119
  See also Cambodia; Vietnam
South Korea, 204
South Vietnam. *See* Vietnam, Republic of
sovereignty, tied to democracy and development, 166
Soviet Union, 2–3
  Afghanistan invaded by, 212, 214
  anti-Communist ideology towards, 112–14
  during Cold War, 53, 56, 109–10, 117–19
  in Cuban missile crisis, 211–12
  dissolution of, 160
  Eastern Europe under dominance of, 96–97
  geopolitical perspective on, 114–15
  influence in Third World of, 220–21
  Korean Airlines (KAL) plane shot down by, 143–44, 212
  Nicaragua and, 94, 95
  post–WW II, 54

Sandinistas on, 93
Vietnam War caused by expansionist policy of, 24–25
See also Russia
space, militarization of, 163–64
Spadafora, Hugo, 171
Spanish American War (1898), 58–59, 111
Srebrenica (Bosnia), 181, 225
state (government), 100–101
    business leaders in positions in, 107–8
    economic interventions by, 166–67
Stevenson, Adlai, 152, 211
Stiglitz, Joseph, 168
strategic hamlets, 27–28
Strout, Richard, 41
structural Marxism, 101, 106, 240n34
Studds, Gerry, 77
"subfascist" states, 236n9
Sudan, 195–97, 215, 227
Suharto
    Chomsky on, 208
    East Timor invaded by (1977), 66, 68–69
    takes power in coup (1965), 62, 96
    US support for, 199
    Wolfowitz support for, 175
Sukarno, 62, 96

Taft, Robert, 113
Taliban (Afghanistan), 193
Tanzania, 195
Task Force on Inequality and American Democracy (American Political Science Association), 104
Taylor, Telford, 234n122
telecommunications, 165
terrorism
    causes of, 192–93
    Chomsky on, 213
    Iraqi invasion and, 175
    of Kosovo Liberation Army, 190
    September 11th attacks as, 192
    US as perpetrator of, 194–201
Tet Offensive (Vietnam), 13, 141
Thailand, 154
Thieu, Nguyen Van, 12–14, 22
Third World
    during Cold War, 53–56, 110, 118
    "fascism" in, 57, 98
    Soviet influence in, 220–21
    US client states in, 215
Time (magazine)
    on Central American elections, 136
    on Vietnam War, 140
Timorese Democratic Union (UDT; East Timor), 66–67
Tirman, John, 198
Tocqueville, Alexis de, 112
torture, in Abu Ghraib, 148
Trilateral Commission, 150–51

Trullinger, James, 22
Truman, Harry S., 157–58, 245n142
Truman administration, 220
    anti-Communism of, 113
    Cold War policies of, 117
Truman Doctrine, 113
Turkey, 175, 197–99, 208
Turner, Stansfield, 92
Turning the Tide (Chomsky), 70, 208, 248–49n2

Ungo, Guillermo, 137, 163
United Fruit Company, 79–83, 238n125
United Kingdom. *See* Great Britain
United Nations, 161
    on Indonesian invasion of East Timor, 67–68
    on Iraqi invasion of Kuwait, 172, 178
    US use of, 214
    veto used by US in, 163
    Vietnam's membership in, 19–20
United Nations Disarmament Committee, 163–64
United States
    academic research funded by, 156
    agreement between North Vietnam and (1973), 14
    Cambodia invaded by, 44–45
    Cold War foreign policy of, 53–57, 109–21
    Diem overthrown by, 11
    Diem supported by, 7
    East Timor and, 67–68, 199–201
    El Salvador and, 70–79
    after end of Cold War, 160–61
    exceptionalism of, 2, 162–63
    in First Gulf War (1990–1991), 172–73, 177–78
    France supported by, in Indochina, 5–6
    at Geneva Conference, 6
    "good intentions" in foreign policy of, 209–10
    Guatemala and, 81–86
    Guatemalan coup of 1954 and, 79–80
    hegemony of, 201–6
    humanitarian intervention by, 182–84
    imperialism and empire of, 58
    Indonesian violence and, 62–66, 237n50
    in Iraq War, 180
    in negotiations with North Vietnam, 13
    Nicaragua and, 86–95
    as perpetrator of terrorism, 194–201
    Philippines under, 58–59
    power structure in, 99–108
    sanctions against Iraq by, 178–79
    September 11th terrorist attacks on, 192
    Turkey and, 198–99
    Washington Consensus of, 164–69
US Chamber of Commerce, 60, 125
US News and World Report, 138

Vaky, Viron, 74, 84
Vance, Cyrus, 13, 190
Vandenberg, Arthur, 113
Vedrine, Hubert, 201

victims, worthy and unworthy, 128–31
Vien, Cao Van, 12
Viet Cong. *See* National Liberation Front (NLF; Vietnam)
Viet Minh, 5–6
    in battles with Vietnamese Army (ARVN), 9
    on elections in Vietnam, 7–8
    Geneva Accords accepted by, 18
    Pentagon Papers on, 42
    popularity of, 21–22
Vietnam
    Geneva Accords on, 18–20
    post-WW II, 54
    reunification of (1975), 14
    before US intervention (WW II to 1956), 5–9
    war in, 11–14
    See also Vietnam War
Vietnam, Democratic Republic of (DRV; North Vietnam)
    as aggressor against South Vietnam, 16–21
    agreement between US and (1973), 14
    antagonism between China and, 24
    bombing of, 26, 39
    Chomsky in, 40
    creation of (1946), 5
    Diem's South Vietnam and, 9–10
    disputes between Cambodia and, 45
    National Liberation Front (NLF) aided by, 12
    in negotiations with US, 13
Vietnam, Republic of (RVN; South Vietnam)
    after Diem, 12–13
    anti-Diem insurgency in, 9–11
    bombing of, 26
    creation of, 8
    fall of (1975), 14
    as invention of US, 18–19
    refugees in, 26–31
    self-determinism for, 21–24
    as victim of aggression from North Vietnam, 16–21
Vietnam, State of, 6
Vietnamese Army (ARVN), 8, 9, 12
Vietnamese Workers Party. *See* Communist Party (Vietnam; Vietnamese Workers Party)
Vietnam War, 1–2
    Chomsky on, 14–17, 39–43, 54, 207, 209, 212, 216, 248n1
    economic origins of, 119
    escalation of US involvement in, 11–12
    expanded into Cambodia, 44–45
    intellectuals on, 151, 155–59
    under Johnson, 12–13
    McNamara on, 210
    under Nixon, 14
    Philippine bases used during, 61
    Propaganda Model on, 138–42
    as "war of annihilation," 25–39
Vietnam War Crimes Working Group (VWCWG), 32, 43

Wall Street Journal, 171
Walzer, Michael, 16, 38
Warburg, J. P., 157
war crimes
    atrocities distinguished from, 234n122
    Vietnam War Crimes Working Group on, 32, 43
war on drugs, 172, 219–20
war on terror
    declared by Bush administration, 192, 193
    Iraq invasion as part of, 174
Washington Connection (Chomsky and Herman), 70
Washington Consensus, 164–69, 204
Washington Post, 137–38, 144
Westad, Odd Arne, 119
Westmoreland, William, 28, 30, 35, 37
What Uncle Sam Really Wants (Chomsky), 217–18
White, Robert, 76
Wicker, Tom, 209
Williams, William Appleman, 111, 154
Wise Men (Johnson's advisers), 13
Wolfe, Alan, 156, 244n129
Wolfowitz, Paul, 175, 180
Woolcott, Richard, 67
Workers Party (Vietnam). *See* Communist Party (Vietnam; Vietnamese Workers Party)
World Bank
    loans to Philippines by, 59, 60
    Nicaragua and, 88
World Court, 163, 218–19
World Trade Organization (WTO), 165
World War I, 56–57
World War II, 111, 115, 210

Young, Marilyn, 10–11, 43